W9-AVQ-835

Morten
Rand-Hendriksen

Sams Teach Yourself

Microsoft
Expression°
Web 3

in **24**
Hours

SAMS   800 East 96th Street, Indianapolis, Indiana, 46240 USA

Sams Teach Yourself Microsoft Expression® Web 3 in 24 Hours

Copyright © 2010 by Sams Publishing

All rights reserved. No part of this book shall be reproduced, stored in a retrieval system, or transmitted by any means, electronic, mechanical, photocopying, recording, or otherwise, without written permission from the publisher. No patent liability is assumed with respect to the use of the information contained herein. Although every precaution has been taken in the preparation of this book, the publisher and author assume no responsibility for errors or omissions. Nor is any liability assumed for damages resulting from the use of the information contained herein.

ISBN-13: 978-0-672-33064-3
ISBN-10: 0-672-33064-4

Library of Congress Cataloging-in-Publication Data:

Rand-Hendriksen, Morten.
  Sams teach yourself Microsoft Expression Web 3 in 24 hours / Morten Rand-Hendriksen.
    p. cm.
  ISBN 978-0-672-33064-3
  1. Web sites—Authoring programs. 2. Microsoft Expression Web. 3. Web site development. I. Title.
  TK5105.8883.R362 2009
  006.7'8—dc22
                                   2009032708

Printed in the United States of America

Second Printing December 2009

Trademarks

All terms mentioned in this book that are known to be trademarks or service marks have been appropriately capitalized. Sams Publishing cannot attest to the accuracy of this information. Use of a term in this book should not be regarded as affecting the validity of any trademark or service mark.

Warning and Disclaimer

Every effort has been made to make this book as complete and as accurate as possible, but no warranty or fitness is implied. The information provided is on an "as is" basis. The author and the publisher shall have neither liability nor responsibility to any person or entity with respect to any loss or damages arising from the information contained in this book or from the use of programs accompanying it.

Bulk Sales

Sams Publishing offers excellent discounts on this book when ordered in quantity for bulk purchases or special sales. For more information, please contact

U.S. Corporate and Government Sales

1-800-382-3419

corpsales@pearsontechgroup.com

For sales outside of the U.S., please contact

International Sales

international@pearson.com

Acquisitions Editor
Loretta Yates

Development Editor
Todd Brakke

Managing Editor
Kristy Hart

Project Editor
Anne Goebel

Copy Editor
Apostrophe Editing Services

Indexer
Larry Sweazy

Proofreader
Keith Cline

Technical Editors
Anna Ullrich
Doug Holland

Publishing Coordinator
Cindy Teeters

Book Designer
Gary Adair

Composition
Jake McFarland
Gloria Schurick

Contents at a Glance

Table of Contents

About the Author

Morten Rand-Hendriksen is the owner and creative director of Pink & Yellow Media, a boutique-style design company providing digital media consulting and creations for individuals, businesses, and broadcast television. He was awarded the Microsoft MVP (Most Valuable Professional) Award for his work with Microsoft Expression in 2008.

In addition to Microsoft Expression Web, Morten is considered an expert on the integration and use of the publishing platform WordPress in conjunction with the application, and he has published numerous articles and videos and done public speaking engagements on the topic.

Sams Teach Yourself Microsoft Expression Web 3 in 24 Hours is his second published book (the first one being *Sams Teach Yourself Microsoft Expression Web 2 in 24 Hours*). He is a regular contributor to the official Microsoft Expression newsletter and has also been published in international design magazines. You can find more tutorials, articles, and other design-related musings on his blog at http://www.designisphilosophy.com and follow his rants on Twitter under the name @mor10 and you might run into him in different forums and newsgroups throughout the Web, usually using the same handle.

If you have any questions relating to the book, you can contact Morten by writing to book@pinkandyellow.com or through the website dedicated to this book found at http://expression.pinkandyellow.com.

Dedication

I dedicate this book to Angela, my love,
without whom none of this would be possible.

Acknowledgments

Nearly one year ago I sat in this same couch writing the acknowledgments for the first version of this book, *Sams Teach Yourself Microsoft Expression Web 2 in 24 Hours*. At the time it felt like I was at the end of some bizarre roller-coaster ride and that after the book was bound and printed everything would go back to normal. That, it turned out, was a big bowl of ignorance with a generous helping of naiveté on my part: Just a few days after the book hit stores, I started getting emails from readers asking questions, providing feedback, and providing suggestions for future projects. I guess I shouldn't have been surprised—after all, I did provide my email address both on the book website and several places in the book itself—but it didn't really connect with me until then that when you publish a book, people will not only buy it but also actually read it and want to tell you what they thought. And it is that feedback I have found to be the most rewarding of the entire process: When I was asked to write the original book, I said I wanted to write something that would help demystify web design and make it available to everyone. And based on the feedback I've gotten, I must have hit the mark dead on.

It may come as a surprise—at least it did to me—but revising and updating a book for the release of new software is almost as much work as writing one from scratch. And as with the writing of the original book, there is an entire cast of characters that have worked behind the scenes to make this book happen. First and foremost is my acquisitions editor, Loretta Yates, who put her unwavering trust and support behind this project and has walked with me every step of the way. Without Loretta you would not be holding this book in your hands, and for that I am eternally grateful.

Apart from making the book up-to-date with the new and exciting third version of Expression Web, one of the main items I wanted to check off on the revision list was to get rid of some of the errors in the first book. And for that, the comments, questions, and suggestions from my readers have been invaluable. In particular I would like to thank Ray Pennoyer and Salvador Torres, who both provided extensive (as in several pages!) feedback and suggestions that have been of great help in shaping this revision.

Another important update in this book is the new and much better looking example project, designed by my loving partner in crime Angela Chih. Demanding only hugs and kisses in return, she produced a great looking site I hope many of my readers will find useful and maybe even use for their own site. Faced with having to rewrite 24 chapters of content, having someone else take care of the design portion was an immense load off my back.

When the first draft of the revision was complete I was lucky enough to have Anna Ullrich from the Expression Web team and Doug Holland sign on as technical editors ensuring that everything I wrote actually made practical sense so that I wouldn't lead you astray. On the development and editing side, Anne Goebel, Todd Brakke, and San Dee Phillips have to be credited for making my sometimes archaic language and run-on sentences make sense.

On the practical side, a big thanks goes out to the Expression Web development team, and in particular to Steven Guttman and Anna Ullrich for giving me unrestricted access to and influence on the application months before it was in its final version. It goes without saying that without access to the prebeta and beta versions of Expression Web 3, there is no way I could have revised my book to have it available at the time of the release of the new software.

I'd also like to thank my friends Paul LaBerge and Qixing Zheng from Microsoft Canada not only for their continuing support and assistance but also for nominating me to receive the Microsoft Most Valuable Professional Award for my work with Expression Web. Receiving the award was an honor, and I can only hope I am living up to it.

There are countless others involved in both the pre- and post-publishing process I have not mentioned, and they should all be gravely offended for not being named by name. Without their contributions, this book would never have made the journey from my mind to the hands of the readers, and they should be acknowledged for their invaluable work.

We Want to Hear from You!

As the reader of this book, you are our most important critic and commentator. We value your opinion and want to know what we're doing right, what we could do better, what areas you'd like to see us publish in, and any other words of wisdom you're willing to pass our way.

You can email or write me directly to let me know what you did or didn't like about this book—as well as what we can do to make our books stronger.

Please note that I cannot help you with technical problems related to the topic of this book, and that due to the high volume of mail I receive, I might not be able to reply to every message.

When you write, please be sure to include this book's title and author as well as your name and phone or email address. I will carefully review your comments and share them with the author and editors who worked on the book.

E-mail: greg.wiegand@pearson.com

Mail: Greg Wiegand
         Associate Publisher
         Sams Publishing
         800 East 96th Street
         Indianapolis, IN 46240 USA

Reader Services

Visit our website and register this book at www.informit.com/title/9780672330643 for convenient access to any updates, downloads, or errata that might be available for this book.

Introduction

About This Book

Because you have opened this book and started reading the introduction, I am assuming that you are interested in learning how to create websites using Microsoft's new and exciting web development application, Expression Web 3. If so, I congratulate you: By choosing this application as your platform, you are already well on your way to creating functional and well-designed sites based on web standards. In other words, unlike me, you are putting the proverbial horse before the cart and starting at the beginning rather than learning things the hard way.

Expression Web 3 is the third version of a web design and development platform that sees Microsoft take a whole new approach to the concept of web standards. The application you work with throughout this book produces standards-based websites right out of the box without requiring any tweaking or custom coding. In fact, using Expression Web 3, you can create advanced standards-based websites with lots of fancy interactive features without ever writing a line of code. And with that, the threshold for learning, understanding, and creating websites that look and behave the same across all browsers and platforms is lowered to a level anyone can manage.

This book is actually a revision of my first book, *Sams Teach Yourself Microsoft Expression Web 2 in 24 Hours*. Well, actually "revision" might be an understatement: In many cases, this book is a complete rewrite of the first book. That means even if you've read the first one, there are a lot of things you can learn from this one. Since the publication of the first book nearly a year ago, I have received a lot of feedback from readers, and I've taken all of it into account. As a result I created an entirely new and much better example project that you can take and use for your own website when you are done. I've also included new and improved tutorials, tricks and tips to make you a better and more effective designer, and an entirely new chapter focusing on the new SuperPreview application included with Expression Web 3 teaching you how to properly test, diagnose, and fix problems you encounter when testing your websites across multiple different browsers and platforms.

When I started writing this book, I spent a lot of time thinking about you, the reader; more specifically how to ensure that after reading this book, you would walk away with not only an understanding of the application but also how to use it to get from an idea to a finalized product. The result of my ponderings was a website called

MyKipple.com that showcases many of the basic and more advanced functions available in Expression Web 3. By following the tutorials in this book, you build the MyKipple.com website from scratch and, in the process, learn how all the different elements come together and how to get the most out of the application. When you finish the last hour and the site is complete, you will have both the tools and know-how to build your own websites using Hypertext Markup Language (HTML), Cascading Style Sheets (CSS), and the many other functions that Expression Web 3 offers. You will also have a basic understanding of how the application deals with more advanced coding languages such as PHP, and you'll learn how to publish a simple Silverlight application.

Accompanying this book is a small website that contains information about the book itself along with the lesson files for each hour and in time a wiki or a forum for you to get further information and showcase your work. The website is located at http://expression.pinkandyellow.com.

Who Is This Book For?

Opening this book you are probably wondering "Is this the right book for me?" So I guess I should tell you who this book was written for. The answer, though it might sound silly, is that I wrote this book for myself—or rather myself 15 years ago.

When I started building websites in the 1990s, I really had no clue what I was doing other than a vision of what I wanted to create. And when I looked around for help in the form of books or tutorials, I couldn't find anything that spoke to me. What was available was either too technical or too superficial. No matter where I looked, I could find only basic algorithms on how to perform simple tasks, never detailed explanations of how to get from point A to point B. As a result, I ended up teaching myself how to do things. Needless to say, I learned the true meaning of the term "taking the long way around."

So, when I signed up to write this book, I had one main goal in mind: to write the book I was looking for and really needed when I started out—a book that took me all the way from a basic sketch on a napkin to a fully working website and taught me how to use the application at the same time.

As a result, this book is written with the novice designer in mind. No, let me rephrase that: As a result, this book is written in a way that I think a novice designer can understand and learn from. I make this distinction because even if you are a seasoned designer or developer, I am certain you can find lots of useful information inside these covers.

Being introduced to Expression Web has had an enormous impact on my business because it reduced what used to take hours or days to only minutes. In particular I am talking about the application's excellent CSS features: More than just a design and development application, Expression Web 3 is a tool that helps you learn, understand, dissect, and modify style sheets with unprecedented speed and accuracy. Getting a firm grasp on these tools and understanding how to use them in real-world scenarios can almost certainly make your work with CSS more efficient and productive, regardless of whether this is the first time you've encountered the term *style sheets* or you are a seasoned professional with years of experience.

So, without further ado, I wish you a pleasant journey and hope you come out on the other side with the skills, understanding, and confidence to take on the wild and exciting world of web design.

Lykke til!

Morten Rand-Hendriksen, June 2009

HOUR 1

Get to Know Microsoft Expression Web 3

What You'll Learn in This Hour:

▶ What Expression Web 3 is and what you can use it for

▶ How to navigate and customize the workspace layout

▶ How to open and close toolbars and panels

▶ How to reset the workspace to the default settings

Opening this book, you probably want to jump right in and start creating websites. But before you start it's a good idea to take the time to familiarize yourself with the program. Whether you are a first-time user or a seasoned web designer, Expression Web 3 has something new to offer. And because you'll be spending a lot of time with the program, learning it before you start working on projects can save you both time and frustration. If you are too impatient, you can always jump ahead to Hour 3, "A Website Is Really Just Text: Build One in 5 Minutes," and come back here later. But as my father always told me, "If you want to bottle an elephant, you better read the manual first." Getting to know your tools before using them makes your life easier in the long run.

Introducing Expression Web 3

Expression Web 3 is a complete web publishing suite bundled into one program. It's an HTML editor, a WYSIWYG editor, an authoring tool, a code debugger, a Cascading Style Sheets (CSS) generator, and a file management tool all wrapped up in one convenient package—a one-stop shop for putting content on the Web. Whether you are a designer with no previous code experience, a developer with no previous design experience, or somewhere between the two, Expression Web 3 can help you work faster and more effectively.

WYSIWYG: What You See Is What You Get. An acronym used for visual web-editing applications in which the user can view and edit the page as it appears in a browser rather than simply viewing and editing code.

As you will see when working with web design, this name is a bit misleading: The fact that a web page looks a certain way in a WYSIWYG editor doesn't necessarily mean it will look the same when viewed through an actual web browser. There are also different kinds of content that cannot be displayed in WYSIWYG editors such as Silverlight applications and dynamic web content. You will be introduced to these components and learn how to deal with this problem later in the book. In spite of this, the WYSIWYG editor is a powerful tool that gives you a fairly accurate picture of what your design will look like on the Web.

Expression Web 3 is a new link in a long chain of web-authoring tools. What makes it unique is that it gives the user the ability to create 100% standards-based sites even without knowing what the term *standards based* means. Expression Web 3 is in many ways a shortcut that opens the world of standards-based code, previously accessible to only the web developer elite, to anyone using it. And because creating standards-based sites is (or should be) the ultimate goal of any web designer, Expression Web 3 gives you a huge advantage. Of course that doesn't mean your sites will be perfect, but you will spend far less time picking at finicky code and solving browser incompatibilities.

With Expression Web 3 you can create new pages and sites from scratch or from templates; view, edit, and alter existing pages and sites; and build new server-based applications with ASP.NET (Active Server Pages .NET) and PHP (PHP: Hypertext Preprocessor; its name is recursive). In short, Expression Web 3 is a complete package for creating and publishing websites whether on a local computer, a network, or the Web.

The terms *standards based* and *web standards* refer to the formal standards and technical specifications set out by the World Wide Web Consortium (W3C) to describe how the World Wide Web works. If you follow these standards, your web page *should* look the same in all web browsers. (I emphasize *should* because not all web browsers follow these standards.) By creating standards-based websites, you avoid many of the problems associated with browser incompatibilities and build clean and functional websites accessible to people with disabilities and anyone on slower connections or older computers. The terms refer to a website's coding, not what it looks like. So, don't worry: A standards-based website does not have to be boring or ordinary, just built properly. If you want more information on web standards, a good place to start is the W3C website: www.w3.org.

Getting and Installing Expression Web 3

Expression Web 3 was launched in July 2009, and is available through most software retailers or through the Microsoft Expression website (www.microsoft.com/expression). If you haven't already, consider purchasing the software as a download from Microsoft rather than through a retailer. Not only is it much quicker than going to a store or ordering from an online retailer, but you save the planet from all the unnecessary waste created in the production and shipping of the product.

If you are new to the field and unsure of whether you want to use this program, you can download from the same site a fully functional trial version that gives you 60 days to make up your mind.

Expression Web 3 is designed for the Microsoft Windows platform and works on Microsoft Windows XP Service Pack 2, Windows Vista, and Windows 7, as well as on Windows Server 2003 and 2008. It also runs on a Mac running the aforementioned Windows operating systems either as a dual boot via Bootcamp or in virtualization software such as VMWare Fusion or Parallels.

Installing the software, whether it's from a download or from a DVD, is straightforward. If you purchased the software from a vendor, your activation key is inside the box. If you purchased the software from the Microsoft Expression website, you received your activation code during the purchase. If you are using a trial version, select the Trial option the first time you run the software.

> If you have any problems with the installation or the program doesn't work after you install it, troubleshooting tips, FAQs, and forums on the Microsoft Expression website can walk you through the troubleshooting process and get you up and running.

Did you Know?

Getting Acquainted with the Workspace

When you open Expression Web 3 for the first time, it presents several views, panels, and toolbars containing tools and information (see Figure 1.1). In the middle, the Code view and the Design view show you the current page. Together, these panes and toolbars give you a complete picture of the project you are working on and multiple ways of working with and editing that project.

The Program Bar

The address and name of the current file you are working with are at the top of the workspace. In Figure 1.1 it says Untitled 1 (untitled_1.html). When you open the program for the first time, it displays this default empty web page. Later you learn how to decide what the program displays when it opens.

FIGURE 1.1
Expression Web
3 as it appears
when first
opened.

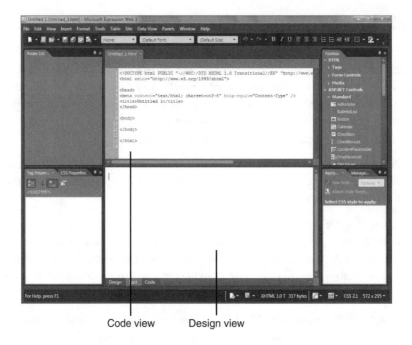

Code view   Design view

The Menu Bar

The menu bar is directly under the address bar. This bar is familiar to anyone who has used a computer program. The menu bar is the program's control center from which you can access any tool, feature, or functionality. Clicking a menu item reveals that item's drop-down menu. Sliding your mouse left and right displays the drop-down menus for each menu item. Some drop-down menu items have an arrow icon to their right. Hovering your mouse pointer over the arrow reveals additional sub-menus. We cover each of these options in later hours. To collapse the menus, simply click anywhere outside the drop-down menu.

▼   **Try It Yourself**

Use the Menu Bar to Close and Open Design View and Code View

If you have never used a web design application like Expression Web 3 before, the window with all its menus and panels and views might seem a bit intimidating. However, when you understand how to use and manipulate them, you will see that they are there for one reason only: to help you get your job done faster and more efficiently.

At the center of the page is the View panel. By default it is split in half horizontally with the Code view on the top and the Design view on the bottom. These views will be explained in detail later but for now let's see how you can use the View menu shown in Figure 1.2 to change them to see only what you want.

FIGURE 1.2
The View menu with the Page submenu open.

1. Click View and hover the mouse pointer over the Page item.

2. Click Design in the submenu that opens to the right (refer to Figure 1.2).

3. Notice that the middle of the workspace now shows only Design view.

4. Repeat step 1 and click Code in the submenu. You now see only Code view.

5. Repeat step 1 and click Split. Notice that doing so restores the workspace to what it was when you started.

Common and Other Toolbars

The Common toolbar is under the menu bar (see Figure 1.3). This toolbar contains the most commonly used functions in the program, such as New, Open, Save, Font,

FIGURE 1.3
The Common toolbar holds the most commonly used tools for easy access.

Alignment, and so on. In addition to being an excellent tool for quick access to frequently used functions, the Common toolbar also displays information about your current selections.

In addition to the Common toolbar are numerous other toolbars that serve different functions (see Figure 1.4). You can activate these toolbars by clicking View on the

FIGURE 1.4
The different toolbars are accessible from the Toolbars sub-menu under View.

Main menu and selecting Toolbars or by right-clicking in the empty area to the right in the Common toolbar and selecting the new Toolbar from the pop-up menu. When you open a new toolbar, it docks directly under the Common toolbar (or whatever is the lowest toolbar visible).

When you hover your mouse over a button or function throughout the program, a small ScreenTip appears explaining what the button or function does and, in some cases, giving you the shortcut for that action. Learning shortcuts not only speeds up your work but also prevents muscle and joint problems caused by excessive mouse use.

Code, Design, and Split View

As you work on your pages you need to switch back and forth between the different views. To make this as easy as possible, the View panel comes equipped with three buttons to toggle the different views on and off, as seen in Figure 1.5.

FIGURE 1.5
The Design, Split, and Code buttons can be found at the bottom of the View panel.

As its name suggests, Code view displays the code or "back end" of the file in which you are working. All web pages are in reality just code documents, and Code view gives you a behind-the-scenes look at the inner workings of your page. Code view has many features to help you in your work, from color coding and line numbering to IntelliSense and snippets. You use this view not only to inspect the code Expression Web 3 created for you but also to make alterations and add your own code. If you work with a strict code file (.css, .php, .js, and so on), this is the only view available.

Did you Know?

When you open a page in your web browser, you are actually looking at the browser's interpretation of the code in the file. Web pages are written in a markup code language that, when interpreted, turns into what you see in your browser. What you don't see is that many of these pages actually consist of several different files, and some of these contain only programming code. These are what I refer to as "strict code files," and they are an important part of functional web design. By placing code in a strict code file, you can use this one file as the code source for multiple pages and thus make sweeping changes to all the related files by editing just one. In this book you learn how to use one such strict code file, known as a Cascading Style Sheet, to control the look and feel of multiple pages at the same time.

Design view is the WYSIWYG editor. This view emulates a web browser and (at least in theory) displays your files as they will appear in a web browser. This is probably where you will do most of your work. In Design view, you can visually edit HTML and other markup files by dragging and dropping content, editing text, and moving borders in much the same way you would work in word processing software such as Microsoft Word. It also features visual aids to help you see how the page functions. Design view provides a much less intimidating approach to web design, and people starting out in the subject often prefer it to Code view.

Split view gives you the best of both worlds: Code view on the top and Design view on the bottom. In Split view, you can see in real time how changes in one view effects the other. For a beginner, working in Split view can greatly enhance the learning process whether you come from a coding background or a design background.

Left and Right Panels

On the left and right sides of the workspace are four panels, described in the following sections. These panels contain tools, information, and content you can use in the design process.

Folder List (Top Left)

The Folder List panel shows the folder and file tree in the project or site you are working within (see Figure 1.6).

FIGURE 1.6
Folder List panel.

Tag Properties and CSS Properties (Bottom Left)

This panel contains two tabbed subpanes. The Tag Properties (see Figure 1.7) and CSS Properties (see Figure 1.8) panes display the current tag or CSS properties of the

FIGURE 1.7
Tag Properties panel.

FIGURE 1.8
CSS Properties panel.

selected object. Clicking different parts of the code in Code view shows how the tag properties change depending on the code you click. We cover both panes in more detail in later hours.

Toolbox (Top Right)

The Toolbox panel contains code segments and tags frequently used while editing in Code view (see Figure 1.9). These make up two main sections, HTML and ASP.NET

FIGURE 1.9
Toolbox panel.

Controls, and each section has multiple subcategories. By clicking the + and – icons, you can explode and collapse the categories to see what they contain.

Apply Styles and Manage Styles (Bottom Right)

This panel contains two tabbed subpanels. The Apply Styles panel displays the CSS styles available to the current page and enables you to apply styles to objects in Design view (see Figure 1.10). The Manage Styles panel has similar functionality

FIGURE 1.10
Apply Styles
panel.

with the addition of a preview area where you can see what each style does to your content (see Figure 1.11). Both panels give you the ability to either apply styles or create new styles.

FIGURE 1.11
Manage Styles
panel.

All the panels are intelligent; they learn from how you use the program. If you use a particular item often, it moves higher on the list to make it more accessible. A rarely used item moves down on the list. The panels also help you by turning currently unavailable functions gray so that you don't waste time trying to do something impossible.

Status Bar

The status bar is at the bottom of the workspace (see Figure 1.12). It provides information about the program itself and general information such as file size and overall settings (what code format you are using and so on) of the page you are working

FIGURE 1.12
The status bar
appears on the
bottom of the
workspace and
gives you con-
stant and current
information
about the file you
are working on.

on. In addition, the status bar has tools that warn you if there is invalid or incompatible code in your page. If you want to close the status bar (not something I recommend), click Tools, Application Options and uncheck Show Status Bar under General.

Changing and Customizing the Workspace

Depending on what you are doing, you might want to have a certain panel or menu
more prominently featured, or you might want to open a new panel with more functions. To accommodate this, the workspace is completely customizable: You can grab
any horizontal and vertical border within the workspace to make a panel smaller or
larger. You can also grab panels and move them around both by repositioning them
within the workspace and by undocking and floating them on top of or outside the
window (see Figure 1.13). This technique is particularly useful if you use a dual-monitor

FIGURE 1.13
The Manage
Styles panel
floating above
the workspace.

setup because you can dedicate the main window to Code view and Design view and leave all the tools on the other screen.

As you saw previously, each panel can contain several subpanels. Each subpanel becomes accessible through tabs. Expression Web 3 groups related subpanels together for convenience, but you are free to move them around in any way you like.

The Panels menu on the menu bar controls the panels (see Figure 1.14). From here you can select what panels are active (marked by a check mark). If you click one not

FIGURE 1.14
You can turn all available panels on and off from the Panels menu.

currently featured in the workspace, the program adds it to the relevant panel. You can remove a panel from view by clicking the small X in its upper-right corner.

New to Expression Web 3 is the ability to pin the panels to the sides of the workspace. This feature allows you to keep the panels handy in the workspace without them taking up much needed real estate. To pin a panel to the side, simply click the pin icon at the top-right corner of the panel (see Figure 1.15).

When a panel has been pinned to the side, the panel name is written vertically down the side. To access the panel, simply hover your mouse over the name of the desired panel and it "pops" out to cover your workspace (see Figure 1.16). In addition to the

Pin icon

FIGURE 1.15
You can pin any panel to the side of the workspace by clicking the pin icon in the top-right corner of the panel.

Pinned panels —

FIGURE 1.16
The pinned panel pops out to cover the workspace when you hover your mouse over the name.

obvious space saving, one interesting benefit of using this pinning feature is that when the panels open when hovered over, they are wider than the default setting. This enables more information to display.

To unpin the panels and place them back in their normal configuration, simply click the horizontal pin in the top-right corner of the currently active pinned panel (see Figure 1.16). If you want to quickly pin or unpin all the panels in your workspace, go to Panels on the Main menu and select Hide Panels. To unpin them again, go back to the menu and uncheck the same function.

▼   **Try It Yourself**

Change the Size and Content of the Panels

As you perform different tasks while working on a page or website, your needs will change in terms of what tools and information should be prominently displayed and what can be hidden. For this reason Expression Web 3 gives you complete control over what panels are available and where they are positioned at any time.

1. Hover your mouse pointer over the vertical line that separates the Code and Design views from the right panels.

2. Click and drag the separator to the left to create more space for the panels.

3. Do the same with the horizontal line separating the top and bottom panels to allow more space for the bottom panel.

4. Hover your mouse pointer over the horizontal line that separates Code view and Design view.

5. Click and drag the separator upward to create more space for Design view.

6. Use the pin icon in the Folder List panel to pin the folder list to the left side of the workspace. Note that when the Folder List is pinned, the Tag and CSS Properties panel shifts up to fill out the space.

7. Pin the Tag and CSS Properties panel to the side to free up space for the View panel (see Figure 1.17).

8. Click and hold the Apply Styles panel and drag it around inside the workspace. Notice how it suggests different docking positions depending on which area you hover over.

9. Drag the Apply Styles panel to the edge of the workspace so that it floats on top before letting go. If you have a dual-monitor setup, drag the panel to the other monitor so that it doesn't cover the main window.

10. Click the Panels button on the menu bar (now on the left side of your workspace) and select Behaviors. Notice that the Behaviors panel appears at its default location in the lower-right corner.

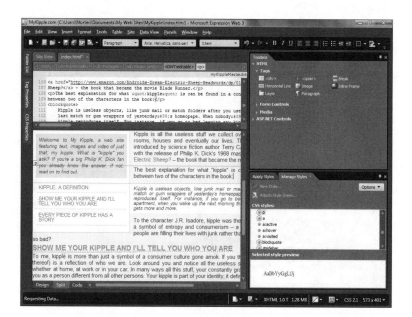

FIGURE 1.17
You can customize the look of Expression Web 3 to suit your specific needs.

11. Click and hold the Behaviors tab in the floating panel and drag it away from the panel until it floats on its own.

Following this exercise, you can see that the workspace is flexible, and there is no "right" or "wrong" in terms of workspace layout: Whatever works for you is the right layout. Figure 1.18 shows my workspace while I was in the middle of working on the demo site for this book. It might look messy and out of control, but at the time it made sense to me.

But what if your workspace gets too "messy" or you accidentally close a panel or lose it altogether? To simplify the process of cleaning up your workspace, click the Panels button on the menu bar and select Reset Workspace Layout to restore its original configuration.

Summary

In this hour, you learned how Expression Web 3 works and how you can customize it to suit your needs. To some readers, this information might seem rudimentary or even redundant. But as you progress through the next 23 hours, you will see that having a solid understanding of the program makes a world of difference when you encounter new challenges. By knowing the basics, your understanding of the more

FIGURE 1.18
There is no right or wrong when it comes to work-space layout. This layout has three toolbars and Snapshot (found under the Panels menu) turned on.

advanced issues will be much easier. And because you'll be spending a lot of time with this program, it's worth your time to get to know it properly first.

For convenience, this book uses the default workspace and panel layout. But now that you know how to customize them, feel free to organize their layout any way you see fit.

Q&A

Q. *The Common toolbar looks a lot like the Formatting toolbar in Microsoft Word. Does that mean that it works the same way?*

A. Both yes and no. The Common toolbar has many of the same functions as Microsoft Word's Formatting toolbar, but when you click a button on the Common toolbar, a change happens through the addition or modification of a snippet in the code or hypertext rather than in the text. (The program refers to these code snippets as *styles*.) So yes, they look similar, but no, what happens when you push a button is different.

Q. *Can I accidentally lose a panel or a toolbar and not be able to open it again?*

A. No. All the panels are accessible from the Panels button on the Main menu. If you accidentally close a panel, you can always open it again from there. Furthermore, you can always reset the original layout of the panels by clicking

Panels and Reset Workspace Layout. All the toolbars are accessible by clicking View and selecting Toolbars.

Workshop

The workshop has quiz questions to help you put to use what you just learned. If you get stuck, the answers to the quiz questions are in the next section. But try to answer the questions first. Otherwise you'll only be cheating yourself.

Quiz

1. What is the proper way to create a web page?

    A. Using only Code view

    B. Using only Design view

    C. Using Split view

    D. None of the above

2. How many panels can you have open at one time?

    A. 8

    B. 14

    C. As many as you like

Answers

1. D. None of the above. There is no right or wrong when it comes to how you create a web page. Some people create spectacular sites using only Notepad, whereas others create just as spectacular sites without ever seeing a line of code. To get the most out of this book, use Split view as much as possible. That way you get to see what happens in Code view when you make changes in Design view and vice versa. But, in the end, what works best is up to the individual user.

2. C. In theory you could fill your entire screen with panels and toolbars, but if you did it would be hard to get any work done. With that said, however, you are free to set up your workspace any way you please.

HOUR 2

Beginning at the End: A Walkthrough of the Finished Project

What You'll Learn in This Hour:

▶ How to import and work with a completed website in Expression Web 3

▶ How to preview a site in your browser

▶ How this book is laid out

▶ How to use the different tools in Expression Web 3 to explore a website and learn how it works

Introduction

When I start to read a book like this, I always want to see the end result of all the lessons before I start so that I know what I'm getting myself into. So, rather than making you go through all the tutorials to see what you can build in just a few hours with Expression Web 3, I've decided to start at the very end by showing you the site you will build through these lessons and use it to showcase some of the many features available in this application.

Because websites consist of many different files linked together, it is important to keep everything organized. But to do this, you first need to understand what the different elements are and how they work and relate to each other. By looking at a completed website and using the tools available in Expression Web 3, you can get a firmer grip on how it all comes together.

The methods you learn in this hour will be useful to you down the road as well. In fact, when you finish Hour 24, "Publishing Your Website," I urge you to come back to this hour for a second look. Because you'll come back with a better understanding of how the website works, you'll have a whole new perspective on the different lessons in this hour.

Working with a Completed Website

To work efficiently in Expression Web 3 (or any web design application for that matter), it is important to understand how the application handles files and file relationships. By working with a completed website, you can experiment and learn how Expression Web 3 works with you to keep everything functioning properly as you edit and reorganize the different elements. That way you get an early start developing techniques and understanding that usually comes only much later in the learning process.

The Import Site Wizard is a helpful tool that saves you a lot of time when you need to work on a website built in a different application or by a different designer. Therefore you will probably use it quite frequently.

▼ **Try It Yourself**

Importing a Completed Website

A website is actually just a folder with a group of files linked together. What makes it a *website* is that the files within that folder can be viewed using a web browser. You get a more thorough explanation of this idea later in this book. By creating a new website in Expression Web 3, you are telling the application that the main (root) folder is the bottom line or foundation and that everything in it relates back to this folder. When you publish your website, the domain name replaces the root folder.

To start, you use the Import Site Wizard to import the finished project into the application as a new website. You can use it to import sites from your local computer or network and from external web servers or even directly from the websites themselves.

1. Go to the book website at http://expression.pinkandyellow.com and download the lesson files for this hour to a central location on your computer.

2. Open Expression Web 3.

3. Go to Site, Import and select Import Site Wizard. This opens the Import Site Wizard dialog, as shown in Figure 2.1.

4. Select the File System option and use the Browse button to navigate to the location where you placed the lesson files for this hour. Select the folder called MyKippleFinal. With the address set, click Next.

FIGURE 2.1
The Import Site Wizard dialog lets you import an existing site from a multitude of different sources both on your computer and on the Web.

5. On the next page (see Figure 2.2), you are asked to define where the local copy of the site should be created. You need to select a folder different from the one the files are in right now. It is always a good idea to keep all your website projects in one location on your computer so that they are easy to find. Many people use the My Web Sites folder under Documents for this. Browse to the location you want the new website to be created in, create a new folder called **MyKippleFinal**, and select it. Click Next.

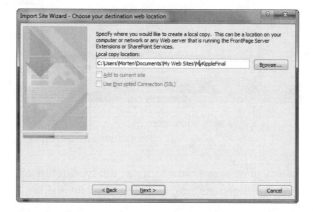

FIGURE 2.2
The second page of the Import Site Wizard lets you define where you want the new website project placed on your computer.

6. Expression Web 3 will most likely flash two warning messages at this point, the first one telling you there is no site at the location you defined in step 4 and the second asking you if you want to set up a site in that location. Click OK to both. The final page of the Import Site Wizard tells you that the website has been set up and that you can now start importing files. Click Finish.

Now that you have defined a location for the new website, Expression Web 3 opens in Site view, and you see all the files in the remote location (the folder you downloaded the lesson files to) on the right and your new site location on the left. To begin with, the left side is blank. To populate your new site with the files from the finished project, press the blue left-pointing arrow between the two views. This button publishes the existing files to your new site. This might seem a bit odd, but if you consider a scenario in which you were downloading files off a web server, it makes more sense.

When the transfer is complete, you see a view like the one shown in Figure 2.3. This view shows you the local website on the left and the remote website on the right. This

FIGURE 2.3
The second page of the Import Site Wizard lets you define where you want the new website project placed on your computer.

Local website addresses

Remote website addresses

is your site management window from which you can synchronize two locations or move files and folders between the local and remote locations either one by one or in groups. Expression Web 3 keeps tabs on what files have been moved and what files have been modified in the program, and whenever you come back to this view, it tells you what files need to be updated on either the local or remote location.

You have successfully imported the new website when you can see that the local and remote websites are identical in terms of files and folders and that the Folder View panel shows all the files and folders.

By the Way

Don't Be Confused by the Names "Local" and "Remote"

As you saw in the preceding lesson, Expression Web 3 separates the website you are working with from the one you are publishing to by naming them *local website* and *remote website*, respectively. But these names can easily be confusing. In the example, you just saw it can be argued that *both* websites are local.

Expression Web 3 considers the website you open in the application as the local website and the one you are publishing the files you have worked on to as the remote website, regardless of the actual location of either. This can lead to some very interesting and confusing results: If you want to, you can set up a website so that the files you are working on are on a web server (technically a *remote* location) and publish these files to a hard drive on your computer (technically a *local* location). In that case, the web server would be considered the *local* website and placed on the left, whereas the folder on your hard drive would be considered the *remote* website and placed on the right.

If you are ever confused about which location is defined as remote or local, you can always check the address bars at the top of each folder tree in Site view (refer to Figure 2.3).

Previewing the Site in Your Browser

Now that you have set up the MyKipple website in Expression Web 3, look at how the site works in real life. One of the most important habits you need to establish when working with web design is to constantly test what you are doing in one (or preferably several) browsers to see that everything is working as it should. For this reason, you have the ability to preview a page in your browser from anywhere inside the application.

To see the new site as it would appear for any visitor when it is on the Web, go to the Folder List panel, right-click on the default.html file, and select the default preview browser (prefixed by a browser icon) from the pop-up menu (see Figure 2.4).

FIGURE 2.4
You can preview any page in your website by selecting a browser from the right-click menu. In this case the default browser is Firefox 3.0.11.

This opens the default.html page of the MyKipple website in your browser. The default.html page is the home page of the website, and from here you can navigate through all the different pages that have been created.

The website itself serves as a good introduction to the different sections of this book. The following sections describe the different functionalities and when you will learn them.

Setting Up a Website and Building Pages

All websites consist of a group of web pages. These pages can contain anything from text to images to interactive elements such as Flash movies or Silverlight applications. In Hours 3, "A Website Is Really Just Text: Build One in 5 Minutes," and 4, "Building a Home Page: A Look Behind the Curtain," you learn how to set up a new site and build simple pages.

Hyperlinks

On the MyKipple website, you can see that several segments of text are highlighted in blue. These are hyperlinks that point the browser to different pages either within the website or in external websites. You learn how to create and manage hyperlinks in Hour 5, "Getting Connected with (Hyper)Links: The Cornerstone of the World Wide Web."

Images

If you scroll down to the last paragraph and click on the link with the text "my collection of cameras," you are taken to a new page with a large image of a collection of cameras. Images are an important part of web design and can serve both as content (such as the camera image), as functional elements such as buttons, or even as design elements. You learn how to insert and manage images in Hours 6, "Getting Visual, Part 1: Adding Images and Graphics," and 7, "Getting Visual, Part 2: Advanced Image Editing, Thumbnails, and Hotspots."

Tables

At the bottom of the camera page, you find a standard HTML table. In the past tables were heavily used as design elements to structure the contents of web pages. But this was never an ideal situation, and it caused a lot of problems for designers and the people visiting their sites. As a result, designers are moving away from using tables as design elements and now use them only for their intended purpose: to display tabular data. Because the focus of this book is to learn how to design standards-based websites with Expression Web 3, you learn how to use tables to display tabular data only. Tables are covered in Hour 9, "Getting Boxed In, Part 1: Using Tables for Tabular Content."

Styling the Content

Go back to the home page by clicking the Home button, and you see that the text in the page has many different styles (see Figure 2.5). The heading is big, uppercase,

FIGURE 2.5
The home page of the MyKipple website features many different text styles defined by Cascading Style Sheets.

and gray; the paragraph text is smaller, darker, and justified. There are subheadings that look different from the main heading, links, a sidebar with a text box and links, and so on. If you were working in a word processing application, you would have applied these different looks or *styles* to each of the sections. But in standards-based web design, you create an external set of styles that define how the different elements look and behave. These styles are created with a code language called Cascading Style Sheets (CSS), and Expression Web 3 is an excellent tool for both learning and working with this language. In Hour 10, "Bringing Style to Substance with Cascading Style Sheets," you learn how to create and manage these CSS styles to give your content more identity.

Page Layout

As you just learned, designers used to use tables to create page layouts, but this practice is on the way out. In its place designers are now turning to CSS as their primary layout tool. In addition to changing the look and feel of text and other content, CSS can build containers or *boxes* that wrap the content. Using this technique, you can group different elements together and create styles and substyles to define how these different elements should look and behave. With the proper use of CSS, you can create visually stunning and easily approachable web layouts that look the same across all browsers and platforms. Hours 11, "Getting Boxed In, Part 2: Knee Deep in CSS," and 14, "Harnessing the Power of CSS Layouts," show you how to create, modify, and apply styles using the built in CSS functionalities of Expression Web 3 and by editing code directly. In these hours, you learn how to use CSS to create advanced layouts for your sites and how external style sheets can control the look and feel of multiple pages from one central location.

Buttons

Buttons are a subgenre of the common hyperlink in which the hyperlink is attached to a visual element such as an image or a text box. Because there are many different types of buttons, there are many different ways to make them, and each serves its own purpose. In Hour 15, "Buttons, Buttons, Buttons," you learn how to create several different types of buttons and also when to use these.

Behaviors

To add increased functionality to your pages, you can include small programs in your pages that perform simple actions when they are triggered by the visitor. Expression Web 3 has a series of these common actions known as *behaviors* built in for easy application. You can see one such behavior if you go back to the camera collection page, click on the top middle camera in the big photo, and click on the small detail image of the camera in the second paragraph on the new page. As seen in Figure 2.6, this particular behavior opens a new small window that shows a larger version of the image. In Hour 16, "Using Behaviors," you learn about the different behaviors available in Expression Web 3 and how to use them to create interactive experiences for your visitors.

Frames and Layers

Back on the Home page, if you hover over the hyperlink named Do Androids Dream of Electric Sheep? you notice that a small window appears inside the page showing an Amazon.com page. This is called an *inline frame* or *iFrame*, and it is a technique that cuts a hole in your current page and places content from a different page inside it. In this example, the iFrame is placed inside a layer so that it hovers over the rest of

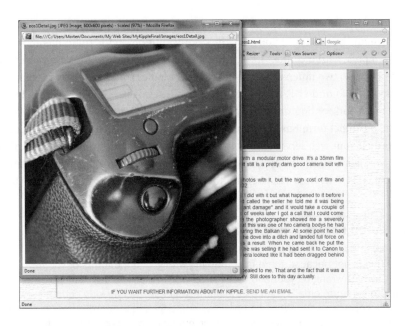

FIGURE 2.6
In Hour 16, you learn how to use behaviors to create effects such as this pop-up window that opens when you click on the smaller image on the main page.

the page rather than appearing alongside it. In Hour 17, "Frames and Layers," you learn how to use frames and layers to place interactive and external content inside or on top of your regular content to make external preview windows and other advanced effects. You also learn how to make a frames-based web page and how these differ from regular web pages.

The Main Menu

Aside from the content itself, I would argue that the navigation is the most important feature of any website. There are many ways to create functional navigation and some are better than others. One of the most intuitive and visually exciting navigational tools you can put on your website is the image-based menu. As with everything else, there are several different ways you can make such menus, and each has advantages and drawbacks. In Hour 18, "Building a Functional Menu," you learn how to create several different CSS-based menus including a drop-down menu. All these menus are highly functional and are used heavily throughout the Web.

Contact Forms

The Internet allows for a two-way conversation between the website owner and the visitor. To facilitate this type of communication, there is a large group of tools known as *forms* built in to the main code language of the Internet, HTML. Using forms you can create anything from a simple email form to advanced forum, blog, and even e-commerce functionalities. If you click the Contact button on the main menu, you are taken to a page with a contact form. In this book you learn how to make this contact form work using two different server-based technologies called FrontPage Server Extensions (FPSE) and PHP. In Hour 20, "Getting Interactive with Forms," you learn how to build and configure web forms and built-in functionality in Expression Web 3 to create a contact form based on FrontPage Server Extensions. However this form works only if your web server has FrontPage Server Extensions installed. As an alternative, you learn how to build an identical email form using a different code language called PHP in Hour 22, "Beyond the Basics, Part 1: PHP in Expression Web 3."

The Email Forms Don't Work!

If you try to use the email form, you immediately notice that it doesn't actually work. This is not because there is something wrong with the forms or you have done anything wrong on your end. Both FPSE and PHP forms use *server-side scripts* to generate emails. And as the name suggests, server-side scripts need to run on a server to work. When you preview your pages in your browser from Expression Web 3, you are not using a web server, but just looking at your local files.

In Hours 20 and 22, you will be introduced to an application known as Expression Development Server and learn how to use it to preview the functionality of the email forms. If you want to see a fully working version of the email forms right now, go to www.mykipple.com.

Flash and Silverlight Galleries

On the main menu there are two buttons named Flash and Silverlight. In Hour 21, "Working with Flash and Silverlight," you learn how to include Flash movies and Silverlight applications into your pages. Both these types of content are created using dedicated applications, and you can use only Expression Web 3 to insert them into your pages and configure their data files. In that hour, you get a glimpse into the world of both Flash and Silverlight to get a basic understanding of how these technologies work and interact with your website. You also learn how to insert Flash-based videos from sites such as YouTube into your site.

Watch Out!

The Silverlight Gallery Doesn't Work!

As with the email forms, the Silverlight gallery doesn't work when you preview it in your browser. This is because Silverlight is a server-side script language and requires a web server to run. You learn how to trick the browser to preview your

Silverlight application in Hour 21, but until then if you want to see a fully working version of the Silverlight gallery right now, go to www.mykipple.com.

Exploring the Website in Expression Web 3

Back in Expression Web 3, you can use the different features to explore the website and understand how it works. The application comes equipped with a set of tools to help you get a quick overview of the different elements the site is made up of and how everything is put together to work.

On the bottom of the Web Site view, you have four tabs: Folders, Publishing, Reports, and Hyperlinks. These are four different ways to view your website:

▶ Folders gives you a regular browser view of the files and folders in your website. In other words, it works the same way as the Folder List panel.

▶ Publishing gives you a view of the local and remote websites side by side and lets you transfer files between the two locations either one at a time or in groups. This is where you actually publish your site to the Web (publishing your site is covered in Hour 24).

▶ Reports gives you a rundown of all the assets in your website and the status of each of these assets. From there you can see, for example, how many hyperlinks are in the site (and how many of them are broken), how many images it contains, and how many files are *unlinked*—meaning they can't be accessed by the visitor.

▶ Hyperlinks creates a visual map that looks a lot like a mind-map, showing your files and how they relate to each other through hyperlinks. This tool makes it easy to understand how the site is organized.

Click on the Reports button to see the stats of the new website you imported. Expression Web 3 produces a list of all the different assets grouped in specific categories, as shown in Figure 2.7.

Two of the most important items on this list are Slow Pages and Broken Links. The Slow Pages report gives you a list of all the pages estimated to take more than 30 seconds to load on a 56Kbps connection. This report is important if you expect a lot of visitors with slower connections and shows you whether any of your pages is unnecessarily large or heavy to load. You can change the default connection speed the report tests for by going to Tools, Application Options and selecting the Reports View tab.

FIGURE 2.7
Reports gives you a complete overview of all the assets on your website and how they relate to each other.

When you click on Broken Hyperlinks, the Hyperlinks report opens displaying all the broken and unverified hyperlinks. By default all external links are considered unverified until they are verified by the application. When you open the Broken or Unverified report, Expression Web 3 asks whether you want it to verify the external links for you (see Figure 2.8). The application goes to each of the hyperlink locations to ensure that they are valid. If so, the hyperlink is checked off as valid. If not, it is checked off as broken.

FIGURE 2.8
Expression Web 3 can help you verify that all your hyperlinks point to real pages or assets.

▼ **Try It Yourself**

Fix a Broken Hyperlink

After running the report, there should be one broken hyperlink pointing to a file called Contact/confirmed.html. You can fix broken hyperlinks right from the report without even opening the page itself.

1. Right-click on the broken hyperlink and select Edit Hyperlink. This opens the
   Edit Hyperlink dialog (see Figure 2.9).

2. From here use the Browse button to find the correct file. It is under the Contact
   folder and is called success.html.

FIGURE 2.9
You can fix bro-
ken hyperlinks
from the Reports
view without
opening the
pages them-
selves.

3. Click the Replace button and the hyperlink is automatically updated in all the
   pages where it is featured.

Keeping Your Pages Functional

As you previously learned, a website consists of a group of files and folders that are
linked together. That means for the individual pages of the site to work, all the links
between them have to be correct and up-to-date. One of the many important features
of Expression Web 3 is that it keeps tabs on your files for you, making the necessary
changes throughout all your files when something is changed.

As long as you make the changes to your pages, files, and folders inside Expression
Web 3, the application makes all the necessary changes to the links within related
files to make everything run smoothly. So, if you want to move a file or folder into or
out of another folder, always use either the Folder List panel or the Folder view, and
the links to your files and folders will be updated automatically. A short example puts
this into context.

Right now the root folder (main folder) of the website contains two files: kippleStyles.css and layout.css. These two files (known as *style sheets*) contain all the CSS or styling code for all the pages of the site, and as a result every page has a link to them. To make the style sheets easier to find, you want to put them in their own folder called Styles.

1. Switch to Folders view and click on the folder icon in the upper-right corner to create a new folder. Give it the name **Styles**.

2. Drag-and-drop the kippleStyles.css and layout.css files into the new Styles folder.

3. A dialog briefly appears telling you that the files are being renamed. This means that all the links that point to these two files from all the pages are being updated to reflect the change in location. When the dialog disappears, preview the default.html page in your browser again to make sure nothing changed.

When you preview the pages in your browser, it appears as if nothing has changed, but in fact the links to the external style sheets have been changed in every page. If Expression Web 3 hadn't changed all the links to the two files you moved, all the pages would have appeared as regular text without the backgrounds and different styles. By using this drag-and-drop technique, you can move any and all files inside your site and be certain that Expression Web 3 updates the links that point to them so that everything keeps working as it is supposed to.

Never Move Your Files Outside of Expression Web 3

A common mistake of new web designers is moving files or folders using the regular browser window in their operating system rather than inside Expression Web 3. If you move a file or folder that way, the hyperlinks that tell the browser where these files are when the pages are displayed will not be updated, and as a result you end up with a page that doesn't work properly. If you want to move a file from one folder to another, you should *always* use the Folder List panel or Folders view to ensure that all your hyperlinks are updated accordingly.

Summary

Expression Web 3 is a powerful web design and management tool that lets you easily build and publish advanced websites based on web standards. In this hour, you explored the final product you will end up with after following all the tutorials in this book and used it to learn how Expression Web 3 works to help you manage your website.

The ability to import an existing website gives you a quick-and-easy way to pick up an old project or take over an existing project from someone else. In this hour, you learned how to import an existing website and move the necessary files from a remote location to your website's folder. You also learned how to use the Reports view to manage the files and folders in your website and track any problems or errors that are present. Expression Web 3 is set up in such a way that you can find and fix problems such as broken hyperlinks without actually having to open the pages and make changes there. This ability is a huge timesaver and gives you intimate control of the site even without knowing or understanding exactly how it works.

Finally, you learned how to use the Folder List and Folders view to rearrange the files within your website without breaking the many links between them by letting Expression Web 3 handle all the details for you.

What you saw in this hour is just the beginning. In the coming hours, you learn how to build the MyKipple website from scratch and through that learn how to get the most out of Expression Web 3.

Q&A

Q. *When I preview the MyKipple site in Internet Explorer, a bar appears on top of the page saying that to protect my security it has blocked the page from running scripts and ActiveX controls that would access my computer. Does this mean I have a virus or that there is something dangerous in the MyKipple website project?*

A. Internet Explorer is a little overprotective when it comes to previewing local websites. By that I mean if the same pages were loaded from the Web, you wouldn't be getting that message. You can safely click on the bar and select Allow Blocked Content. There is nothing in the MyKipple website project that would harm your computer in any way.

Q. *The contact pages/Silverlight gallery doesn't work at all! There's something wrong with these files.*

A. The contact forms and Silverlight gallery all work by utilizing server-side scripts. When you preview these pages directly from Expression Web 3, the scripts cannot run. If you want to test these pages properly in your browser from the local location, you can do so by triggering Expression Development Server. For more information on this, check Hour 21 for the Silverlight gallery, Hour 20 for the FrontPage Server Extensions form, and Hour 22 for the PHP form.

Workshop

The workshop has an exercise to help you put to use what you have just learned.

Exercise

Open the Hyperlinks view by clicking the button on the bottom of the view and select any of the pages in the Folder View panel to see how it relates to other pages and files. You see that all the pages that link *to* the page are placed on the left and all the pages the selected page links to are placed on the right. You can click on any of the other icons in the view to see how these files relate to further files as well.

A Website Is Really Just Text: Build One in 5 Minutes

What You'll Learn in This Hour:

- ▶ How to create a new website
- ▶ How to create a new page
- ▶ How to create and edit simple text content using Design view
- ▶ How to test your first web page in multiple browsers
- ▶ How to use SuperPreview to test your pages against Internet Explorer 6 and other browsers

Introduction

Now that you have seen what this program can do, it's your turn to make your own project. You start at the beginning with a blank site and one Hypertext Markup Language (HTML) page, and work your way from there to the fully functional site you saw in Hour 2, "Beginning at the End: A Walkthrough of the Finished Project."

Creating a New Website

As you saw in Hour 2, a website is a grouping of related files and folders under one main folder. In fact, a website such as www.designisphilosophy.com is little more than a folder on a server you can access through the Internet. By creating a new website in Expression Web 3, you tell the program "This folder is where I will put all the text, images, and other files I want to share with everyone in the world when they visit the website. Please keep track of them for me." In response, Expression Web

3 keeps tabs on what you do and makes appropriate changes to your files to reflect the changes you have made in related files and keep the website working properly. It does so by creating a set of hidden metadata files that describe the site and its contents. That way the information about how your site functions is stored even if you delete the program from your computer or hand over the project to another Expression Web 3 user.

The first thing to do when you start a new project is to create a new website. You can do this from the Site menu or from the New Site icon on the Common toolbar. This opens the New Web Site dialog, which displays the different options available to you (see Figure 3.1).

FIGURE 3.1
The New Web Site dialog gives you the ability to create new websites from scratch, from templates or by importing an existing site.

<table>
<tr><td colspan="3">**By the Way**</td></tr>
</table>

Expression Web 3 makes a more deliberate separation between Sites and Pages through the introduction of the New Site button on the Common toolbar and the moving of the New Site, Open Site, Recent Site, and Close Site functions from the File menu to the Site menu.

From the New Web Site dialog, you have the option to make a basic website with no content, one from a template, or you can import an existing site using the Import Site Wizard. Under General are three more options: One Page Web Site, Empty Web Site, and Import Web Site Wizard. The One Page Web Site option creates a website with a home page file called default.html. The Empty Web Site option creates a website folder with no files. The Import Web Site Wizard lets you import an already existing site from a local folder, a network folder, or the Web.

By the Way

Don't take titles such as One Page Web Site and Empty Web Site too literally. People often think of computer programs as rigid and inflexible and start to worry when they see definite descriptions like these. A common question that arises when people open the New Web Site dialog for the first time is "What option do I choose if I want to create a site with *more* than one page?" It might seem a silly question to those well traveled in the world of web design, but this confusion is completely understandable in much the same way that my old high school teacher could never understand that the computer casing was not the hard drive. It's all a matter of perspective. In reality, programs are (at least for the most part) very flexible and titles such as these are merely general descriptions. Using a One Page Web Site template in Expression Web 3 just means that you start with a folder with one file. In fact, strictly speaking, a one-page website isn't a website at all—it's just a single web page. Likewise, an "Empty Web Site" is a website folder that starts with no files in it with the expectation that more files will be added later.

At the bottom of the dialog is the suggested location for your new website. The suggested location varies depending on your computer's operating system and setup. To avoid confusion, you should always create a new folder with the same name as your project and use it as your website folder. You can use the Browse button to select any folder on your hard drive, on a local network, or on an external server, such as your website or root folder, but keeping your files on one of your local hard drives is usually the best solution.

It's a good idea to have a central location where you keep all your websites. Expression Web 3 suggests you use the My Web Sites folder located under Documents, but you can use any folder you want. This book uses the My Web Sites folder as the central location for all projects.

Try It Yourself ▼

Create a New One-Page Website

Creating a new website should always be the first step when starting a new project. In this task, you create a new website with one HTML page.

1. Click the New Site icon (second from the left on the Common toolbar) or click Site and select New Site from the main menu.

2. In the New dialog, select General and One Page Site.

3. Click the Browse button next to the Location box on the bottom of the dialog and navigate to the My Web Sites folder under Documents. Create a New Folder and name the new folder **MyKipple**.

4. Click the MyKipple folder to highlight it and click Open. The Site Name automatically matches the folder name you created, unless you want to give the site a different identifying name.

5. Make sure the Add to Managed List box is checked and click OK.

Did you Know?

> **Title**
>
> When you start Expression Web 3 again after closing it, by default the program opens the last project you were working on. This function is great if you are working on only one project but can be annoying if you have several projects going at once. If you want the program to start without opening a website and create a blank web page instead, you can change the settings under Tools, Application Options.

Expression Web 3 has now created a new site with one page called default.html (see Figure 3.2). This is the blank canvas you work with from here on out.

FIGURE 3.2
MyKipple site as it appears after creation.

As you make changes to the files in the website, Expression Web 3 keeps tabs on what you do and makes sure your hyperlinks are up-to-date even if you change them to keep everything working properly.

Creating Your First Web Page

Now that you have created a website, the Site view appears in place of the Split view you previously saw. You explored the different functions of this pane in Hour 2. For now, let's focus on creating your first web page.

As you can see, your new website contains one file called default.html. In the web world, particular filenames signify a home page: index and the less common default or main. All versions of Expression Web use default.html as the home page, A *home page* or *root page* is the page the browser looks for in a folder if the visitor does not specify a particular filename in the address bar.

Default.html is an HTML file that contains all the code a web browser needs to display the web page.

HTML is the most prevalent markup or publishing language for creating websites. A markup language is a set of code snippets that define for a browser how it should lay out and format text. Used correctly, HTML is a powerful tool to organize and display large amounts of content in a simple and accessible way. For further information on HTML, visit http://en.wikipedia.org/wiki/HTML.

Double-click the filename and make sure you are in Split view (see Figure 3.3). As you can see, although it contains some code, it has no content. If you were to open the file

FIGURE 3.3
Even though there are several lines of code in Code view, default.html is empty in Design view because there is no content yet.

in a browser at this point, all you would get is a white page. So, before going any further, you need to add some content.

To see how easy it is to create a simple web page, switch to Design view so that all you see is the blank page. When set to Design view, Expression Web 3 works in much the same way as a word processing application, such as Microsoft Word. This is great when you want to edit content quickly. Click anywhere inside Design view and start typing text. The text appears in a dotted box with a P hovering over it. This box is a visual aid called Block Selection, and it gives a visual representation of what content a particular element applies to (in this instance P or "paragraph"). If you click on the dotted line itself, Expression Web 3 adds pink shading above and below it, providing a visual representation of the default margins the paragraph has. You can turn Block Selection and all other visual aids on and off from the Visual Aids menu under the View menu or from the Visual Aids button on the status bar (see Figure 3.4).

FIGURE 3.4
The Visual Aids button on the status bar lets you turn on and off visual aids as you work.

If you click somewhere else on the page, the Block Selection box disappears and you see the text as it appears in a browser. By moving the cursor to the end of this line, you can continue your current paragraph. If you press Enter, the cursor shifts down approximately two lines to start a new paragraph, and Expression Web 3 creates a new Block Selection box.

On the first line, enter your page title and select Heading 1 <h1> from the Style drop-down menu (see Figure 3.5) in the toolbar.

FIGURE 3.5
The Style drop-down menu works much the same as the style menu in a word processing application such as Microsoft Word.

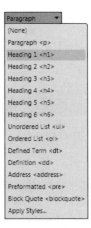

With the cursor at the end of the first line, press Enter to create a new paragraph, and a new P box will appear under your heading. Enter some more text—enough to fill at least three full lines. If you can't come up with anything to write, simply replicate some text out of this book or any other written material lying around.

Create a new paragraph by pressing Enter and typing a subheading. Use the Style drop-down menu in the toolbar to set the tag to Heading 2 <h2>. Directly underneath, type one more paragraph, this time using the *I* (italic) and **B** (bold) buttons in the toolbar to *emphasize* and **strongly emphasize** parts of the text.

You need two more elements: a bullet (unordered) list and a numbered (ordered) list. As in a word processor, press Enter to create a new line and click the Numbered List button (see Figure 3.6).

FIGURE 3.6
The Numbered List and Bulleted List buttons work in much the same way as they would in a word procession application.

A number appears on the left, the Block Selection box shifts to the right, and its tag changes to LI (list item). Type a series of list items separating them by pressing Enter. To end the list, simply press Enter to create a new list item and then either click the Numbered List button again to deactivate it or press the Backspace key on your keyboard. Doing so changes the new list item to a new paragraph.

Creating a bulleted list is done in the same way: Click the Bulleted List button and create a series of list items.

Finally, click the Save button or press Ctrl+S to save the file and pat yourself on the back: You have created your first web page (see Figure 3.7).

Four Browsers You Should Have on Your Computer

By the Way

A web designer should always have the end user in mind. But you don't know what browser or even what kind of computer the visitor will use when viewing your websites. Making an educated guess is the best you can do.

The majority of the computers connected to the Internet run some version of Microsoft Windows, and most of these computers have Internet Explorer as their default browser. So, Internet Explorer should be at the top of the list. Because Expression Web 3 works only on Windows-based computers, you probably already have Internet Explorer installed by default. If not, you can get the latest version of Internet Explorer free from Microsoft by visiting http://www.microsoft.com/ie.

FIGURE 3.7
The result as it
appears in
Design view in
Expression
Web 3.

In the last few years, Mozilla's Firefox browser has gained enormous popularity and it is now the biggest competitor to Internet Explorer. In comparison with Internet Explorer 6 and 7, Firefox is a far more "reasonable" browser when it comes to code interpretation because it follows web standards pretty closely, although with the release of Internet Explorer 8 that gap has narrowed substantially. For these reasons, you should also have Firefox installed. You can get it free from Mozilla by visiting http://www.firefox.com.

Most Mac (Apple) users use the default Mac OS browser called Safari. Apple released a Windows version of this browser last year. To ensure that Mac users get the same experience as Windows users, you should also test everything in Safari. You can get it free from Apple by visiting http://www.apple.com/safari/.

In 2008, Google released a new browser on the market called Chrome. This browser is entirely JavaScript based and is meant to run "lighter and faster" than any other browser available today. In the short time it has been available it has managed to build up a large following, and even though it is still in its infancy it is becoming a true contender that has to be considered. In addition Chrome has some interesting and often annoying idiosyncrasies that need to be tested against when a site is published. And even though its user base might be small now, we can expect it to grow exponentially simply because it is a Google product. You can get it free from Google by visiting www.google.com/chrome.

Finally, there is the Opera browser. Although it doesn't have a large market share, Opera is a popular alternative to the mainstream browsers and has an extremely loyal following. It works on many cell phones and other portable devices. Opera is strict when it comes to web standards and can be an excellent tool for uncovering bad code that other browsers glance over. You can download Opera for free by visiting www.opera.com.

Testing Your Web Page in Multiple Browsers

When you are designing for the Web, it's important to continually test your pages in multiple web browsers to ensure that they work and appear the way you intend. A web browser is nothing more than a program that renders or interprets the code in your page and displays it accordingly. But like human interpreters, there can be large discrepancies among browsers when it comes to interpretation. The WYSIWYG editor in Expression Web 3's Design view is a custom browser built to mimic standard browser behavior but it is not perfect and there is some standard markup that is not rendered accurately. Likewise, not all browsers are particular about web standards or they interpret web standards differently and, as a result, your page can look different depending on which browser you use.

To help with the testing process, Expression Web 3 can be set up to preview your page in all the different browsers installed on your computer, and in multiple different window sizes. This can be done from the File menu or from the new Preview button on the Common toolbar.

To preview the current page in your default browser, simply click the Preview button on the Common toolbar. If you want to select a different browser or preview the page in multiple browsers, click the down arrow next to the Preview icon to get the Preview in the browser drop-down menu, as shown in Figure 3.8. By default the list includes

FIGURE 3.8
By clicking the down arrow next to the Preview icon, you can test your page in one or multiple different browsers (and windows sizes) installed on your computer.

the currently installed version of Internet Explorer and your default browser if different from Internet Explorer. If you have installed more browsers on your computer, you can add these to the list by selecting Edit Browser List from the bottom of the drop-down menu.

The quickest way to test your current page against the last browser you tested in is to press F12. By pressing F12, the browser opens and you see the local instance of your page just as you would if it were stored somewhere on the Web. As you can see from Figure 3.9, the page looks the same as it did in Expression Web 3. Because you use

FIGURE 3.9
Your first web page as it appears in Internet Explorer 8.

only the standard styles h1, h2, p, and li, the text fills the entire width of the window. If you grab the edge of the window and resize it, the text reorganizes itself to fit the smaller or larger space.

Watch Out!

When Browsers Go Bad: Internet Explorer

If you've worked with web design before or you've surfed the web using different browsers, you've no doubt run into the infamous Internet Explorer problem where pages that look fine in Internet Explorer are "broken" in other browsers or vice versa. Internet Explorer 6 and 7 have a tendency to display pages, and especially those using CSS, differently from other browsers. This problem is often misconstrued as a problem with the other browsers, but in reality it is the result of Internet Explorer interpreting web standards in a nonstandard way (no pun intended). This has lead to the rise in popularity of other browsers such as Firefox, international campaigns to phase out Internet Explorer 6 (like my own pet project found at www.StopLivingInThePast.com), and a phenomenon known as "IE Hacks" in which designers and developers have been forced to come up with special code hacks to circumvent these problems so that their sites appear identical across all browsers.

Fortunately, the Internet Explorer development team finally realized the error of their ways and, with the release of Internet Explorer 8 in April 2009, they seem to have resolved many of these issues and gotten "in line" with the other browsers.

Unfortunately, in the short run this does little to solve the browser compatibility problem as Internet Explorer 6 and 7 hold 17% and 25% of the market share respectively (as of March 2009) and it is estimated that users will "hang on to" Internet Explorer 6 for years to come.

SuperPreview: A Sneak Preview

At this point, you are probably thinking two things: First of all, it seems awfully cumbersome to keep testing all your pages in all these different browsers. Second, how are you supposed to test your pages against older browsers you don't have? After all there is no simple way of installing Internet Explorer 6 and 7 on your computer now that you have Internet Explorer 8 up and running!

To curb this problem designers have turned to one of three strategies: virtual machines (where you set up virtual computers with older operating systems within your current operating system and run older browsers in them), multiple computers (in which you have several different computers running at the same time, and you test the pages on all of them), or web-based "browser shot" applications (that produce screen shots of what the page looks like in multiple different browsers and configurations). The problem with all these is that they are cumbersome, time-consuming, and not very effective.

Fortunately, now there is a fourth option, and it is built right in to Expression Web 3! When you installed Expression Web 3, you also installed a new application called SuperPreview that makes cross-browser testing both simple and effective and gives you a series of tools previously unavailable to find, diagnose, and remedy browser inconsistencies and incompatibilities. Additionally (and this is revolutionary), SuperPreview comes with a full working model of Internet Explorer 6 installed, giving you the ability to test your sites against this old but resilient browser without having to install it.

You learn how to use SuperPreview to its full potential in Hour 23, "Test Twice, Publish Once: Introducing SuperPreview," but if you want to, you can take a sneak peek at it right now by pressing the SuperPreview button on the Common toolbar. This opens SuperPreview as a separate application, and from here you can pick what browsers you want to preview your page in and get a quick look at the differences, if any, in the way the browsers display the page. At this point your page is too basic for SuperPreview to have any real value, but as you progress through the book you can use this application instead of or in addition to regular browser testing to get a better idea of what browser compatibility testing is all about.

Summary

In this hour, you learned to create a one-page website from scratch and discovered how to edit an HTML file to make your first web page. You saw that editing simple text content in Design view is no different from editing text in a word processor. You also learned how to test your page in multiple browsers and why, in this case, quantity improves quality. Finally, you got a sneak preview of the new and revolutionary browser testing application SuperPreview that is discussed at length in Hour 23. I urge you to use SuperPreview to test your pages throughout this book to get used to the interface and make browser testing a part of your general routine.

From here until the end of the book, you work with this project to make the final site you saw in Hour 2. Starting from scratch is a great way to learn how to do things properly the first time around. In Hour 4, "Building the Home Page: A Look Behind the Curtain," you expand on the first page by introducing more text content and standard style elements. You see what goes on in the code and learn a bit about the HTML code language.

Q&A

Q. *What is the difference between a website and a web page?*

A. Simply put, a website is a group of web pages in a folder. A website is a dedicated space on the Web and contains a number of web pages that relate to each other. In practical terms, the combined content at www.pinkandyellow.com is a website, whereas a single page under the same domain, such as http://pinkandyellow.com/photography/index.htm, is a web page.

Q. *Can I build a website without knowing anything about HTML and other code?*

A. Yes you can. But as you see in the following hours, understanding the inner workings of a web page can save you a lot of time and energy and help you create better sites faster. That doesn't mean you have to become a code guru. You can get a lot done with a rudimentary understanding of HTML.

Q. *Why does SuperPreview appear as a separate application in my program list?*

A. SuperPreview was built to work both as an integrated part of Expression Web 3 and as a standalone unit. This is to give you, the designer, an easy way to test pages and sites from your computer, your network, or on the web without having to import them into Expression Web 3 first. There is no qualitative difference between the SuperPreview you see inside Expression Web 3 and the SuperPreview you see when you use it as a standalone application.

Workshop

The workshop has quiz questions to help you put to use what you just learned. If you get stuck, the answers to the quiz questions are in the next section. But try to answer them first. Otherwise you'll be cheating yourself.

Quiz

1. How do you preview a web page in a browser from within Expression Web 3?

2. Why is it important to test a page in multiple browsers?

Answers

1. From within Expression Web 3, there are many ways to preview a web page in a browser. The easiest one is to simply press F12; doing so opens the current page in the default browser. You can also open the page in a browser with a specific window size by selecting File, Preview in Browser and clicking the size you want to use. Finally, you can preview the page in multiple browsers simultaneously by clicking Preview in Multiple Browsers on the same menu.

2. No browser is created equally. As a result, your web pages might look different depending on the configuration of the visitor's computer. To put it into perspective, Internet Explorer versions 6, 7, and 8 handle web pages in entirely different ways, so although a page looks great in Internet Explorer 8, it might be unreadable in Internet Explorer 6. The best way around this problem is to create standards-based websites, but even then you might run into browser incompatibilities. Continually testing your pages helps you catch problems early and figure out ways to fix them.

HOUR 4

Building a Home Page: A Look Behind the Curtain

What You'll Learn in This Hour:

▶ How to read and edit basic HTML code in Code view

▶ How to import text from Microsoft Word and other documents

▶ How to clean up imported code using Code and Design views

▶ How to use Find and Replace on many instances of code at the same time

Introduction

In Hour 3, "A Website Is Really Just Text: Build One in 5 Minutes," you built a basic web page using functions similar to those in a word processing program. But that is just half the story: In web design, what happens behind the curtain is what really matters. It's time to learn some basic HTML and see how the code affects the content. To do this, you build the basic structure of the home page of the MyKipple site.

Opening and Editing an Existing File Using Code View

If you haven't already done so, open the default.html file you worked on in Hour 3. The MyKipple site should open automatically when you open Expression Web 3. If not, you can find it by selecting Open Site from the Site menu or from the drop-down menu of the Open icon on the Common toolbar (see Figure 4.1).

FIGURE 4.1
The drop-down menu under the Open icon on the Common toolbar gives you quick access to open files and sites without having to go to the Main menu.

The Open Site dialog lists all the sites created in Expression Web 3 (see Figure 4.2). When you create or manage a website with Expression Web 3, the program automatically generates a shortcut to facilitate easy access to the site from this list. If you can't find the project on this list, you can navigate to it as you normally would. If you followed the directions in Hour 3, the project is in the My Web Sites folder under Documents.

FIGURE 4.2
The Open Site dialog displays all the websites you created in Expression Web 3; here seen with the My Kipple project.

Did you Know?

The Open Sites dialog isn't restricted to local sites. You can also use it to open and manage external websites both through Hypertext Markup Language (HTML) and File Transfer Protocol (FTP) if you have the necessary permissions to access the sites. If you use the Browse button or insert an address that Expression Web 3 does not already have on the list, the Add to Managed Sites box becomes active, and you can give the site a friendly name. In fact, you can use Expression Web 3 to make changes to live websites in real time.

Before going any further, let's look at what is happening in the page's code. Select Split view using the button at the bottom of the pane to reveal both Code view and Design view. Click anywhere on the heading, and then click the h1 tag on the Block

Selection box. This highlights the content affected by the h1 style in both Design view and Code view (see Figure 4.3). In Design view, you see a box with pink shading above and below. The pink areas are the default top and bottom margins for the h1 tag. In Code view, you see the text buffered or wrapped on both sides by code tags. These tags tell the browser to display the text in the h1 heading style.

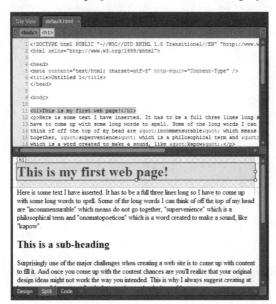

FIGURE 4.3
When you click on an element in either Code or Design view, that object is high-lighted in both views for easy reference.

HTML is a basic markup language that can be summarized in one simple rule: Everything is wrapped between a beginning and an end tag. All beginning tags consist of a less-than bracket (<), the tag name and/or function, and a greater-than bracket (>). End tags look much the same, but with the addition of a forward slash (/) before the content. In this example, <h1> tags wrap the heading like this:

```
<h1>This is my first web page!</h1>
```

You now have two ways to change the appearance of your content. You can use the Style drop-down menu as you learned in Hour 3, or you can go into Code view and change the style manually. Try changing the heading <h1> and </h1> tags to paragraph <p> and </p> to see what happens in Design view.

To use Design view to see changes you made in Code view, you need to click inside the Design view area or save the page. This is because as you change the code in Code view, you are temporarily breaking the code. Rather than trying to display broken code, Expression Web 3 waits for you to tell it when you finish editing before it refreshes the WYSIWYG (What You See Is What You Get) editor.

Notice that when you change the beginning tag, Expression Web 3 highlights the end tag in yellow and red to tell you that your code is broken (see Figure 4.4). Likewise,

FIGURE 4.4
When Expression Web 3 discovers a code error, it highlights the error with a yellow background and red text and shows a warning sign in the status bar.

Error highlighted in Code view

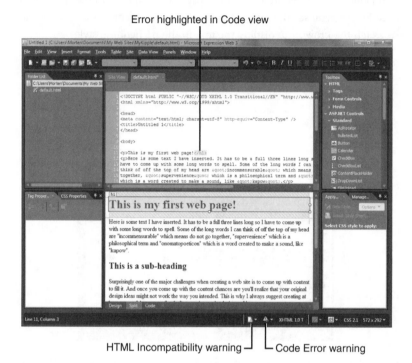

HTML Incompatibility warning ⏤ ⎿ Code Error warning

the status bar on the bottom of the workspace puts up two warning signs: The first one tells you that it detects an HTML incompatibility; the second one tells you that it detects a code error. When you change the end tag to match the start tag, the errors go away.

By studying the code, you see that all the different styles you applied in Hour 3 are actually just code tags:

- ▶ Heading 1 `<h1>`
- ▶ Heading 2 `<h2>`
- ▶ Paragraph `<p>`
- ▶ Italicized (emphasized) `<em>`
- ▶ Bold (strongly emphasized) `<strong>`
- ▶ Bullet (unordered) list `<ul>`

▶ Numbered (ordered) list <ol>

▶ List item for both lists <li>

Looking at the rest of the code, the <body> tag, which wraps all the content, tells the browser that this is the content to display. The <head> tag contains all the meta information that is available to the browser but that the browser does not display within the page. Meta information includes the page title displayed at the top of the window, info about the designer, and so on. Finally, the <html> tag, which tells the browser that the following content is written in the HTML language, wraps both the <head> and <body> sections. Scroll to the bottom of the Code view and you can see the </body> and </html> tags that close the page.

Importing Styled Text from a Document

What is a website if not a source of information? You need some real content to work with. Right now the default.html file contains whatever text you inserted during Hour 3. The next step is to introduce some real content. In most cases, you will either be provided with or write your own content in some form of word processing software. Your first instinct is probably to cut and paste this content straight into your page. The problem is that depending on what word processor you use, it is likely to attach a large amount of legacy formatting to the documents—code that becomes difficult to work with after importing it into an HTML file. Newer versions of word processors such as Microsoft Word 2007 have less of this code clutter, but you are still faced with a bit of a cleanup when you move the content from paper to web. To get rid of this superfluous code, you need to do a bit of code surgery.

In the lesson files for this hour downloaded from the book site is a Microsoft Word document called homePageText.doc (see Figure 4.5). Open this document in Microsoft Word, and you see a standard document with headings, subheadings, and some text.

The next step is to move all this content over to the default.html file and translate the styling to standards-based markup.

With the default.html file open in Design view, select and delete all existing content. Then go to the homePageText.doc file in your word processing software, select all the text and press Ctrl+C (universal shortcut for copy) to copy the content. Next go back to the default.html file in Expression Web 3, place your cursor at the top of the page, and press Ctrl+V (universal shortcut for paste) to paste the content into the page. What you get is a page that looks almost the same as the document. But the fact that

FIGURE 4.5
Homepagetext.
doc as it
appears in
Microsoft Word.

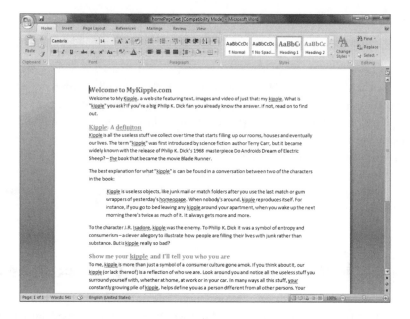

it looks almost the same means there is style code attached, and that style code has to
go if you want to stay on the standards-based path.

> You don't need Microsoft Office or Microsoft Word to open Word (.doc) docu-
> ments. If you don't have one of these applications installed, you can still access
> the lesson file by downloading and installing OpenOffice—an open source office
> suite that contains much the same kind of programs as Microsoft Office 100%
> free of charge. OpenOffice can be downloaded from www.openoffice.org.

Cleaning Up Imported Text

Although the new imported content looks the same in Design view as it did in
Microsoft Word, the code tells a different story (see Figure 4.6). By highlighting the
heading at the top of the document, you see that the code is no longer as clean as it
was earlier.

Depending on what word processing software was used to create the original .doc
file, you can get anything from basic style elements like in this example (.doc file created using Microsoft Word 2007) to hugely cluttered styles and deprecated elements
and inline hard coding. Expression Web 3 tries its best to get rid of the worst of the
clutter, but if clean and tidy markup is what you want, it's up to you to make the
document that way.

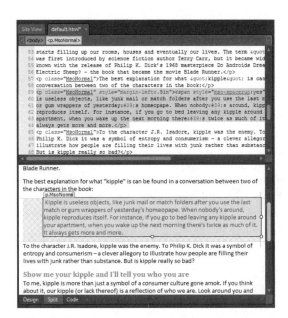

FIGURE 4.6
Although the new content looks right in Design view, the content imported from the Word document is littered with style code that should be removed.

The easiest way to clean up the code is to open the page in Split view and use the Code view toolbar that is explained in detail in Hour 8, "Cracking the Code: Working in Code View." Using these tools you can easily navigate through the content in the Design view panel and clean up the code in the Code view panel. What you want in the end is clean tags such as <h1> and <p> without any additional style coding.

To start off, open the Code view toolbar by clicking View on the Main menu, selecting Toolbars, and clicking Code view from the pop-out menu. The Code view toolbar docks directly under the Common toolbar. There is no right or wrong way to do this, so let's just start from the top. In Code view, scroll to the top of the page and find the string of code that reads

```
<style type="text/css">
```

This is the beginning tag of the Cascading Style Sheets (or CSS) code that defines what the different elements look like in the document. You learn about CSS and how they work from Hour 10, "Bringing Style to Substance with Cascading Style Sheets," and forward in this book. Right now you want to delete all the style code from the document. To highlight all the style definitions in one easy motion, place your cursor anywhere inside the preceding string listed and click the Select Tag button on the Code view toolbar (see Figure 4.7).

If you scroll up and down inside Code view, you see that the Select Tag function highlighted all the code between the beginning <style> and end </style> tags. All you

FIGURE 4.7
The Code View Toolbar has a series of tools that make navigating, selecting and editing code quick and easy.

Select Tag button

have to do now is press the Delete button and the style code is gone! To make sure, click inside the Design view area and note that the headings that were blue just a moment ago are now black and bigger. That's what you want.

Next you need to make sure all the content has the correct tags attached to them. The headings (<h1>,< h2>) and paragraphs (<p>) are fine, but the long quote is not. In HTML, long quotes like this have a special tag called *blockquote* that uses the tag <blockquote>. But right now the section is defined as a paragraph with some added style code like this:

```
<p class="MsoNormal" style="margin-left:.5in">
```

To apply the correct tag, use the Quick Tag Tools built in to Expression Web 3. You get a full description of the Quick Tag Tools in Hour 10. To edit the tag, place your cursor anywhere inside the preceding tag code and move your mouse to the box that reads *p.MsoNormal* found directly under the page tabs at the top of the view panel (see Figure 4.8). Hovering over the box brings out a down arrow. Click on the down arrow

FIGURE 4.8
The Quick Tag Editor gives you instant access to editing tools for the selected tags.

to display the Quick Tag Selector tools and select Edit Tag from the menu. This opens the Quick Tag Editor dialog. You can also open the Quick Tag Editor from Edit on the main menu.

In the Quick Tag Editor replace all the content within the two brackets with the word *blockquote* (see Figure 4.9). To apply the change, click the green check mark on the

FIGURE 4.9
The Quick Tag Editor dialog lets you edit single tags without messing with the code.

right side of the dialog. In response Expression Web 3 changes the code in the beginning tag and also changes the end tag to match so you don't have to do it manually. This simple substitution ensures that your code stays valid and makes the Quick Tag Editor an incredibly useful and powerful tool.

To finalize the cleanup of the indented section, find the <span> code that inserts a further indent on the first line (<span style="mso-spacerun:yes"> </span>) and delete it using the Select Tag tool or highlighting the entire code string.

The final step is to get rid of the calls to the style code you just deleted. If you take a look at one of the paragraphs in Code view you'll note that they each start with a tag like this:

```
<p class="MsoNormal">
```

Try It Yourself ▼

Use Find and Replace to Change Multiple Tags at Once

With the blockquote created only, a few more edits are necessary to make the code absolutely clean. If you look at the paragraphs, you see that each of the tags has an added style class call like this:

```
<p class="MsoNormal">
```

You already deleted the MsoNormal style class earlier in this hour, so this call is no longer necessary. You could use the Quick Tag Editor to remove each of these calls manually, but because there are several instances of the same call, it is quicker and easier to use the Replace function instead.

Find and Replace is a great tool to find content and make multiple changes to a document with only a few mouse clicks.

1. In Code view highlight the entire <p> tag (<p class="MsoNormal">).

2. Open the Replace dialog by clicking Edit, Replace under on the menu bar or by using the shortcut Ctrl+H.

3. In the Find What box, Expression Web 3 has already entered your highlighted selection **<p class="MsoNormal">**. In the Replace With box, type **<p>** (see Figure 4.10).

FIGURE 4.10
The Find and
Replace dialog
lets you find and
replace any con-
tent within both
Code view and
Design view just
like the similar
function would in
a word process-
ing application.

4. Click Replace All if you are confident you want to replace all the tags, or click Find Next and then Replace for each instance. You should replace a total of six instances.

You have now successfully imported and converted the contents of a Word document to standards-based code. The final step is to save the page on top of your old one (Ctrl+S) and test it in multiple browsers to ensure that it looks the way it's supposed to.

Summary

In this hour, you took a trip behind the scenes and learned a bit about how an HTML page works. You saw that the code boils down to wrapping the content in a begin- ning and an end tag and that changing these tags can be done from Code view and Design view and also by using Find and Replace. You got a preview of some of the code editing tools available in Expression Web 3, including the Code view toolbar, the Quick Tag Selector, and the Quick Tag Editor, and you also learned how to import text content from external files and clean up the code so that it works properly. In Hour 5, "Getting Connected with (Hyper)Links: The Cornerstone of the World Wide Web," you create a second page and add hyperlinks to your pages to make them interactive.

Q&A

Q. *Why can't I simply cut and paste the content from a Word document straight into my web page?*

A. A word processor, such as Microsoft Word, inserts a large amount of hidden style code in documents. When you copy and paste text from these programs, all that code quite literally tags along. One example of this is long quotes. When you press the Tab key in a word processor to visually distinguish a long quote by indenting it, you actually insert a block of style code defining how far in to indent the content. So, when you copy and paste the content to Expression Web 3, that style code follows along and clutters up the code. This indentation code is unnecessary in HTML because there is already a dedicated tag for long quotes called blockquote. There are many ways of getting around this problem. One is to use the Paste Text command found under Edit on the main menu. This command strips the style code from copied text and inserts it as plain text with only the tags you request. But this approach can cause a lot of confusion and extra work because it strips away all the style information and gives you only plain text. There is nothing technically wrong with cutting and pasting content from word processors to Expression Web 3, but it creates a lot of extra work.

Workshop

The Workshop has quiz questions and exercises to help you put to use what you just learned. If you get stuck, the answers to the quiz questions are in the next section. But try to answer them first. Otherwise you'll be cheating yourself.

Quiz

1. In Code view, how do you tell the browser to treat one line of text differently from another?

Answer

1. To separate and group content, HTML uses *tags*. Any content placed between a beginning and an end tag is semantically defined by that tag so that browsers understand paragraphs as paragraphs, headings as headings, unordered lists as unordered lists, and so on. When you apply a particular style to content in Design view, you are actually telling the browser to find content wrapped by a certain tag and then apply the defined styles to this content.

Exercise

Find a Word document you already have on your computer or write a new one. Make sure it has several headings and subheadings along with bold and italicized content and a few lists. With the default.html file open in Expression Web 3, choose Save As under File and select a new name, like **myTest.html**, and save it. Delete all the content in your new file and import the content from the Word document. Clean up the code so that it has only styles you can find in the Styles drop-down menu, and all bold and italicized content is strong and emphasized instead. Save the file and test it in your browser to verify that it works properly.

Getting Connected with (Hyper)Links: The Cornerstone of the World Wide Web

---

What You'll Learn in This Hour:

- ▶ How to import and work with a completed website in Expression Web 3
- ▶ How to import a new page and link to it
- ▶ How to create links between pages on your website
- ▶ How to create links to other websites
- ▶ How to create links that open in new windows
- ▶ How to create bookmark links within your page

Introduction

Hyperlinks (also known simply as *links*) are an integral part of any website. Hyperlinks work as both navigational tools within your website and pathways to further resources in your network or on the World Wide Web. They can also perform actions such as opening an email program and sending commands.

The hyperlink in its basic form appears on a web page as a colored and underlined segment of text with a web page address attached. When you click the text, the browser goes to that new page. But hyperlinks don't have to be only text. You can attach them to images and behaviors, and even empty areas within a web page. By knowing the capabilities and limitations of hyperlinks, you can build intuitive, functional, and visually compelling navigational tools and menus to make it easy for visitors to navigate and interact with your site.

For the most part, you use hyperlinks to navigate within your website or link to other websites. But you can also use hyperlinks to give visitors access to other types of files such as documents, compressed archives, and other files. Although a web browser is limited in the file types it can display, it can be set up to interact with other programs on your computer to handle these file types. One such file type encountered often on the Web is *Portable Document Format* (Adobe PDF). If you click a PDF file, your browser asks whether you want to save the file or, if you have Adobe Reader or a similar PDF-capable program on your computer, if you want to open it. Then the browser automatically calls for the program to open and display the file. The same goes for documents, spreadsheets, and numerous other types of files.

The two most commonly used links are internal links that point to other pages within a website and external links that point to other websites. To start this hour, you make an internal link. But before you can do that, you need to have a new page to which you can link.

Import a New Page and Create an Internal Hyperlink

The lesson files contain a file called myCameras.html. Follow these steps to import that file into your project:

1. From the menu bar, select File, Import, File (see Figure 5.1).

FIGURE 5.1
Importing a new page or other document can be done from the File option under Import in the File menu.

2. In the Import dialog, click Add File and browse to the location where you stored the downloaded lesson files on your computer.

3. Click Hour 5 and select the myCameras.html file. Click Open; myCameras.html is now visible in the Import dialog (see Figure 5.2). If you did

FIGURE 5.2
myCameras.html
file selected
in the Import
dialog.

not complete the default.html page in Hour 4, "Building a Home Page: A Look Behind the Curtain," or you want to ensure that you are working with an identical version of the file to the one I used to write this book I've also added the default.html file in the lesson file for you to use.

4. Click OK and the myCameras.html file shows up in the Folder List task pane.

Now you have two files in the My Kipple website project: default.html and myCameras.html. The next step is to link the two pages to each other with hyperlinks. Open default.html by double-clicking the filename, and then select Design view from the buttons at the bottom page. The first hyperlink you make is an inline link—a segment of text that links to a further explanation of the topic.

> Inline links are prevalent throughout the Web and are just as useful as menu links because they mainly point directly to highly relevant information or further reading. For example, whereas a menu link might be quite generic and titled something such as "Norwegian Mythological Creatures" or "Scandinavian Christmas Traditions," an inline link would be titled "The Norwegian Nisse" with a link to a page exclusively about this mythical creature.

Scroll to the bottom of the page and find the last paragraph. On the second line, highlight the words *my collection of cameras*. These four words will be the link to the new

myCameras.html page. Right-click the highlighted text and select Hyperlink from the
menu that appears. Doing so opens the Insert Hyperlink dialog (see Figure 5.3).

FIGURE 5.3
The Insert Hyper-
link dialog can be
opened by high-
lighting one or
more words,
clicking the right
mouse button,
and selecting
Hyperlink from
the pop-up menu.

From this dialog, you have complete control of your hyperlinks. On the left, you have
four options that set where you are linking to:

▶ **Existing File or Web Page**—Lets you link to a file within your current site or
enter a URL to an external web page.

▶ **Place in This Document**—Lets you link to bookmarks (also known as anchors)
within the document. A *bookmark* is a destination within a document that can
be targeted by a link. Longer documents such as Frequently Asked Questions
(FAQ) lists and registries make heavy use of bookmarks.

▶ **Create a New Document**—Lets you link to a new page you have not created
yet. You define a name for the new file and have the option to edit it right away
or simply link to the blank page now and edit it later. This is useful if you build
a menu but haven't created the target pages. The reason for this option is obvious: You can't link to something that doesn't exist!

▶ **E-mail Address**—Creates the code necessary for the browser to open the default
email program on the computer and insert a recipient address and even a
default subject line if you so choose.

URL means *uniform resource locator*. A URL is the web address that takes you to
a web page, a file, or a specific server location. The URL to the site I built to
accompany this book is http://expression.pinkandyellow.com and the URL to my
blog is http://www.designisphilosophy.com.

In this case you are linking to an existing file, so pick the first option. The Text to Display field shows the text you previously highlighted. This text becomes the link and is
visible on the page. If you change the text here, the text in the page changes as well.

Directly underneath is a standard file browser window where you can find and select the file you want to link to. As you can see, the main window lists both default.html and myCameras.html.

Did you Know?

Expression Web 3 assumes that you intend to link to other files within your website, so these files are the first option you get. You can navigate away from this folder and link to other files, but any file you link to should always be either inside your website folder (or one of its subfolders) or a file that is already on the Web. Never link to a local file on your computer that is not in your website folder unless your website is only for use on your computer—the link will not work anywhere else.

Select myCameras.html. Its address shows up in the Address box. The last step is to add a ScreenTip to the link. This is not strictly necessary for the link to work but is required if you want your site to be accessible. A *ScreenTip* is the title attribute for a link (a short line of text that pops up next to the mouse pointer when you hover over a link). It gives the user more information about the link. In terms of accessibility if the visitor uses a text-to-speech browser, the ScreenTip is read out loud to tell the user that there is a link and what the link points to. To add a ScreenTip, click the Screen-Tip button in the upper-right corner of the Insert Hyperlink dialog. In the Set Hyperlink ScreenTip dialog that opens, type **Learn more about my camera collection and what I use them for** and click OK (see Figure 5.4). Click OK in the Insert Hyperlink dialog to finish the hyperlink.

FIGURE 5.4
The Set Hyperlink ScreenTip dialog lets you add a detailed description to your hyperlinks and is necessary to make your links accessible.

The text you highlighted before is now blue and underlined, indicating to the visitor that it is a link. Save the file and test it in your browser (see Figure 5.5).

If you hover over the new link, a small box with the ScreenTip appears. And if you click it, the browser navigates to the linked file myCameras.html. But there's a small problem: After you get to myCameras.html, you have no way to get back unless you use the navigation buttons in the browser. To address this problem, you need to create a Home link in the myCameras.html file to link back to default.html.

FIGURE 5.5
default.html with the new link and its ScreenTip as it appears in Firefox.

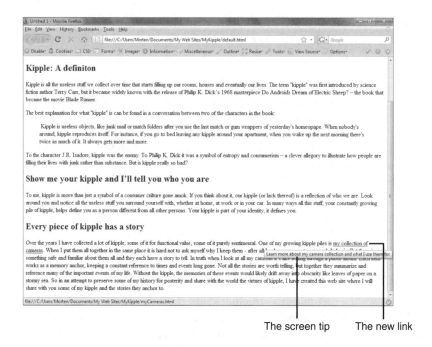

The screen tip   The new link

▼   **Try It Yourself**

Create a Home Link in myCameras.html

It's important to give the visitor an easy way to get back to the main page of any website. The easiest way to do this is to create a Home link.

1. Open myCameras.html in Design view by double-clicking it in the Folder List task pane.

2. With the cursor at the beginning of the first line of the heading, press Enter once to shift the heading down one line, and then put your cursor up on the new first line. Use the Style menu to change the style of the new line to Paragraph.

3. Type the word **Home** and double-click the word to select it. Then right-click the selected word and select **Hyperlink** from the menu that appears.

4. In the Insert Hyperlink dialog, select the default.html file and use the Set Hyperlink ScreenTip dialog to give it the ScreenTip text **Go back to My Kipple**.

5. Click OK. Save and test the file in your browser, making sure the ScreenTip works and that it links back to default.html.

▲

Hyperlink Syntax: Absolute, Relative, and Root-Relative

As you are creating hyperlinks in Expression Web 3, you will notice that the syntax of the link address in the Code view changes depending on what you link to. There are actually three different ways of writing a hyperlink address, all of which are used for different purposes:

Absolute hyperlinks are complete addresses that contain all the elements of a URL. They always start with some version of http:// followed by the domain name (for example, www.designisphilosophy.com) and optionally a page/folder. Absolute hyperlinks are used when linking to pages outside of the current site that have a different domain name.

Relative hyperlinks are addresses that are relative to the current domain or location. They only contain the name of the target page prefixed with any necessary folder moves (for example, default.html). The browser sees that this is a relative hyperlink and adds the domain and folder location of the current page to the beginning of the link to complete it. If you use relative hyperlinks and you want to navigate from a page stored in one folder to a page stored in a different folder you add the folder prefixes to the hyperlink. For instance, a relative link from a page in Folder 1 to a page in Folder 2 would be ../Folder 2/page.html, where the ../ tells the browser you want to go out of the current folder and into a new one. When you create hyperlinks between pages in Expression Web 3, they are always inserted as relative links so that the application can easily update them if you choose to move files around. However, if you move the files around on your computer outside of the Expression Web program, the hyperlinks break.

Root-relative hyperlinks are a subset of relative hyperlinks in which all the links are assumed to start from the root folder (domain name) of the site. They differ from the relative hyperlinks in that the address is prefixed by a forward slash (for example, /default.html). The browser applies only the domain to the beginning of this link. Root-relative hyperlinks are used in place of relative ones in large sites in which there is a chance the files will be moved around without using an application such as Expression Web 3 to update them. Because they refer to the root of the site rather than the current location of the page they are placed in, they work regardless of where the file is placed as long as they remain under the right domain.

Creating External Links and New Windows

Now that you have created some internal links, it's time to link your website to other external websites. You do this in much the same way that you created your internal links, but instead of selecting a file from your computer, you go to the link's destination and find its URL to insert.

In the second paragraph of the home page (default.html) is a reference to the book *Do Androids Dream of Electric Sheep?* Some of the readers of this website might want to buy this book. Why not give them a link to the book's page on Amazon.com? To do this, you first need the address. In your browser, go to www.amazon.com and search for *Do Androids Dream of Electric Sheep?* Click one of the search results to get to the book's main page. Highlight the entire address in the address bar and copy it by using Ctrl+C (the universal copy shortcut), or right-click the address and select Copy (see Figure 5.6).

FIGURE 5.6
Copying the Amazon.com URL for the book can be done by right-clicking and selecting Copy from the context menu.

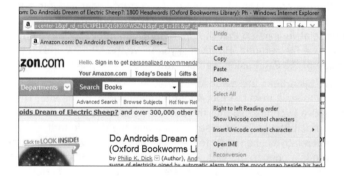

Back in Expression Web 3, select the book title in the second paragraph, right-click the selection, and select Hyperlink as you did before. In the Insert Hyperlink dialog, select Existing File or Web Page and paste the Amazon.com URL into the Address field by clicking in the text box and either pressing Ctrl+V (universal paste shortcut) or right-clicking and selecting Paste (see Figure 5.7).

Open the ScreenTip dialog and type **Do Androids Dream of Electric Sheep? is available from Amazon.com**. Click OK twice and save the new file. Test it in your browser.

But here is a new problem: After the visitor clicks the link, she goes to Amazon.com. How does she get back to your site? Unlike the myDesk.html file, you can't insert a home link in the Amazon.com page. How do you keep your visitor on your site and

FIGURE 5.7
Pasting the Amazon.com URL for the book by right-clicking and selecting Paste from the menu.

Using the Browsed Pages Option to Obtain Hyperlinks

If you don't want to copy and paste the URL from the browser, there is an alternative built in to Expression Web 3: The application connects to the Internet Explorer browser history that means you can get the URL from right inside the program itself. To use this option go to the desired target location in Internet Explorer before creating the hyperlink. When inside the Insert Hyperlink dialog, click the Browsed Pages option (see Figure 5.8) in the main window to get the browsing history. From here you can select any of the pages you have visited with Internet Explorer recently, and Expression Web automatically inserts the URL to that page for you.

FIGURE 5.8
The Browsed Pages option gives you access to the recent browser history from Internet Explorer.

still let her visit other sites? One solution is to edit your link so that the external page opens in a new window.

1. Right-click the *Do Androids Dream of Electric Sheep?* link you just created and select Hyperlink Properties.

2. In the Edit Hyperlink dialog, click the Target Frame button on the right.

3. In the Target Frame dialog, select New Window under Common Targets. This tells the browser to open a new window (see Figure 5.9).

FIGURE 5.9
The Target Frame dialog within Hyperlink Properties lets you define where the linked page opens.

4. Click OK twice, save the file, and test it in your browser.

Now when you click the link to the book, the page opens in a new window or tab in your browser. This is a basic way to make links open in new windows. In Hour 16, "Using Behaviors," you learn how to use behaviors to make more advanced new windows and pop-up windows.

Creating Internal Links Within Documents Using Bookmarks

Another type of link you can create is a *bookmark* (also known as an *anchor*), a hyperlink that points to a specific position in the current page. Designers most often use this type of link to help people navigate longer web pages by providing a menu that leads to different sections. Bookmarks are also effective for linking directly to footnotes.

Before you make bookmark links, you have to insert the bookmarks in your document. In default.html, select the first subheading (Kipple: A Definition). Select Insert, Bookmark from the menu bar, or click Ctrl+G. This opens the Bookmark dialog. From here you can set the bookmark's name. The name becomes the address of the bookmark and is included in the hyperlink. For that reason, underscores replace all spaces (see Figure 5.10).

FIGURE 5.10
The Bookmark dialog lets you define a so-called "slug" for your bookmark anchor. Note the underscores between each word.

> You can change the bookmark name to whatever you want, but it's a good idea to keep it consistent and meaningful, especially if your document has many bookmarks.

Did you Know?

When you click OK, you see that the title now has a dotted underline in the Design view of the page. This is a visual reminder that the text has a bookmark attached and is visible only within Expression Web, not in the web browser. Follow the same process and attach bookmarks to the two other subheadings.

Now all you have to do is make a menu with links to the bookmarks. This menu should go directly under the main heading. Make a new paragraph under the main heading by clicking the beginning of the first paragraph and pressing Enter. In the new first paragraph, create an unordered (bulleted) list. Each list item should be identical to the subheadings, like this:

- ▶ Kipple: A Definition
- ▶ Show me your kipple and I'll tell you who you are
- ▶ Every piece of kipple has a story

Highlight the first bullet point and right-click to open the Hyperlink dialog. By selecting Link to Place in This Document from the left-side menu, you open a list of the three bookmarks you created. Select the one that matches your title (see Figure 5.11). As before, attach a ScreenTip such as Jump to Kipple: A Definition to keep your page accessible. Finally, click OK and save your changes.

Do the same with the two other menu items. When you are done, save and test in your browser. You see that when you click the links, the browser jumps to the bookmarked section. Because the document is relatively short, it might not look like anything is happening when you click a link. But if you reduce the width of your

FIGURE 5.11
The Bookmark option under the Insert Hyperlink dialog lets you link to a bookmark within the same page.

window to about half the size of your screen and then click the links, you should see the page jump.

Note that because a bookmark link is no different from any other link, the navigation buttons in your browser work on it as well. This makes more sense if you look in the address bar after clicking on one of the bookmark links: When a bookmark link is clicked, the browser is directed to the page in question and the bookmark within that page, which is signified by a # symbol followed by the bookmark name like this:

"My Web Sites/MyKipple/default.html#Kipple:_A_definiton"

Creating an Email Hyperlink

The final option in the Hyperlink dialog is the E-mail Address link. With this option, you can create a link that opens the visitor's preferred email program and sets the To address and Subject line. This is the easiest way to provide contact information to your visitors because they don't have to copy and paste or type out the email address themselves.

To create an email hyperlink, you first need some text to work as a link. On the bottom of the home page, add a new paragraph and type **If you want further information about my kipple, send me an e-mail**. Highlight the *send me an e-mail* portion of the text and open the Insert Hyperlink dialog. Select E-mail Address from the left-side menu to open the email options. In the E-mail Address line, enter the email address to which you want the message to go. When you start writing, the program automatically inserts a block of code, `mailto:`, directly in front of your address. This code tells the browser that this is not a regular link but an email link. In the Subject line, type the default subject line that you want emails generated from the website to have (see Figure 5.12). The Recently Used E-Mail Addresses option displays

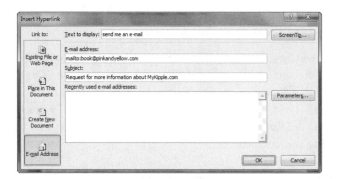

FIGURE 5.12
The E-Mail Address option under the Insert Hyperlink dialog lets you insert a receiving email address and a default subject line.

the most recent email addresses you linked to within Expression Web 3. Remember to set a ScreenTip for your email link and click OK.

When you test the page in your browser and click the new link, your computer opens your default email program and starts an email with the address and subject line you chose.

Summary

Hyperlinks are what set the World Wide Web apart from other informational sources. By enabling the user to quickly navigate through large amounts of content and instantly move from one source to another, hyperlinks have revolutionized the way we find and use information. In this hour, you learned how to create hyperlinks within your own site, to the outside world, and even within one document. Hyperlinks are core components of any website and create navigation and links to the rest of the Web. You also learned how to create links that open in new windows. In Hour 16, you learn how to expand on this technique using Expression Web 3's built in behaviors.

Q&A

Q. When I copied and pasted the subheading into my unordered list, the text kept the dotted underline. Is this a problem?

A. If you copy and paste content such as text in Design view, all the associated attributes come with it. In this case, you copied not only the text itself but also the bookmark. To get rid of the bookmark, highlight the text, right-click, and select Bookmark Properties. Simply click Clear and Expression Web 3 removes the bookmark.

Q. *Why are all my links blue and underlined? I don't like blue and I don't like the underline either. Can I change them?*

A. As with headings, paragraph, block quote, and other default styles, the link or anchor <a> tag has default properties in all browsers. That default is blue and underlined. Likewise, a previously visited link has a purplish color. In Hour 10, "Bringing Style to Substance with Cascading Style Sheets," you learn how to style your links by changing their color, font style, and size, and by adding underline and other effects.

Q. *What is the difference between a menu and a link?*

A. A menu is just a series of links styled to look a certain way. On a website, any item that takes you somewhere else when you click it is just a link created in the same way you created links in this hour. The reason menus look different is that they have heavy styling and usually use graphics instead of just text.

Workshop

The Workshop has quiz questions and exercises to help you put to use what you just learned. If you get stuck, the answers to the quiz questions are in the next section. But try to answer them first. Otherwise you'll be cheating yourself.

Quiz

1. What kind of content can a hyperlink be applied to?

2. What are the three different types of hyperlinks and when are they used?

3. How does a bookmark differ from a "regular" hyperlink?

Answers

1. Hyperlinks can be applied to any and all content in a page although it is advisable to restrict them to smaller items like short text segments or images.

2. The three types of hyperlinks are absolute, relative, and root-relative. Absolute links are used to link to pages that are not inside your current site. Relative links are used to link to pages that are within your site. Root-relative links are used to link to pages that are within your site when there is a chance the pages will be moved around without using Expression Web 3.

3. Bookmarks make the browser navigate to a certain location within the current page, so instead of loading a new page, it jumps down or up in the current page to a different location.

Exercise

Throughout the default.html page are several items that you can link to sites with further information. For instance, you could link the name Philip K. Dick to the Wikipedia.org page about the author and the name Blade Runner to the imdb.com page about the movie. Use the Web to find further information on these items and make links that point to these sources. Make sure you attach a ScreenTip to each link and that each one opens in a new window.

HOUR 6

Getting Visual, Part 1: Adding Images and Graphics

What You'll Learn in This Hour:

▶ How to import and work with a completed website in Expression Web 3

▶ What the main image file types are and when to use them

▶ How to import an image into Expression Web 3

▶ How to insert an image into a page

▶ How to change the placement and appearance of an image in a page

Introduction

Because the World Wide Web is a visual medium, making your website visually pleasing is important. The easiest way to do this is by adding images and graphics to the text. But images can be so much more than just eye candy. As hinted at in Hour 5, "Getting Connected With (Hyper)Links: The Cornerstone of the World Wide Web," an image can also be used as a link or even as a navigational tool. If you dissect websites, you find images used as borders, backgrounds, buttons, underlines, and even text. The possibilities are endless.

In the past, heavy use of images in websites was frowned upon mostly because people were on slow dial-up connections, and the images made the pages heavy and slow to load. But now that broadband Internet is becoming more and more prevalent throughout the world and image compression technology has evolved to a point where web-quality images take up little memory, web designers rely heavily on image elements to make their sites look better.

The bottom line is this: Used correctly, images can be a great tool to enhance the look and feel of your website.

Images on the Web: Three File Types for Three Uses

At first glance, it looks like all images on the Web have the same format. But in reality they are different. Web designers choose different file formats, with different attributes, depending on how they plan to use an image. That choice in turn affects how a page looks and works.

There are three main image formats that most current browsers support. They are GIF (Graphics Interchange Format), JPEG or JPG (Joint Photographic Experts Group), and PNG (Portable Network Graphics). Each format has advantages and limitations:

> ▶ The GIF format produces the smallest files for quick downloads. Unfortunately, the image quality of a GIF file is quite poor. When introduced, the GIF format was the only format that supported transparency. It gave designers the option to create graphics that could display on top of other graphics or display without an unsightly box around them. But this transparency is coarse and effective only with images that have clean lines. In addition, the GIF format can display only up to 256 colors, severely limiting the kinds of images that designers can use it for. For these reasons, the GIF format is best suited for computer-generated content and line drawings. Today's designers use the GIF format mostly to display small icons and buttons (see Figure 6.1).

FIGURE 6.1
A GIF image with transparency on a white background and a transparent background. The file size is 3.82KB.

> ▶ JPEG or JPG is the most common image format on the Web. Its success stems from its high compression rate and low image noise. JPEG has become the standard format for images not only on the Web but also in digital cameras and other devices. JPEG is a compression format that uses advanced algorithms to recalculate the image data and remove content that is not easily noticed by the human eye. Among the many different things a JPEG compressor does is evening the colors, duplicate similar looking areas, and compress the actual image code to make it shorter. At high-quality (and low-compression) settings,

JPEG compression can be excellent, but if you set the compression too high, the image can end up looking a bit like a paint-by-numbers painting (see Figure 6.2). The JPEG is "solid" and cannot be made transparent.

FIGURE 6.2
A JPEG image with minimum compression to the left and maximum compression to the right. At minimum compression, the file size is 21KB; at maximum compression, it is 14.2KB.

▶ PNG is the newest of the formats. What sets the PNG format apart is that it has an alpha layer that tells the browser what portions of the image are transparent. As a result, you can superimpose PNGs on top of other images with full transparency. Unlike the GIF format, PNG transparencies are clean (see Figure 6.3), but this ability comes at a price: PNGs are often much larger files than the

FIGURE 6.3
A PNG image with transparency on a white background and a transparent background. Note that unlike the GIF format, the transparency in the PNG is clean. The file size is 7.1KB.

two other formats. Even so, the ability to create advanced transparencies makes the format ideal for logos and other superimposed and hovering graphics in websites. Some older browsers, in particular Internet Explorer 6, do not support PNG transparencies.

Importing and Inserting an Image

Images are the most common nontext elements featured in web pages. And because images are so heavily used, there are many different ways to handle them depending on how the designer plans to use them.

The easiest use is simply inserting an image into a page. To do that, you need to import the image file into your project. But before you do, it's a good idea to start thinking about how your site is organized. Look at the Folder List panel, and you see that your site currently consists of two pages: default.html and myCameras.html. Now you are adding image files to your site, which means they appear alongside your two HTML files. If you were adding just two or three images, this wouldn't be a problem. But as you saw in Hour 2, "Beginning at the End: A Walkthrough of the Finished Project," the final site has a large number of images and files. So, before things get too complicated, it's a good idea to start organizing everything in folders. In other words, you need to make a folder for your images.

Create a New Folder and Import a New Image

Folders serve as effective tools for keeping your site organized. Websites have a tendency to fill up with files fast, and it's important to think about file organization early. The Folder List panel gives you easy access to all the files and folders in your site, and you can use it to create new files and folders and organize them.

1. With the Folder List panel selected, click the arrow next to the New Document icon on the Common toolbar and select Folder (see Figure 6.4), or right-click inside the panel and select New, Folder.

FIGURE 6.4
One of several ways to create a new folder is to select Folder from the New drop-down menu on the Common toolbar.

2. Name the new folder Images and double-click it.

3. Select File, Import, File as you did in Hour 5. In the Import dialog, click Add File and browse to the location where you stored the downloaded lesson files on your computer.

4. Click Hour 6 and select the file called camerasSmall.jpg. Click Open, and then click OK. Expression Web 3 copies the file and stores it in the Images folder. You

can see it in the Folder List panel by clicking on the + icon next to the Images folder (see Figure 6.5).

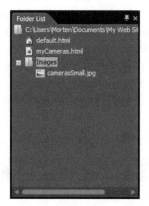

FIGURE 6.5
The imported image file as it appears under the Images folder in the Folder List panel when the + icon has been clicked. If you click the – icon, the folder is closed and the + icon reappears.

Expression Web 3 is quite finicky when it comes to image files. If you add images into your website without importing them through Expression Web 3, they might not work properly in Design view, and you see a small square with a red X instead of the image. This doesn't mean that there is anything wrong with the image; in fact, if you preview the page in a browser, you see that the image is there. The problem has to do with how Expression Web 3 handles files internally. The best (and only) way to avoid this problem is to make a habit to import all image files properly through the Import File dialog.

Now that Expression Web 3 has imported the image into your project, it's time to insert it into a page. You can do this in Design view by dragging and dropping the image into the text. To start, open the myCameras.html file. In the Folder List panel, click and hold the camerasSmall.jpg file and drag it to Design view. You see a gray dotted marker jump around inside the text indicating where the image insertion point will be. Place the image at the beginning of the first paragraph under the heading and let go. Doing so opens the Accessibility Properties dialog (see Figure 6.6).

FIGURE 6.6
The Accessibility Properties dialog lets you customize the information attached to the image for those who can't view the image itself.

The Accessibility Properties dialog gives you the option to attach alternative text and a longer description to your images. Some visitors cannot see the images in your page because they are using a text-only browser, portable device, or text-to-speech browser. The alternative text displays in place of the image for these users and helps to explain what the image shows. It also appears if, for one reason or another, the image doesn't load properly when the page is opened by someone using a regular browser. The alternative text should be a description of what the image is. In this case, enter **Most of my cameras together** in the Alternate Text text box, and click OK. Expression Web 3 inserts the image in the text at the beginning of the first paragraph (see Figure 6.7).

FIGURE 6.7
The inserted image as it appears in Design view.

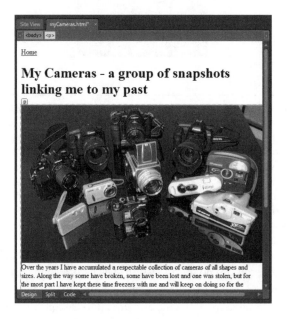

Save the file and preview the page in a browser. Something is a bit off; the image breaks the text and leaves a large empty area to the right (see Figure 6.8).

This big void appears because, by default, web browsers consider images to be "inline" elements, meaning they appear alongside the other elements on the line just like a letter or word. If you've ever placed images in a Word document, you are probably familiar with the concept of "text wrapping." The solution to the problem is similar when we work with websites: Tell the browser that the image should not be considered part of the text but rather an object around which the text should wrap. This can be done using the Picture Properties.

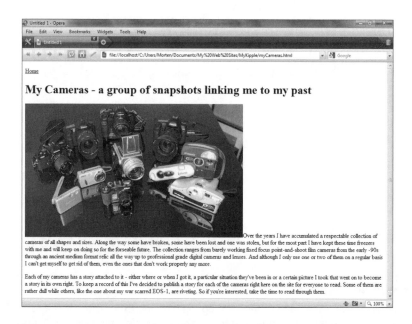

FIGURE 6.8
The page with the inserted image as it appears in Opera.

Using Picture Properties to Change the Appearance of an Image

After an image is part of a web page, there are properties and functions available to tell the browser how to display the image and how the image should relate to the surrounding content. In addition to simple HTML properties, Expression Web 3 gives you access to some basic image-editing options normally found only in dedicated imaging software. You can access some of these options by right-clicking the image in Design view and selecting Picture Properties from the context menu. Doing so opens the Picture Properties dialog (see Figure 6.9).

The General Tab

Under the General tab, the Picture field tells you the file with which you are currently working. You can change the file by using the Browse button or by typing a new filename in the Picture text box. The Edit button opens the source file in the default image editor on your computer.

FIGURE 6.9
The General tab of the Picture Properties dialog.

<table>
<tr><td>

Picture Properties   ?   X

General | Appearance

Picture:

| Images/camerasSmall.jpg | Browse...   Edit...

Picture File Type...

Accessibility

☑ Alternate Text: Most of my cameras together

Long Description: | | Browse...

Hyperlink

Location: | | Browse...

Target Frame: | | ✏ Parameters...

OK   Cancel

</td></tr>
</table>

Watch Out!

Expression Web 3 Is Not an Image Editor!

Even though you are presented with the option of using Expression Web 3 to change the file formats for images, it is not something I suggest you do. Expression Web 3 is not an image editing program, and the options you are given are both restrictive and potentially destructive. By changing the file formats of your images—from a transparent PNG to a low resolution JPEG image, for example—you can inadvertently reduce the quality of your images to the point where they are unusable.

As much as possible, you should try to use a dedicated image editor to make changes to your images and then import the final product into Expression Web 3.

Directly underneath the Picture text box is the Picture File Type button. If you click this button, a new dialog opens (see Figure 6.10). From here you can convert the file you are working with to any other main image format with a few mouse clicks. If you change the file type in this dialog, Expression Web 3 automatically replaces the image on your page. When you save the page, a dialog asks you where you want to store the new image file.

The next section of the General tab of the Picture Properties dialog is Accessibility. This displays the same options that appeared when you inserted the image.

The final section is Hyperlink. Here you can make the entire image into a hyperlink pointing to a different page, a different site, or a file.

FIGURE 6.10
The Picture File Type dialog lets you change the file type of your images without having to open a separate image-editing application.

The Appearance Tab

The Appearance tab contains the most commonly used code controls for the image (see Figure 6.11). This is where you instruct the browser how to handle the image in relation to other content as well as specify border thickness, margins and dimensions,. The functions under the Appearance tab are styles that Expression Web 3 applies to the image. In later hours, you learn how to create styles that apply to all images in a site so that you don't have to set them for each individual image.

FIGURE 6.11
The Appearance tab of the Picture Properties dialog controls the image in relation to the other content on the page and sets the image dimensions, border, and margins/padding.

▶ The Wrapping Style options define how the surrounding text wraps around the image. The three buttons provide good illustrations of what the different options mean. None (the default) tells the browser to handle the image as if it were part of the text. This means that the image lines up with the rest of the text like a large letter and pushes the remaining text to the right to make room. Left means that the image lines up against the left side of the window and the text wraps on its right. Right works the same way as the Left option, except the image is now on the right with the text wrapping on the left.

▶ Alignment settings apply only if the wrapping style is set to None. In the Layout section, the Alignment option gives you control over where the image lies in relation to the remaining text on the line. For example, if you set the alignment to Top, the top of the image aligns with the top of the text line. If you set the alignment to Middle, the middle of the image aligns with the middle of the text line (see Figure 6.12). And if you set the alignment to Bottom, the bottom of the image aligns with the bottom of the text line. Expression Web 3 gives you eight different positions in addition to Default.

FIGURE 6.12
The Alignment attribute is set to Middle, centering the image vertically in relation to the line of text.

The Layout section also contains the Border Thickness setting (which defines a border or outline that can be applied to the edges of the image) and the

Horizontal Margin and Vertical Margin settings (which create empty space on the four sides of the image).

▶ The final section of the Appearance tab is Size, where you can manually set the dimensions of the image either in pixels or in a percentage of the original size. You can also toggle the Keep Aspect Ratio option on and off. As a rule of thumb, always keep the image size the same as the file itself and never change the aspect ratio. If you change the image size, you leave it up to the browser to resize the image, and its quality drops dramatically as a result. Changing the aspect ratio distorts the image by making it either too squished or too stretched out. In Hour 7, "Getting Visual, Part 2: Advanced Image Editing, Thumbnails, and Hotspots," you learn how to use one of Expression Web 3's built-in functions to create a thumbnail (small version of your image) that links to the larger version, thereby avoiding the need to manually resize your images.

Try It Yourself   ▼

Change the Properties of the Image

By default, an image inserted into a page appears directly next to the line of text in which the designer placed it, and the image breaks the text. To make the page more appealing, it is necessary to separate the image from the text and give it some breathing room.

1. Right-click the image in Design view and select Picture Properties. Select the Appearance tab.

2. Click Left in the Wrapping Style section to align the image to the left and wrap the text to the right.

3. Set the border thickness to three pixels using the up and down buttons or by typing 3 in the box.

4. Set the horizontal and vertical margins to five pixels by using the up and down buttons or by typing 5 in the boxes, and click OK. Save the file and preview the page in your browser.   ▲

The image now appears to the left with the text wrapped to the right. The image has a 3-pixel black border with a 5-pixel space between the image and the surrounding text (see Figure 6.13).

FIGURE 6.13
With styling applied, the image floats to the left with the text wrapping to the right.

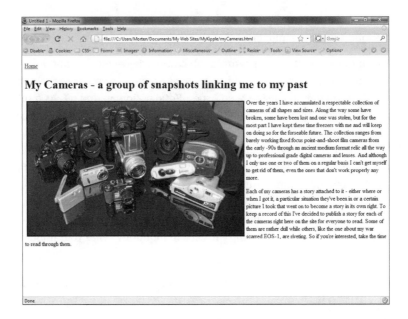

Summary

Images are an important part of any website. Not only do they increase the visual appeal of the site, but they can also help make the content more interesting and informative. In this hour, you learned that three main image formats are in use on the Web and that each has advantages and disadvantages. You also learned how to import images into your project and organize them in folders. At the end of the hour, you learned how to insert an image into a page using Design view and how to manipulate that image with the functions available in the Picture Properties dialog. You now have the basic building blocks to create a page with text and images.

Q&A

Q. *When I imported an image into Expression Web 3, it didn't end up in the Images folder but was stored alongside the files in the main folder. Why did this happen and how can I fix it?*

A. If the file you imported was stored in the main (or root) folder, you didn't select the subfolder before you started the import process. To avoid this problem, before you start the importing process, always double-click the folder you want to import files to. If a file ends up in the wrong folder, simply go to the Folder List panel or the Folders view in the Web Site pane and drag the file into the right folder. Expression Web 3 automatically updates all the files that link to the file and ensures that they still point to the right place.

Q. *When I inserted an image into my page, I accidentally grabbed one of the image sides and changed its size. Now it looks all weird and stretched. How do I fix it?*

A. If you make a mistake and notice it right away, the easiest way to fix the problem is by selecting Edit, Undo on the menu bar or using the shortcut Ctrl+Z. You can also reset the image to its original size and dimension by opening Picture Properties and unchecking the Specify Size box. Doing so returns the image to its original size. Then reselect the Specify Size option so that the image dimensions are specified in the markup. Even though your image still displays in a web browser even when you do not specify the image dimensions in the markup, it's good practice to specify the dimensions. Doing so helps the browser render the page layout correctly before the image has downloaded and appeared on the page.

Q. *When I dragged and dropped an image into a page, it ended up in the wrong place. What do I do now?*

A. The image you placed can be moved anywhere on the page simply by grabbing it with the mouse and dragging it to a different location. Because an image acts like part of the text, you can place it anywhere within the text in the same way you move around words and paragraphs. When you grab an image and move the cursor outside its border and into the text, a small, fuzzy gray vertical line indicates where the image will land.

Workshop

The Workshop has quiz questions and exercises to help you put to use what you just learned. If you get stuck, the answers to the quiz questions are in the next section. But try to answer the questions first. Otherwise you'll be cheating yourself.

Quiz

1. Why is it important to always provide alternative text when inserting an image into a web page?

2. What are the differences among GIF files, JPEG files, and PNG files? When would you use each format?

Answers

1. The alternative text displays whenever the image is not loaded because the connection is too slow, the image is not available, or the visitor is using a text-only or text-to-speech browser. The alternative text is both a courtesy to these users and a necessary substitute if your images do not load.

2. A GIF is a small file size, low-resolution image that can display coarse transparencies. GIFs mainly display smaller icons and simple line graphics. JPEG is the predominant image file format used to save photos and images with continuous tones, such as gradients. Most digital cameras and most other devices save images in this format. The JPEG format has good compression and relatively small file size. PNG is an image file format that has image quality the same as or better than the JPEG format, with the added bonus of clean transparencies. Unfortunately this comes at the price of a larger image file. Some older browsers, most prominently Internet Explorer 6, do not support PNG transparencies.

Exercise

Insert a second copy of the camerasSmall.jpg image into the myCameras.html page anywhere you want. Give it alternative text of your choice. Use the Picture Properties dialog to position the image on the right side of the screen to give the image a thin border and to provide more margin space than you gave the other image.

Getting Visual, Part 2: Advanced Image Editing, Thumbnails, and Hotspots

---

What You'll Learn in This Hour:

▶ How to import and work with a completed website in Expression Web 3
▶ How to use the Pictures toolbar to insert and edit images
▶ How to create thumbnails using the Auto Thumbnail function
▶ How to create and edit hotspots

Introduction

Now that you know how to import and insert an image, it's time to look at the image-editing tools featured in Expression Web 3. The program goes beyond the norm and gives you several quick-and-easy tools to make "quick and dirty" changes to your image files—changes that would normally require an image editor. One such feature is the ability to make thumbnails with a few mouse clicks. In this hour, you learn how to use these tools to make changes to image files you have already inserted into your page.

In addition to being visual elements, images in a web page can be functional elements if you turn them into links and buttons. You can even designate separate areas within an image to interact with the user either by highlighting when the user hovers over them or by linking to other images or pages. You do this by creating hotspots in your image.

Exploring the Pictures Toolbar

In Hour 6, "Getting Visual, Part 1: Adding Images and Graphics," you learned how to insert an image into a page and how to use the Picture Properties dialog to change the way the image relates to the other content on the page. But what if you want to change the appearance of the image itself? Maybe after you insert it into the page, you notice that it is too bright or that it needs cropping. Normally this requires you to open the image file in an image editor such as Photoshop or Expression Design, make the necessary changes, reimport the image into Expression Web 3, and finally replace the image on your page with a new one. Well, those days are over. Expression Web 3 has a built-in set of tools to help you do simple image editing without leaving the program. The Pictures toolbar conveniently contains these tools (see Figure 7.1).

FIGURE 7.1
The Pictures toolbar gives you instant access to all the image editing features in Expression Web 3.

As you learned in Hour 1, "Get to Know Microsoft Expression Web 3," all you have to do to open the Pictures toolbar is select View, Toolbars on the menu bar and click Pictures. The Pictures toolbar opens directly under the Common toolbar, and you can move it within the toolbar area to reposition it if you like.

If you haven't already done so, open the myCameras.html file. To activate the functions of the Pictures toolbar, click the image you inserted in Hour 6. Expression Web 3 always tells you which functions are available by fading out those that are unavailable. Place your cursor anywhere inside the page and notice that the icons in the toolbar fade out and become unavailable as is applicable.

With the image selected, hover over each button to view its ScreenTip and see what function the icon represents.

▶ Insert Picture from File ▣ is the only button that remains active no matter where you are in the document. Clicking this button lets you insert a new image in the current cursor location or replace the selected image with a different image.

▶ When you click Auto Thumbnail ▣, Expression Web 3 creates a small version of the selected image and inserts it on the page in place of the larger one. The smaller image (the thumbnail) is fitted with a hyperlink that displays the larger image.

▶ The Bring Forward ▣ and Bring Backward ▣ buttons tell the browser to change the stacking order of your content. A good analogy is to think of the page as a deck of cards; when you click the Bring Forward or Bring Backward button, you move the current card up or down in the stack. You use these functions when you start placing content on top of other content—for example, text on top of an image.

▶ The orientation buttons change the orientation of the image. They are Rotate Left 90° ▣ (counter-clockwise), Rotate Right 90° ▣ (clockwise), Flip Horizontal ▣, and Flip Vertical ▣. These buttons are useful if you import an image from a digital camera in which the orientation is incorrect—for example, a photo taken with the camera in a vertical orientation but the image in a horizontal orientation.

▶ The More Contrast ▣ and Less Contrast ▣ buttons bring the contrast levels of the image up or down. If you add more contrast to an image, the bright colors become brighter, and the dark colors become darker. If you reduce the contrast, the difference between bright and dark colors becomes more even. The More Brightness ▣ and Less Brightness ▣ buttons bring the overall brightness level up and down. If you bring up the brightness level, you usually also need to bring up the contrast level to prevent the image's colors from fading.

▶ The Crop ▣ button lets you cut out an area of the image and discard the rest, much as if you used a ruler and a knife to cut out part of a photo.

▶ The Set Transparent Color ▣ button lets you set a specific color to be transparent. This function works only with GIF images. If you apply the function to a non-GIF image, Expression Web 3 converts the image to the GIF format and reduces its color depth. Expression Web 3 warns you about this before performing any changes.

▶ The Color ▣ button changes the image in one of two ways: grayscale or "washed-out," which in image editing terms means desaturated, increased brightness, and reduced contrast. The washed-out look in particular is good if you are making buttons and you want a "faded" look when the button is inactive.

▶ Bevel ▣ puts a beveled border on your image to make it look as if it's standing up from the page. Designers often use this function when creating buttons from images.

▶ The Resample Image ▣ button becomes available only if you change the dimensions of the image in Design view or through the Picture Properties dialog. When you click this button, the image permanently changes to the new dimensions rather than simply resizing in the browser.

▶ The next set of tools let you insert and modify hotspots in the image. Select ⬚ lets you select the whole image or the respective hotspots on it. The Rectangular Hotspot ▢, Circular Hotspot ⬤, and Polygonal Hotspot ⬚ tools set the hotspots within an image. The Highlight Hotspots ⬚ button displays the image as an imagemap in which the hotspots are black and the rest of the image is white. This tool is a visual aid to help you find the hotspots and makes no actual changes to the image.

▶ The most important button on the Pictures toolbar is the Restore button ⬚. It restores the image to its original state and undoes all the changes you made to the image since you last saved the page. Be aware that if you save the page you are working in, Expression Web 3 saves the new edited version of the image on top of the old version and the Restore button can no longer restore the older image.

Watch Out!

All the editing functions on the Pictures toolbar (orientation, contrast, brightness, crop, color, and so on) are destructive image-editing tools. *Destructive* means the function permanently changes the file it affects and you cannot reverse the change. For that reason, it is paramount that you always keep backup copies of your original image files in case you make changes you are not satisfied with. Likewise, if you use the same image several times throughout your site and you make a change to one of these instances of the image using the Pictures toolbar, the change affects all other instances of that image. If you intend to make a change to an image you are using in multiple locations, you must first make a copy of the image and then apply the change to only the copy.

Using the Pictures Toolbar to Add and Change an Image

Now that you know what the different tools on the Pictures toolbar do, it's time to put them to use. But first you need a page to put some more images in. In the project files for this hour, you can find an HTML file called eos1.html. Create a new folder called Pages using the same technique you used in the last hour, and import the eos1.html file to that folder. In the lesson files there is also an image straight from my digital camera called eos1.jpg. As you learned in Hour 6, the first step when dealing with an image file is to import it into Expression Web 3 by selecting File, Import File in the menu bar. Make sure the new image is stored in the Images folder in the Folder View task pane. If it isn't there, simply drag and drop the file into the Images folder.

After you import the image, open the eos1.html file. There are now three different methods to insert the image into the page. In Hour 6, you used the drag-and-drop option. You can also insert an image by putting the cursor where you want to place the image, opening the Insert, Picture submenu on the menu bar, and selecting From File (see Figure 7.2). Finally, you can use the Insert Picture from File button on the Pictures toolbar. The last two methods are the same function. Both approaches open a standard file browser window from which you select the file you want to insert.

FIGURE 7.2
You can use the Insert Picture from File option on the menu bar to insert an image at the current cursor location.

In Design view, place the cursor at the beginning of the heading in the eos1.html page. Press Enter to make a new line over the heading and change the new line to a Paragraph using the Style menu on the Common toolbar. With the cursor in the new line, use one of the two options previously described to open the Insert Picture dialog. Navigate to the Images folder and select the eos1.jpg file you just imported.

From time to time, you might notice that recently imported images or files don't show up in the Insert Picture dialog or other file browsing dialogs within Expression Web 3. To solve this problem, refresh the dialog by right-clicking in the file browser dialog and selecting Refresh or by pressing the F5 key.

The same thing goes for the Folder List panel: After images have been imported properly, they don't always appear in the file list. To refresh the Folder List task pane, click inside it and press the F5 key.

Did you Know?

When you click OK, the Accessibility Properties dialog opens, as it did when you inserted the camerasSmall.jpg image in Hour 6. Enter the alternative text **Canon EOS-1** and click OK. At this point, you might think you made a mistake because the Design View pane fills with an image that is a murky gray/brown color, much like Figure 7.3.

What you are seeing is the corner of a large image. This is a common problem: The image is not an appropriate size for the Web; therefore, it doesn't fit on a web page. In fact, the image you just inserted is more than three times as tall as a regular computer screen! If you click the image and look in the Tag Properties task pane on the bottom left, you can see that the image is 3744 pixels high and 5616 pixels wide. A

FIGURE 7.3
The page as it appears in Design view after you insert the eos1.jpg image.

good rule of thumb is that an image in a web page should never be more than 600 pixels at the longest side. So, before you do anything else, you need to drastically reduce the size. To do so, right-click the image, open the Picture Properties dialog, and select the Appearance tab. In the Size section, enable the Keep Aspect Ratio check box, and change the Width setting (the longest side) to 600 pixels (see Figure 7.4). The height changes accordingly.

FIGURE 7.4
You can change the image to an exact size from Picture Properties.

When you click OK, Expression Web 3 reduces the image to a workable size. Now you can alter the image to make it work better within the page. First, I took the image through a mirror so that it is mirrored. To turn the image the right way, click the image to select it, and then click the Flip Horizontal button on the Pictures toolbar.

The framing of the photo isn't very good and it could use some cropping. With the image still selected, click the Crop button on the Pictures toolbar. This produces a dashed rectangle that indicates the crop area within the image (see Figure 7.5).

FIGURE 7.4
The crop area inside the image is indicated by a dotted line with handles.

Using your mouse, you can either draw a new crop area within the image by clicking and dragging the mouse to create a new rectangle, or simply resize the existing rectangle by grabbing the handles (marked by small squares) in the corners or at the middle of all four sides. Resize the rectangle so that you cut a bit off the top and the left and right sides. When you are satisfied with your crop area, press Enter and Expression Web 3 crops the image.

Now that the image is cropped, it is smaller than it was before. To bring it back to the 600 pixel wide size, right-click the image, go to the Advanced tab under Picture Properties, and set the width to 600 pixels just like you did before.

The photo is a little dark. To lighten the image, select it and click the More Brightness button one or two times and bring up the contrast one step by clicking the More Contrast button as well. This brings up the brightness of the image slightly.

If you are not satisfied with your alterations, this is the time to start over. If you want to undo any of your changes or just want some practice, click the Restore button to return the image to its original state. If you click the Restore button by mistake, simply go to the Edit menu and select Undo Edit Picture, or press Ctrl+Z on your keyboard.

There is one final step left. You might remember from earlier in the hour that the Resample button becomes active only if you change the size of the image. You might also remember from Hour 6 that you should never make the browser resize your images for you. When you resized the eos1.jpg image earlier in this hour, you asked the browser to squish the large image down to make it fit certain dimensions. Now you want to resample the image so that the picture in the image file is of the correct dimensions. You can do this in two ways: Either click the Resample button on the Pictures toolbar, or select Resample Picture to Match Size from the Picture Actions drop-down menu found under the small icon attached to the image (see Figure 7.6).

FIGURE 7.6
You can resample the image from the Picture Actions drop-down menu found under the inserted image.

This function overwrites the old image file and replaces it with the reoriented, cropped, and resized image as it appears in Design view. To make the changes permanent (a.k.a. The Point of No Return), simply save the page. Expression Web 3 opens the Save Embedded Files dialog and asks you whether, where, and how you want to save the changed image file (see Figure 7.7). When you are sure the image looks the way you want it to look, click OK, and the new image replaces the original one.

FIGURE 7.7
The Save Embedded Files dialog appears every time you make changes to other external files while modifying the page. you are currently saving.

Try It Yourself ▼

Creating a Thumbnail Using Auto Thumbnail

Because most web pages contain a lot of content and not all visitors are on high-speed connections, using smaller versions of images (commonly referred to as *thumbnails*) that link to the larger version of the image is common. Using thumbnails helps the page load faster because the browser doesn't have to download large image files. In addition, thumbnails can help designers create manageable layouts because they can link to large images rather than inserting them in the page.

More than just eye candy, you can use images to supplement the text. In this page a detail image of some of the damage on the camera seems fitting and lends more reality to the story. A second image called eos1Detail.jpg is in the lesson files. Using the same method as before, import this image and place it in the Images folder. When imported, place your cursor at the beginning of the third paragraph, and insert the new image there using one of the three methods previously described in this hour. You now have a page with two images, one on top and one in the body of the text.

But as you can see, even though the new image is a web-friendly size (600 by 600 pixels), it's much too big and makes the page difficult to read. What you want is a small thumbnail of the eos1Detail.jpg image that links to the bigger version. In Expression Web 3, you can do this with a single-click of your mouse: With the eos1Detail.jpg image selected, click the Auto Thumbnail button on the Pictures toolbar or use the Ctrl+T shortcut.

This creates a 100-pixels-wide thumbnail with a blue outline that, when clicked, opens the original full-size image in the same window. Because the thumbnail inherits whatever styling you applied to the original image (and you didn't apply any styling to the image), it appears at the top of the paragraph as part of the first line of text. You can quickly fix this by using the Picture Properties techniques you learned in Hour 6; on the Appearance tab set the Wrapping Style to Left and Horizontal Margin to 10. When you click OK the thumbnail places itself nicely to the left with the text wrapping around it, as shown in Figure 7.8.

FIGURE 7.8
With the Wrapping Style and margins applied, the thumbnail appears as part of the paragraph.

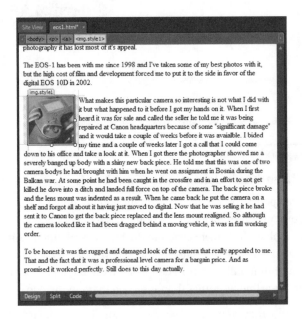

To finalize this process, it is necessary to save the page. When you save the page, the Save Embedded Files dialog you saw in Figure 7.7 opens and asks you to save a new file called eos1Detail_small.jpg. This is the smaller thumbnail file that Expression Web 3 created and inserted in your page. By default Expression Web 3 saves the thumbnail in the currently open folder, but you can pick a different folder by clicking the Change Folder button in the dialog. I recommend placing all images in the Images folder and maybe even separating the thumbnails by making a subfolder called Thumbs. Finally, click OK and preview the page in your browser.

If you don't want the thumbnail to have a blue border or you want it to be a different size, you can modify the Auto Thumbnail default settings from the Page Editor Options dialog. To do this, open the Page Editor Options dialog from the Tools button on the menu bar and select the Auto Thumbnail tab. From here you can define the size of the thumbnail by setting the width, height, shortest side, or longest side to a specific pixel length, changing the thickness of the border around the image (0 for no border), and even give the thumbnail a beveled edge.

Note that changes to the Auto Thumbnail settings apply only to new thumbnails and not to ones that already exist.

Creating Hotspots

A *hotspot* is a defined area or region within an image that has a hyperlink attached to it. There is no limit to how many hotspots with different hyperlinks you can set in a given image. Hotspots are a great tool if you want to provide further information about a certain element within an image or use an image as a navigational tool.

Just so there is no confusion: What Expression Web 3 calls a hotspot is more commonly called an *imagemap*.

Try It Yourself ▼

Create a Hotspot and Link It to a File

In Expression Web 3, you can create and edit hotspots from the Pictures toolbar using the hotspot buttons:

1. In the myCameras.html file, click the camerasSmall.jpg image to activate the Pictures toolbar.

2. Click the Rectangular Hotspot button, and click and drag the image to draw a rectangle around the top middle camera (see Figure 7.9). This opens the Insert Hyperlink dialog.

3. In the Insert Hyperlink dialog, find and select the eos1.html page under the Pages folder. Set the ScreenTip to **Learn about the camera that went to war** and set the target frame to New Window. Click OK.

Save the page and preview it in your browser. Note that although the camerasSmall.jpg image looks unchanged, if you hover your mouse over the top middle camera, the mouse pointer changes to a hand indicating a hyperlink and a ScreenTip appears. If you click the hotspot, the browser navigates to the eos1.html page.

To edit the hyperlink or ScreenTip attached to the hotspot, simply right-click the hotspot in Design view and select Picture Hotspot Properties. If you want to resize the hotspot, you can do so by clicking it, grabbing the resizing handles on any side of the

FIGURE 7.9
Creating a rec-
tangular hotspot
around the top
middle camera.

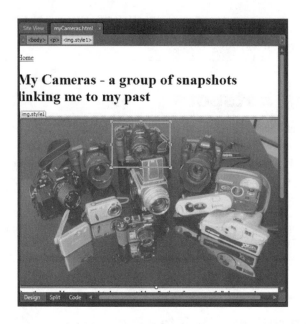

hotspot, and moving them. You can also reposition the hotspot by clicking and dragging it to a different location within the image.

Hotspots can also be circular or even polygonal. To create a circular hotspot, click the
Circular Hotspot button, and draw the circle on the image in the same way you created the rectangle earlier. To create a polygonal hotspot, click the Polygonal Hotspot
button, and use the mouse to define each corner of the hotspot until you outline the
desired area. To finalize a polygonal hotspot, you have to set the last corner point on
top of the first one. Doing so opens the Insert Hyperlink dialog.

Because it can be hard to see exactly where all your hotspots are located, the Pictures
toolbar features a Highlight Hotspots function. Clicking the Highlight Hotspots button replaces the image with an imagemap in which the hotspots have black outlines
and the remaining image is gray. If you select one of the hotspots, it turns solid black
(see Figure 7.10).

This tool is only a visual aid and does not affect the image in any way. To close the
imagemap and see the original image, simply click the Highlight Hotspots button
again, or click anywhere outside the image.

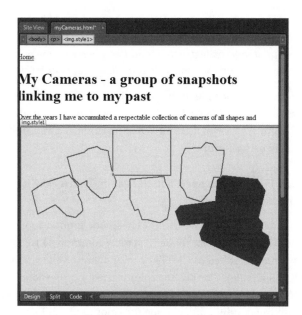

FIGURE 7.10
The cameras
Small.jpg image
with the High-
light Hotspots
function

Summary

The ability to make quick alterations to images without having to leave the program is a feature that puts Expression Web 3 above the fold. Not to mention that it can be a real time saver as long as you think things through and make backups of your image files before changing them. In this hour, you learned how to use the powerful tools in the Pictures toolbar to edit the appearance of images in your page. You saw that the Reset button on the toolbar gives you the ability to experiment with different effects without ruining your files, and that scaling down large photos to make them fit in your page is a relatively simple task.

You also learned how to use the Auto Thumbnail function to make linked thumbnails of your images with one click. Finally, you learned how to set and edit hotspots within an image to create a more interactive and immersive experience for your visitors.

You now have all the tools necessary to create and edit the content of your website. In the next hours, you learn how to style the content to make it more visually pleasing and easier to read.

Q&A

Q. *I imported the image as instructed, and I can see the image in the Folder List panel, but when I open the Insert Picture dialogue, I can't find it anywhere.*

A. If you can see the image file in the Folder List panel but it doesn't appear when you browse for it, try right-clicking in the browser window and selecting Refresh. This works 95% of the time. The remaining 5% is usually caused by the image file being corrupt.

Q. *I placed the image in the page, but all I get in Design view is a box with a red X in it.*

A. There could be two reasons for this: 1) The image is not a supported image file or is not in a supported color mode. The most common cause for this problem is that the image is stored as CMYK (cyan, magenta, yellow, kelvin) instead of RGB (red, green, blue). CMYK is the color mode for professional printing and does not translate to screen graphics. To correct this, you need to open the image in an image editor and change the color mode; 2) Expression Web 3 didn't import the image properly. To test if this is the problem, preview the page in your browser. If the image appears in your browser, it means Expression Web 3 messed up while importing the image and you need to reimport it.

Workshop

The Workshop has quiz questions and exercises to help you put to use what you just learned. If you get stuck, the answers to the quiz questions are in the next section. But try to answer the questions first. Otherwise you'll be cheating yourself.

Quiz

1. There are three different methods to insert an image into your page. Name them and explain how they are used.

2. Why should you always use the Resample Picture function when resizing an image on a page?

3. How many hotspots can you insert into an image?

Answers

1. To insert an image into a page, you can drag and drop it directly from the Folder View task pane, use the Insert Picture from File function found under Insert on the menu bar, or use the Insert Picture button on the Pictures toolbar.

2. If you insert a large image on a page and resize it using the Picture Properties dialog, you force the browser to resize the image for you. That means that the browser downloads far more image information than it displays. As a rule of thumb, you should always reduce the amount of information downloaded by the browser to an absolute minimum. That means you need to resample all your images so that the actual image dimensions match the displayed image dimensions.

3. In theory, there is no limit to how many hotspots an image can contain. In reality, however, the number of hotspots is limited to the number you can fit within the borders of the image. There is not much sense in inserting so many hotspots that the user can't find them or discern one from another.

Exercise

Use the Polygonal Hotspot tool to create hotspots around the different cameras in the photo. Set the hyperlinks to whatever you want; for instance, the camera manufacturer websites (the cameras are all Canon, Nikon, or Polaroid except for the huge one in the middle, which is a Hasselblad). Give the hotspots descriptive ScreenTips and set the hyperlinks to open a new windows.

HOUR 8

Cracking the Code: Working in Code View

What You'll Learn in This Hour:

▶ How to use IntelliSense to write quick and error-free code
▶ What specialized tools are available to you in Code view and how to use them
▶ How to use Code view as a learning tool
▶ How to dissect code in Split view

Introduction

Until now you have worked almost exclusively in Design view using the WYSIWYG (What You See Is What You Get) editor without paying much attention to what goes on behind the scenes. This isn't actually a problem because the code Expression Web 3 creates is clean and tidy enough that you don't need to worry too much about it. But if you want to get a full understanding of how websites work and move beyond the basics, understanding at least the fundamentals of coding becomes vital. To this end, Expression Web 3 is a great learning tool because it generates standards-based code out of the box.

You might consider Code view the exclusive domain of web developers and code experts, but the tools Expression Web 3 provides make it easy even for a novice to work in Code view. Not only is it helpful to understand the code end of your site when something doesn't work properly, but you might also want to add custom elements into your site that require access to the back end.

Tools in Code View

As with Design view, Expression Web 3 has an arsenal of tools available to help you work faster and more effectively in Code view. These tools can be found on the Code View toolbar, in the Toolbox panel, and inside Code view itself. We leave the last one—called IntelliSense—to the end of this hour.

Code view has a dedicated toolbar you can open from the Toolbar menu under view on the menu bar (see Figure 8.1). When opened it docks under the Common toolbar

FIGURE 8.1
The Code View toolbar appears directly under the Common toolbar when it is opened.

Code View toolbar

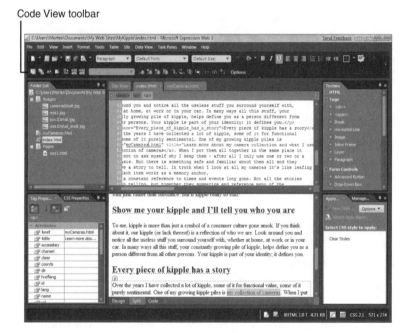

on top of your workspace. If the Pictures toolbar is still open from the last hour, close it from the same menu.

The Buttons of the Code View Toolbar and What They Do

The Code View toolbar has a set of useful tools that can help you write code or understand what is going on inside your code. In this and the following hours, you use most of them, so you might as well acquaint yourself with them right away.

▶ The List Members ⬚ button tells IntelliSense to provide a shortcut menu for the word or segment your cursor is on, so if you write <a and click the button, a drop-down menu with all the possible tags starting with the letter a appears.

The Parameter Info ▣ button opens a list of the valid script parameters for the same segment. (This applies only to script languages such as JavaScript, ASP.NET, and PHP.) The Complete Word ▣ button completes the word you type based on an educated (and surprisingly accurate) guess.

▶ The List Code Snippets ▣ button opens a list of shortcuts to your custom code snippets. Code Snippets is a smart feature in Code view that lets you store frequently used segments of code for easy retrieval through this menu. You can also access the menu by pressing Ctrl+Enter while in Code view. You can add, modify, and delete whatever code snippets you want in the Code Snippets menu by double-clicking the Customize List option and selecting Add.

▶ The Follow Hyperlink ▣ button lets you navigate to the destination of the selected hyperlink within Expression Web 3. The Previous Code Hyperlink ▣ and Next Code Hyperlink ▣ buttons work in much the same way as the Back and Forward buttons in a browser, taking you back and forth through hyperlinks you have already visited with the Follow Hyperlink button.

▶ The Function Lookup [< Select a function > ▾] box directs you to the function you select from the drop-down list of the available functions (such as JavaScript or PHP) in your document. This box works only if your document contains functions (small programs) that are present in the code. You create and use functions in Hour 16, "Using Behaviors."

▶ In Code view, Expression Web 3 lets you insert temporary bookmarks that you can use to quickly navigate between segments of your code. The bookmarks appear as small blue boxes on the far left side of the panel next to the line numbers (see Figure 8.2). The Toggle Bookmark ▣ button inserts a bookmark at the current line of code. The Next Bookmark ▣ and Previous Bookmark ▣ buttons navigate between the set bookmarks. The Clear Bookmarks ▣ button removes all bookmarks from the document.

▶ Based on the current location of the cursor, the Select Tag ▣ button selects and highlights the active beginning and end tags and the content between them. This tool is helpful to see what content a certain tag affects. The Find Matching Tag ▣ button finds the beginning tag of the selected content when you first press it and the respective end tag when you press it again. This is an excellent tool if you are confused about where your tags begin or end, and you can use it to clean up code if beginning or end tags are missing.

▶ The Select Block ▣ button works the same way as the Select Tag button except it finds and selects code blocks bracketed by braces rather than tags. The Find Matching Brace ▣ button works the same way as the Find Matching Tag button except it looks for braces rather than tags.

FIGURE 8.2
A Code View bookmark is a small blue box beside the line numbers.

Code View bookmark

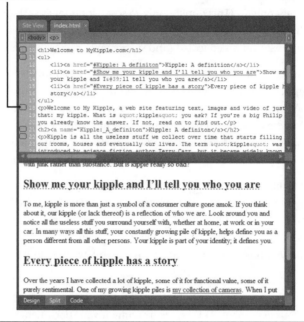

Watch Out!

The temporary bookmarks in Code view are solely a visual and navigational aid to help in the coding process. They have no actual function in the document itself. These bookmarks should not be confused with HTML bookmarks that were covered in Hour 5, "Getting Connected with (Hyper)Links: The Cornerstone of the World Wide Web."

▶ The Insert Start Tag [<>] button inserts an empty start tag at the current location. The Insert End Tag [</>] button inserts an empty end tag at the current location. You must manually enter the names for these tags.

▶ The Insert Comment [¦¦] button inserts the beginning and end tags for nonfunctional code comments. A code comment is text that is visible only in the code itself and has no function other than as a descriptive tool for the developer or anyone else looking at the code. Designers commonly use comments to keep track of changes or explain how or why certain parts of code work.

▶ The Options [Options ▾] button gives you direct access to the code viewing options that define how code is displayed in Code view. You can also access these options by opening the Page Editor Options from the Tools menu and selecting the General tab. The options (see Figure 8.3) are Word Wrap, which wraps the lines of code to fit inside the window (removing the need to scroll sideways to read all the code); Auto Indent, which keeps the indentation from the current line when a new line is created by hitting Enter; Line Numbers (self explanatory); Selection Margin, which adds a space between the line numbers and the content so that you can click and drag in the margin with the mouse to select multiple lines of code; Highlight Invalid HTML, which displays invalid

FIGURE 8.3
The Options but-
ton on the Code
view toolbar give
you quick and
direct access to
the code viewing
options control-
ling how code is
displayed in the
editor.

HTML code as red font with a yellow background; and Highlight Incompatible HTML, which displays incompatible HTML with a wavy underline like the one commonly used to highlight typos.

Common HTML Tags in the Toolbox

To help in the coding process, Expression Web 3 provides a source of commonly used code through the Toolbox panel (see Figure 8.4). Under HTML, you find commonly used tags, form controls, and media insertion tools. To use any of these, simply place

FIGURE 8.4
The Toolbox task
pane provides
easy access to
the most com-
monly used
HTML tags.

your cursor where you want to insert the code in Code view and double-click the desired element. You can also drag and drop the elements directly into the code from the panel. If your Toolbox panel is closed, you can access the same commonly used code elements along with all other available elements under Insert on the menu bar.

Using Code View as a Learning Tool

More than just a design and development tool, Expression Web 3 is an excellent learning tool for designers and developers of all levels. It's a poorly kept secret that web designers and developers learn from what other people create. By using Design view and Code view, you can do the same no matter what level you are at. Web pages are a bit unusual in that after they are published, the code (or blueprint) is available for all to see. That means if you find something you like on a website, you can look at the code to see what is going on and learn from it. In Expression Web 3, you can even open websites from the Internet without downloading them first. All you have to do is click Open from the File menu and insert the URL to the site you want to take a closer look at. When it is open in Split view, you have full access to all the code and other elements that make up the page, and you can see how everything fits together. Just remember that you should never copy code from someone else's page and pass it off as your own. If you use someone else's code, be sure to seek permission and credit them for it.

In the last four hours, you built a website with three pages containing a variety of content. Now you use Code view to answer that burning question: How do the pages really work? For a novice, opening a page in Code view can be intimidating. Fortunately there is the option of using Split view, so you can see the code and the WYSIWYG editor at the same time.

To start, open the default.html file in Split view. In Hour 4, "Building a Home Page: A Look Behind the Curtain," you learned that if you click an item in the WYSIWYG editor while in Split view, Expression Web 3 highlights the relevant section of code in Code view. You already know how basic styles such as headings and paragraphs appear in Code view, so let's concentrate on the new elements in the page.

Dissecting Hyperlinks in Code View

In Hour 5, you added several hyperlinks to the page. Now you can use Code view to see how they work. Click the hyperlink with the words *my collection of cameras*. This highlights the same text in Code view. When you click the highlighted text in Code view and press the Select Tag button on the Code View toolbar, all the code within this particular tag is highlighted (see Figure 8.5). In this case, that is the hyperlink or <a> tag:

```
<a href="myCameras.html" title="Learn more about my camera collection
 and what I use them for">my collection of cameras</a>
```

The highlighted code shows the basic elements of a hyperlink:

▶ The visible hyperlink text is contained between the <a> and </a> tags.

▶ The brackets of the first wrapper contain all the attributes relating to this specific link, separated by spaces. For example, <a attributeOne="attribute
value" attributeTwo="attribute value" attributeThree="attribute
value">.

▶ The destination address is set using the href attribute.

Highlighted code

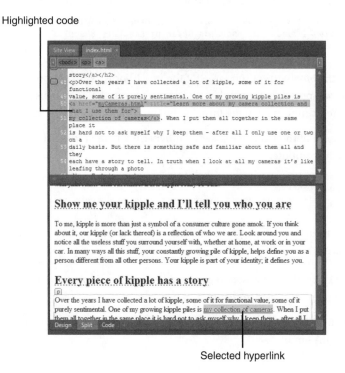

FIGURE 8.5
Using the Select
Tag button on
the Code view
toolbar to high-
light the code
within the
selected tag.

Selected hyperlink

▶ The ScreenTip is set using the title attribute.

> HTML, like most code languages, is littered with weird acronyms and abbreviations. Many of them need to be placed in a historical perspective to make sense. Case in point is the <a> tag and its href attribute. While we commonly use the <a> tag to create links, the original use—from which it gets its name—was actually to refer to other places within the document through Bookmarks that back then were referred to as "anchors." It makes sense if you think about it: You place an anchor at a specific location and then link a chain to it so that you can get there. To this day, some web authoring tools still use the iconography of an anchor and a chain to signify bookmarks and links. The href attribute name harks back to the same era and stands for "hypertext reference."

If you look at the code for the link to the book on Amazon.com you created earlier in the page, you see that an added attribute, named target, is set to _blank:

```
<a href="http://www.amazon.com/Do-Androids-Dream-Electric-Sheep/(...)"
target="_blank" title="Do Androids Dream of Electric Sheep? is available
from Amazon.com">Do Androids Dream of Electric Sheep?</a>
```

This tells the browser that the target of the link (that is, what window it should open in) is a new empty (blank) window. If no target is set, the link opens in the current window. You can also force the target to be the current window by setting it to _self.

At the bottom of the page you inserted a hyperlink to open the default email program on the computer:

```
<a href="mailto:kippleinfo@pinkandyellow.com?subject=Email generated from
the MyKipple website"
title="Send all your questions about this site here">send me an email</a>
```

The href attribute in this hyperlink contains a code rather than an address. This code has two sections:

▶ mailto: tells the browser that the following is a recipient email address for insertion into the default email program.

▶ ?subject= tells the browser that the following text is the subject line to insert into the email.

You also created several bookmarks within default.html. They are the headings with the dotted underlines in Design view. If you click one of these headings and look at them in Code view, you see that the <a> tag wraps them, too. But unlike the hyperlinks, they don't have an href attribute. Instead they have a name attribute that matches the bookmark name you set in the Bookmark Properties dialog:

```
<h2><a name="Kipple:_A_definition">Kipple: A definition</a></h2>
```

Inspecting the code for the menu items you created at the top of the page, you can see that the name attribute preceded by a # works as the hyperlink address to the bookmarks within the document:

```
<a href="#Kipple:_A_definiiton" title="Jump to Kipple: A definition">
Kipple: A Definition</a>
```

Hyperlink code can wrap around many elements, not just text. In the eos1.html file, you created a hyperlink attached to an image. To see an example of this, open eos1.html in Split view, and click the thumbnail of the detail photo you created using Auto Thumbnail. By highlighting the relevant code using the Select Tag function in Code view, you can see that the only difference between this hyperlink and the previous examples is that an image has replaced the content between the <a> and </a> tags:

```
<a href="../Images/eos1Detail.jpg">
<img alt="Canon EOS-1 detail" class="style1" height="100"
src="../Images/eos1Detail_small.jpg" style="float: left" width="100" />
<!-- MSComment="autothumbnail" xthumbnail-orig-image=
"file:///C:/Users/Morten/Documents/My Web Sites/MyKipple/Images/eos1Detail.jpg"
-->
</a>
```

Note the commented section, which is shown in gray in Code view. Expression Web 3 inserted this nonfunctional code to explain the origins of the thumbnail. The comment is wrapped inside a special tag that starts with <!-- and ends with -->.

Images in Code View

In Hour 3, "A Website Is Really Just Text: Build One in 5 Minutes," you learned that all web pages are text documents filled with code. But how does that work when it comes to images? When you inserted images into the page, you didn't convert them into code first. And when you click them and inspect them in Code view, all you get is what looks like a hyperlink. So, how do images appear in web pages?

The answer is simple: Images in web pages belong to a group of elements known as replaced elements. A replaced element is a segment of code that has no content in it but instead points to external content that the browser displays in its place. So, when you insert an image into your web page in Design view, you are inserting a small piece of code that tells the browser to find a specific image file, insert it in place of the code, and apply a set of attributes to it.

Select the camera detail thumbnail in Design view and look at the section of code highlighted in Code view:

```
<img alt="Canon EOS-1 detail" class="style1" height="100"
 src="../Images/eos1Detail_small.jpg" style="float: left" width="100" />
```

Unlike the tags you saw earlier, the `<img>` tag doesn't have a corresponding `</img>` tag but rather ends with `/>`, telling the browser that it is closed. This makes sense because, as you previously saw, any text content between a beginning and an end tag is visible in the browser, but there is no such content in the case of an image. Within the tag you find all the information you inserted using the Picture Properties dialog: the `alt` attribute defines the alternative text; the `height` and `width` attributes define the height and width; and the `src` attribute defines the location of the external image file. The remaining attributes, `class` and `style`, are explained in future hours.

When the page opens in a browser, the browser reads the information in the image tag and performs the necessary replacements: In this place, insert the eos1Detail_small.jpg image, located under the Images folder, with the alternative text **Canon EOS-1 detail** and a height of 100 pixels. The image belongs to style class `style1` and should float to the left with the adjoining text flowing around it to the right.

Other replaced elements include, among other things, Silverlight applications and Adobe Flash movies (.swf files), both covered in Hour 21, "Working with Flash and Silverlight," and inline frames (iFrames), covered in Hour 17, "Frames and Layers."

Unordered and Ordered Lists in Code View

Working with lists in Design view can get complicated, especially if you have lists within lists. Fortunately, lists have an organized code structure that makes Code view ideal for advanced list editing.

As you learned in Hour 4, there are two types of lists. Unordered lists, signified by the `<ul>` tag, are what we usually refer to as bullet lists. When the browser finds a `<ul>` tag, it assumes that each list item should have a bullet in front of it unless otherwise specified. Ordered lists signified by the `<ol>` tag are what we usually refer to as numbered lists. When the browser finds an `<ol>` tag, it assumes that each list item should have a consecutively higher number in front of it than the previous one.

The items in ordered and unordered lists are usually prefixed by either a number or a bullet, but in many cases these elements don't work well with your design. In Hour 13, "Getting Visual, Part 3: Images as Design Elements with CSS," you learn how to turn the numbers and bullets on and off or swap them for image files using CSS.

The HTML list structure, regardless of whether it is an unordered or an ordered list, is quite simple. It starts with the `<ul>` or `<ol>` tag telling the browser what kind of list it is and then wraps each list item between `<li>` and `</li>` tags. The end of the list is indicated by the closing `</ul>` or `</ol>` tag. The structure looks like this:

```
<ul>
    <li>First List Item</li>
    <li>Second List Item</li>
    <li>Third List Item</li>
</ul>
```

To change this list from an unordered list to an ordered list, all you need to do is change the `<ul>` and `</ul>` tags to `<ol>` and `</ol>`.

You can build lists within lists just as easily. The following is an unordered list with three list items in which the second one is an ordered list with three subitems:

```
<ul>
        <li>First List Item</li>
        <li>
           <ol>
              <li>First Sub List Item</li>
              <li>Second Sub List Item</li>
              <li>Third Sub List Item</li>
           </ol>
        </li>
        <li>Third List Item</li>
</ul>
```

Try It Yourself ▼

Introducing IntelliSense—Your New Best Friend

Joining the Code view toolbar and the Toolbox panel on the list of tools to help you navigate and write code in Expression Web 3 is IntelliSense. In my view, IntelliSense is the most powerful and helpful tool in the application, and I am certain that when you see how it works, you will agree with me. In short, IntelliSense is a tool that helps you write proper code faster. The best way to understand exactly what it does is to see it in action. In this example, you insert an image in Code view with the help of IntelliSense:

1. With the myCameras.html file open in Split view, find the second paragraph wrapped by `<p>` tags. Place the cursor next to the `<p>` tag before the text.

2. Still in Code view, type a less-than bracket: `<`. A drop-down menu appears below the bracket—this is IntelliSense presenting you with all the available code snippets that start with a less-than bracket. You are inserting an image, so you want the img tag. To find this, enter an **i** and IntelliSense brings up all the available tags that start with `<i` (see Figure 8.6). Use the arrow keys to skip down to `<img` and press Enter to insert the `<img` tag.

FIGURE 8.6
IntelliSense
pops up in Code
view to suggest
possible code
segments you
could insert.

3. Next you need a source for your image. Press the spacebar and IntelliSense pops up with new options. This time it gives you only available attributes for the img tag. As you previously learned, the image location is set with the src attribute, so type **s** to narrow the search. IntelliSense takes you straight to src and all you need to do is press the Enter key.

4. Because the src attribute requires a URL (uniform resource locator), IntelliSense inserts the necessary code and asks you for the location of the image. Click the Pick URL button shown in Figure 8.7 and navigate to the desired file, in this case eos1Detail_small.html located under the Images folder.

FIGURE 8.7
IntelliSense fin-
ishes the code
and provides a
button to open a
browser to
select an URL
for the image.

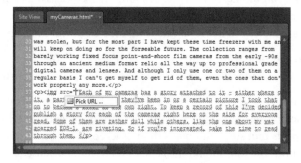

5. Before you close the tag, remember to add the alternative text using the alt attribute. This is done by following the same steps as in the preceding steps, but

starting with the letter a. If you want to, you can add more attributes to your image using IntelliSense.

6. To close the img tag, simply type `/>`. The final code looks like this: `<img src="Images/eos1Detail_small.jpg" alt="Another thumbnail" />`.

If you click outside the active text or accidentally press Backspace, IntelliSense closes. To open it again, click the List Members button on the Code view toolbar or use the Ctrl+L shortcut.

IntelliSense helps you write a number of different code languages including HTML, CSS, PHP, JavaScript, ASP.NET, and even Visual Basic. More important, it keeps tabs on your code to prevent you from making errors. For instance, if you insert a beginning tag, IntelliSense automatically inserts a matching end tag. The same goes for braces and quotes. The code output of IntelliSense matches the code settings for the current document. The status bar at the bottom of the work area tells you what code language and version you are working in. If you want to change the IntelliSense settings, open the Page Editor Options under Tools on the menu bar, and select the IntelliSense tab.

You will be introduced to CSS in Hour 10, "Bringing Style to Substance with Cascading Style Sheets," PHP in Hour 22, "Beyond the Basics, Part 1: PHP in Expression Web 3," and ASP.NET in Hour 25, "Beyond the Basics, Part 2: Building a Site with ASP.NET."

▲

Summary

Understanding the code that makes up a web page can greatly enhance your ability to create professional-looking and functional sites for yourself and your clients. Expression Web 3's Code view is an excellent tool not only to write flawless and standards-compliant code but also to understand and learn how this code works. With its arsenal of tools, such as IntelliSense, the program keeps tabs on what you are doing and makes sure your code remains valid by inserting all the necessary little extra pieces. It's like having an assistant that looks over your shoulder and makes subtle changes and additions as you work.

In this hour, you learned how to use Code view and Split view to get a better understanding of how the code works. You got an introduction to the many tools for use in Code view, such as the Code View toolbar, IntelliSense, and the Toolbox task pane. You learned how to use those tools and their functions to make quick and error-free changes and additions to your page.

You used Split view to learn a great deal about HTML semantics; that is, how the HTML language is put together. Using the Code view tools, you inspected and altered hyperlinks and images, and by doing so you learned how these code elements work to produce the desired output.

In the upcoming hours, you use both Code view and Design view to continue building the MyKipple website. That way you learn not only how the code works but also why it's better to handle some tasks in the back end rather than in the front end.

Q&A

Q. *Why doesn't the* `<img>` *tag close with a separate* `</img>` *tag like the other tags I have used?*

A. Unlike the other tags you have learned about, the `<img>` tag does not affect any visible text but works instead as a replaced element. Any text contained between two tags is visible in the browser. The way you closed the `<img>` tag by simply ending it with `/>` is a shorthand version of the tag code. Ending the tag by closing the beginning tag and following it directly with an end tag produces the same results: `<img src="Images/eos1Detail_small.jpg" alt="Another thumbnail"></img>`.

Q. *When I insert new code into Code view, other segments of code turn red or are highlighted in yellow. Why is that?*

A. While you are inserting new code in Code view, you often temporarily break the code. When this happens, Expression Web 3 immediately highlights the incorrect code to tell you something is wrong. You'll note that when you break the code, only small segments of code actually highlight. Usually these are beginning or end tags. This is because Expression Web 3 tracks the source of the error rather than highlighting the affected area. This makes it easier to clear out any mistakes quickly. On a side note, this function is excellent for debugging websites other developers and designers have created because any errors pop out immediately upon opening them in Code view and can be easily remedied.

Q. *There are all these strange code snippets in my text in Code view, such as* " *and* '. *What do they mean?*

A. If you look closely at the code, you see that it is full of symbols you would often use in text—symbols such as quotation marks, ampersands, apostrophes, and so forth. These symbols are functional code elements, and if they appear as themselves in the code, the browser interprets them as code rather than text elements. To avoid this, all special characters displayed in the text are assigned HTML entities; that is, alternative snippets of code that tell the browser which symbol to insert. The most common entities are " for a quotation mark, & for an ampersand, ' for an apostrophe, © for the copyright symbol, and   for a nonbreaking space (used in the same way you would normally press the spacebar if you want to insert an empty paragraph or an empty space). If you don't know the HTML entry for a particular symbol, the easiest way to find it is to simply type in the symbol in Design view to see what it produces in Code view. You can find complete lists of all available HTML entries by searching for HTML entries on the W3C (World Wide Web Consortium) website at www.w3.org.

Workshop

The Workshop has quiz questions and exercises to help you put to use what you just learned. If you get stuck, the answers to the quiz questions are in the next section. But try to answer them first. Otherwise you'll be cheating yourself.

Quiz

1. How do you find out what tag is affecting a particular portion of the content of your page?

2. In this hour, you were introduced to two tools that help you write code. What are they and how do you use them?

Answers

1. To find the relevant tags for your content, place the cursor anywhere within the content in question in Code view and click the Select Tag button on the Code view toolbar. Doing so highlights the current tags and all content within them.

2. There were two code-writing tools introduced in this hour: IntelliSense and the Toolbox task pane. IntelliSense helps you write proper code by constantly suggesting the closest matching code snippets when you write them and giving you Screentips about what elements this code needs to include to work properly. The Toolbox task pane provides you with drag-and-drop HTML elements for easy insertion into your document.

Exercise

With the help of IntelliSense, use only Code view (not Split view) to insert the eos1Detail_small.jpg file in the default.html page. Locate the reference to the movie *Blade Runner* in the same page, and use Code view to link the text to the IMDB.com entry for the movie. Remember that the active visual link text must be between the <a> and the </a> tags. If you are uncertain about the syntax, look at the code for the other links on the page.

Getting Boxed In, Part 1: Using Tables for Tabular Content

What You'll Learn in This Hour:

▶ How to create a table from scratch
▶ How to change the appearance of a table
▶ How to use the Tables toolbar to work with tables
▶ How to use table and cell properties to change the appearance of tables
▶ How to use AutoFormat to quickly change the appearance of your tables

Introduction

So far you have learned about simple text elements such as the headings, paragraphs, blockquotes, lists, and links. But these let you display your content in only a linear manner. What do you do if you want to introduce more structured content into your web page or control the position or relation between certain content? In many cases, the answer is tables. Just like in a word processing application, Hypertext Markup Language (HTML) tables can display content in a well-organized and structured way. And they work in much the same way as the other text elements, too.

Tables are composed of cells organized in rows (horizontal lines) and columns (vertical lines) just like a spreadsheet. You can style each element inside the table to achieve the desired look and feel. You can control the color, size, and appearance of the borders, cells, rows, and columns. Thus, when used correctly, tables can greatly enhance the experience for the visitor by making your content more visually appealing and meaningful.

One-Minute History of Tables in Web Pages

When HTML originated in the 1980s, it was as a simple standardized markup language for use by physicists to share research data and results on the Web in an easy and manageable way. Much of the data was contained in tables, so tables became an important addition to HTML. But as designers, developers, and the public started to see the potential in HTML and the World Wide Web, the content made available quickly moved beyond simple text documents with a few images and some tables to more advanced designs with background graphics, menus, and advanced interactivity. As the demands of the new users expanded, so did the capabilities of the markup language. As a result, what began as a simple way to communicate text content grew into a hugely complicated code set with heavy focus on the visual aspects of presentation rather than on the content.

One of the big elements of this development was the use of tables as a layout tool. If you have ever tried to make content look nice in a word processing application, you know you can use tables to make backgrounds, separate text, and insert other eye candy. This quickly became the standard for web design at the cost of legibility: Nonessential information, such as layout and design code, cluttered the simple HTML markup.

To solve this problem, a new language, called Cascading Style Sheets (CSS), developed. The idea behind CSS was to separate the HTML code from all the styling and layout code and return it to its intended use as a markup language. As CSS became more prevalent, the standard-setting body of the Internet weeded out or deprecated the styling elements that had made their way into HTML.

The idea behind standards-based code, which is what you make by using Expression Web 3, is to return HTML to its intended use as a markup language and separate it from the styling. In other words, tables are to display tabular data and nothing else. For example, rather than making a menu consisting of a series of table cells with graphic buttons inside, you make a menu using an unordered list styled using CSS. (You learn how to make such a menu in Hour 18, "Building a Functional Menu.")

There is an ongoing battle within the design and development community over the use of tables as design elements. I stand firmly on the side of standards-based code and CSS, and only briefly touch on how to use tables as a layout tool. That's not to say doing so is wrong—you are free to design using tables if you choose. But you will not learn how to do so here. With that said, it's time to make tables!

Creating a Table from Scratch

The most common use of tables is to display some form of statistical data in which each item has several variables. Good examples of tables are address lists with name, address, phone number, and email address as variables; archives of your books, music or movies; or purely statistical data such as temperature variances and financial data. In truth, a table can display any type of information that needs some form of structure.

In this lesson, you create a table based on the photo of all the cameras. In that table you list their variables. The following steps show you how to create a table in Design view:

1. Open the myCameras.html file in Design view. Scroll down to the bottom and make a new h2 subheading with the text **Camera Inventory**.

2. Make a new paragraph under the heading and click the Insert Table button on the Common toolbar. This opens a drop-down panel consisting of empty boxes (see Figure 9.1). By sliding your mouse over the boxes, you can highlight the number of rows and columns you want. In this example, you want 12 rows and 5 columns. Because the drop-down panel allows only for tables up to 6 rows and 7 columns, you need to click the More Options button to open the Insert Table dialog and set the rows and columns manually. We cover this dialog in more detail later. For now, just set Rows to 12 and Columns to 5, and click OK.

FIGURE 9.1
Use the Insert Table button on the Common toolbar to easily create tables with different row and column configurations.

You now have a 12-by-5 table in your page. By default HTML tables are invisible, meaning they have no color and no borders. They simply separate the content within them, as indicated by the dotted lines.

You can control how tables appear in your page by using the functions found under Table on the menu bar or by right-clicking the menu and accessing the options from there. But the easiest way to edit your tables is by using the Tables toolbar found under View, Toolbars. If you haven't already done so, close the Code View toolbar from Hour 8, "Cracking the Code: Working in Code View," and open the Tables toolbar (see Figure 9.2). It docks underneath the Common toolbar.

FIGURE 9.2
The Tables toolbar contains most of the tools you need to edit your table.

Before going any further, the table needs some content. The five columns represent the five values **Camera Name**, **Camera Type**, **Recording Medium**, **Lens Type**, and **Year of Purchase**. To insert these titles into the first row, select the upper-left corner cell by clicking inside it and start typing. As you write, the cells expand to the right. This is because the cell width and height in a default table is set to auto so that it conforms to whatever content you insert. To move to the next cell, press the Tab key on your keyboard, click the next cell with the mouse, or use the arrow keys. Fill in the next two headlines.

To save you the time of filling in the rest of the table, I have created a version of the lesson file completed to this point that you can install directly from the lesson files for this hour. Simply close the myCameras.html file, import the new myCameras.html file from the lesson files, overwrite the old one, and open the new file.

Changing the Appearance of a Table

When you create a table from scratch, it is set to default. That means all the text in the cells aligns to the left and centers in the vertical space and that all the text looks the same. With the tools built into Expression Web 3, you can easily change these settings to change the look of your tables.

Creating Table Headings

The first row of your table contains the headings that explain the content below. As such it should stand out. To change the heading row, you first need to select all the cells in the row. You can do this in two ways: Click and hold inside the first cell and drag your mouse over the two others. When the mouse pointer is out of the first cell, it changes to a plus sign indicating that you are selecting more than one cell. You can use this technique to select groups of cells from rows, columns, or both. Alternatively, you can right-click any of the cells in the row and click Select, Row (see Figure 9.3).

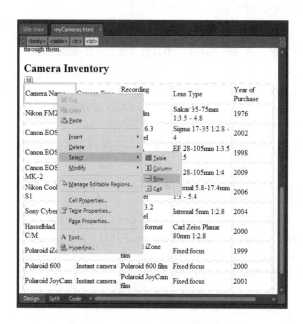

FIGURE 9.3
You can select a row by right-clicking a cell and choosing Select, Row.

With the row selected, you can change the style to Heading 3 to make the headings stand out. You can also change the background color of the cells by clicking the Fill Color button on the Tables toolbar and selecting a new color (see Figure 9.4).

FIGURE 9.4
The Fill Color button on the Tables Toolbar lets you pick the background color for the cells selected from a selection of pre-defined colors or with a color picker.

Changing the Vertical Alignment of Cell Content

By default all the content in a table centers vertically in the cells. This looks strange when some cells have one line of text and others have several. To change the vertical alignment of the cells, select the remaining cells using the click-and-hold technique and click the Align Top button on the Tables toolbar. You can choose to align text to the top , center , or bottom of the cells .

Adding Rows and Columns to the Table

When you create a table, you often find that you need to add more rows or columns. If you want to add one or two, the quickest way is to use the Tables toolbar. To add a new row below the last row of your table, select any of the bottom cells and click the Row Below ▦ button on the Tables toolbar. You can also add a row above the selected row by clicking the Row Above ▦ button. To add a column, you click either the Column to the Left ▦ or Column to the Right ▦ button.

If you want to add several rows or columns, select the cell in which you want to create new rows or columns next to and choose Table, Insert, Rows and Columns from the menu bar, or right-click and select Insert, Rows and Columns from the context menu. This opens the Insert Rows or Columns dialog in which you can set how many rows or columns you want, and whether to insert them above, below, to the left, or to the right of your selection (see Figure 9.5).

FIGURE 9.5
The Insert Rows or Columns dialog lets you insert multiple rows or columns in your table.

Merging and Splitting Cells

Sometimes it is necessary to merge cells to display certain types of content within the table. Let's say you want to insert a subheading in the table to go underneath the heading and across the whole table. If you simply insert a new row underneath the heading, you still have five columns to work with when you need only one. To insert a subheading in your table, first insert a new row underneath the heading using the Row Below button. Note that if you chose a fill color for the heading row, the styling (color) is automatically copied down to the new row. After inserting the new row, select all the cells in that row and click the Merge Cells ▦ button on the Tables toolbar. Doing so merges the five cells into one. Now you can insert a subheading that goes across the whole table.

Likewise, you can split a cell into several new rows or columns using the Split Cell
button. After you select a cell and click the button, Expression Web 3 asks how
many rows or columns you want to create within that cell.

You can also merge and split cells by highlighting them, right-clicking, and selecting Modify and Merge Cells or Split Cells from the pop-up menu.

Did you Know?

Deleting Cells, Rows, and Columns from the Table

Now that you know how to add rows and columns to a table, you need to know how
to remove them. To delete a cell, right-click the cell and select Delete, Cell from the
context menu or click the Delete Cells button ![] on the Tables toolbar. Both actions
delete the cell in question, and the remaining cells shift to the left to accommodate
the deletion. Deleting a cell leaves an empty space filled with the background color.

To delete a row or column, right-click inside a cell on the row or column you want to
delete, and select Delete, Row or Column or select all the cells in the row or column
you want to delete and click the Delete Cells button on the Tables toolbar. Expression
Web 3 deletes the row or column and the remaining rows or columns realign themselves to fill the void.

If you delete a cell, row, or column, you also delete all the content within it.

Watch Out!

To delete an entire table, you can right-click anywhere inside the table and select
Delete Table; Expression Web 3 deletes the table.

Changing Row and Column Sizes

When you first entered text into the cells in your table, you noticed that the width of
the columns changed accordingly. The same thing happened with the height of the
rows when you entered several lines of text in one of the cells. This is because both
row, height, and column width are set to AutoFit by default. In most cases, you want
to manually control the height and width of your rows and columns to achieve a certain look. You can do this in several ways:

The first method uses the Distribute Rows Evenly ![] and Distribute Columns Evenly
![] buttons on the Tables toolbar to make changes to the whole table. To use these
buttons, simply place your cursor anywhere inside the table and click the button. The
program gives the rows or columns an even distribution based on their content and

gives them a fixed height or width. To revert back to AutoFit, simply click the AutoFit to Contents button .

The second method is a more direct approach in which you manually set the width and height of each row or column by grabbing the margins of the table cells by clicking and holding them with the mouse and pulling them up, down, left, or right. When you let go, the width and height are permanent just like in the first method, but they are now set to your specifications rather than evenly distributed.

You can also use the second method to resize the entire table. By default the table width setting is 100% so that the table fills whatever area it is in (no area is yet defined, so the table fills the entire width of the screen), but you can change it by grabbing the sides of the table and resizing it.

By the Way

The table's content defines the minimum size of a table and its cells. In other words, a cell cannot be smaller than the size of what is inside it. For example, a cell with three lines of text can not be the height of a cell with two lines of text. Even if you set the height in pixels to be smaller, the cell remains tall enough to fit its contents. And because rows are the height of the largest cell, the content of the largest cell, not the pixel value, decides how tall each row will be. The same goes for the table as a whole. You cannot make the table smaller than the size of its contents no matter how hard you try. This is one reason why tables are not ideal as layout tools.

Using Table Properties to Change the Appearance of Your Table

If you want to make changes to the size or appearance of the entire table, you need to open Table Properties by right-clicking anywhere inside the table and selecting Table Properties or selecting Table, Table Properties on the menu bar. From here you can change all the main aspects of your table (see Figure 9.6).

The Size setting lets you define how many rows and columns the table should have. The Layout setting sets the `alignment` and `float` of the entire table in relation to the page, the width and height of the table in pixels or percentages, and the cell padding and cell spacing.

Watch Out!

The `alignment` and `float` attributes serve the same purpose: to place the table on the left or right side of the page. The `alignment` (or `align`) attribute is deprecated and is replaced by the CSS `float` attribute. Therefore, I recommended that you use `float` to align your table.

FIGURE 9.6
From the Table Properties dialog you can make changes to the table as a whole.

Cell padding is the space between the walls of the cell and the content within it (see Figure 9.7). Cell padding of 0 pixels means that the content of the cell is touching the

Table 1: Cell Padding 5 pixels	
Cell 1	Cell 2
Cell 3	Cell 4

Table 2: Cell Padding 0 pixels	
Cell 1	Cell 2
Cell 3	Cell 4

FIGURE 9.7
Other than the use of cell padding, these two tables are the same. The cells have a white background color, and the tables have a gray background color.

four walls, whereas cell padding of 10 pixels leaves an empty 10-pixel "buffer zone" between the walls and the content. Cell spacing, as shown in Figure 9.8, is the space

Table 1: Cell Spacing 5 pixels	
Cell 1	Cell 2
Cell 3	Cell 4

Table 2: Cell Spacing 0 pixels	
Cell 1	Cell 2
Cell 3	Cell 4

FIGURE 9.8
The cells in these two tables use different values for cell spacing. The cells have a white background color and the tables have a gray background color.

between the cells that separate them from each other. Cell spacing of 0 pixels means that the cells touch each other, whereas cell spacing of 10 pixels means there is a 10-pixel gap between each cell. Cell spacing is especially useful if you want to create a table with clearly defined borders between the cells because the cell spacing area is transparent and shows the background color of the table.

The Borders setting values define the thickness and color of the border of the table. The border is a box that surrounds the entire table (see Figure 9.9). By default, the

FIGURE 9.9
Borders in real life: Table 1 as it appears in Figure 9.10 but with the addition of a three-pixel border that wraps around the outside of the table.

Table 1: Cell Spacing 5 pixels, Border 3 pixels	
Cell 1	Cell 2
Cell 3	Cell 4

border is invisible (0 pixels). Depending on the settings, the border can be unique in that it has a 3D look to it: The top and left sides are slightly lighter in color than the bottom and right sides. The Collapse Table Border check box changes the relationship between the table border and the outer cell spacing.

The Background setting sets the background color or background image of the table. By default tables are transparent, and the background color or image shines through. If you define the color of a cell or group of cells, they will no longer be transparent. To make a table with white cells and blue lines around each cell, set the table background color to blue and the cell background color to white. The cell spacing remains transparent and lets the blue color shine through, and the white cells block the background color.

The Set value lets you define the current table layout as the default layout for future inserted tables.

Using Cell Properties to Change the Appearance of Your Cells

You can also change the appearance of a single cell, or group of cells, in a table by highlighting the cell and selecting Cell Properties from the context menu or choosing Table, Cell Properties on the menu bar. This opens the Cell Properties dialog, as shown in Figure 9.10.

From here you can change the layout, borders, and background of each cell or a group of cells. The Borders and Background settings work in much the same way as in the Table Properties dialog, but there is some new functionality in Layout.

FIGURE 9.10
The Cell Properties dialog lets you control the appearance of individual or groups of cells independently of the other cells in the table.

The Horizontal and Vertical Alignment settings define where the content appears within the cell. Horizontal Alignment works just like alignment in a word processor (left, right, center, justified), and Vertical Alignment defines whether the content within the cell should be positioned on the top, middle, or bottom of the cell.

The Rows and Columns Spanned setting changes the layout of the table by letting the cells span more than one row or column. If you let one cell span two rows, the displaced cells in the row below shift to the right to make room. As a result, the right-most cell protrudes from the right side of the table. If you let one cell span two columns, the remaining cells in the row shift to the right, and the leftmost cell protrudes from the right side of the table. These functions can easily make your table very confusing, so use them with care.

The Specify Width and Height setting gives you the ability to specify the width or height of the selected row or column in pixels or percentages. The effect is the same as when you used the mouse to drag the width and height of the rows and columns but is more precise because you set the values manually.

The Header Cell setting changes the content of the cells to center-aligned and bold as is normal in table headers. The name *Header Cell* is a bit misleading because you can apply the effect to any cell in a table, not just the header.

The No Wrap attribute tells the cell not to split lines even if they don't fit within the cell. If No Wrap is checked, lines of text that are too long to fit on one line do not continue on the next line but instead hide behind the next cell.

By the Way

When you insert content in a HTML page, the order of the elements applied to that content matters; the closer an element is to the actual content, the more important it is. In practical terms this means that the *cell properties* are more important and take priority over the *table properties* because they are closer to the cell content. You will meet this principle, referred to as the *cascade*, again when you are introduced to CSS in Hour 10, "Bringing Style to Substance with Cascading Style Sheets."

Using AutoFormat to Quickly Change the Look of Your Tables

Making tables more interesting to look at can be an arduous task. To help ease the workload, Expression Web 3 has a long list of prepackaged table layouts at your disposal through the AutoFormat option. To apply one of these layouts, all you have to do is select the table you want to change and click the Table AutoFormat button or the AutoFormat Combo drop-down menu on the Tables toolbar 📇. Clicking the AutoFormat button opens the Table AutoFormat dialog, as shown in Figure 9.11.

FIGURE 9.11
Use the Table AutoFormat dialog to make your tables look great with a few mouse clicks.

From here you can preview the various layouts available and make changes to them using the check boxes. All these table layouts are different, and the check boxes affect them in different ways depending on the layout, so it's a good idea to experiment to get that perfect look. When you are satisfied with what you see in the preview, click OK, and Expression Web 3 applies the AutoFormat. If it is not what you want, simply press Ctrl+Z or select Edit, Undo from the menu bar and try again.

If you already know what Table AutoFormat you want, you can select it from the Table AutoFormat Combo drop-down menu on the Tables toolbar. This bypasses the Table AutoFormat dialog and applies the AutoFormat directly.

Table AutoFormat creates a series of different CSS styles and applies them to the table. To change the final look of your table, you need to change these styles. In upcoming hours, you learn how to modify existing styles and create new ones from scratch.

Did you Know?

Using the Table Layout Tool to Make Nonstandard Tables

Sometimes you might want to make less structured tables or use a table to create a certain layout. This is where the Table Layout Tool comes in. The Table Layout tool gives you the option to resize individual cells without affecting the other cells on the column or row (as long as you don't try to make them bigger than the row or column or smaller than the content of the individual cell). You can use the Table Layout tool to edit an existing table, or you can draw new tables and cells using the Draw Layout Table and Draw Layout Cell functions, all found on the Tables toolbar.

To activate the Layout tool, place the cursor anywhere inside the table, and click the Show Layout Tool button. This changes the appearance of the table in Design view by giving the table a green outline and each of the cells a blue outline. It also tells you the actual pixel size of each of the rows and columns (see Figure 9.12). Hovering the mouse close to the corners or the left and right edges of each cell turns the pointer into an angled symbol to indicate that you can change the size or shape of that cell. If you click and drag the sides or corner of a cell to resize it, the Layout tool creates new cells to accommodate the new layout. You can achieve the same results by splitting cells and changing their widths and heights manually, but the Layout tool makes this process much easier. Be advised that editing an existing table with the Table Layout tool can be difficult because tables are quite inflexible. In many cases it's easier to create a new layout table from scratch than to edit an existing table.

FIGURE 9.12
The table as it appears with Show Layout tool activated.

Try It Yourself ▼

Creating a Nonstandard Table Using the Layout Tool

Although you can use the Layout tool to change your existing tables, it is far more useful to create new and nonstandard tables.

1. In Design view, click the Draw Layout Table button on the Tables toolbar. This changes the mouse pointer to a pencil. Draw a new table underneath the old one by clicking and dragging the mouse across the page. Make it slightly smaller than the first table.

2. Click the Draw Layout Cell button on the Tables toolbar and draw a series of cells within the new table. You need to click the Draw Layout Cell button again each time you want to draw a new cell. Make sure the cells are of different sizes and that they don't line up, as shown in Figure 9.13.

With this method, you can create tables that bear little resemblance to the normal structured ones. But if you click outside of the new table, you can see that what you created is nothing more than a complicated table with a series of split and merged cells.

There are some limitations to drawing new cells in a table using the Draw Layout Cell function: First, the cells can't overlap. Second, you can draw cells only in the

FIGURE 9.13
You can create a nonstandard table by drawing cells using the Draw Layout Cell button.

empty areas of the original table. Last, the cells snap to nearby rows, columns, and the outer edges of the table. After you create the new nonstandard table, you can use all the tools and functionalities described earlier to change its appearance.

Summary

Tables are an integral part of web design, both as a tool to display data and as a means to create layouts. In recent years, designers and developers have moved away from using tables as a design tool and started using them exclusively for their intended purpose: to display tabular data.

In this hour, you learned how to create tables and how to modify their appearance using the many tools available in Expression Web 3. You learned how to change the sizes of tables and cells, how to add and remove cells, and how to change the background color of both the table as a whole and individual or groups of cells. Finally, you learned how to create nonstandard tables using the Table Layout tools.

In upcoming hours you learn how to create page layouts without using tables, and how to use CSS to style your tables to create layouts like the ones you applied with AutoFormat.

Q&A

Q. *It seems cumbersome to first insert a table and then set all the properties. Is there a way to perform both actions at once?*

A. Yes, there is. If you place your cursor where you want the table to appear and select Table, Insert Table from the menu bar, an Insert Table dialog opens with the same options as the Table Properties dialog. Using this function lets you set the table properties before inserting the table.

Q. *You said that the `align` attribute is deprecated and that I should use the `float` attribute instead. But `float` has only an option for left and right and no center. What do I do if I want to center my table on the page?*

A. In the coming hours, you dive headfirst into the world of Cascading Style Sheets. The idea behind CSS is to move all styling elements out of the main body of the page and into its own section. This applies as much to tables as anything else. In fact, most of the styling you did in this hour was CSS, although you didn't know it. In the next hours, you learn how to control the styling of your document, and an important part of this is to learn how to position and align content on the page. If you are in a hurry and want to get your table centered right away, go to Hour 11, "Getting Boxed In, Part 2: Knee Deep in CSS," and read about centering an image using CSS.

Q. *Even though I grabbed the edge of my table and made it smaller, it still appears larger when I preview the page in my browser. What am I doing wrong?*

A. By default the table width setting is 100%. When you change the width by dragging it in Design view, you are not changing it to a pixel width but changing the percentage width. If you want your table to be a set or fixed width, you need to go to the Table Properties dialog and change the width from percent to pixels. Keep in mind that 100 or fewer pixels is a very small size, so you need to change the pixel size to something larger. After you change the size of pixels in the Table Properties dialog, you can resize the table in Design view, and the size stays the same when you preview the page in your browser.

Workshop

The Workshop has quiz questions and exercises to help you put to use what you just learned. If you get stuck, the answers to the quiz questions are in the next section. But try to answer them first. Otherwise you'll be cheating yourself.

Quiz

1. There are three different methods for changing the height and width of rows and columns. Name them.

2. What is the difference between cell padding and cell spacing?

Answers

1. To change the height and width of rows and columns, you can use the Distribute Rows and Columns buttons on the Tables toolbar; resize the rows and columns manually by clicking and dragging the dividing lines; or use cell properties to change the height or width of individual cells by entering the desired value in pixels or percentages.

2. Cell padding is the space between the cell walls and the content within the cell. Cell spacing is the space between the cells.

Exercise

Add more rows and columns to the table and insert new content. Change the background color of the table and set the color of the cells to white. Make the table 600 pixels wide, and change the column widths so that the first and last columns are smaller than the middle one. Use the Table AutoFormat function to restyle the table so that the rows have alternating colors.

HOUR 10

Bringing Style to Substance with Cascading Style Sheets

What You'll Learn in This Hour:

▶ What Cascading Style Sheets are

▶ How to create new styles from scratch

▶ How to modify existing styles using the style tools

▶ How to use styles to change the appearance of words, sections, or even the whole page

Introduction

Although it might be informational, a website with no style is plain boring and probably won't get many visitors. Now that you have a firm grasp on how to create content for your website, it's time to make it look good. Enter Cascading Style Sheets (CSS), a code language that lets you change the appearance of your pages and sites without messing up the Hypertext Markup Language (HTML) code. This is where Expression Web 3 really excels. With Expression Web 3's built-in CSS capabilities, creating standards-based and cross-browser-compatible styles is easier than ever before, even if you don't understand exactly what's going on.

Expression Web 3 gives you a multitude of ways to create and apply styles, many of which don't require you to write a single line of code. In fact, you can make highly advanced and elaborate styles and layouts using these tools without even glancing at the actual code!

CSS—The Driving Force Behind the New Web

Whenever I start talking about CSS and how powerful a tool it is, I see people's eyes starting to glaze over. And no wonder—almost every designer and developer I know (me included) did the same thing when we first started. Why? Because CSS is so cryptic and foreign. With HTML at least with you have some form of logical structure and meaning. When it comes to CSS, it is just endless lines of seemingly similar code repeated over and over with no rhyme or reason. And deciphering style sheets—especially ones you have not been involved in writing—can be a real headache. I'm really selling it aren't I? Well, there's a point to all this, and what I'm about to tell you is the honest truth: Before I started using Expression Web, CSS was a bit of a mystery to me! I could use it; I could hack it; but it never really made any sense.

I'm telling you this because I think it's important that you understand that CSS is not as complicated as it looks. It's all about perspective. And I will try my best to introduce you to this phenomenal coding language in a way that helps you understand it.

Why do I think it's so important that you get a firm handle on CSS? Because right now CSS is the most powerful tool on the web. I dare say it is what is driving the new web. And if you understand CSS, and I do mean really understand it, you are well equipped to build a career in web design.

CSS, and with it the separation of style and content, is one of the central building blocks of what is known as Web 2.0 or the social web. CSS lies in the foundation of pretty much every new web invention you can think of. From blogs like my own (www.DesignIsPhilosophy.com was built from the ground up in Expression Web 2 and is entirely CSS-based) to the new WhiteHouse.gov website to Facebook and CNN.com, style and content have been successfully separated. As a result visitors can ingest the content in any way they want—from RSS feed readers, on their cell phones, by email updates or by visiting the sites. And for every method available, the content conforms to fit the display medium providing a more user-friendly experience and better communication.

It might sound a little pompous but I'm telling you: CSS is the wave of the future. And it's here right now. So jump on and enjoy the ride!

Styles can apply to individual objects, sections of a page, or even an entire site. It all depends on what you, the designer, want to do. Styles can do simple things such as change the font or color of a heading, or advanced things such as position content and set behaviors and multiple styles at the same time. Right now CSS is probably the most powerful tool in a web designer's arsenal, and it is the basis of most modern websites and blogs. Designers and developers with strong CSS skills are in high demand, and because Microsoft built Expression Web 3 specifically to handle and generate proper standards-based code and CSS, you already have a leg up just by using the program.

CSS Sans Code

Because of Expression Web 3's setup, you don't need to know anything about CSS code to create styles in your document. In fact, creating and applying styles to documents can be as easy as a couple of mouse clicks.

Creating Styles with a Click of Your Mouse

In this example, you change the style or look of the subheadings in the default.html document. The idea of this exercise is to show you that changing one style can affect multiple sections within the page. If you haven't already done so, open the default.html page in Design view.

1. With the default.html page open, click the New Style button in the Apply Styles panel in the lower-right corner (see Figure 10.1). This opens the New Style dialog.

FIGURE 10.1
The Apply Styles panel from which you can create new styles or apply existing styles to your content with a single mouse click.

2. In the New Style dialog, shown in Figure 10.2, open the Selector drop-down menu and scroll down to h2. Select h2 or, alternatively, type **h2** in the Selector bar. Doing so means the style you are creating applies to all the text that has Heading 2 as its style.

3. With the Font category selected, change the font-family to Arial, Helvetica, sans-serif with the drop-down menu. Set the font-size to 1.2 and change the units to em. Set the font-weight to bold and text-transform to uppercase. Finally change the color to gray using the drop-down menu (see Figure 10.3).

FIGURE 10.2
The New Style
dialog showing
the Selector
drop-down menu
with h2 chosen.

FIGURE 10.3
The New Style
dialog provides
point-and-click
access to most
style variables
and an instant
preview of the
style and the
style code.

As you make these changes, you see the changes in real-time in the Preview
box and see the code being generated in the Description box. Click OK to apply
the changes.

By looking through the page in Design view, you can see that the subheadings you styled with Heading 2 have changed. They are now a different font, all uppercase and gray in color. Now that you've changed the subheadings, you probably want to change the main heading as well. To do so, simply click the New Style button again, and follow the same procedure you used to change the subheadings but change the Selector to h1 instead of h2. Because h1 is the primary heading, it should be slightly larger than h2, so a size of 1.4em is appropriate.

Font Sizes and How to Use Them

By the Way

When you changed the font size of the styles, you probably noticed that you had many different units from which to choose: px, pt, in, cm, mm, pc, em, ex, and %. You are probably familiar with px (pixel), in (inch), cm (centimeter), mm (millimeter), but pt (point), em (em space; historically the width of the letter m but now the height of the letter m), and ex (x height; the height of the lowercase letter x) are new to most people. To be quite honest it is confusing that there are so many options. When you work in a word processing application, you just set the font size, so why do you have to decide what kind of measurement to use when it comes to websites? The answer is both simple and complicated: The content of a website, although most often viewed on a computer monitor, can be displayed on a multitude of different media—from cell phones to text readers and even paper printouts. CSS gives you the ability to define different styles depending on what type of media the viewer is using. So, although it makes sense to size content displayed on a computer monitor using pixels, it might make more sense to size content intended for printouts in centimeters or inches.

There is also the issue of absolute and relative sizes. Inches, centimeters, and millimeters are absolute sizes, meaning that they should always be the same size no matter what medium is displaying them. Pixels, em spaces, and ex heights are relative sizes, meaning they will vary in size depending on the medium displaying them and the settings in the program used to display them. (Pixel measurement is a bit different because it is relative based on the pixel size and resolution of the display unit; that is, better resolution means smaller pixels.)

So, how do you decide which unit to use? There is no definite answer to this question, but you are relatively safe if you go by these two rules:

- ▶ Use px for content that must have a set size (images, tables, fancy headings, menus, and so on).
- ▶ Use em for content that the user can resize to facilitate readability.

Many users have browsers that enable them to increase the size of the font on the page; em facilitates this sizing. In contrast, older browsers do not allow resizing of text sized with px.

The downside to using em as the sizing unit is that it is not consistent throughout different fonts, so a size of 1.2em in one font might be small but in another font might be large. On average, 0.8em equals 10px to 12px.

For further reading on the em size and why you should use it, I recommend the article "The amazing em unit and other best practices" found at http://www.w3.org/WAI/GL/css2em.htm.

Creating Inline Styles

The previous example demonstrates how to make styles that affect all the content to which they apply, including new content you add later. If you want to make a style change to just one section of the page and do not use the style elsewhere, you create what is called an inline style.

1. In Design view, place the cursor anywhere inside the first paragraph to select it. Click the New Style button in the Apply Styles panel as before.

2. In the Selector drop-down menu, select (Inline Style). Below the Selector you see that Define In field is Current tag: <p>, meaning that this inline style applies to only the content inside this paragraph.

3. In the Font category, set the `font-size` to 1.1 em and `font-weight` to bold. In the Border category, uncheck the Same for All boxes and set the `Border-bottom-style` to solid, the `Bottom border-width` to 2px, and the `Border-bottom-color` to gray (see Figure 10.4). Click OK.

FIGURE 10.4
Under Border in the New Style dialog, you can set the style, width, and color of each of the four border sides.

As you can see in Design view, the font in the first paragraph is now Bold and there is a 2-pixel thick line separating it from the rest of the text. This style is inline because it affects only one tag or segment of content rather than the whole page.

Styling Small Selections

In the extreme, you can even set the style of just a small selection of words or even one word or one letter within a word by creating spans within the text and applying styles to them. You can do this in two ways.

Either

1. In Design view, select the word *kipple* on the second sentence of the second paragraph.

2. Using the tools available from the Common toolbar, change the font to Courier New, give the word an outside border using the Outside Borders button, and change the font color to green using the Font Color button.

Or

1. In Design view, select another word in the second paragraph.

2. Click New Style in the Apply Styles panel to open the New Style dialog. Check the Apply New Style to Document Selection box to ensure that the style applies only to the word you selected (see Figure 10.5).

FIGURE 10.5
The Apply new style to document selection check box ensures that the style only applies to the content you highlighted in Design view.

3. Under the Font category, change the font-family to Arial, Helvetica, sans-serif and change the font-color to Red.

4. Under the Border category, set `border-style` to solid, `border-width` to 1px, and `border-color` to Black.

These two methods produce two new style classes: `.style1` and `.newStyle1`, which change the appearance of the two words you highlighted. The first method is quick and easy if you are making rudimentary changes and produces a class called `.style1`.

The second method is more cumbersome but gives you far more flexibility in terms of the final product and produces a class called `.newStyle1`. One illustration of the difference between the two is that when using the first method, the color of the box is the same as the color of the font. In the second method, you can set the color of the box to whatever you want and even set each side of the box to a different color. Save the file and test it in your browser to see the result of your style applications so far (see Figure 10.6).

FIGURE 10.6
Default.html as it appears in Firefox with the inline style and the span styles applied.

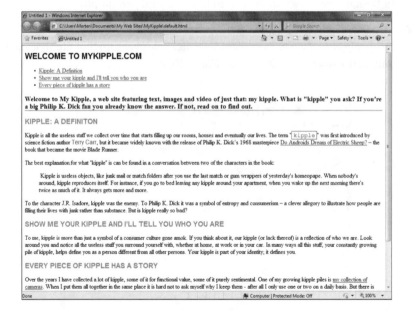

Setting the Font Family for the Entire Document

Now you know how to make changes to preset styles, sections, and individual selections of a document. But what if you want to define certain attributes for the entire page, such as setting all text to one particular font family unless otherwise specified? By default, unstyled HTML text displays in Times New Roman. You can override the default by applying styles to any tag within the HTML code of the page, even the <body> tag that wraps all the content. By creating a body style, you can affect all the content within the <body> tag (that is, all the visible content on the page).

Here is how to change all the text in the document to Arial, Helvetica using the <body> tag:

1. Click New Style in the Apply Styles panel to open the New Style dialog. You do not need to select or highlight any portion of the document to create the body style.

2. In the Selector drop-down menu, select body or type body in the Selector area.

How Exactly Does CSS Work?

This last example begs the question "Why does the word kipple retain its special font-family even when the font-family for the entire document changes?" The short answer is that this is where CSS gets its name: CSS works based on a cascade, meaning that the last style or rule in the sequence has the highest priority and is the one applied. This is, of course, a simplified version of events, and it doesn't always apply, but for now it is sufficient. For an in-depth look at CSS, pick up a copy of Eric A. Meyer's book, *CSS: The Definitive Guide*.

---

3. Under the Font category, change the font-family to Arial, Helvetica, sans-serif. Click OK.

   ▶ By setting the font-family of the <body> tag, you changed to the new font any text that has not had its font-family defined by a custom style. In this example, because you created a special style for the word kipple, it retains the Courier font. The same is true for the headings, although you can't see it because the body font and the heading fonts are the same.

Styling Links (a.k.a. Getting Rid of the Blue Underline)

You probably noticed that even though you changed the font-family for the entire document, the links retain that garish blue color and underline. The first things new web designers want to know are how to get rid of the underline and change the color of links. As you might have guessed, the answer is by using styles.

In Hour 7, "Getting Visual, Part 2: Advanced Image Editing, Thumbnails, and Hotspots," you learned that all links are defined using the <a> tag. So, it follows that if you create an a style, you change the links.

1. Click New Style in the Apply Styles panel to open the New Style dialog. You do not need to select or highlight any portion of the document to change the link style.

2. In the Selector drop-down menu, select a or type **a** in the Selector area.

3. Under the Font category, check the none option under text-decoration. (Even though it is not checked, the default setting for links is underline, so you have to explicitly tell the browser to not apply this option.) Click OK.

Now the underline is gone but the links are still blue. Most designers want their links to be a different color; to change the color, you need to modify the style you just created. You can do this using the Modify Style function.

1. To access the styles you have already created, click the Manage Styles tab in the Apply Styles panel (see Figure 10.7). The Manage Styles panel gives you a list of

FIGURE 10.7
The Manage Styles panel gives you information about available styles, active styles, and what style is applied to the current selection.

all the styles relating to the current document and uses visual aids to tell you what styles are active and what styles are applied to the current selection. If you place the cursor on a link, you see that the a style is highlighted, telling you that this is the last style in the cascade applied to your selection.

2. To edit the existing style, right-click the a style and select Modify Style from the context menu. This opens the Modify Style dialog, which is the same as the New Style dialog.

3. Under the Font category, change the font-color to a calmer blue using the More Colors option (see Figure 10.8). Click OK.

Now all the links are a nicer shade of blue. But so are the subheadings!

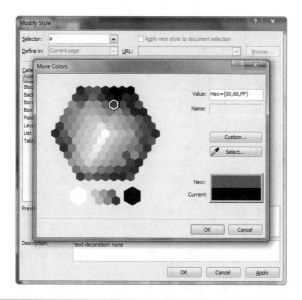

FIGURE 10.8
The More Colors option is always available whenever you set a color. From here you can pick a color from the expanded palette or use the eyedropper tool to pick a color from anywhere on your screen (even outside Expression Web 3).

Try It Yourself ▼

Using the Cascade to Override Styles

In Hour 5, "Getting Connected with (Hyper)Links: The Cornerstone of the World Wide Web," you set the subheadings as bookmarks using the <a> tag, and now the color of the a style is overriding the color of the h2 style. This is where the cascade shows its true strength: Using CSS you can define multiple attributes to the same content, and the browser picks the one that is most relevant based on a set of rules. In this case, you want to create a style that applies only to text that is both a subheading and a link.

1. Click the New Style button in the Manage Styles panel to open the New Style dialog.

2. In the Selector bar, type **h2 a**. This literally means Heading 2 links. In the Font category, change the font-color to gray and click OK.

Now the subheadings return to their gray color because the browser picks the most specific style in the cascade. (h2 a is more specific than either h2 or a.)

Caveat: Not Everyone Has Your Fonts!

You might have noticed when you select a font style that off the top Expression Web 3 offers you font families rather than particular fonts, and the remaining single fonts appear underneath. This is because Expression Web 3 knows that not

Watch Out!

every computer has every font, so it gives the browser a variety of similar-looking fonts to choose from. There are three main font families based on the most common fonts that almost all computers have installed by default:

▶ Arial, Helvetica, sans-serif

▶ Times New Roman, Times, serif

▶ Courier New, Courier, monospace

All these families work the same way. The browser looks for the first font to see whether the computer has it installed. If not, the browser goes to the second font. If the computer has neither of the two fonts installed, the browser looks for the first font that falls under the category (sans-serif, serif, or monospace).

You can set your text to any font you want, but if you go outside the three main font families, you increase the chance that the computers used to view your page don't have the necessary fonts, and the page will not display properly. If the browser cannot find the defined font, it picks one of the default fonts—in certain cases that can lead to strange results.

To be certain your page appears the same across all computers and browsers, I strongly advise you to stick to the three main font families for HTML text.

CSS Tools in Expression Web 3

Expression Web 3 has a variety of built-in tools to help you create CSS correctly and efficiently. You already used some of them in earlier examples, and now it's time to take a closer look and familiarize yourself with each of them individually.

The Quick Tag Tools

Working with HTML documents, it can be hard to remember, or even figure out, exactly what is going on because most of the content is in tags within tags within tags. Trying to navigate through this mishmash of code can be a daunting task for even an experienced developer. To fully understand why a certain element or segment of text looks and behaves the way it does, you need to know exactly what tags are applied and in what order. Doing this manually is a lot of work. But with the Quick Tag tools, it is so easy it borders on the absurd. To get a complete ordered list of all the tags applied to an element in Design, Split, or Code view, simply place the cursor on that element and look at the top of the view pane. There the Quick Tag tools list the entire sequence of tags and give you the option to edit each of them individually (see Figure 10.9).

The Quick Tag tools also interact with other tools, such as the Tag and CSS Properties panels and the Apply and Manage Styles panels, to give you a complete picture of what Expression Web 3 is doing to the content.

FIGURE 10.9
The Quick Tag tools list all the tags applied to the selected content in order.

The Quick Tag Selector is the bar itself. After you click something in the page, the Quick Tag Selector displays all the applied tags. By hovering over each of the tags displayed on the bar, you cause a box in Design view to highlight the affected area of that tag. From here you can click any tag in the Selector to display its tag or CSS properties or to show what style is applied. You can open the Quick Tag Tools dropdown menu by clicking the arrow button next to the tag and make changes to the tag without navigating through all the code (see Figure 10.10).

FIGURE 10.10
You trigger the Quick Tag tools drop-down menu by clicking the down arrow next to each tag.

From here you can open the Quick Tag Editor that lets you edit the tag by clicking Edit Tag, insert new HTML, and even wrap the existing tag in a new tag. You can also remove the tag altogether, change the positioning of the content, or select just the content or the whole tag in Code view.

> Not only are the Quick Tag tools excellent for helping you keep track of your own work, but they also make short process out of dissecting complicated websites designed by others. I regularly use the Quick Tag tools in combination with the Code View toolbar to quickly track down and fix errors in large web pages because they give me instant access to only the elements I care about.

Did you Know?

The Quick Tag tools are an important part of the CSS creation and editing process because all tags have attached styles, and you need to know what tags are at the end of the cascade to see what styles apply to a tag and what if anything needs to be changed.

If you can't find the CSS Properties panel, go to Panels on the main menu and select CSS Properties. It appears in the bottom-left corner.

The CSS Properties Panel

The CSS Properties panel gives you a more detailed breakdown of what styles are applied to the selected elements and exactly what they do.

The top half of the panel provides a list of all the applied rules or styles (the cascade), and the bottom part lists the attributes applied to the selected rule. You can select individual rules by clicking them in the top half of the panel or by clicking the tags in the Quick Tag Selector. By default the bottom half of the CSS Properties panel displays a list of all the available attributes for the selected style. If you want to see only those attributes that have a value, click the Summary button.

As you have learned, CSS allows the same attribute to have many different values, and the browser picks the one furthest down the cascade. The CSS Properties panel shows you which attribute values are applied and which are ignored by using a red line to strike out the ones not in use. To see this in action, place the cursor on one of the subheadings (see Figure 10.11). This way you can easily see how the cascade is flowing and track errors in value attribution.

FIGURE 10.11
The red lines show that the Expression Web 3 is ignoring the original and colors and applying the third defined color.

The CSS Properties panel lets you make direct changes to the selected CSS style by entering new values for all the attributes. This is a quick way to make the same kind of changes you made in the Modify Style dialog, but it doesn't give you the same kind of trial-and-error environment because all the changes are immediate. The CSS Properties panel works in direct conjunction with the Apply and Manage Styles panels.

The Apply Styles Panel

The Apply Styles panel, as shown in Figure 10.12, provides a visual representation of the applied and available styles by previewing them in a list. The primary function of this panel is to provide an easy way to apply styles to the selected content. To do so, simply select the content in Design view and click the desired style. You can also use the Apply Styles panel to remove styles from the content and select all the content to which the style is applied on the page.

FIGURE 10.12
The Apply Styles panel displays all the applied and available styles and provides an easy way to apply new styles to the selected content.

The Manage Styles Panel

The Manage Styles panel, as shown in Figure 10.13, works in much the same way as the Apply Styles panel, with the one major difference that you can't simply click a style to apply it to a page. (You need to right-click it and select Apply Style from the context menu.) The Manage Styles panel provides a complete list of all the styles available in the page and a preview of the selected style. As the name suggests, the Manage Styles panel is an excellent tool for managing styles both when you want to

FIGURE 10.13
The Manage Styles panel displays a complete list of all styles related to the open page and is an excellent tool for managing these styles.

edit a particular style and also when you start dealing with styles stored in different locations such as multiple external style sheets. The combination of these functionalities makes Expression Web 3 an incredibly powerful tool when it comes to creating, editing, and troubleshooting CSS code. By familiarizing yourself with them, you can work not only quicker and more effectively but also learn how to use CSS in a fun and hands-on way.

By the *Way*

Color Coding in Apply and Manage Styles Panels

A colored dot that sometimes has a gray ring around it prefixes the styles in both the Apply and Manage Styles panels. The dot's color indicates the category to which each style belongs:

▶ Blue means the style affects regular tags such as p, h1, a, or blockquote.

▶ Yellow means the style is an inline style.

▶ Red means the style is a CSS ID (prefixed by #).

▶ Green means the style is a CSS class (prefixed by a period [.]).

▶ A gray circle surrounds the colored dot if the style is in use in the current page.

You learn what CSS IDs and classes are in Hour 11, "Getting Boxed In, Part 2: Knee Deep in CSS."

Using Various CSS Tools to Apply and Change Styles

Now that you know all the different CSS tools available, it's time to put them to use. In this example, you use the various panels to apply styles to content and then change the styles without using the Modify Style dialog.

1. In Design view, find and highlight the word *homeopape* in the blockquote.

2. With the Apply Styles tab selected in the panel, click the .newStyle1 style to apply it to the selected text.

3. Click the <span.newStyle1> tag in the Quick Tag Selector to select the correct tag. If Summary is active in the CSS Properties panel, click the button to deactivate it so that you get a list of all available attributes.

4. Pin the Folder List panel to the side to get full access to the CSS Properties panel. Use the CSS Properties panel to change the font-color to Maroon by

clicking the drop-down menu under Font and Color. Scroll down to `font-variant` and set it to small-caps.

5. To change the border, scroll down until you find the `border` attribute and click the + sign to see all the available attributes. Delete the current attributes by clicking the `border` attribute value and pressing the Delete key or the Back-space key on your keyboard. Scroll down to `border-bottom` (you might have to change the layout of your workspace to see the whole name) and set the `Border-bottom-color` to Maroon, the `Border-bottom-style` to dotted, and the `Border-bottom-width` to 1px.

The changes you just made to the `.newStyle1` style are instant and affect both words that Expression Web 3 applied the style to. This technique is effective for making smaller adjustments or changes to your styles, but be careful: Unlike the Modify Style dialog, you cannot reset multiple changes with a simple click. If you make many changes to your style, it can be hard to retrace your steps even with the Undo button.

Summary

Using Cascading Style Sheets gives you precise and easy control over how your content appears to the visitor. And with Expression Web 3's many integrated CSS tools, even a novice can create advanced and standards-based styles without writing a single line of code. In this hour, you learned how to use these tools to edit existing styles and create new ones and how to apply styles to the whole page, sections of a page, and individual words. You saw how easy it is to modify existing styles using the Modify Style dialog and the CSS Properties panel, and how the Quick Tag tools can help you find the relevant tags and styles quickly and decipher complicated code to see how and why elements in the page look the way they do.

Cascading Style Sheets apply to the page in a cascade. In this hour, you got a basic understanding of what this means and how to use this knowledge to style your content and solve problems. But so far you have scratched only the surface of what CSS is capable of. In the next hours, you learn how to use CSS as a layout tool and unlock its true potential and how to move beyond simple point-and-click page styling to full-fledged CSS authoring and the creation of separate style sheets.

Q&A

Q. *I changed my text size from 12 px to 12 em but now the text is incredibly large! What is the correct equivalent to 12 px in ems?*

A. One em is the width of the letter m that is defined as standard in the browser the user uses. So 12 em is the width of 12 m's next to one another, thus the huge size. Because em is a relative size measurement, there is no correct answer to this question. Depending on what font you use, a 12 px equivalent is usually between 0.8 and 1 em. To get the perfect size you need to do a bit of trial and error. Just remember that when dealing with ems, you should always use decimals rather than full integers.

Q. *I followed the tutorial and applied a class to some text but nothing happened!*

A. If you created a class and nothing happened, one of two things went wrong: Either you didn't actually create the style (by accidentally pressing Cancel perhaps?) or the style wasn't applied to the content. First check if the style is listed in the Manage Styles panel. If it is, click on the element you wanted to style, and check the Quick Tag Selector to see if the correct selector or class is applied. If you created a new class and the selector says only <p> or <h1>, you need to apply the class manually by selecting the selector and clicking on the class in the Apply Styles panel.

Q. *When I select the different colors from the drop-down color options, they are replaced by a weird code starting with # and followed by six letters and numbers. What is this?*

A. When working with colors in the digital realm, every shade has a distinct hexadecimal code preceded by #. That way the color is interpreted the same way by all applications whether it is an image editor, web browser, or word processor. In CSS, you set colors by using their hexadecimal codes.

Workshop

The Workshop has quiz questions and exercises to help you put to use what you have just learned. If you get stuck, the answers to the quiz questions are in the next section. But try to answer them first. Otherwise you'll be cheating yourself.

Quiz

1. What part of the document does a CSS style apply to?

2. What happens if several styles with different values for the same attributes are applied to the content?

Answers

1. CSS styles are applied to the content within their respective tags; that is to say, a p style will be applied to any content within the <p> tags, an a style will be applied to any content within a <a> tag, and so on. You can also create spans around content and apply styles to them as well.

2. If several different attribute values are applied to the same content from different styles, the browser goes through the cascade and selects the attribute that is furthest down the line or is most specific. In most cases, this means the style that is attached to the closest tag.

Exercise

Two other selectors in the default.html page were not styled in the earlier examples: the paragraph and the blockquote. Use the techniques you learned in this hour to create a p style and a blockquote style, and apply some different attributes to them. Remember that because the font-family has already been set in the body style, you don't need to change it. Try experimenting with background colors, borders, and text decorations and explore the many different options available under the Font category.

HOUR 11

Getting Boxed In, Part 2: Knee Deep in CSS

What You'll Learn in This Hour:

▶ How to create and apply classes to individual tags
▶ How to use divs to define sections of content
▶ How to apply classes and IDs to divs to style sections of content
▶ How to use pseudoclasses to give visual cues to the visitor
▶ How the box model works and how to use it to create layouts

Introduction

In the last hour, you learned how to use Cascading Style Sheets (CSS) to style text content. But that's just one small part of what CSS can do. You realize the true strength of the CSS styling language only when you use it not only to style individual elements but also to define different sections within a page that have different styles, and to create and manage layouts and position content.

CSS lets you build a hierarchy of the styles applied to different portions of your page so that a paragraph in one part of the page can have a completely different style from a paragraph in another part of the page. Likewise, CSS can organize content within the page so that certain content appears to the left or right of other content even though it is not in a table.

To understand how CSS operates as a layout tool, you first need to understand the box model. In this hour, you explore the box model to see how it interacts with your content. Through this knowledge you get a firm understanding of how CSS puts everything in boxes and how you can use these boxes to create advanced and visually stunning layouts without destroying the markup.

CSS Classes—Because Not All Content Should Be Treated Equally

In Hour 10, "Bringing Style to Substance with Cascading Style Sheets," you learned how to apply styles to a page using the standard tag selectors such as p, h1, h2, and a. But these styles applied to the entire page, so you had to make an inline style to change the style of just one section of the page. This is an acceptable solution if the change happens only once, but if you plan to use this special style again somewhere else in the page, this approach quickly becomes cumbersome. You need a way to group the content into separate classes so that each section can get its own style even though the same selectors define them all—enter CSS classes.

Create a Class and Apply It to the Content

A CSS class defines a subsection of the content that has its own set of styles. An example illustrates this best: Right now there is no clear separation between the beginning part of the default.html page and the rest of the content. To remedy this, you can make a class to style this portion of the page:

1. With the default.html page open in Design view, place the cursor inside the first paragraph to select it. In the Apply Styles task pane, right-click the inline style you created in Hour 10, and select Remove Inline Style from the context menu. This returns the paragraph to its original appearance.

2. Click the New Style button and change the Selector name to `.abstract`. The punctuation mark in front of the name defines this style as a class.

3. In the Font category, set `font-family` to `Times New Roman, Times, serif;` `font-size` to `1.2em`; `font-weight` to `bold`; and `font-style` to `italic`. In the Block category, set `text-align` to `justify`.

4. In the Border category, uncheck all the Same for All Boxes and change the `bottom` values to `solid, 2px,` and `#000000` (black). Click OK to create the new style class.

5. To apply the new class to an existing element within the page, place the selector on the element; in this case the first paragraph, and click the `.abstract` class in the Apply Styles task pane.

When you click the first paragraph after applying the new class, you can see that the p tag in the Quick Tag Selector has changed to include the new class. It now reads `<p.abstract>`, as shown in Figure 11.1.

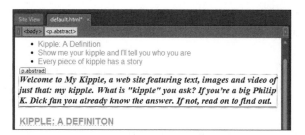

Using the method described here to apply a new class results in the class being applied to the last tag in the chain of the selected items. This means that when you have grouped objects such as lists, you need to pick which tags you want to apply the class to. If you click one of the list objects on the top of the page and apply the class, it affects only the selected list item. If you highlight the entire list or select the <ul> tag from the Quick Tag Selector, Expression Web 3 applies the class to the list as a whole.

Using CSS Classes to Center an Image

This way of using classes is often preferred when positioning content like images in pages. You might recall from Hours 6, "Getting Visual, Part 1: Adding Images and Graphics," and 7, "Getting Visual, Part 2: Advanced Image Editing, Thumbnails, and Hotspots," that the align attribute is deprecated. And although you can position elements left and right using the float attribute, there is no option to position items in the center of the page. To properly center nontext content with standards-based code, you need to use CSS. But although you want the *option* to center your images and other content, you don't want to center every image. Making a class to center content is the perfect solution to this problem.

Before you start, replace the current myCameras.html file with the fresh one from the lesson files for this hour. You should do this because when you inserted and changed the properties for the images in Hours 6 and 7, you created a series of styles. This new file has no styles and gives you a fresh start.

1. With the myCameras.html page open in Design view, click the New Style button and change the Selector name to **.alignCenter**.

2. In the Box category, uncheck the Margin: Same for All box and set right and left to auto. (Leave top and bottom empty.)

3. In the Layout category, set display to block. This tells the browser that whatever content this class is applied to is to appear as a separate block or box independent of the rest of the content (that is, on its own line). Click OK to create the new class.

4. Click the image of the cameras thumbnail and click the new `.alignCenter` class to apply it.

Save the page and test it in your browser, and you see that with the new `.alignCenter` class applied, the image centers itself on its own line in the page, as shown in Figure 11.2.

FIGURE 11.2
The photo of the cameras is centered on the page using the `.alignCenter` class.

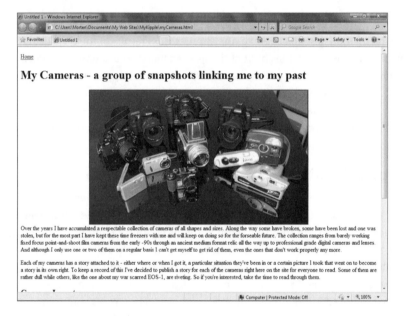

The clever thing about using the method to set the left and right margins to auto is that you leave it to the browser to decide where the center of the page is by telling it that the two side margins are to be identical.

You can create similar classes for `.alignLeft` and `.alignRight` by setting the `display` attribute under the Layout category to `inline` (to keep the image on the same line as the text) and setting the `float` attribute to `left` for `.alignLeft` and `right` for `.alignRight`. That way you don't have to use the Picture Properties dialog to position your images, but you can apply classes to them individually instead.

Using Boxes to Separate Content

Using CSS classes in the ways described in the previous section is an excellent way to apply changes to multiple individual objects throughout a page. But sometimes you want a whole section of a page to have a different look from the rest. You can use classes for this purpose, too, but rather than applying them to selectors such as p, h1, a, and img, you now apply them to a new tag called `<div>`.

By the Way

I am not entirely sure what <div> actually means. In my research, I have found many suggestions, some more vulgar than others, and the one that sounds the most reasonable to me is that div is short for divider. But it has recently been suggested to me that it stands for division, so I guess the search for the actual meaning continues.

To understand what the <div> tag does, you need to delve a little deeper into the inner workings of tags and CSS. When Expression Web 3 applies a tag to content, it draws an invisible box around the content. You can see a visual representation of this phenomenon when you hover your mouse over the tags on the Quick Tag Selector bar, and the corresponding boxes are outlined in Design view. When you create a style using CSS, you are, in reality, telling the browser to apply a set of variables to this box and what's inside it. This is why when you open the New or Modify Style dialog, you always have the option to create top, bottom, left, and right borders around the content even if it is a single word in a sentence. The <div> and <span> tags create such boxes that wrap around the content and their tags so that attributes such as size, background color, and positioning can be applied to the content as a whole. In short, creating a div and putting content into it is like drawing a box around content on a page.

Creating a Div and Placing It Around Content

To understand when and how you would use divs to wrap content, you apply the .abstract class to all the content before the first subheading in default.html. As you saw in the previous example, adding the .abstract class to individual sections of the page causes Expression Web 3 to treat each section as a separate entity (refer to Figure 11.1). Now you want to create a box that contains both the first paragraph and the list above it and treat them as a single entity. You use the Toolbox panel to assist you in the next task. The Toolbox should be visible on the top-right side of the workspace. If it is not, you can activate it by clicking Panels from the main menu and selecting Toolbox.

1. With the default.html page open in Design view, drag and drop a <div> instance (found under HTML, Tags in the Toolbox task pane) into the page and place it at the end of the first heading. This should create a new empty horizontal box directly under the heading (see Figure 11.3).

2. To move the content into the div, simply highlight the first paragraph and drag and drop it into the div. For layout purposes, which will make sense later, you

FIGURE 11.3
An empty div can
be dragged from
the Toolbox panel
directly into
Design view and
placed anywhere
within the text.

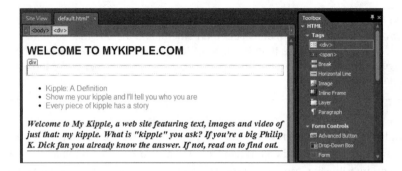

want the list to appear underneath the first paragraph, so select it and drag
and drop it inside the div underneath the text.

Now the first paragraph and the list are both contained within the new div (see
Figure 11.4), and when you place your cursor on either, the Quick Tag Selector shows
that the div comes before any of the other tags in the cascade.

FIGURE 11.4
The first para-
graph and the
list are now both
contained within
the div selector.

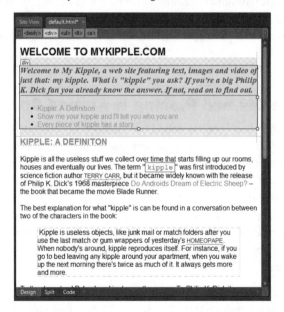

In addition to style classes, you also have style IDs. The ID differs little from the
class—so little, in fact, that many wonder why it exists at all.

Now that we have separated some of the content from the rest of the page, it is time
to make that content appear separated visually and in the code. To do this you use a
different kind of style element called an ID.

Introducing ID—Class's Almost Identical Twin

The ID works in the same way as the class: You can apply attributes to it, apply it to any tag, and create custom styles that appear only within divs that belong to this ID. The only difference between the class and the ID is that although you can use the class many times throughout a page, you can use the ID only once. (Or rather, if you want your page to remain compliant with web standards, you can use an ID only once per page—most browsers allow the repeated usage of the same ID in a page even though it's technically a breach of the standards.)

So, what is the point of using IDs or having them at all? From a designer and developer standpoint, the ID is a great tool for separating content and making the code more readable. As an example, a common practice when designing blogs is to use IDs to define the main sections of the page and classes to define components that repeat several times within these sections. For example the front page of my blog (http://www.designisphilosophy.com) has an ID called content that holds all the articles, and each article is kept in a class called post. For someone looking at the code, it is far easier to understand what is going on in large pages if the developer lays out the code this way.

Creating a Sidebar Using an ID

To make the page layout more interesting, let's make the new div you just created into a sidebar that appears on the left side of the screen. To do this, you assign it an ID called #sidebar and style that ID to make it float to the left.

1. Click the New Style button in the Apply Styles panel to open the New Style dialog. Set the Selector to #sidebar. (The # symbol prefix tells the browser that this is an ID.)

2. Under Background set the background-color to #CCCCCC (a light gray) using the More Colors swatch or by inserting the hex value manually.

3. Under Border leave the Same for all boxes checked and set the borders to solid, 1px and #808080 (a darker gray).

4. Under Position set the width to 250px. By default the width of a div box is 100%. This sets it manually to a fixed size.

5. Under Layout set float to left. This pushes the box to the far left, letting the remaining text float around it as you saw with the images earlier. Click OK to create the new ID.

To apply the new ID, select the div by clicking the `<div>` box in the Quick Tag Selector, and click the new #sidebar ID in the Apply Styles panel. When the #sidebar ID is applied to the div, the browser creates a gray box around the content and shifts it to the right, as shown in Figure 11.5.

FIGURE 11.5
With the #sidebar ID applied, the div floats to the left and is styled with a gray background and a border.

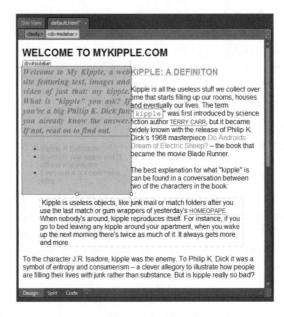

Using an ID to Center the Page

A common question from new web designers is how to center the contents of a page using CSS. There is a lot of confusion about how to do this, and most of it results from the fact that people think of web design tools as word processing applications on steroids. But, as you have seen, this couldn't be further from the truth. In the past, a common way to center the content on a page was to put it in a one-cell table and center the table using `text-align`. This is not an ideal solution because by putting the content inside a table, you are inadvertently restricting the options for future layout changes and fancy styling. In addition you learned in Hour 9, "Getting Boxed In, Part 1: Using Tables for Tabular Content," that tables should be used only for tabular content, and it would be quite a stretch to argue that all the content of an entire page is tabular data that should be displayed in one cell!

Even so, the table idea is a good one; it's just using the wrong type of box. If you paid close attention to the earlier sections of this hour, you might already have figured out how to do this using only CSS.

1. Go to Code view and drag and drop a `<div>` instance found under Tags in the Toolbox task pane into the page directly before the line that reads `<h1>Welcome`

to MyKipple.com</h1>. Go back to Design view and a new box appears at the top of the page.

2. Create a new style and give it the Selector name **#wrapper**.

3. In the Box category, uncheck the Margin: Same for All box and set left and right to auto. Leave top and bottom blank (see Figure 11.6).

FIGURE 11.6
Setting the left and right margins of the #wrapper ID to auto.

4. In the Position category, set width to 800px. This will be the total width of the content on the page. Click OK to create the new ID.

5. In Design view, highlight all the content underneath the new div including the sidebar, and then drag and drop it into the div you just created at the top of the page.

6. Select the div tag belonging to the new div from the Quick Tag Selector bar and click the new #wrapper ID in the Apply Styles task pane to apply the ID. The tag changes to <div#wrapper>. Save and press F12 to preview the page in your browser. The content of the page should now be restricted to the center of the page and remain so even if you resize your browser window (see Figure 11.7).

When you apply this ID to your div, Expression Web 3 reduces the width of the div to 800px and tells the browser to place the div within two equally wide margins: one on the left and one on the right. Naturally, this results in the div box appearing in the middle of the screen. To position the content to the left or right of the screen, simply remove the two margin attributes and set float to left or right instead.

FIGURE 11.7
The #wrapper
ID applied to the
outermost div
reduces the
width of the box
to 800 pixels
and centers the
content in the
browser window.

This is the pure CSS method for centering content in the browser. In extremely rare cases it doesn't work properly because some older browsers don't follow or understand proper CSS code and become confused by the margins set to `auto`. Nevertheless, this is the correct way to perform the task.

Creating Custom Styles Within IDs and Classes

When you have content that is contained within a div that has an ID or class, you can create custom styles that affect only the tags within that class. You do so by making the tags a subelement of the class. To do so, create a new style but give the tag a prefix in the form of the class name. For example you can make a custom version of the `.abstract` class that applies only to content within the #sidebar div. To do so, create a new style and give it the selector name **#sidebar .abstract**. In the Font category, set `font-size` to `1em` and `font-weight` to `normal`. When you click OK to create the new style, you see that attributes from both of the `.abstract` classes are applied to the content but that the attributes from the `#sidebar .abstract` class has preference. That is because the more specific style is further down the cascade and closer to the content.

You can apply this technique to any standard tag of class whether it is a heading, paragraph, link, blockquote, or something else. If you ever wondered how you can create several different paragraph styles within one document, now you have the answer!

Classes Within Classes: Micromanaging the Content

In the earlier example, you saw that you can create special styles for content within IDs and classes. There is no limit to how far you can take this technique by applying multiple IDs, classes, and tags within each other. See the layout in Figure 11.8 as an example.

FIGURE 11.8
A layout using multiple IDs and classes to separate the content. IDs are outlined with a solid line, and classes are outlined with a dashed line.

In this figure, multiple IDs and classes divide different parts of the content. By understanding how to properly name your style selectors, you can micromanage the content within these IDs and classes for a highly customized look. You do so by creating selector names that have the relevant IDs, classes, and tags listed with spaces between them. Here are some examples of different selector names:

- ▶ p styles all paragraphs on the page, both inside and outside the IDs and classes.

- ▶ #wrapper p styles all paragraphs within the wrapper ID.

- ▶ #wrapper #top p and #top p style paragraphs within the top ID only.

- ▶ .header p styles all paragraphs within the header class regardless of ID.

- ▶ #wrapper #top .header p and #top .header p style paragraphs within the header class inside the top ID only.

> You can experiment with different selector names by using the boxExample.html
> file found in the lesson files for this hour.

Using Classes to Control IDs

To see just how flexible the tag, class, and ID structure is, consider this trick used by professional designers for quick-and-easy prototyping:

Right now the sidebar floats to the right because the ID contains a float variable. But you can also use a class and apply it to the ID to do this! Earlier in the hour you were asked to create two alignment classes called `.alignLeft` and `.alignRight`. If you haven't already done so, create the two classes and give them the following attributes:

- `.alignLeft`: Set margin-right to 10px and float to left.

- `.alignRight`: Set margin-left to 10px and float to right.

Next open the Modify Style dialog for the #sidebar ID by right-clicking the style in the Apply Styles panel and selecting Modify style from the pop-up menu. In the dialog go to the Layout category and remove the `float:left` attribute. Click OK to save the change, and the text should no longer wrap around the sidebar.

Now comes the fun part: Place your cursor anywhere inside the sidebar box and select the `<div#sidebar>` box in the Quick Tag Selector to select the whole div. Then go to the Apply Styles panel and click the `.alignLeft` style to apply it. With the application the sidebar floats to the left with a nice 10px margin as a buffer against the other content. Without doing any changes, click the `.alignRight` style instead and, as if by magic, the sidebar jumps to the right with the text floating to the left. This is because Expression Web 3 won't let you apply two styles to the same div, so it overwrites the last one you applied. This way you can quickly see which layout you like better. And this trick doesn't just apply to the sidebar—you can do the exact same thing with images and other elements on the page.

Pseudoclasses

In addition to tags, classes, and IDs, HTML supports something called *pseudoclasses*. These specialized versions of selectors come into play when the user interacts with the page; that is, when the user hovers over or clicks content or a link. There are five such pseudoclasses, all of which are normally used in conjunction with the <a> tag:

- `:active` refers to an element that is currently active. For example, a link during the time the user is holding the mouse button down and clicking it.

▶ :focus refers to an element that currently has the input focus, meaning that it can receive keyboard or mouse input. To understand focus, think of an input table with the current cell highlighted—that cell has the focus. When you press the Tab button, the focus changes to the next cell.

▶ :hover refers to an element being hovered over by the mouse pointer.

▶ :link refers specifically to an element that is an unvisited hyperlink. Unlike the preceding pseudoclasses, :link applies to the a tag only.

▶ :visited refers to a link that has already been visited. Like the :link pseudo-class, :visited only applies to the a tag.

Use Pseudoclasses to Style Links

If you do not define an a style, browsers will style hyperlink so that :link is set to blue, :active is set to red, and :visited is set to purple. If you define only an a style, it overrides all the default settings and the link appears the same regardless of what the user does. To give the visitor a visual guide to what she is doing, it is a good idea to style the main pseudoclasses for links within your page. To use pseudoclasses, all you need to do is attach them directly after the tags in the selector name.

1. With default.html open in Design view, create a new style. In the Selector area, use the drop-down menu to find a:active or type a:active.

2. In the Font category, set the color to red (**#FF0000**). Click OK to finalize the new style.

3. Create a new style and give it the selector name **a:hover**. In the Font category, check the underline box under text-decoration. Click OK to finalize the new style.

4. Create a new style and give it the selector name **a:visited**. In the Font category, set the color to gray (**#808080**). Click OK to finalize the new style.

You will not see any changes in Design view, but when you save and preview the page in your browser, you will see that the links on the page are blue when they have not been visited and are not being hovered over. They have an underline when they are being hovered over, turn red when you press and hold them, and turn gray if they have already been visited. Note that because you attached the pseudoclasses to the general a style, they are applied to all the instances of the <a> tag in the page including the subheadings that work as bookmarks. And because the pseudoclasses are more specific, they override the h2 a link as well. If you want the h2 links to have separate pseudoclasses from the other links on the page, all you have to do is create a new style with a selector name such as **h2 a:hover**.

Did you
Know?

You can apply the pseudoclasses `:active`, `:focus`, and `:hover` to many tags, not just links. For example, the `:hover` pseudoclass is sometimes used to highlight sections of lists, tables, and paragraphs to help with readability. When doing this, it is important to make the nonlink components visually different from the links to avoid confusing the visitor. The `:hover` style applied to nonlink content commonly changes the background color of the content rather than the font color.

For even more advanced control, you can combine several pseudoclasses by stacking them. As an example, right now when you hover over a link, it retains the current color and displays an underline regardless of whether you visited it before. By creating a separate style with the selector name `a:visited:hover`, you can display hovered-over visited links in a different color. Just as with tags, classes, and IDs, you can attach any styling attribute to pseudoclasses.

Understanding the Box Model

Previously in this hour, you learned that when you attach tags to your content, Expression Web 3 creates an invisible box around the content. To understand how the content behaves and how you can style it, you need a firm understanding of the box model. Fortunately, the clever people in the Expression Web development team considered this and built a box model reference right into the New and Modify Style dialogs so that you don't need to remember how it works.

To get a better understanding of what the box model is and how you use it, let's take a closer look at the #sidebar ID you created in default.html. To do so, right-click the #sidebar ID in the Apply or Manage Styles task pane, and select Modify Style to open the Modify Style task pane. The box model reference is located under the Box category, as shown in Figure 11.9.

All content wrapped inside tags has four main areas. In the center is the content itself, and surrounding the content is the padding. The padding is the "breathing space" that separates the content from the next area, the border. The padding retains the same background color or image as the content. The border is the outer edge of the box. It can be given any color, be solid, or have a number of different textures. Outside the border is the margin. The margin works as the buffer area between the outer edges of the box (the border) and the other content on the page. The margin is transparent and you cannot give it a distinct color.

You can set the values of each of the four sides of the padding, border, and margin independently or in groups. To set all four sides of the padding, border, or margin, check the corresponding Same for All box and enter the desired value in the first box.

FIGURE 11.9
The New and Modify Style dialogs include a CSS box model reference guide under the Box category.

To set the values for each side independently, uncheck the Same for All box and set each value. If you leave any values empty, the default value applies. The default value is usually 0px.

The tricky part about the box model is the calculation of width and height. Generally, the width and height of any boxed element are equal to the distance from side to side or top to bottom of the content area before the padding is applied. The thickness of the padding, borders, and margins add to the total width and height of the box. This means that if you create a div with a width of 800px, as you did earlier, and give it a border of 2px on each side and a padding of 10px on each side, the total width of your div becomes 824px. As a result, if you want to keep the total width of your div at 800px, you need to subtract both your border width and your padding width and set the width of your div to 776px. It's not rocket science, but if you forget this little piece of information, you could easily end up with content that doesn't fit and not understand why.

Try It Yourself ▼

Using the Box Model to Style Content

Now that you know how the box model works, you can use it to create layout elements that are far more functional than tables. In this example, you change the appearance of the sidebar default.html page by changing the `#sidebar` ID style.

1. With default.html open in Design view, right-click the `#sidebar` ID and select Modify Style to open the Modify Style dialog.

2. Right now there is no space between the edge of the div box and the text, so the text appears attached to the left wall. To solve this problem, change the padding of the div: Under the Box category, uncheck the Padding: Same for All box and set `padding right` and `padding left` to `10px`. This creates some breathing space between the inner edge of the box (the content) and the borders. You can use the Preview box to make sure the space is created correctly. Click OK to apply the changes to the style.

When you save and preview the page in your browser, you can see that the breathing space inside and around the sidebar (previously added with the alignment class) gives the entire page a much nicer layout (see Figure 11.10). Because the outer

FIGURE 11.10
By utilizing your knowledge of the box model, you can create visually pleasing layouts without using graphics or tables.

`#sidebar` ID has a specific width defined and you have now added padding, you have to reduce the width attribute if you want to keep it at 250px width.

Summary

As you can see, CSS is a powerful tool that goes far beyond merely changing the color and size of fonts. In this hour, you got a glimpse of how you can use CSS to create highly complex and visually compelling layouts and how easy it is to make dramatic changes to the look of the page without destroying the content in the process. The examples in this hour merely scratch the surface of what is possible when you use CSS as a layout tool, but they give you a good idea of what you can do. Finishing this hour, you have better ideas of why having strong CSS skills gives you an advantage in the web design market and why Expression Web 3 is an excellent tool not only to create but also to learn CSS.

In this hour, you learned how to move beyond simple text styling to create classes that change the appearance of specific elements within a page. You also learned how to group sections of the page using divs and how to assign IDs and classes to these divs to get detailed control of your content. You learned how to set selector names so that certain styles apply to only certain elements within an ID, class, or subclass, and how to apply and modify those styles to change the overall look of your page. In addition, you got an introduction to pseudoclasses and learned how to use them to style active content within a page to give the visitor a more interactive experience. Finally, you learned how the box model works and how you can use it to create layouts and style content. In the next hour, you look at the CSS code and learn how to manipulate the code to achieve the same results you saw in this hour. You also learn how to completely separate the style from the content by creating standalone style sheets and how to apply the styles you have already created to other pages you build.

Q&A

Q. *I can't find this Quick Tag Selector bar you keep talking about! Where is it?*

A. By default, the Quick Tag Selector is on, but you might have accidentally turned it off. If it is not visible directly under the tabs at the top of the View pane, open the View menu from the menu bar and click Quick Tag Selector to activate it. The Quick Tag Selector has an orange box with a check mark to its left when it is active.

Q. *I changed the name of a style/class/ID I created and now it isn't applied to the content. Why is that?*

A. If you change the name of a style, class, or ID, you also need to change the name in the tags that the style, class, or ID that you applied it to. You can do this by selecting the tag using the Quick Tag Selector and opening the Tag Editor.

Q. *I followed the tutorial and created pseudoclasses for my links, but I still can't see them in Design view. Am I doing something wrong?*

A. Design view displays only the plain link style, not the pseudoclasses. To test the pseudoclasses you created, you have to preview your page in a browser.

Workshop

The Workshop has quiz questions and exercises to help you put to use what you just learned. If you get stuck, the answers to the quiz questions are in the next section. But try to answer them first. Otherwise you'll be cheating yourself.

Quiz

1. What is the difference between styles, classes, and IDs?

2. Can you apply multiple styles, classes, or IDs to the same item?

3. What is the difference between padding, border, and margin in the Box model?

Answers

1. A style is a set of styling parameters applied to a specific selector such as p, h1, ul, li, or td. A class is an independent set of styling parameters that can be applied to any selector and divs and spans. An ID is similar to the class except each ID can be used only once per page.

2. Yes, you can apply multiple styles, classes, and IDs to an item, but not all at the same time. To do this, you need to place the different styles, classes, and IDs in concentric circles around the item. For instance if you want a block of text to be affected by an ID, a class, and a specific style, you need to place the content inside a div with the class applied that is surrounded by a div with the ID applied.

3. The padding is the space between the content and the inner sides of the box. The border is the demarcating line that separates the inside and the outside of the box. The margin is the space between the outer sides of the margin and the surrounding content.

Exercise

Create a new div and place all the content except the main heading and the sidebar inside it. Create a new class called **.content** and apply it to the div. Use your knowledge of the box model to position the text so that the space below the sidebar box is empty.

Styling with Code: Fully Immersed in CSS

What You'll Learn in This Hour:

▶ How to read CSS code

▶ How inline styles differ from other styles

▶ How to apply styles, classes, and IDs to tags in Code view

▶ How to create external style sheets and apply them to multiple pages

Introduction

In Hours 10, "Bringing Style to Substance with Cascading Style Sheets," and 11, "Getting Boxed In, Part 2: Knee Deep in CSS," you learned how to create styles and apply them to content in Design view. But that's just half the story. To fully grasp what Cascading Style Sheets (CSS) is all about, you need to go to the source and learn how to read the code.

Fortunately CSS code is quite simple to learn, especially when you have Expression Web 3's many CSS tools available whenever you get confused. Just as in Design view, you have full access to the CSS panels when you work in Code view, and all the tools you used in the past two hours are available for use in the same way.

The main purpose of this hour is to go beyond the basics and learn how styling actually works and how to create, apply, and modify styles without using the tools every time. Because the tools Expression Web 3 provides are excellent, they are sometimes cumbersome to use, especially if you make quick, minor changes and already know what to do. Other benefits to using Code view are that you have more control when it comes to the placement and attribution of tags, and you can get a better overview of what is happening to your code. And you get a much clearer picture of the meaning of the phrase separating the style from the content.

In addition to learning how to read, write, and dissect CSS code, this hour covers how to create separate style sheets and apply them to multiple files. You also see how easy it is to move styles from one file to another and apply a style created in one file to other files without having to re-create it. By the end of this hour, you will have the necessary tools and understanding to use CSS not only as a styling tool but also as a platform to create visually stunning websites with clean and concise code that looks the same across most, if not all, browsers and platforms.

Introducing CSS: The Code Version

In the last two hours, you created a series of styles, classes, and IDs. In this hour, you inspect and expand on these, so if you didn't do all the tasks in earlier hours, you should replace the default.html file and the myCameras.html file with the ones supplied in the lesson files for this hour.

To work, CSS requires two sets of code: the styles and the tags to which the styles are attached. Let's take a closer look at the styles as they appear in code form. Expression Web 3 gives you multiple ways to view the CSS code. By far the easiest way of doing so is simply to hover over the style in question in the Manage Styles panel. When you do so, a ScreenTip opens to display the entire style code in a pop-up window (see Figure 12.1).

FIGURE 12.1
Hovering the mouse pointer over a style in the Manage Styles panel brings up a ScreenTip that displays the CSS code for that style.

With the default.html file open, hovering over the h1 style gives you the following output:

```
h1 {
    font-family: Arial, Helvetica, sans-serif;
    font-size: 1.4em;
```

```
    font-weight: bold;
    text-transform: uppercase;
    color: #333333;
}
```

This is a typical style. It consists of the style name followed by a set of curly braces. The braces contain all the actual styling code: Each attribute followed by its respective values after a colon. A semicolon separates the attributes.

As you can see, the CSS code Expression Web 3 generates is easy to read. The only reason why each attribute is on a separate line is for readability. If you want to, you could remove all the line breaks and write the entire style on one line, but as you can see it would be much harder to read:

```
h1 {font-family: Arial, Helvetica, sans-serif; font-size: 1.4em;
 font-weight: bold; text-transform: uppercase; color: #333333;}
```

By the Way

> Because of the limited physical width of this book the entire line doesn't fit on one single line when printed. Normally if you look at the line in Expression Web 3, it would appear on one line. Just like in this book, there are times when CSS confined to a single line is arbitrarily divided into multiple lines by the application you use to look at the code. Even so, the style works the exact same way. The information you should walk away with here is that it is the semicolons that define when a line of code ends, not the line breaks.

Now that you know what the CSS code looks like, the next logical question is, "Where is it located?" If you paid close attention when you created the styles in the last two hours, you might already have a good idea. Directly under the Selector box in the New and Modify Style dialog was the Define In box, which was set to Current page. That means all the styles you created so far are stored in the same page as the content—more specifically at the top of the page inside the <head> tag. The <head> tag contains functional but nonvisual content and information about the current page.

To see where the styles are stored, switch to Code view and scroll to the top of the page. Directly under the <meta> tags is a tag that says <style type="text/css">. You can find all the styles within this tag (see Figure 12.2).

In Hour 8, "Cracking the Code: Working in Code View," you were introduced to the Code View toolbar. Now is a good time to use it. To get an idea of how much code Expression Web 3 created for you when you created the styles, place your cursor on any of the lines with CSS code, and click the Select Tag button on the toolbar. This highlights all the CSS code. Likewise, to highlight the code within one style, you can use the Highlight Block button. But reading this code can still be quite daunting. Currently you have 16 styles defined, and many style sheets have hundreds or even thousands of styles.

FIGURE 12.2
You can find the CSS code at the top of the default.html page inside the <head> tag in Code view.

To find a particular style in Code view, all you need to do is click the style in question in the Manage Styles panel, and Expression Web 3 highlights the style for you. While in the Manage Styles panel, you can even use the arrow keys to navigate between styles for quick-and-easy access to the particular style, class, or ID on which you want to work.

The Value of Separation

Throughout this book there have been several mentions of the styles being separate from the content. Now, for the first time, you see what this means in real life: The style code is quite literally separate from the rest of the content in the page. There are several reasons for this. First, keeping the styles separate means that style code does not clutter the content portion of the page. Second, it makes it easier to make changes to both the styles and the content because they are easily distinguishable. Last, it means that you don't have to insert styling code in the page whenever you add new content.

When you add CSS code to the head of an HTML page, the browser reads it and applies it to whatever content it finds below. In practical terms, it works kind of like a coin sorter. If you just dump various coins in a bucket, they have no order. But a coin sorter sorts, separates, and puts each different coin size in its own collector. In HTML, the CSS code becomes the different coin slots, and as the content flows through the filter, the different kinds of content fall into their appropriate slots. So rather than sorting each piece of content individually by applying styles directly to it, CSS works as a template from which all the content sorts simultaneously.

Understanding Inline Styles

But what is a rule without an exception? In Hour 10 you created an inline style that applied to just one section of the page. You removed that inline style and replaced it with a class in Hour 11, so you need to make a new one. But this time you see what goes on in the code and, through that, learn how the inline style gets its name.

1. With the default.html page open in Split view, scroll down to the bottom of the page and place the cursor anywhere inside the last paragraph. Click the New Style button to create a new style, and use the drop-down menu to set the selector name to (Inline Style).

2. In the Font category, set the font-size to 0.8em and the font-variant to small-caps. In the Block category, set text-align to center. Click OK to apply the new inline style, the result of which you can see in Figure 12.3.

FIGURE 12.3
You can use inline styles to create specialized styles for small segments of content that should appear different than the regular content.

The last paragraph of the page changes appearance after you apply the inline style. But what matters is what happened in Code view. Look at the tag for this particular paragraph:

```
<p style="font-size: 0.8em; font-variant: small-caps; text-align: center">
```

Rather than creating a new style and adding it to the list at the top of the page, Expression Web 3 added this style inside the tag of the affected paragraph. The style is in the same line as the content—hence the name inline style. This explains not only why the style you just created affects only this particular paragraph but also serves as a good example of why you should always try to keep your styles separate from your content. Just imagine what your HTML code would look like if every tag had to contain the necessary style attributes! With that said, inline styles are useful if you need to apply a special style featured only once in the entire page or site.

▼   **Try It Yourself**

Create a New Style in Code View Using IntelliSense

In Code view, you can make direct changes to the CSS code or create new styles with the help of IntelliSense. In this example, you create a new img style from scratch to give the image the appearance of having a white background with a gray border.

1. With the myCameras.html page open in Code view, find the `<style type="text/css">` tag and create a new line directly below it.

2. To create the new style, type **im** and IntelliSense suggests img. Press the Enter key to accept img, press the spacebar, and type a **beginning curly bracket** {. In response, IntelliSense automatically moves you to the next line, inserts the end curly bracket on the line below, and brings up a list of all available attributes that apply to the img tag (see Figure 12.4).

FIGURE 12.4
IntelliSense automatically closes any bracket you start and gives you a list of the available attributes.

3. To create five-pixel padding around the image, type **pa**. IntelliSense suggests padding. Press Enter to complete the word.

4. IntelliSense now opens a ScreenTip to tell you what kind of information the padding attribute requires. Because you want five-pixel padding on all four sides, you can type **5px** and be done with it. If you want different values for each side, follow the ScreenTip and type, for example, **5px 4px 4px 10px** (top, right, bottom, left). Complete the line by entering a **semicolon** and pressing Enter to create a new line.

To create a border, you need to set three attributes: `border-style`, `border-width`, and `border-color`. To help you remember this, IntelliSense reminds you and helps you set all three variables on one line: On the new line, type **border:**. This opens the ScreenTip for the `border` attribute. IntelliSense now asks you for the values it needs. First up is `border-width`. Type **1px** and press the spacebar. The ScreenTip automatically jumps to the next variable, `border-color`, and opens a drop-down menu of colors for you (see Figure 12.5). Pick the gray color and press the spacebar. IntelliSense

FIGURE 12.5
Depending on which variable is required, IntelliSense provides a drop-down menu of options for you to choose from. In this case, it provides a list of colors for the border-color variable.

now asks you for the `border-style`. Select solid from the drop-down menu and finish the line with a semicolon. The two new lines should read `padding:5px;` and `border: 1px gray solid;`.

To see the effects of your changes, click anywhere inside Design view to apply the changes. The image now has a one-pixel solid gray border and five pixels of white padding. This example shows you how easy it is to write and make changes to CSS code in Code view and also how IntelliSense works with you to simplify the code-writing process.

Applying Classes to Tags in Code View

In Hour 11, you learned to apply special styles to certain content with the use of classes. In one example, you used classes to change the position of the image in the myCameras.html page. This example provides a good basis for learning how Expression Web 3 applies classes to tags in Code view. If you open myCameras.html in Split view and click the image, the relevant code highlights in Code view (see Figure 12.6).

```
<img alt="Most of my cameras together" height="355" src="Images/camerasSmall.jpg"
width="600" class="alignCenter" usemap="#FPMap0" />
```

Inspecting the tag code you see a new attribute toward the end: `class="align Center"`. This is how Expression Web 3 applies classes to tags, whether they are

FIGURE 12.6
The img tag for the image highlights in Code view when you click the image in Design view.

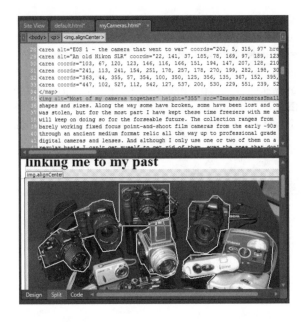

selectors, spans, or divs. To change the class, all you need to do is edit the class name in Code view. In Hour 11, you learned how to create two more alignment classes. To apply one of these instead, simply change the class name to either `alignLeft` or `alignRight` and immediately see the changes in Design view. Adding a class to an existing tag is just as easy: Simply type the word **class** before the end bracket of the beginning tag, and IntelliSense gives you a drop-down list of all available classes.

To see the CSS code for the class in Code view, right-click the class in the Manage Styles panel and select Go to Code, or simply double-click the class to go right to it. No matter where you are in the program, these functions take you straight to the relevant CSS code in Code view.

Using Divs and Spans to Separate Content

We touched on both the `<span>` tag and the `<div>` tag earlier, and now it's time to take a closer look at these separators. The main difference between the two is that span is an inline separator, whereas div is a block separator. In other words, span's display attribute is `inline` by default, whereas div's display attribute is `block`. You saw the difference between the two when you used the `.centerAlign` class to center the thumbnail earlier: The `inline` value means that the content, although separated from the surrounding content, is still on the same line as the rest. In contrast, the `block` value creates a block or box on its own line that holds only the content inside the tag.

The default.html page contains two instances of the <span> tag that you created to highlight the words kipple and the random word you chose in the first paragraph. If you find the words in the Design portion of Split View and click them, you can see the corresponding <span> tags and how they are applied in Code view:

```
<span class="style1">&quot;kipple&quot;</span>
```

As you can see, the class application is no different in the span tag than in any other tag. But because you were just starting to learn how to create styles, you didn't give the class a proper name, so it has the nondescript name style1. It's important to give all your styles, classes, and IDs proper descriptive names so that you know what they do. But how do you do so without afterward going into the code and manually changing all the references to the style?

Rename Styles and Apply the Change to All Tags in a Page

When you work with large pages or sites, you often run into situations in which you need to rename a style, class, or ID. The problem is that Expression Web 3 already applied these elements to many tags within your pages, and if you change the name of the style, class, or ID, all the references have to change as well. To help simplify this process and save you from the trouble of tracking down every reference to your now changed style, class, or ID, Expression Web 3 can make all the substitutions for you.

1. With the default.html page open in Split view, navigate both the Code and Design views so that you can see both span instances you created earlier by clicking on one of them.

2. In the Manage Styles panel, right-click the .style1 class and select Rename Class "style1" from the context menu. This opens the Rename Class dialog.

3. In the Rename Class dialog (see Figure 12.7), give the class the new name highlight. Be sure to enable the Rename Class References in This Page box and click OK.

FIGURE 12.7
The Rename Style, Class, and ID dialogs give you the option of renaming all references to the renamed element in the current page or in all pages affected by it.

When you click OK, not only does Expression Web 3 rename the class, but it also changes the references to the class in the page, as you can see in Code view. Changing all the references to a style, class, or ID to correspond with a name change extends to external style sheets, meaning that when you learn how to create an external style sheet and apply it to multiple pages, Expression Web 3 changes all references to the changed name throughout all these pages for you, even if they are not open!

In Hour 11, you used divs to create blocks that separated and sectioned the contents of the page. default.html now has two divs: one outer box with the ID wrapper and an inner box with the ID sidebar. To see how Expression Web 3 applies those divs, click the sidebar in Design view to see all the tags applied to it. By clicking the <div#wrapper> tag in the Quick Tag Selector, all the content affected by the tag highlights both in Code and Design view. To find only the beginning tag, click the Find Matching Tag button on the Code View toolbar. As you can see, the application of an ID is similar to that of a class: <div id="wrapper">.

Because divs box in larger sections of content, it can be hard to see exactly where they apply and how much content they contain. You already saw how to use the Quick Tag Selector to highlight all the content affected by a tag. Another way is to use the Select Tab button on the Code View toolbar. If you need to see where the end </div> tag is located, click the Find Matching Tag button again, and Code view jumps to the end tag.

Creating Divs in Code View

As you may have experienced in Hour 11, dragging and dropping divs into Design view can be a bit tricky. A much easier and more effective way of applying divs is to use Code or Split view because in Code view, you can see exactly what content you are wrapping and place the beginning and end tags in the precise location you want them. You already inserted two divs in the default.html page, and now you are going to insert the same divs in the myCameras.html page.

1. With the myCameras.html page open in Split view, click the Home text button you created earlier to navigate both views to the top of the page.

2. From the Toolbox panel, drag an instance of the <div> tag into Code view and place it directly under the <body> tag. This creates a beginning and an end div tag: <div></div>.

3. Highlight and cut out the `</div>` end tag by pressing Ctrl+X. In Code view, navigate to the bottom of the page. There you can see that the `</body>` tag is now red with a yellow background, indicating that the code is broken. Paste the `</div>` tag you just cut out into the line directly above the `</body>` tag. If you click an element within the page, you can see that the `<div>` tag is now present in the Quick Tag Selector.

4. Now add the sidebar to the page. Just like in the default.html page, the sidebar should appear alongside the content off the top, so in the markup it should appear right after the `<div>` you just created. Find the beginning div tag and add a new line directly underneath it. Drag and drop a new `<div>` tag into the new line or enter `<div>` manually. IntelliSense creates the end tag for you to keep the code from breaking. Again highlight and cut out the end tag. Because this page doesn't have a descriptive section, the sidebar should contain only the Home link, so place your cursor at the end of the line containing the Home link, and press Enter to create a new line. Paste the `</div>` end tag you cut out into this new line or enter `</div>`.

The myCameras.html page now has two divs just as the default.html page does. But the classes and IDs you used to style the divs are still in the default.html file. To apply them to myCameras.html as well, you need to create an external style sheet.

Creating External Style Sheets

By far the most powerful feature of CSS is that it gives you the ability to create styles, classes, and IDs stored in one central location and applied to many different pages or entire sites. This is where the Sheets part of the name Cascading Style Sheets comes from.

An external style sheet is a dedicated file with the extension .css that contains only style code. Until now Expression Web 3 has inserted all the style code you created into the head of your HTML pages, but doing so limits their application to that particular page. Now you need to move the styles from the HTML page to a new style sheet so that you can apply the same styles to multiple pages.

To create an external style sheet, you first have to create a .css file. The easiest way to create a .css file is to click the down arrow next to the New icon on the Common Toolbar and select CSS in the context menu. This creates a new file named Untitled_1.css. In most cases the style sheet name is simply styles.css, but it is often a good idea to be more specific in naming to ensure that you know which site each sheet belongs to.

After creating the new file, go to File, select Save As and give it the name kippleStyles.css. When saved it appears in the Folder panel, as shown in Figure 12.8.

FIGURE 12.8
It's usually a good idea to give your .css files site-specific names to make sure you know where they belong.

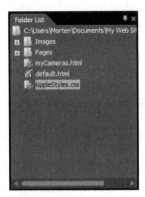

Opening the new CSS file, you can see that it is completely empty. That is because unlike HTML and other markup files, a CSS file doesn't need any code other than the actual styles to function. And because it's a new file, there are no style definitions yet.

The next step is to attach the style sheet to your pages by using the Attach Style Sheet button in the Apply and Manage Styles panel. With the default.html page open, click the Attach Style Sheet button to open the Attach Style Sheet dialog (see Figure 12.9).

FIGURE 12.9
The Attach Style Sheet dialog lets you attach an external style sheet to the current page or all pages in the site using either the link or import method.

From here you can browse to the style sheet you want to attach and choose whether you want to attach it to all the pages in your site or just the current page. (The Selected pages option becomes available if you highlight a series of pages in the Folders panel before opening the Attach Style Sheet dialog.) You also have the choice of whether to attach the style sheet using the link method or the import method. They produce nearly the same results, but use the Link option for the most consistent results.

Browse and select the kippleStyles.css file you just created, select Attach to All HTML Pages, and Attach as Link. This attaches the new style sheet to all the HTML pages within your site by inserting the following line of code in the <head> tag:

```
<link href="kippleStyles.css" rel="stylesheet" type="text/css" />
```

The attached style sheet now appears in the Manage Styles panel under the styles embedded in the current page (see Figure 12.10).

Newly attached style sheet ———

FIGURE 12.10
The newly attached style sheet appears in the Manage Styles panel underneath the locally embedded styles.

The Difference Between Linking and Importing

There are two methods for attaching a style sheet to an HTML file: linking and importing. The difference between the two is subtle and comes into play only in special cases.

The linking method simply tells the browser that styles stored are in the linked file for application to the content below. If you want to attach another style sheet to the page, you add a new link and so on. The linking method works across all browsers, no matter how old.

The importing method is somewhat different. First, you can use it within a style sheet to import another style sheet so that instead of calling two style sheets from the HTML file, you call one, and then the first style sheet calls the second one. But more important, the importing method does not work with some older browsers, and this can be used to prevent older browsers from trying to read style code they can't understand. However, this applies only to very old browsers and should not be a deciding factor in picking one method over the other. For all intents and purposes, both methods work the same way.

Moving Styles to and from the External Style Sheet

After attaching the external style sheet to all the pages in your site, the styles set in the kippleStyles.css file affect all the pages instead of just one. You have already created many styles in different pages, but they are stored in the head of each page and not in the style sheet. The obvious way to solve this is to cut and paste the code out of the pages and into the style sheet, but this method is both cumbersome and prone to error. Expression Web 3 provides a better solution in the form of the Manage Styles panel.

1. With the default.html file open, click and drag the body style from the Current Page area down the kippleStyles.css area. When you let go, the style appears below the kippleStyles.css heading.

Did you Know?	For this exercise it is a good idea to pin the Toolbar panel to the side and let the Manage Styles panel cover the entire height of your screen. You can always unpin the panel later.

2. Using the same method, move the rest of the styles, classes, and IDs from the Current Page area to the kippleStyles.css area (see Figure 12.11).

FIGURE 12.11
You can move styles, classes, and IDs from the current HTML file to the new .css file by dragging and dropping them into the new file area in the Manage Styles panel.

3. When you finish moving all the styles, classes, and IDs to the kippleStyles.css area, scroll to the top of default.html in Code view. Note that all the style code is gone. All that is left is the `<style>` tag. In the Manage Styles panel, right-click any of the styles and select Go to Code. The new kippleStyles.css style sheet opens, and you can see that all the code previously housed in the head of the HTML file is now in the style sheet.

4. Open myCameras.html. Note that the styles you just moved from default.html now appear under kippleStyles.css in the Manage Styles panel for this page. Using the same technique, move the styles from myCameras.html to kippleStyles.css.

5. Press Ctrl+S to save the changes. This opens the Save Embedded Files dialog, which asks whether you want to save the changes to the kippleStyles.css file (see Figure 12.12). Click OK.

FIGURE 12.12
When saving an HTML file after making changes to styles contained in an external style sheet, Expression Web 3 always open the Save Embedded File dialog to ask whether you want to save the changes made in the style sheet as well.

The kippleStyles.css file now contains all the styles from both default.html and myCameras.html. Expression Web 3 still applies the styles to the content of those pages, and they appear the same in Design view and in any browser you preview them in.

Inspecting the code in kippleStyles.css, you can see that the order of the styles corresponds with the list of styles in the Manage Styles panel. If you change the order of the styles in the panel, the code reorganizes in the same manner. This is because the order of styles in the style sheet is relevant to the cascade: The lower in the sheet the style is, the more weight it has in deciding what the content should look like.

If you want to keep a style, class, or ID in both style sheets, you can use the same drag-and-drop technique to copy them. To do so simply press and hold the Ctrl key on your keyboard while dragging and dropping the element. Just keep in mind when you do so that you will now have two styles with the same name, and the one in the style sheet that is listed furthest down in the cascade has precedence.

Did you Know?

In some cases a style, class, or ID applies to only one page. In that case, it is a good idea to keep the element in the relevant page rather than in the style sheet. For example, in default.html you created a class called `highlight` that applied to two words as an inline style. Now the style sheet contains this class, but because only the default.html page uses it, the class should be only in that file. To return this particular class back to its original location, simply open default.html and drag and drop the `.highlight` class back to Current Page (see Figure 12.13).

FIGURE 12.13
The final style structure of the styles for default.html.

Applying External Styles to a Page

Styles nested in an external style sheet act in the same way as styles nested in the current document. Therefore Expression Web 3 applies them in the same way. Earlier in this hour, you created two divs to section out the content in the myCameras.html page. Now that you have attached the external style sheet, you can apply the same IDs and classes you used to change the layout of default.html to change the layout of myCameras.html.

1. With the myCameras.html file open in Split view, click anywhere inside the page in Design view, and click the first `<div>` tag in the Quick Tag Selector to select the div that wraps all the content. This highlights all the content in both Code view and Design view.

2. In the Manage Styles panel, right-click the `#wrapper` ID, and select Apply Style from the context menu (see Figure 12.14). The tag in the Quick Tag Selector and in Code view changes to `<div#wrapper>` and the wrapper ID is applied.

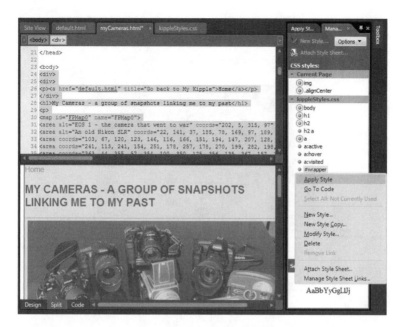

FIGURE 12.14
Applying a style from an external style sheet is no different from applying a style nested within the file itself.

3. In Code view, move the cursor one line down to select the next <div> tag, right-click the #sidebar ID in the Manage Styles panel, and select Apply Style. The tag changes to <div#sidebar> and the #sidebar ID is applied.

4. Because, the position of the sidebar is no longer defined by the #sidebar ID you also need to apply a class to the div. This action can also be done from the Apply Styles panel by selecting the relevant div (now <div#sidebar>) and clicking the appropriate alignment class (.alignLeft or .alignRight) in the Apply Styles panel. The tag changes to <div#sidebar.alignRight> and the alignment class is applied. Save the file and preview it in your browser (see Figure 12.15).

By previewing the page in a browser, you can see the styles you created for default.html applied to myCameras.html.

Summary

Even though Expression Web 3 creates proper standards-based CSS code out of the box, understanding the CSS code can make your life as a designer a lot easier. In fact, in many cases, it makes more sense to work directly with the code rather than to use the point-and-click tools in the application. Fortunately you can choose either way and customize your work process depending on the task.

FIGURE 12.15
The layout IDs and classes created for default.html applied to myCameras.html. By navigating back and forth between the two files, you see they now look consistent when previewed in Opera.

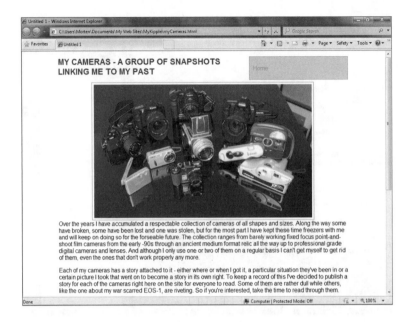

In this hour, you learned how to build a CSS style using code and how to edit it in Code view with the help of IntelliSense. You also learned how to insert spans and divs in your page from Code view, and why doing so is often easier than doing it in Design view. In addition you saw how inline styles differ from other styles and where the name inline stems from. You also learned how to rename both inline and other styles without going through all the code and renaming each instance afterward.

Most important, you learned how to completely separate the styles from the content by creating an external style sheet and how this makes styling groups of pages or an entire website much easier. Understanding this process is fundamental; it dramatically reduces your workload and makes changing and upgrading the look and feel of large websites an easy and straightforward process.

At this point you should begin to realize the true power of standards-based web design and the use of HTML and CSS. In upcoming hours, you use this knowledge to turn up the "wow" factor of the myKipple site by creating advanced layouts and menus.

Q&A

Q. *When I try to apply an inline style to a single word, it is applied to the entire text block instead. What am I doing wrong?*

A. When you create an inline style, the new style is applied to the closest tag. That means that unless you have separated the single word from the rest of the block using the <span> tags, the inline style will be applied to the block tag. To apply the inline style to a single word, you have to wrap it in <span> tags first and then create the new inline style.

Q. *I followed the tutorial to create divs in code view, but everything looks the same as it did before!*

A. When there is a problem with content being wrapped with <div> or <span> tags and nothing looking any different, the answer is usually answered by the following three questions: Does the <div> or <span> actually wrap anything? A common mistake when inserting these elements it to forget to place the end tag at the end of the content. This is because both IntelliSense and other tools automatically place the end tag right after the beginning tag before the content. The second question is do the tags close properly? You might have forgotten to paste the end tag in after cutting it out, or you might have placed it in the wrong spot. If so the code will be broken, and you should see the little warning sign in the status bar and find highlighted code further down in the document. Finally did you actually apply the class or ID to the tag? If you click on the content that should be styled by the class or ID and the Quick Tag Selector reads <div> or <span> without the class or style attached, you need to apply the style or ID to make everything work properly.

Workshop

The Workshop has quiz questions and exercises to help you put to use what you just learned. If you get stuck, the answers to the quiz questions are in the new section. But try to answer them first. Otherwise you'll be cheating yourself.

Quiz

1. What is the difference between a `<span>` tag and a `<div>` tag?

2. What are the two main methods used to make new styles, classes, and IDs you have been introduced to?

3. What is the benefit of moving styles to an external style sheet?

Answers

1. The `<span>` tag is an inline tag meaning that if applied to content in a line, the content stays on the same line. The `<div>` tag, on the other hand, is a block tag meaning it creates a new block or line that the content it wraps is placed on. For this reason `<span>` is used to highlight words or elements whereas `<div>` is used to group sections.

2. You now have two methods to create styles: You can use the New Style button on the Apply and Manage Styles panel and create a new style through the dialog, or you can create a new style from scratch in Code view with the help of IntelliSense.

3. By placing your styles in an external style sheet, you can now use the same styles to control the look of several pages. It also means you can make changes to one style and see those changes applied to all the pages it is attached to without ever opening them.

Exercise

Using the techniques you learned, change the layout of the eos1.html page by adding divs and styling them with IDs and classes to match the default.html and myCameras.html pages.

Getting Visual, Part 3: Images as Design Elements with CSS

What You'll Learn in This Hour:

▶ How to apply images as backgrounds

▶ How to use repeating background images to achieve a consistent look

▶ How to use background images as style elements

▶ How to replace list bullets with images

▶ How to import and change .psd files directly inside Expression Web 3

Introduction

In Hours 6, "Getting Visual, Part 1: Adding Images and Graphics," and 7, "Getting Visual, Part 2: Advanced Image Editing, Thumbnails, and Hotspots," you learned how to insert images as objects in a web page. But if you have spent any length of time on the Web, you know that images are used for so much more and most prominently as design elements. In fact, most of the nontext content you find on a website is an image in some form or another. This is because the basic building blocks of a web page (Hypertext Markup Language [HTML] and Cascading Style Sheets [CSS]) can do only rudimentary tasks such as build boxes with borders. If you want a drop shadow or something more advanced, the only way to make them is to introduce an image. Fortunately, HTML and CSS give you a huge variety of ways in which you can introduce images as design elements by adding them as backgrounds, replaced items, or even buttons without thereby displacing the actual content on the page. Understanding how to achieve this means you can take your site from a plain looking boxes-and-borders layout to a graphics-heavy visual masterpiece.

When creating graphics-heavy websites, you move out of the realm of strict web authoring and into that of a designer. This is because, for all their virtues, no web-authoring software yet includes full-fledged design capabilities; they can't make graphics from scratch. Microsoft Expression Studio includes a powerful design application in Expression Design, but most designers are already using Adobe Photoshop as their base of operations. For this reason Expression Web 3 includes a powerful Photoshop import feature that lets you import .psd files and slice them into workable pieces right in the web-authoring application. This feature is a huge timesaver if you know its capabilities and limitations. The lessons of this hour show you how to use graphics and CSS to create visual design elements for your site and then how to use the Photoshop import feature to generate workable graphics.

Images as Backgrounds: A Crash Course

In Hours 6 and 7, you learned how to insert images into the content of your page. But as you saw, these images were content elements. What you want now are design elements and that requires a somewhat different approach.

As you have already learned, when you insert an image into a web page, you are actually inserting a replaced item, a link that is replaced with an external file. This same technique can be used to replace items such as CSS backgrounds, meaning that rather than giving your box a flat color (or no color) background, the background is the image of your choice.

Furthermore, you can control the way in which this image displays to achieve different effects. As with the content images, any image used as a background must be RGB and of one of the three main formats: GIF, JPEG, or PNG.

Use an Image as a Background with CSS

In the lesson files for this hour is a series of image files. Before going any further, you need to create a new folder called Graphics and import these files into it using the technique you learned in Hour 6.

In this first lesson, you apply an image as a background to see how you can easily change the look of an entire page, even with a small image file.

1. With the default.html page open in Design view, open the Modify Style dialog for the body style you created previously.

2. In the Background category, use the Browse button next to the background-image attribute to navigate to the Graphics folder you just created. Select the

file called demoTile.jpg and click OK. In the Preview box, you see a red-and-black texture appear behind the text (see Figure 13.1). Click OK.

FIGURE 13.1
When the tile.jpg file is defined as the background image for the body style, you can preview it in the dialog.

In Design view, you now see that the entire background of the page has been over-taken by a red-and-black texture. But if you open the demoTile.gif file you just inserted as a background in your regular file explorer outside of Expression Web 3, you see that it is, in fact, just a 20-pixel by 20-pixel image. So, how is it covering the entire background? By default, if you set an image as a background for any style, the image automatically repeats or tiles both horizontally and vertically from the upper-most left corner down to the end of the page. This gives the designer the ability to use a tiny image to cover a large area. Otherwise the background image would need to be as wide as the display on the largest monitor imaginable and as tall as the longest page you could come up with, and that would be a very large image indeed.

The Background Attributes

To see how this tiling works in real life, you can turn it off. To do so, go back to the Background category of the body style and set the background-repeat attribute to no-repeat. Now only one instance of the background appears in the upper-left corner (see Figure 13.2).

The background-repeat attribute can be set to one of four values that give you a variety of options in terms of how to display your background image. You've already seen what no-repeat does; repeat is the default setting by which the image is tiled

FIGURE 13.2
With the background-repeat attribute set to no-repeat, the background image appears only once in the upper-left corner of the area.

Background Image

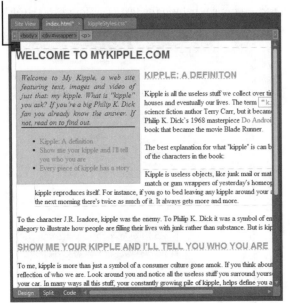

both horizontally and vertically; repeat-x tiles the image only along the x-axis, meaning there will be one line of tiles along the top going from left to right; repeat-y tiles the image only along the y-axis, meaning there will be one line of tiles along the left side going from top to bottom.

You can further specify the location of the background image using the (x) background-position and (y) background-position attributes in which you can give the background image an absolute position with a numeric value, or you can set it to left, center, or right for the x value and top, center, or bottom for the y value. For example, by setting both the (x) background-position and (y) background-position attributes to center, the image will be located in the middle of the area relative to the total width and height of the area within the tags (see Figure 13.3).

The Background category also lets you set the background-attachment attribute for the image. The default value of this attribute is scroll, meaning that the background is affected if you scroll up, down, left, or right in the page just like the rest of the content. If you set this attribute to fixed, the background image is fixed in the same location relative to the browser window, so the image stays even if you scroll through the content.

The background-color attribute comes into play whenever you use a background-repeat value other than default or repeat and when the image does not display for

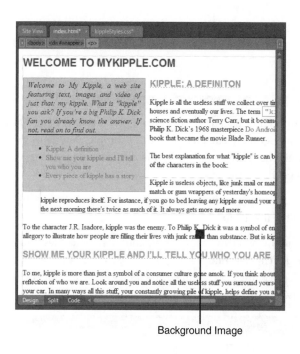

Background Image

whatever reason. All the area not covered by the background image has the color defined by the background-color attribute.

> As a rule of thumb, you should always set the background-color of the body because you never know if the visitors have images turned off or has set their browser to apply a color other than white to pages with no background color defined. To drive this point home, some designers have started posting screen grabs of sites with their "underwear showing" (that is, no background color defined) in a Flickr group by the same name. To see the growing list of such sites and what happens when you forget to give your site underwear, visit http://www.flickr.com/groups/underwearshowing/.

Did you Know?

How Backgrounds Relate to the Content and the Page

Background images work exactly the same way that background colors work in styles, meaning they cover the area within the confines of the box that contains the content within the beginning and end tags. In the preceding example, you gave the style that governs the body tag a background image, meaning that the image is applied to the background of the entire page. If you define a background image for any other style you have created, the attributes act in the same way, but they will be applied in relation to each individual object to which they are applied.

Applying a Background Image to an ID

To fully understand how background images in CSS work, you need to see how they relate to the content and to each other. In this example, you apply two background images: one to the body style and one to a new ID you are going to create to contain the individual page content.

1. Open the Modify Style dialog for the body style and change the background image to the file tile.jpg.

2. Remove all the other styling to ensure that the image tiles throughout the entire page. The new image is a gray-and-white texture on which the page will be built (see Figure 13.4). At the same time, set the background-color to #FFFFFF (white) to ensure that the page looks great even if images are disabled.

FIGURE 13.4
Clicking Apply rather than OK in the Modify Style dialog gives you the ability to see the style applied without closing the dialog.

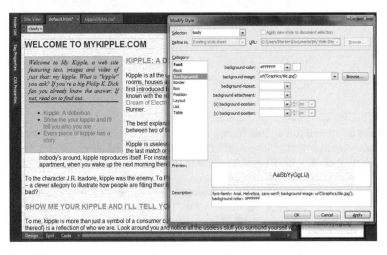

3. In Hour 14, "Harnessing the Power of CSS Layouts," you learn how to use CSS to section off different parts of the page to create flexible layouts. Here's a little sneak peek: To separate the header area of the page (where the title and menu will go) from the rest of the content, you need to wrap the main content in a new ID. In Split view find the line wrapped in <h1> tags and create a new line directly below. Type **<div id="mainContent">** and IntelliSense creates the end </div> tag for you (see Figure 13.5). Select and cut out the end </div> tag, scroll to the bottom of the page, and paste it in just before the end </body> tag. Now the content of the page is wrapped separately and can be styled separately as well.

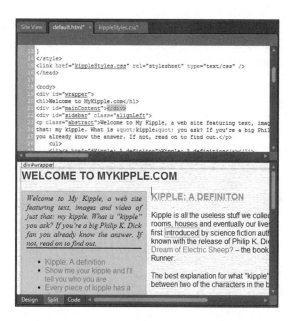

FIGURE 13.5
Inserting new
<div> tags is
usually easier in
Code view.

As you can see from the bottom of the code page, after a while you start to get a lot of end tags that are hard to tell apart because they are identical. An easy way to keep track of what end tag belongs to what beginning tag is to use code comments to name them. What I do is select an end tag such as </div> and click the Find Matching Tag button on the Code view toolbar to find the beginning tag. I note the name, click the Find Matching Tag button again to go back to the end tag, and place a comment directly after it to keep track. In HTML, comments are wrapped in special tags starting with <!-- and ending with -->. For example, in my page the two div end tags look like this:

```
</div> <!-- END #mainContent -->
</div> <!-- END #wrapper -->
```

4. Create a new ID called #mainContent to match the <div> you just created. Make sure it is defined in the kippleStyles.css style sheet.

5. In the Background category, use the Browse button to set background-image to paperTile.png. Set the background-repeat attribute to repeat-y so that the image tiles only vertically.

6. When you click Apply, you see that the background image has an edge to it and that the text is currently overflowing it. To realign the text so it fits on the inside of the graphic, go to Box and set padding-right and padding-left to 15px. Click OK to apply the changes, and then save and preview the page in your browser (see Figure 13.6).

FIGURE 13.6
With the new background images applied to the page, it looks dramatically different.

As you can see, the backgrounds are relative to the tag to which they are applied; the body background covers the entire page regardless of how wide or tall the window is, whereas the #mainContent background is constrained inside the div.

Background Images and the Box Model

To see how the background images relate to the box model, open the Modify Styles dialog for the h2 style, set the background-image to underline.png and background-repeat to no-repeat. Click OK to apply the style change. By looking at the headings in Design view, you see that they now have a gray line behind them toward the top. But there are two problems: First, the image is called "underline," so it is obviously meant to be an underline, and second, the image is missing from the top h2 title.

Let's tackle the last one first. If you click on the top title and look at the tag selector box, it is obvious why you can't see the underline graphic behind the text: Even though the sidebar box pushes the text to the side, the h2 box still stretches to the far-left side of the page and the background with it (see Figure 13.7). To solve this problem, you need to change the display attribute for the h2 style. By default, all headings have the display attribute set to block, meaning they appear on their own line and span the width of the box in which they are placed (in this case the #mainContent div). To make the box shift to the side to accommodate the sidebar, open the Modify Style dialog for the h2 style, go to Layout, and set display to inline-block.

FIGURE 13.7
By default the headings are defined as blocks, meaning any background images span the width of the entire containing box rather than just behind the text itself.

The first problem is less cryptic and can be solved with some common-sense thinking: To move the line to the bottom of the box, simply set the (y) `background-position` to bottom and the (x) `background-position` to left. But, even so, the line still appears behind the text, not under it. This is where the box model comes into play.

As you learned in Hour 12, "Styling with Code: Fully Immersed in CSS," the background spans the entire area inside the box drawn by the tags. The same thing goes for the background image. You also learned that the padding defines the space between the content and the inner edges of the box. This means that if you want an image to appear above, below, to the left, or to the right of your content, you need to increase the padding to leave room for it in whatever direction you want the image to appear.

In this case, you want the background image to appear below the text content of the h2 headings. You set the (y) `background-position` attribute to bottom, which means the image hugs the bottom of the box. So, if you increase the bottom padding, the image shifts down relative to the text. To do so, open the Modify Style dialog for the h2 style, and go to the Box category. The next step is a bit of trial and error: Uncheck the Same for All box for Padding, and set bottom-padding to 5px. Click Apply and move the Modify Style dialog to the side to see whether this produced the result you were looking for. In this case, the image didn't move far enough down, so use the up and down buttons to increase the `bottom-padding` value to 10px and click Apply again. If you are satisfied with what you see, click OK to finalize the change.

Stacking Order Means You Can Pile Your Images

Because background images are style elements contained within the box model, they act just like any other feature in the box. The most obvious advantage of this is that it gives you the ability to stack multiple images on top of each other, just like a pile of photos, by setting them as backgrounds for different elements. This method also preserves any transparencies (if the browser supports them), meaning you can place one transparent image on top of another one and see one through the other. In fact, using this method, there is no limit to how deep your stack of images can be except the capabilities of the computer that displays them.

As with all other style elements, the cascade decides the stacking order of images used as backgrounds: The tag closest to the content has top position, followed by the second closest, and so on. This way the background of the most relevant object ends up on top. While you were following the lessons earlier in this hour, what you were actually doing was stacking one image on top of another. When you test the current page in your browser and look at the h2 headings you see the underline.png image stacked on top of the paperTile.png, which in turn is stacked on top of the tile.jpg image. And as you can see from Figure 13.8, the transparencies of the two topmost images stay intact throughout the page.

FIGURE 13.8
Default.html now has three background images stacked on top of one another: tile.jpg, paperTile.png, and underline.png. Each appears on top of the other because of their order in the page hierarchy.

underline.png

title.jpg   paperTile.png

Using Images as List Bullets

In addition to using images as backgrounds, they have another extremely useful application: replacing list item bullets with image files.

Did you Know?

When you change the style of lists, keep in mind that depending on what you want to achieve, there are three different tags to which you can attach styles. An ol style affects all the list items in ordered lists as a group. A ul style affects all the list items in unordered lists as a group. An li style affects all list items individually regardless of whether they are in an ordered or unordered list. You can target only list items in ordered lists by creating an ol li style and an unordered list with an ul li style. Of course, you can also make these styles subsidiary to any class, ID, or group of classes or IDs.

By default, a bullet precedes all unordered list items. However, this is but one of many different options. Figure 13.9 shows how the eight main list styles appear in a browser

Commonly used list styles:
- disk (unordered list default)
- circle
- square
4. decimal (ordered list default)
v. lower-roman
VI. upper-roman
g. lower-alpha
H. upper-alpha

FIGURE 13.9
The eight main list styles as they appear in a browser with no additional styling.

when no additional styling has been applied. But for all their convenience and functionality, these items are very basic and exchanging them for images is a quick-and-easy way to bring your design to that next level.

Switching out the bullet for an image is similar to changing the bullet style. Because list items are a special type of content in HTML, there is a separate section for them in the New and Modify Style dialogs.

1. With the default.html page open in Design view, create a new style with the selector name **ul**. This style affects all list items in unordered lists. Make sure Define In is set to Existing Style Sheet and kippleStyles.css is the URL.

2. In the List category, use the Browse button to select the arrow.gif file (see Figure 13.10). Click OK to create the new style.

FIGURE 13.10
The List category
in the New and
Modify Style
dialogs controls
the appearance
of both ordered
and unordered
list items.

The new style you made replaces the bullets in front of the list items with small arrows. As with the backgrounds, any image file can be used as a list bullet. (Although for obvious reasons I advise you to use small ones.) But unlike the backgrounds, the bullet image is not directly related to the box but rather to the first line of text in each item. In practical terms, this means that if you add left padding, the distance between the bullet image and the text increases, but if you add bottom padding, the bullet stays on the line. This situation can produce some strange results if you use a large font size because the bullet image stays in its original position in relation to the first line of text rather than grow with the font size. Figure 13.11 demonstrates how both regular bullets and bullet images react to different styling of the li tag. Note that standard HTML bullets size according to the font size.

Watch Out!

The height of the image itself decides the vertical positioning of a bullet image, not the font size or any other style element. If you want a bullet image to appear higher in relation to the text, you need to make it physically taller in your image-editing program by adding more space at the bottom of the image.

FIGURE 13.11
Two identical lists show how the standard HTML bullet and a list-style-image behave in relation to the list item text when different style attribute values are applied. To show the bullet in relation to the box, each list item has a one-pixel gray border on all four sides.

The List category in the New and Modify Style dialogs also includes the `list-style-position` attribute. It can be set to either inside or outside. (Outside is default.) This attribute describes the position of the bullet in relation to the box. If it is set to outside, the bullet or bullet image appears outside of the box. If it is set to inside, the bullet or bullet image appears inside the box. This value does not change the actual distance between the bullet and the text, however. As you can see in Figure 13.11, the distance remains the same and is changed with the `padding-left` attribute. The difference between the two becomes apparent when the list item has more than one line of text because if the `list-style-position` is set to inside, the bullet is treated as if it is part of the text, and the second line of text lines up with the edge of the box underneath the bullet.

> **Did you Know?**
>
> Because of the somewhat odd behavior of list-style-images, many designers set the list-style-type for the list to none and create an `li` style using a regular no-repeat background image with the `(x)` `background-position` set to left and the `(y)` `background-position` set to center instead. Unlike the list-style-image, this background image centers vertically with the box for each line. Keep in mind that if you do this, you have to apply the background to the `li` style. If you apply it to the `ul` or `ol` style, the background image is applied to the list as a whole and not the individual list items.

Importing Adobe Photoshop Files

The term *web design* is a somewhat confusing one, especially when talking about the tools used. You can question whether the actual design of a page or site takes place in web-authoring software such as Expression Web 3 or whether the designing occurs in other applications, and Expression Web 3 and similar programs merely build the framework to display the design. Regardless of where you stand in this debate, you cannot dismiss one fact: Pure design applications such as Expression Design and Adobe Photoshop play an integral part in creating visually stunning websites.

More than just a tool for photographers to manipulate and clean up their photos, Adobe Photoshop has grown into a design platform from which you can create everything from artwork to broadcast graphics and websites. But creating graphics for a website using Photoshop always involved cropping and exporting images that you then imported into the web-authoring application. And because the two applications were not connected, any change required in the image required a new round of exporting and importing the altered image. With Photoshop Import, the Expression Web development team has done away with this cumbersome process, at least partially.

In addition to regular file imports, Expression Web 3 has a dedicated function for importing Adobe Photoshop .psd files. And because .psd files usually contain several layers, you are given the ability to select which layers to include in the import so that you can produce several different images out of one file.

1. With the default.html page open in Design view, click File on the menu bar and select Adobe Photoshop (.psd) under Import. This opens a browser dialog where you select the .psd file you want to import. Select the file named myKipple sticker art.psd from the lesson files and click Open. This opens the Import Adobe Photoshop (.psd) File dialog (see Figure 13.12).

FIGURE 13.12
The Import Adobe Photoshop (.psd) File dialog gives you a series of options for importing and converting Adobe Photoshop files to web-ready images.

2. By default the Check All Layers to Import option is checked, meaning the output will be the image as it appears with all the layers activated. By unchecking individual layers you can select which layers to include in the final export.

Although you can't see it the total area covered by the exported image changes with the content you choose to export, so if you uncheck the Background layer, the image size shrinks to contain only the remaining content.

3. When you are satisfied with your layer selection, you can choose whether to export the image as a GIF, JPEG, or PNG from the Encoding drop-down menu. If you choose JPEG, you have the further option of deciding how much compression to apply (lower quality means higher compression). Sliding the bar back and forth gives you a real-time preview of what the different compression settings do to the image. Choose the lowest possible quality that doesn't produce artifacts that ruin the image, as is the case in Figure 13.13. For this particular image, you can go as low as 33% without losing much in terms of quality.

FIGURE 13.13
Setting the JPEG quality too low can lead to unsightly image artifacts. Use the slider to find a good middle ground between compression and quality.

4. With the Background layer unchecked, set the encoding to PNG and click OK. This opens a standard Save As dialog. Give the compressed image file the name MyKippleSticker.png and place it in the Images folder. The image is added to your file tree in the Folder List task pane.

5. In the default.html file, delete the heading, and drag and drop the new image into the h1 box instead. Give it the alternative text **MyKipple.com sticker**. Save the file and preview the page in your browser (see Figure 13.14).

After placing the image on your page, you might find that it doesn't quite work with the rest of the elements, or maybe you need to omit more layers or even change

FIGURE 13.14
The imported Photoshop image is inserted in place of the original heading.

another element within the image. Because you created the image using the Photoshop import option, Expression Web 3 retains a link to the original .psd file, so if you want to make changes to the image, you can do so directly from Design view.

When you right-click an image imported from a .psd file, there is a new item called Adobe Photoshop (.psd) in the drop-down menu. From this submenu, you can choose Edit Source to open the original .psd file in whatever software is set as your default .psd editor (probably Photoshop), or you can choose Update from Source to reopen the Import Adobe Photoshop (.psd) File dialog. From here you can perform all the same functions as when you first imported the image, and those changes will be applied to the imported file. If you have made changes to the .psd file outside of Expression Web 3 and want to update the image in the page to reflect these changes, click Import again.

Although it is a great tool for easy management of imported images from .psd files, the Photoshop Import function is far from perfect. It does not support some of Photoshop's more advanced features, such as blending options and certain effects. To get the most out of this function, it is necessary to flatten blending and adjustment layers and blending options in Photoshop before importing the file into Expression Web 3. Otherwise you might end up with some strange results. Fortunately the Preview window is accurate; if an effect is not supported, you see it immediately.

Summary

For your websites to go to the next level, they need to have some visual elements included in the design. That means including images as noncontent elements. You can do this by adding images as backgrounds in your styles, classes, and IDs.

In this hour, you learned how to use images in different ways to make backgrounds work for different purposes. You saw that, through the use of tiling, a small image can be used to cover a large area. Depending on how you choose to repeat these background images, you can achieve many different looks with the same image. Using a set of simple background images, you gave the entire page a new look, main content a new background, and even added an image-based underline to the h2 style. These diverse applications of background images should give you an idea of how far you can take your designs using more than just colored backgrounds.

Images can also style list items, and in this hour, you learned how to use the List category in the New and Modify Style dialogs to change the overall appearance of lists to include list-style-images as bullets. Moreover you learned how lists function differently from the other elements of a page and how to use this knowledge to your advantage.

Finally you got an in-depth look at the new Adobe Photoshop import function that lets you import and edit already imported .psd files right inside Expression Web 3 to significantly simplify the process of going from designing to authoring. With a firm understanding of this feature and its limitations, you can make your use of these two different programs far more effective.

Q&A

Q. *I added one of my own images as a repeating background, but I can see where each image ends and the next image begins like if I put tiles on a wall. How do I get that seamless floating feel to my backgrounds?*

A. The tricky part about using tiled images as backgrounds is that the left side has to match the right side, and the top has to match the bottom. Otherwise you can see the "seams" between each of them. There is no magical snap-of-the-fingers way to make these images, and it requires a lot of trial and error. It is often easier to find free tiling images by searching for "seamless background" on the Web and use them.

Q. *I imported a transparent Photoshop file, but when it is placed in the page, it is no longer transparent. How do I preserve the transparency?*

A. As you learned previously to preserve transparency, you have to use either the GIF or PNG file formats. By default, imported Photoshop files are saved as JPEG files with no transparency. To make your image transparent, open the Photoshop Importer dialog again and resave the file as a PNG.

Workshop

The Workshop has quiz questions and exercises to help you put to use what you just learned. If you get stuck, the answers to the quiz questions are in the next section. But try to answer them first. Otherwise you'll be cheating yourself.

Quiz

1. Given an image that has a 10-pixel wide solid box on the left, how do you use it as a background for a heading without the text appearing on top of the black box?

2. What is the maximum number of images you can pile on top of one another in a web page?

Answers

1. To avoid having the text appear on top of the box, you need to move the text to the right compared to the background image: Set the x-background-position to left, and set the left padding to 15px. That way the text appears 15 pixels to the right of the left edge and 5 pixels to the right of the box.

2. In theory there is no limit to how many images you can pile on top of one another. However, in reality, you are limited by the connection speed and processing power of the visiting computer: If you start stacking a lot of images, the page will be slow to load, and the browser might not display the page properly. That doesn't mean you shouldn't do it; just think about how many images are actually necessary. I find that in most cases you can get away with flattening most of the images into one and only using one or two images in the final design.

Exercise

The arrows with which you replaced the bullets in the list are too close to the text. Change the distance between the arrows and the text to give them some more breathing space.

Change the myKipple.com sticker image to a low-resolution JPG to see what this does to the background transparency using the Photoshop import functionality.

HOUR 14

Harnessing the Power of CSS Layouts

What You'll Learn in This Hour:

▶ How to design the layout of your page using pen and paper

▶ How to separate the elements of the layout using boxes

▶ How to understand and use CSS positioning

▶ How to create CSS layouts using the prepackaged layouts featured in Expression Web 3

▶ How to apply a separate layout style sheet to existing pages

Introduction

Designing a web page or website is more than just adding content and applying styles. Layout is also an important consideration. A good layout means better readability and, from that, better communication between the author and the reader. Likewise, a bad layout can easily lead to the message getting lost and the reader ending up with a poor understanding of what the author meant to communicate.

So far you have focused mainly on content and learned how to style it. Now that you have a firm grasp on how to do that, it's time to start thinking about how to position the content on the page to make it more accessible, more pleasant, and easier to read. And you want to do this without adding any unnecessary content into your markup. You can do this in several different ways, but in this book the focus is on using groups of divs to contain and separate the content into a cohesive and intuitive layout.

In past hours, you have made some small layout changes to pages using Cascading Style Sheets (CSS). But in this hour, you fully immerse yourself in CSS layouts and learn how to apply them to existing content. You are also introduced to the CSS reset and see how it works to make your layouts cross-browser compatible.

Starting with Pen and Paper

This might come as a bit of a surprise, but it is often a good idea to start designing a website by sketching it out on a piece of paper (see Figure 14.1). Not only is a sketch

FIGURE 14.1
Drawing a sketch of your site layout on paper is a good starting point that gives you an idea of how to section out the page.

faster and easier to change than any other design method, it also gives you a blueprint of sorts to go by when you start building the framework to display the content of your site.

The benefit of starting with a sketch is that you can see almost right away whether the overall layout works and, if it does, what sections you need to define to make it work. As you learned previously in this book, creating layouts using CSS means creating boxes within boxes within boxes, and you need to know and understand the relationship between these boxes before you build them.

Figure 14.1 shows a rough sketch of the layout of the main page of myKipple.com. The layout has several different elements that need to be treated separately: the corkboard background that hovers in the center behind the content, the header (containing the page title and main menu), the pageContent (containing all the text and images of the respective page including the sidebar), and finally the footer. All the page content is centered and should, therefore, be placed in a separate container. From this information, you can draw a set of boxes to indicate how to separate the content (see Figure 14.2).

FIGURE 14.2
With the sketch of the page complete, it is easy to draw boxes around content and get a clear picture of how the site will come together.

Build the Framework from Boxed Parts

Now that you know how you want to section the page, it's time to build the actual framework. In Hour 13, "Getting Visual, Part 3: Images as Design Elements in CSS," you already started the process of boxing in the content, but to get a firm idea of how this process comes together, let's start again from scratch.

There are many ways of doing this, and none of them is wrong. Many designers prefer to build the framework by hand, but it can be nice to get some help if you are new at design. Expression Web 3 has a series of ready-to-use, prepackaged CSS layouts that give you a bit of a head start.

1. Click New, Page from the File option on the menu bar. This opens the New dialog with the Page tab selected.

2. Click CSS Layouts in the first list to open the prepackaged CSS layouts in Expression Web 3. By clicking each of the options in the second list, you get a short description of the layout along with a preview (see Figure 14.3).

FIGURE 14.3
From the New dialog, you can select a series of different prepackaged layouts for different applications including CSS.

3. Select the layout closest to the framework you drew in your sketch. In this case, it is the Header, Nav, 1 Column, Footer design. Select this option and click OK.

After you click OK, Expression Web 3 opens two new files: Untitled_1.css and Untitled_1.html. Both are empty except for the layout styles. This gives you the ability to work with the layout boxes without content and to match the overlay drawings you previously created. Because you already have a series of styles defined for your pages, what you do is create a separate style sheet that contains only the layout portions of the pages (so that you end up with two style sheets: one for content styles, one for layout styles). That way you can make quick changes to the layout without touching all the other styles.

Employing CSS Reset

Before you make any changes on your own, it is a good idea to insert a CSS reset into your style sheet. A CSS reset is a block of CSS code that removes all the preconceived notions that a browser might have about your page by setting everything to zero.

Eric A. Meyer created the most comprehensive CSS reset around, and you can find it at http://meyerweb.com/eric/tools/css/reset/.

To apply the CSS reset, simply copy the code in its entirety from the web page and paste it into the top of the Untitled_1.css file you just created. Save the CSS file as **layout.css**. Because the Untitled_1.html file already links to the CSS file, the link updates automatically. Save the Untitled_1.html file as **layoutTest.html**.

Updating the ID Names

The next step is to change the ID names to match your drawing. You can do so directly in the CSS file or using the Modify Style option from the Manage Styles task pane. Change the name of #masthead to **#header**, #top-nav to **#mainMenu**, and #page-content to **#pageContent**. Leave #footer as it is. In layoutTest.html, go to Split view and make the same changes to the div IDs.

According to Figure 14.2, the mainMenu ID should reside within the header ID. Go to Code view and move the </div> end tag for the header ID below the one for the mainMenu ID—now the header div wraps the mainMenu div.

The drawing also calls for two new IDs, #centeredBG and #wrapper. To wrap all the existing IDs, create a new <div> on the line before the first div and give it the ID wrapper. Then create another box to contain the #wrapper ID and give it the #centeredBG ID. With all the changes made, the page's code inside the <body> tags should look like this (comments added to make it easier to read):

```
<body>

<div id="centeredBG">
<div id="wrapper">
<div id="header">
<div id="mainMenu">
</div> <!-- #end mainMenu -->
</div> <!-- #end header -->
<div id="pageContent">
</div> <!-- #end pageContent -->
<div id="footer">
</div> <!-- end #footer -->
</div> <!-- end #wrapper -->
</div> <!-- end #centeredBG -->

</body>
```

Now that you have inserted calls to the #centeredBG and #wrapper IDs, you need to add these styles in the layout.css file. You can do this manually in Code view with the help of IntelliSense or by using the New Style button in the Manage Styles pane. For now, just create the styles without any style code.

Styling the Layout Boxes

With the layout boxes created, it is time to style them to make the page match the sketch. This requires the use of all the techniques you learned in earlier hours and some new ones. The goal here is to remove all the layout styling from the kippleStyles.css file and store it in the new layout.css file. You can choose to make the following style modifications using the Modify Style dialog, directly in the layout.css file using IntelliSense, or both.

1. You already did this step in Hour 13, but there is no harm in repeating it: The layout drawing calls for a tiled graphic background that covers the entire page. In the new page layoutTest.html create a new style with the selector body, set background-image to the tile.jpg file found in the Graphics folder, and set the background-color set to #FFFFFF (see Figure 14.4). Note that you want to

FIGURE 14.4
Change the body style to add a tiled background that repeats throughout the page.

create a new body style even though the CSS reset already has one. Always leave the CSS reset code alone.

2. The content of the page hovers in the middle of the page with a specific width. Center the content by setting the #wrapper ID margin-left and margin-right attributes to auto. Set the width attribute to 810px (see Figure 14.5).

The design calls for a background image that spills outside of the edges of the wrapper. This is a popular effect that is heavily used in blog design (my blog found at http://www.designisphilosophy.com uses this technique), and I have

FIGURE 14.5
It's often just as easy to make quick changes to the styles in a CSS page by editing the code directly. Here the width attribute in the #wrapper style is set using IntelliSense.

gotten many requests for instructions on how to make it. The premise is that you have a background graphic that spills beyond the outer-left and right edges of the content yet moves with the content when the window is resized. This is achieved using the CSS attribute min-width that is not available in the New and Modify Style dialog.

3. To achieve the hovering centered background image effect, first import the corkboard.png file from the lesson files for this hour and place it in the Graphics folder. In Code view of the layout.css file, find the #centeredBG style and set the background-image attribute to the corkboard.png file with the help of IntelliSense. Set background-repeat to none and background-position to center top. Now the corkboard image hovers in the center of the screen behind the content even when the window is resized. Unfortunately, it insists on hovering in the center also when the window is smaller than the width of the image, which will ruin the effect. To prevent this, set min-width to the exact width of the image, in this case 1000px (see Figure 14.6). This tells the browser that the #centeredBG box should not be reduced to a width less than 1,000 pixels.

4. The header of the page has to be set to a fixed height to ensure that the relationship between the header and the main content remains the same regardless of the size of the main content. To do this, set the #header style height to 285px.

5. On the drawing, the #mainMenu ID is along the bottom and aligned to the left of the #header box. To make this happen, you need to make some changes to

FIGURE 14.6
Although the New and Modify Style dialogs are extensive, they do not cover every CSS attribute available. To curb this problem, those attributes not covered by the dialogs are still covered by IntelliSense.

```
67  #centeredBG {
68      background-image: url('Graphics/corkboard.png');
69      background-repeat: none;
70      background-position: center top;
71      min-width: 1000px;
72  }
```

the position attributes of both #header and #mainMenu. First change the position of the #header ID to relative. Then set the position attribute for the #mainMenu ID to absolute and the bottom and left attributes (under the Position category in the Modify Style dialog) to 0px.

As you can see from Figure 14.7, you now have the basic framework for the page as it appears in the drawing. And all this was done using only CSS, which means the HTML markup has not changed.

FIGURE 14.7
When everything is set correctly, the #mainMenu ID should hover to the lower-right side of the #header box, independent of the remaining content.

In step 4, you used the position attribute to force the mainMenu div down into the left corner of the header. This gives you a first glimpse of the powerful and often misunderstood CSS tool called positioning. Understanding positioning means you have the power to control your content in ways you could never do before.

Understanding Positioning

In the last part of the preceding example, you used the position attribute to place a div in the lower-left corner of another div. This is a nice segue into the confusing and often misunderstood issue of positioning in CSS.

If you open the Modify Style dialog for any of the current styles, classes, or IDs, you see that the position attribute (found under the Position category) has five options: absolute, fixed, relative, static, and inherit (see Figure 14.8). The physical position of

FIGURE 14.8
You can set the position attribute found under the Position category in the New and Modify Style dialog to absolute, fixed, relative, static, or inherit.

any object in a page depends on what this attribute is set to in the current style and whatever style that wraps it.

position: absolute;

The easiest way to explain an element with an absolute position is to think of it as an image (or any other object) pasted onto a page and ignore the rest of the content. The physical placement of an element with an absolute position is decided by setting the pixel value of its distance from the nearest positioned container with the top, right, bottom, and left attributes. In other words, an object with absolute position that has a top value of 20px and a left value of 30px appears exactly 20 pixels from the top and 30 pixels to the left of the edge of the page or the closest container box that has a position value other than static. Setting an object's position attribute to absolute removes it from the flow of the page. That means unless you pay close attention, you might accidentally place objects with absolute positions directly on top of other content.

In the layoutTest.html page, the #menu div has an absolute position zero pixels from the bottom and zero pixels from the right side of the #header div because the #header position is set to relative. If you change the #header position attribute to static, the #menu div is positioned absolutely in relation to the nearest parent with a position other than static, in this case the body, which means it aligns itself with the edge of the page and ends up in the lower-right portion of the window.

If you set the position attribute of a style, class, or ID to absolute without setting values for top, right, bottom, and left, the object appears in the default upper-left corner position (see Figure 14.9).

FIGURE 14.9
In this example, the image style has its position attribute set to absolute. Because the containing div has its position set to relative, the position of the image is relative to this div rather than to the page as a whole.

position: fixed;

Fixed positioning works similarly to absolute positioning except that where the physical position of an object with an absolute position can relate to other positioned objects, the physical position of a fixed object is always based solely on the outer edges of the page as a whole (see Figure 14.10).

Watch Out!

The first version of Microsoft Internet Explorer to support the fixed value for the position attribute was Internet Explorer 7. Older versions of Internet Explorer do not understand the value, and your layout will not work properly in them.

FIGURE 14.10
In this example, the image style has the position attribute set to fixed. Unlike Figure 14.9, the positioning of the image in this page is relative to the page as a whole.

position: relative;

The easiest way to explain relative positioning is to imagine that you cut an image out of a printed page and repositioned it somewhere else on the page. Because you cut out the image from the page, there is a hole where it was, and the image covers content wherever you glue it.

Placement of an object with a relative position is in relation to its original location in the flow of the page. As an example, that means an image with its `position` attribute set to relative and its bottom attribute set to 20px appears 20 pixels above its normal location where it was originally inserted, and the space it would have occupied remains empty (see Figure 14.11).

FIGURE 14.11
In this example, the image style has its position attribute set to relative. The space the image would normally occupy is left empty, but the image is shifted to the right and down because of the top and left values.

position: static;

Static is the default setting for any style. Setting an object's `position` attribute to static places the object in the flow as normal. The object is unaffected by the `top`, `right`, `bottom`, and `left` attributes (see Figure 14.12).

FIGURE 14.12
In this example, the image style has its position attribute set to static. The image lines up with the rest of the text and is not displaced despite the top and left attribute values being the same as in Figures 14.8, 14.9, and 14.10.

position: inherit

If you look closely, you'll see that the value inherit appears in almost every drop-down menu when you create CSS. Inherit literally means that the current elements inherits this style from whatever elements are directly above it in the cascade.

Applying the Framework to Existing Pages

Now that you have created the framework for the myKipple site in a different style sheet from the one you were working on before, you need to alter the existing markup files and style sheet. Because default.html is the home page, it is a good place to start. Before you go any further, remove the big sticker graphic in the header, and replace it with the text **Welcome to MyKipple.com**.

The first step is to remove some of the styles you created in Hour 13 to avoid the new styles clashing with the old ones. Editing style sheets in Expression Web 3 is easy. You can delete these styles directly from the Manage Styles panel by highlighting them and pressing the Delete button on your keyboard or by right-clicking and selecting Delete from the context menu. Delete the body style and the #wrapper style.

With the old styles removed, it is time to apply the new ones. To do this, you need to attach the new layout.css style sheet to the page. As you previously learned, you do this by clicking the Attach Style Sheet button in the Apply and Manage Styles task panes. Select the layout.css file with the Browse button and be sure to enable the Attach to All HTML Pages option.

With the new style sheet attached, you see a dramatic change in how the page appears in Design view. That is because the new style sheet contains the CSS reset that removes all default styling from the content (see Figure 14.13). Furthermore,

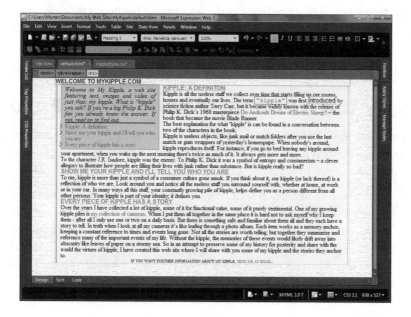

FIGURE 14.13
After applying the CSS reset to your page, all the content that has not been styled will be crammed together. It might look weird, but this is actually what you want because it means you now have a clean slate to work with.

when you attach a second style sheet, you insert it below the first one in the HTML code, and this means it gets more weight or importance in the style cascade. The CSS reset affects all default selectors, but in the kippleStyles.css file, you have already styled several of these, so you want your old styles to have more weight. To give kippleStyles.css more weight than layout.css, simply change the order of the two styles as they appear in the HTML code so that layout.css is first and kippleStyles.css is second. After the change, the two lines of code directly before the </head> end tag should read:

```
<link href="layout.css" rel="stylesheet" type="text/css" />
<link href="kippleStyles.css" rel="stylesheet" type="text/css" />
```

If you preview the page in your browser at this point, you notice three things: First, the header graphic you spent so much time aligning earlier is nowhere to be seen. Second, all the text is bunched together; that is, there is no breathing room between the paragraphs, headings, and blockquotes except for the h2 headings. This might look like a big problem, but it is exactly what you want: If the different selector boxes are stacked directly on top of one another (meaning there is no breathing room between the paragraphs, headings, and so on), the browser is not making any assumptions about your styles if you do not provide a style. In other words, your page looks the same in all browsers. Third, the text has reverted back to the Times New Roman font. This is because you deleted the old body styles that contained the font-family definition for the entire page. This last one is the easiest one to fix, so let's do it before you get into the meat of things: Find the second body style in the layout.css style sheet (the one that has the background tile image defined), open the Modify Style dialog, and set font-family to Arial, Helvetica, sans-serif. Click OK to apply the change, and the font switches back to Arial.

Apply the New Framework to the Page

Now that you have attached the new style sheet, you can apply the new framework to the page. Most of it is already there because you added it in Hour 13, but there are elements that are still missing:

1. With default.html open in Split view, find the <body> tag in the Code area, and create a new line directly below it before the #wrapper div. On the new line, insert a new div with the ID #centeredBG. When you close the tag, IntelliSense automatically inserts an end </div> tag. Cut it out as before, scroll to the bottom of the code page where the #mainContent and #wrapper divs are being closed, create a new line directly over the </body> end tag, and paste the </div> end tag in giving it the comment <!-- END #centeredBG -->.

2. Find the <h1> tag that contains the heading you previously inserted. Create a new line directly above it, and insert a new div with the ID #header. Place the closing </div> tag on a new line directly after the </h1> tag.

Save and preview the page in your browser, and you see that the page now has the corkboard background off the top and the header has plenty of space before the page content begins (see Figure 14.14).

FIGURE 14.14
With the framework applied, the page has started to look like the drawing in Figure 14.1.

Looking back on the drawing in Figure 14.1, there is still one element that has not been added to the page: the footer. Adding this element is done in the exact same way as before: Scroll to the bottom of the page and find the paragraph that starts with "If you want further information...." Place your cursor anywhere on the line and look at it in Code view. You see that the <p> tag is littered with style code. Remove all the style code, leaving only the clean <p> tag. Create a new line directly over it and insert a new div with the ID #footer. Place the closing </div> tag directly after the closing </p> tag before the closing tag for the #mainContent ID. Find the #footer style in the layout.css file, and set the font-variant to small-caps and font-size to 0.8em. To align the text to the center, go to Block and set text-align to center. Click OK to save the new style and the footer text should look exactly as it did before; however, this time it is styled from the layout.css style sheet rather than an inline style.

Now you have a decision to make. Although the drawing in Figure 14.1 calls for the header of the page to have plain text, you can choose to replace the plain text with the sticker image you imported earlier. I give you this option because although it is becoming more popular to use plain text for headings, the vast majority of sites designed these days use fancy images and graphics for the site name and headings. The site works the same either way, so I leave it up to you to decide what kind of heading you want. That said you should still learn how to insert and use images as headers, so even if you want to keep the site name as plain text, do the exercise below anyway, and then you can revert back later.

Adding a Header Image and a Menu

In the sketch of the page layout (refer to Figure 14.1), the header features a large MyKipple.com sticker and a menu. These are important elements of any website—the header image (or site name) provides an intuitive link back to the home page and the main menu. In effect, the header functions as a primary navigational tool for the visitor.

1. First, remove the <h1> tag along with the heading inside it. Because the header contains the sticker, there is no need to have the text there as well. The Images folder contains the image file MyKippleSticker.png that you created earlier. Click and drag the image into the header in Design view, and give it the alternative text Welcome to MyKipple.com.

2. When inserted, the image has both padding and a one-pixel gray border (see Figure 14.15). This is because it is being styled by the img style you created in a

FIGURE 14.15
When inserted, the kippleSticker.png image has both a border and padding applied by the img style created in an earlier hour.

previous hour. To ensure that the img style applies only to images within the #mainContent area, use the Manage Styles task pane to change the Selector Name of the img style to #mainContent img. When you change the style name, the kippleSticker.png changes position to hug the upper-left corner of the #header box.

3. To line up the sticker image with the background, you have to create a new style. Click the New Style button in the Manage Styles task pane, and set the Selector Name to #header img. This style applies only to images within the #header ID. Change the Define In field to Existing Style Sheet, and select kippleStyles.css from the drop-down menu. Under the Box category, set padding-top to 90px. Click OK to apply the style. The top of the header image now lines up with the background image (see Figure 14.16).

FIGURE 14.16
With the new #header img style applied, the image lines up with the background image.

4. Right now the sticker is too big. To change, right-click on the picture and select Picture Properties from the pop-up menu or double-click on the picture to open the same dialog. In the Picture Properties dialog, go to the Appearance tab, and change the Height to 130px making sure that the Keep aspect ratio box is checked. Click OK to apply the change, and use the Picture Actions button that appears on the bottom of the picture to Resample the picture to match size.

5. To make the image link back to the home page, right-click it again, select Hyperlink from the pop-up menu, and set the hyperlink to the default.html page and the Screen Tip to Home.

With the new image heading inserted and formatted, save and preview the page. Expression Web 3 asks you if you want to save the attached files because you changed both the style sheets and the kipple sticker file. When previewed in a browser, the page should now look like Figure 14.17.

FIGURE 14.17
With the new
#header img
style applied, the
image lines up
with the back-
ground image.

Summary

When it comes to communicating a message with visual media, whether printed or on screen, design and layout are paramount. If the content doesn't look inviting, no one will give it a second look. Nowhere is this truer than when it comes to the Web. With the millions upon millions of websites out there, your site has to stand out if it is to generate an audience. To do that, it needs to have a solid and easy-to-understand layout, and it has to look the same no matter who is viewing it.

In this hour, you learned to use CSS to create layouts. By using CSS, you are separating the layout information from the content information and thereby making it easier for everyone to access the information you are communicating through your site. You learned how to use the prepackaged CSS layouts as a starting point to create a proper framework to house all your content, and you learned how to apply this framework to existing pages using a variety of methods in Code view and Design view.

To ensure that your page looks the same across all browsers, it is necessary to remove all assumptions that a browser might make about the styling of your content. You can achieve this by inserting a CSS reset in your style sheet. This code resets all the styles on the page so that you have a clean slate to start with. And because of the cascade, applying a CSS reset in the top of your CSS file means you can restyle all the content further down in the cascade to get the results you want.

CSS positioning is a topic that can be confusing even to seasoned professionals. This hour presented a thorough walkthrough of what the four different positioning values (absolute, fixed, relative, and static) mean and how they work. Understanding these values, and how to use them, means you can easily create advanced layouts that go outside the norm.

In the next hour, you learn about buttons and how to use Expression Web 3's built-in functions Expression Web 3 to create advanced buttons.

Q&A

Q. *When I create a new CSS layout, all I get is a series of empty boxes. Why is that?*

A. The prepackaged CSS layouts in Expression Web 3 are little more than empty divs with some basic positioning in them. The intention is to give the user a clean slate to work with, but in reality there is little difference between using the prepackaged layouts and creating the layouts from scratch. The one advantage of using the layouts is that all the divs have proper names and positions, so you don't have to keep tabs on absolutely everything.

Q. *When I added the new layout.css style sheet, I noticed that there are now many different versions of the styles, such as* body *and* p. *Isn't that a problem?*

A. The new style sheet includes the CSS reset, which has all the available selectors listed and set to 0. Further down in the style sheet and in the kippleStyles.css style sheet, the same selectors are styled a second and sometimes even a third time. This isn't a problem as much as a deliberate exploitation of the cascade: You reset the styles to 0 at the start and then create new styles that apply fresh styles further down the line. This piling of styles is a good illustration of how the cascade works and is something you should take note of for future reference: The farther down in the style sheet a style is, the more weight or importance it has.

Workshop

The Workshop has quiz questions and exercises to help you put to use what you have just learned. If you get stuck, the answers to the quiz questions are in the next section. But try to answer them first. Otherwise you'll be cheating yourself.

Quiz

1. What is the benefit of using CSS to create page layouts?

2. What is a CSS reset and why should you always use it?

3. Given an image placed in the middle of a block of text, briefly describe what happens to the image when its position is set to absolute, fixed, relative, and static.

Answers

1. CSS layouts have many benefits, but the most important one is that they enable you to completely change the layout of multiple pages without actually changing the pages themselves. You can also create multiple layouts visitors can choose from to suit their preference without cluttering the markup. Finally you can "port" a good layout to a new page easily by attaching the existing style sheet to the new page and just adding some classes and IDs to the `<div>`s in the new page.

2. A CSS reset is a block of CSS code that sets all the different styles, browsers usually make assumptions about to zero. By applying it to your designs, you ensure that different browsers don't start changing your designs or layouts on a whim just because the browser designer thinks all paragraphs should have a 15px top padding for instance.

3. With absolute positioning, the image is taken out of the flow of the page and appears in the top-left corner of the page or whatever containing element has a positioning other than static. With fixed positioning, the image is taken out of the flow of the page and appears in the top-left corner of the page no matter what. With relative positioning, the area the image takes up remains in the flow of the page, and the image itself appears in a set position relative to its original location. With no other values attached, it appears where it was placed. Static positioning is the default position, and the image appears in the flow of the text where it was placed.

Exercise

The new layout.css style sheet includes a CSS reset that removes all the regular styling from the content within your page. As a result most of, if not all, the text is crammed together. Create and modify styles to space out the text and make it more approachable by using what you learned in this and previous hours. In particular, create or modify the styles for #content p, #content ul, and #content blockquote.

Using what you learned about positioning, try to change the location of different content in the page. For example, see whether you can move the menu in the header to the upper-right corner of the page.

HOUR 15

Buttons, Buttons, Buttons

What You'll Learn in This Hour:

▶ How to create buttons using Expression Web 3's Interactive Buttons feature

▶ How to create simple box buttons using CSS

▶ How to make the simple box buttons more advanced by using background images

▶ How to use the sliding doors technique to use one background image for multiple button stages

▶ How to hide the button text from the browser without removing it entirely

Introduction

What makes a website different from all other visual media is the ability to navigate through content with the use of hyperlinks. But plain text hyperlinks are not always the best option. If you want to showcase a particular link or if you create a menu, you need to turn those links into buttons.

There are many ways to create buttons, some easy and some more complicated. This hour explains how to use some button-making techniques and describes their advantages and disadvantages.

As before, accessibility is a primary focus of this chapter. In other words, if you strip away all the styles, graphics, and scripting, there should still be an understandable hyperlink left in the markup. Designers often ignore this aspect and that can, in some cases, prevent the visitor from navigating through a site when the images, Flash movies, or other elements don't load properly. But because making buttons accessible is easy, there is no good reason not to do it.

Buttons: A Brief Definition

What is a button in web terms? In the absolute basic form, a *button* is a clearly defined and contained visual object on a web page that functions as a hyperlink. This object can be plain text with a background, text with an image background—just a static image or an interactive or animated graphic element that changes with the mouse behaviors. A button differs from a hyperlink in that it is not merely a string of text but is some form of graphic element with a clearly defined active area.

Of course, as with all definitions, experts can question and dispute this one. For this book, however, this definition suffices.

Creating Interactive Buttons Using Expression Web 3

Expression Web 3 has a built-in feature that enables you to build advanced and modern-looking buttons without creating graphics or importing images from a different program. The Interactive Buttons feature works by creating several different images for the different button states that switch out depending on how the user interacts with the button. At the base of the image switching lies some custom JavaScript code. As with everything else in Expression Web 3, the code generated for the Interactive Buttons is standards-based and, as a result, the buttons look and work the same in all browsers as long as they support JavaScript. If the user turned off JavaScript or the browser is too old, the viewer sees only the inactive state of the button, but the links within it still work.

Make an Interactive Button

The Interactive Buttons function in Expression Web 3 enables to create advanced interactive buttons without ever leaving the program or importing graphics or images.

1. Create and open a new HTML page called buttons.html in Design view. Give it the h1 heading **Button Examples** and create the h2 subheading **Interactive Buttons**. Press Enter to create a new line underneath the subheading.

2. To create a new interactive button, open the Insert menu and scroll down to Interactive Button. Click the option to open the Interactive Buttons dialog.

3. The Interactive Buttons dialog has three main tabs: Button, Font, and Image. The first step in creating a new button is to select the look of the button from the Buttons menu. The different designs are grouped in categories such as

Border, Corporate, Glass, Jewel, and Metal, and each category has subcategories. Most of the designs feature text contained inside some form of box, but a few of them are icons with text next to them. Pick the one called Glass Rectangle 1.

4. Insert the text that you want to display on the button in the Text box and set the link manually, or use the Browse button to navigate to a page in the site you are working on or one on the web. For this example, give the button the text **Interactive Button** and link it back to the buttons.html page (see Figure 15.1).

FIGURE 15.1
Under the Button tab in the Interactive Buttons dialog, you can pick the design of your button, set the text to display on the button, and define the link to which it should point.

5. Under the Font tab you can control the font family, style, and size for the text inside the button. Because the button with the font will be converted to an image, you are not restricted by the web-safe fonts, and you can pick whatever font you have on your computer. Below the font, style, and size options, you can set the font color for each of the three main states of the button: original font color, hovered font color, and pressed font color. Set the original font color to gray, hovered front color to black, and pressed font color to silver. Below these options, you can set the horizontal and vertical alignment of the text in relation to the button. The Preview window lets you test the button in real-time to see the changes you have made (see Figure 15.2).

6. The last tab is Image. From here you can change the overall size of the button by using the Width and Height attributes. As long as the Maintain Proportions box is checked, the button retains its shape. Leave the Maintain Proportions box checked, and change the width of the Change the Size of the Button to 125px so that the text fits well within the button area (see Figure 15.3).

FIGURE 15.2
The Font tab gives you easy control of the text in your button.

FIGURE 15.3
From the Image tab, you can control the size, background color, and file type of the images created by the function.

Did you Know?

The horizontal and vertical dotted lines in the Preview window are guides to tell you whether your text is properly placed within the button. If the text spills over the lines, the button is too small or the text is too long. You can change the size of the button from the Image tab to make it fit the text.

7. Below the size settings, you can choose whether you want the program to create separate images for each of the three button states and whether these images should be preloaded by the browser when the page loads. By default Expression Web 3 creates three images: one for the button in its resting state, one for when the user hovers over it, and one for when the user clicks it. By unchecking one or more of these boxes, you can reduce the number of images created, and one of the remaining images displays in place of the missing image. If you turn off Create Hover Image, for example, the regular state image appears when the visitor hovers over the button. If you turn off Create Pressed Image, the hover image appears when the button is pressed. Leave the boxes checked.

Watch Out!

If you uncheck the Maintain proportions box and resize the button, the graphic elements stretch. This makes little difference in the case of square-cornered buttons, but if you work with circles or oval corners, unchecking this box makes the button look strange.

---

8. The final two options let you decide the background color and file type of the button images after export. If you leave the default option checked, you can pick a background color from the drop-down menu. If you want the button background to be transparent, you need to select the GIF option. When choosing this option, pay close attention to the Preview window to ensure that the outer borders of the button are not too jagged. Leave the background color as it is and click OK. The button is inserted into your page.

Did you Know?

The Interactive Buttons function goes through your existing page and finds all the colors you have used so far. These colors display in the color drop-down menus under Document Colors and help you keep the colors throughout your site consistent.

Saving and Editing Interactive Buttons

The interactive button you just created is now on your page, but if you look at your file tree in the Folder List task pane, you can see that no image files have been created. To finalize the process to create an interactive button, you need to save the page. This opens the Save Embedded Files dialog from which you can define where to save the new button images (see Figure 15.4).

After you save the files, they behave like any other image on the page, which means that even if you delete the button from your page, you do not delete the image files from your file tree.

As with the Photoshop Import feature, Expression Web 3 keeps track of the interactive buttons you create in your pages. This means that if at some point you want to make changes to the interactive buttons, you don't need to make new ones or open each image file individually. To edit an interactive button, all you have to do is right-click it while in Design view and select Button Properties from the context menu. This

FIGURE 15.4
When you save the page, you also save the images you created using the Interactive Buttons feature.

opens the Interactive Buttons dialog. From this dialog, any changes you make to a button are applied to the page when you click OK. When you save the page again, the new images overwrite the old ones.

Creating Buttons from Scratch Using CSS

Although the interactive buttons that Expression Web 3 creates are great, they don't always work with the design you envision. Designers often need to create their own buttons from scratch to achieve a particular look in their sites. Using the techniques you learned in previous hours, you can use Cascading Style Sheets (CSS) to make advanced buttons that both rival, and sometimes even outdo, the interactive buttons you just created.

Creating a Basic Box Button

When designers first started to focus on buttons as a navigational tool, they could rely on only basic functionality. The most basic button of all is a string of text with a colored box around it (see Figure 15.5).

Although you could use tables to make this type of button, the "proper" way is to build the button is through the use of CSS, like in this next tutorial:

1. In the same page as before, create a subheading and name it **CSS Buttons**. Under that heading, create a new paragraph with the text **Basic Box Button**.

2. Highlight the button text and make it a hyperlink pointing back to the current buttons.html page.

3. Click the New Style button and create a new class called `.basicBox`. In the Font category, set `font-family` to Arial, Helvetica, sans-serif, `font-size` to 0.8em,

FIGURE 15.5
The basic box button was the staple of web design for many years.

font-weight to bold, text-transform to uppercase, font-color to white (#FFFFFF), and check the None box under text-decoration to get rid of the line under the text.

4. Under Background, set background-color to a light blue (#99CCFF). Under Border, set border-style to solid for all, border-width to 2px for all, the border-top and border-left colors to a medium blue (#0F87FF), and the border-bottom, and border-right colors to a dark blue (#004F9D) (see Figure 15.6). This gives the button the appearance of popping out from the screen.

5. In the Box category, set padding to 5px for all four sides. Click OK to create the new class.

6. Select the button text you created, and use the Apply Styles task pane to apply the new class.

7. To make the button react when the user hovers the mouse over it, you also have to make a :hover pseudoclass with different styles. Because you want to retain most of the styles, the easiest way to make a new and similar class is to copy and paste the CSS code in Code view and give the new class the selector name **.basicBox:hover**. After doing this, you can open the new pseudoclass from the Apply Styles task pane using Modify Style and make changes to it.

8. With .basicBox:hover open in the Modify Style dialog, change font-color to black (#000000), and invert the border colors so that the lighter blue is on the right and bottom sides while the darker blue is on the top and left sides. This

FIGURE 15.6
Setting different colors for the top and left borders and bottom and right borders can create the illusion of the button hovering or being pushed into the page.

gives the appearance of the button being pressed down when it is hovered over. Click OK to apply the changes, and then save and test in your browser (see Figure 15.7).

FIGURE 15.7
The two button states as they appear next to one another.

Regular state　　　:hover state

As with all other styles, you can create separate styles for each pseudoclass for more advanced visual interaction with the button.

In this example the actual styling of the button came from applying a class to the <a> tag. But this is not the only way to create box buttons. You can easily group one or several buttons within a <div> or <span> class or ID, and create a styles instead. The result would be the same.

Creating an Advanced Box Button with Images

The basic box button might be easy to create, but it is also dull to look at. Although prevalent in the 1990s, you rarely see this type of button in modern web design. Fortunately you can easily modernize the look of the box button without much extra effort. The key is to replace the background color with a background image, as shown in Figure 15.8.

FIGURE 15.8
The basic box button gets a modern look by swapping out the background color for a background image. Button 2 is in the :hover state.

In this example, you use a different styling technique to apply the same style to multiple buttons:

1. Below the basic box button, create a new headline and name it **Advanced Box Button**. Underneath that, create an unordered list with three buttons: **Button 1**, **Button 2**, and **Button 3**. Make each list item into a hyperlink back to the current page.

2. Make a new class called **.advancedBox** by using the New Style dialog. Under the List category, set the list-style-type to none. Click OK to create the class and apply it to the <ul> tag using the Quick Tag Selector (see Figure 15.9).

FIGURE 15.9
The menu list is created and the .advancedBox style applied.

3. Import the images named blueButtonUp.gif and blueButtonOver.gif from the lesson files and save them in a new folder called buttonGraphics.

4. Make a new style and give it the selector name **.advancedBox a.** In the Font category, set `font-family` to Arial, Helvetica, sans-serif, `font-size` to 0.8em, `font-weight` to bold, and `text-transform` to uppercase, `font-color` to white (#FFFFFF). Check the None box under `text-decoration` to get rid of the line under the text.

5. In the Background category, set `background-image` to the blueButtonUp.gif image you just imported, and set `background-repeat` to no-repeat. Because the image is larger than the text and you want it to surround the text, go to the Box category and set `padding` to 13px on all sides. Click OK to apply the style.

6. In Design view, you can see that the new button background is applied, but the buttons are covering each other (see Figure 15.10). This is because the list items

FIGURE 15.10
The .advancedBox a style is applied to the new buttons, but they cover each other because the list item style has not been modified yet.

have not yet been styled, and the browser assumes that the list items are the height of the text without the padding.

To fix this problem create a new style with the selector name **.advancedBox li** and set the `padding-top` and `padding-bottom` attributes to 13px to match the link style you just created. Click OK to apply the new style, and the buttons no longer overlap.

7. To create a hover-over effect, create a new style with the selector name **.advancedBox a:hover**. Because the :hover pseudoclass inherits all the

styling from the main a class, all you need to do is change background-image to blueButtonOver.gif. Click OK, and then save and preview in your browser.

Now instead of the background color changing when the mouse hovers over the button, the background image swaps out. And because the background image is part of the a style, the entire image is clickable, not just the text itself.

The problem with this technique is that it requires two images to work. This might not seem like a big deal, but if the user is on a slow connection, the page is on a slow server, or if there is something else that slows the system down, the user might experience noticeable lag between hovering over the button and the new background image being loaded. One way around this problem is to preload the images using behaviors, but this requires JavaScript to work properly.

Create Text-Free Buttons with Sliding Doors

The problem of preloading content has become more prevalent with the emergence of blogs because many blogs have a lot of scripts running at the same time, and it is important to reduce the load on both the network and the computer as much as possible to make things work smoothly. A technique often referred to as *sliding doors* was developed to enable the designer to use one image file as two different backgrounds. This is done by creating a file that has two versions of the background, either on top of or to the side of one another. The name *sliding doors* refers to the action of literally sliding the background from one side to the other to display only half of the image at a time (see Figure 15.11).

FIGURE 15.11
The name sliding doors refers to the action of sliding the background image so that only half of it is visible depending on how the mouse interacts with the button.

You can use a similar technique to hide text content. As you have seen, the regular method of creating buttons requires there to be text superimposed on the background. If you don't want the text to appear, the quick answer is to simply swap out the text for an image and use it as a button. But if you do this, the link is not visible if the image doesn't load or the visitor uses a text-only browser. The way to solve this is to push the text out of the way so that only the background image appears. Another reason to use this technique is that designers often want to use custom fonts or font effects in their buttons. To do this and retain full accessibility, they need to hide the regular HTML text first. In this example, you create a button that uses the sliding doors technique and hides the text at the same time.

1. Import the file named slidingButtons.gif into the buttonGraphics folder from the lesson files. Under the three buttons you just created, add a new subheading and call it **Sliding Doors Button with Hidden Text**. Below it, add a paragraph with the text **Button** and make it into a hyperlink pointing back to the current page.

2. Make a new class called **.slider**. Create a span around the new button text using the Toolbox panel (make sure the <span> tags go on the outside of the <a> tags), and apply the .slider class to it using the Quick Tag Selector (see Figure 15.12).

FIGURE 15.12
The new button
text is wrapped
in a <span> tag
and the
.slider class
is applied.

3. Make a new style and give it the selector name **.slider a**. Because you are going to hide the text you don't need change any of the Font attributes. In the Background category, set background-image to slidingButtons.gif and background-repeat to no-repeat.

4. To create the sliding effect, you need to change the position of the background image and define the visible area within the page. The image has two buttons on it: The top one is for the regular state, and the bottom one is for the :hover state. Set the (x) background-position to 0px and the (y) background-position to 0px. This locks the image in place.

5. To define the visible area of the button, you need to first set the display attribute under the Layout category to Block to create an independent box in which to display the content and then change the size of the box under the Position category. The height of the image is 88px and because you will be displaying half of it at one time, the height attribute should therefore be 44px. To contain the active area of the button to the area of the image, set the width attribute to 92px, which is the width of the image. Click OK to apply the style, and the button appears in Design view, as shown in Figure 15.13.

FIGURE 15.13
After styling, the button appears as it should, but the text is still visible.

6. As you can see, the button looks the way it should, but the text is still visible. To hide the text, open the Modify Style dialog for the style, go to the Block category, and set the text-indent attribute to -9999px (see Figure 15.14). Click OK to save the change.

7. Finally create a new style with the selector name **.slider a:hover**. Because of the cascade, any pseudoclass inherits all the styling from its parent unless the style is changed. Therefore you need to make changes to only the

FIGURE 15.14
Setting the text-indent attribute to -9999px places the text of the button 9999 pixels to the left of the screen, making it invisible to the visitor.

background-position attributes, and the rest of the attributes will stay the same. Set (x) background-position to 0px and (y) background-position to -44px. This shifts the background image up 44 pixels, and the bottom half is shown in place of the top half. Click OK, and then save and preview in your browser.

Designers frequently use the sliding doors technique to create eye-catching rollovers without load times getting in the way. In this example, the background image only had two versions, but you could have an image with more instances. Likewise, you can place the images next to one another instead of on top of each other and change the (x) background-position value instead.

You can find more information and tutorials on how to use the sliding doors technique at the A List Apart website: www.alistapart.com.

Summary

Buttons are an integral part of a website, both as navigational tools and as design elements. Knowing how to make and when to use different styles of buttons makes your life easier as a designer and your sites easier to navigate for the visitors.

Buttons can be anything from simple colored boxes with text inside them to advanced image-based elements with different graphics for each state. The layout and design of the page, and what the designer wants out of it, drive the choice of what kind of button to use.

To simplify the process of creating interactive buttons, Expression Web 3 has a built-in Interactive Buttons function that lets you choose a design and set properties for a wide range of prepackaged buttons. In this hour, you learned how to create and customize these interactive buttons and insert them into your page. The major benefit of the interactive buttons is that even after inserting them in your page, you can always go back to the Interactive Buttons dialog and change the design and font attributes of the button without creating a new one. This high level of flexibility is great when you design pages on-the-fly and you're not sure what the end product will look like. The downside of interactive buttons is that they are limited in the button design.

If you want to move beyond the designs of the prepackaged interactive buttons, the best way to go is to create CSS buttons instead. The advantages of CSS buttons are that they are text-based and standards-compliant, and a visitor who uses a text-only browser can still see the hyperlinks within the buttons. In this hour, you learned how to create simple box-type buttons with interactive features using CSS. You also learned how to take these buttons to the next level by replacing the solid color backgrounds with images. Finally, you learned how to use the sliding doors technique to use one image as the base for multiple different button states by sliding it in the background to show different versions of the same button image.

Q&A

Q. *I inserted an interactive button in my page, but all I see is a small box with a red X in it. What is wrong?*

A. When you make an interactive button, Expression Web 3 creates a series of images to correspond to the different button states. If you are seeing a red X, the link to the image or images is broken, probably because you deleted the images accidentally, didn't save them when you saved the page before closing the application, or moved them to a different folder outside of Expression Web 3. To fix the problem, simply right-click the interactive button in Design view and select Button Properties from the context menu. From here, you can make changes to the button or, if you just want to reestablish the images, simply click OK, and the button shows up as it is supposed to.

Q. *I created a second copy of the sliding doors button, but it shows up underneath the first one no matter what I do. Why can't I make these buttons show up next to each other?*

A. Although sliding doors buttons can easily be lined up next to one another, the one you made in this example cannot do so without putting each of the buttons in a separate table cell. The reason for this has to do with the hiding of the button text, not the sliding doors function.

Workshop

The Workshop has quiz questions and exercises to help you put to use what you just learned. If you get stuck, the answers to the quiz questions are in the next section. But try to answer them first. Otherwise you'll be cheating yourself.

Quiz

1. What is the advantage of using Interactive Buttons generated by Expression Web 3?

2. When creating the basic and advanced box buttons, do you need to create separate styles for each of the buttons?

Answers

1. The Interactive Buttons created by Expression Web 3 are accompanied by macros that help the application remember its settings. That means you can completely change the look and functionality of the buttons from the Interactive Button Properties dialog even after they have been inserted.

2. No, not unless you want to. The idea of using CSS to create box buttons is that you can apply the same styling and background (either color or image) to multiple buttons with one set of styles. That way you can make quick changes to multiple buttons throughout your site by changing only a few styles rather than having to change each individual button separately. You can, however, make individualized buttons with individual backgrounds or styles by wrapping each button instance in a <span> tag.

Exercise

Using the Interactive Buttons feature, create a series of new buttons with different designs and layouts. After inserting them, pick one design you like and change all the buttons to that look by changing their button properties.

To give the visitor a visual cue that the button has been pressed before, make styles for the :active and :visited pseudoclasses for all the different CSS buttons you created. The :active style usually has a bold appearance (bright colors and dark font), whereas the :visited pseudoclass is usually more muted than the other styles.

Using Behaviors

What You'll Learn in This Hour:

▶ How to apply behaviors to elements in your site
▶ How to edit existing behaviors
▶ How to change the events that trigger behaviors
▶ What the different behaviors in Expression Web 3 are and how they work

Introduction

Hypertext Markup Language (HTML) and Cascading Style Sheets (CSS) are powerful tools that can take you a long way to making a great website. But for all the virtues of those tools, many tasks are impossible or far too cumbersome to do using them alone. To help simplify some of these tasks, Expression Web 3 comes complete with a set of behaviors to insert into your pages. *Behaviors* are small pieces of JavaScript that, when inserted, perform actions within the page and give the visitor a more powerful interactive experience.

Behaviors: An Introduction

The behaviors in Expression Web 3 can be accessed from the Behaviors panel, which when selected from the Panels menu on the toolbar, opens in the lower-right corner of the workspace next to the Apply and Manage Styles panels (see Figure 16.1).

When you insert a behavior into your page, you are actually adding a block of JavaScript code to it. *JavaScript* is a basic script language that enables you to perform many tasks that are not available or are otherwise hard to achieve using HTML and CSS alone.

FIGURE 16.1
The Behaviors
panel docs to
the bottom-right
panel when it is
opened.

Boiled down to its basic components, a behavior consists of two elements: an event and an action. An *event* is an interaction, usually performed by the user, which tells the browser that something happened and asks it to respond by running a script. Events are standardized code segments that, in most cases, describe themselves pretty well. Here are some examples:

- `onclick`—When the object is clicked

- `ondblclick`—When the object is double-clicked

- `onload`—When the object is loaded by the browser

- `onmousedown`—When the mouse button is pressed

- `onmouseover`—When the mouse pointer is over the object

When triggered, an event sends a set of predefined arguments to the browser that it passes on to the action. In short, the event describes what needs to happen for the action to trigger.

An *action* is a JavaScript function (tiny program) that executes when the corresponding event occurs. The action receives the arguments from the event, and the script performs the programmed task with these arguments.

Creating a Swap-Image Behavior

The easiest way to understand how a behavior works is to see it in action. So, before you immerse yourself in all the different behaviors available, you apply a simple behavior to an image:

1. Create and open a new HTML page called behaviors.html in Design view.

2. From the buttonGraphics folder, drag and drop the blueButtonUp.gif file into the page. Give it the alternative text **Behavior button**.

3. Click the image to select it, and click the Insert button in the Behaviors panel to open the Behaviors menu (see Figure 16.2).

FIGURE 16.2
Clicking the Insert button in the Behaviors panel opens a menu with all the available behaviors.

4. Select the Swap Image behavior from the menu. This opens the Swap Images dialog.

5. In the Swap Images dialog, click the Browse button and select the blueButtonOver.gif image. Click OK and the image location now appears in the Swap Image URL column. Leave Preload Images checked and check Restore on Mouseout Event as well. Click OK to apply the new behavior (see Figure 16.3).

FIGURE 16.3
The Swap Image URL is set, and the Preload Images and Restore on Mouseout Event options are checked.

After clicking OK, you see that there are now two behaviors visible in the Behaviors panel. The first one has the event onmouseout and the action Swap Image Restore, whereas the other has the event onmouseover and the action Swap Images (see Figure 16.4).

FIGURE 16.4
After you add a behavior to an object on the page, it appears in the Behaviors panel when you select the object.

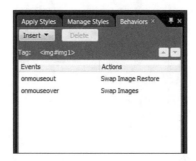

If you click anywhere else in the page, you see that a different behavior shows up with the event onload and the action Preload Images. To see what the combination of these three behaviors does, save and preload the page in your browser. When you hover your mouse over the image (the onmouseover event), it is swapped for the other image you defined (the Swap Images action). When you move your mouse away from the image (the onmouseout event), the original image is restored (the Swap Image Restore action). The third behavior is triggered when the page loads (the onload event) and preloads the second image into the browser memory so that it is readily available when it is needed (the Preload Images action).

Modifying Behaviors

Each of the three behaviors you inserted into the page has three components: the event, the action, and the variable. To change the event, hover over the event name in the Behaviors panel and click the drop-down arrow. This opens a full menu of all available events that you can choose from (see Figure 16.5).

To change the variables of a behavior, double-click the behavior in the Behaviors panel and the dialog for that behavior opens.

The only thing you can't do to a behavior is change its action. To do that, you have to add a new behavior to the object and delete the old one, if necessary.

Experienced designers and people familiar with JavaScript can make modifications of the different behaviors in Code view. Although this book does not cover the

FIGURE 16.5
After applying a behavior, you can change the event by opening the Event sub-menu from the drop-down arrow.

modification of JavaScript in Code view, it is worth your time to look under the hood to understand how exactly behaviors work.

If you click the image you inserted into the page and switch to Split view, you see that the image code is much longer than what you have seen before:

```
<img id="img1" alt="Behavior button" height="44"
onmouseout="FP_swapImgRestore()"
onmouseover="FP_swapImg(1,1,/*id*/'img1',/*url*/
'buttonGraphics/blueButtonOver.gif')"
src="buttonGraphics/blueButtonUp.gif" width="92" /></p>
```

In addition to familiar components such as id, alt, src, height, and width, the image now has a series of new code elements attached. Those new code elements are the behavior events. Let's take a closer look at the onmouseover event:

```
onmouseover="FP_swapImg(1,1,/*id*/'img1',/*url*/
'buttonGraphics/blueButtonOver.gif')"
```

The first part of this code is the event itself. The next part, FP_swapImg, is the name of the action or function the event is triggering. Every JavaScript function has a name and a set of arguments contained within parentheses and separated by commas. In this case the variables are 1, 1, 'img1', 'buttonGraphics/blueButtonOver.gif', and they tell the script what image to swap out (img1) and what image to put in its place (buttonGraphics/blueButtonOver.gif).

The actual action or function is in the head of the page (see Figure 16.6):

```
function FP_swapImg() {//v1.0
var doc=document,args=arguments,elm,n; doc.$imgSwaps=new Array();
for(n=2; n<args.length; n+=2) { elm=FP_getObjectByID(args[n]); if(elm) {
doc.$imgSwaps[doc.$imgSwaps.length]=elm;

 elm.$src=elm.src; elm.src=args[n+1]; } }
}
```

FIGURE 16.6
When you attach behaviors to objects in the page, you also add small programs called functions into the head of the page.

This is highly technical JavaScript code, and you do not need to understand what it means and how it works. What you can do, however, is examine the sequence of events: When the page loads in the browser, the image on the page loads as normal, and the browser loads a second image into memory as per the onload event. When the visitor moves the mouse over the image, the onmouseover event triggers the FP_swapImg action and sends it the arguments img and buttonGraphics/blueButtonOver.gif. The action runs the tiny program with these arguments and replaces the image. When the visitor moves the mouse off the image, the onmouseout event triggers the FP_swapImageRestore action. This action has no arguments because it just restores the old image.

To put this example into context, the interactive button you created in Hour 15, "Buttons, Buttons, Buttons," used the same events and actions along with some additional ones to achieve its hover and click effects.

The Many Behaviors of Expression Web 3

The preceding example introduced you to the Preload Images, Swap Image, and Swap Image Restore behaviors. Those are just three of a series of behaviors you can use to increase interactivity for your visitors. To get the full use out of the program, you should know each behavior and what it does.

Call Script

The Call Script behavior calls a script that is not featured in the prepackaged behaviors in Expression Web 3. To put it simply, Call Script is a behavior where you define the action. When you apply Call Script to an object, a dialog opens asking you for the JavaScript/JScript code (see Figure 16.7). This behavior is for advanced users with previous knowledge of JavaScript.

FIGURE 16.7
The Call Script dialog.

Change Property

The Change Property behavior lets you change the styling properties of the object to which it is applied. These properties include Font, Position, Borders and Shading, and Visibility.

1. Below the image you previously inserted, write a couple of lines of text in a new paragraph. With the cursor inside the text, apply the Change Property behavior by clicking the Insert button in the Behaviors panel and selecting Change Property. This opens the Change Property dialog (see Figure 16.8).

FIGURE 16.8
The Change Property dialog.

2. In the Change Property dialog, you can choose whether you want to change the properties of the current element or selected element. The Selected Element option lets you pick any of the defined elements within the page. Leave Current Element checked.

3. For this exercise you want to create a box with a gray background around the paragraph when the visitor hovers over it. Click Borders to open the Borders and Shading dialog. From here you can pick the border style and shading (background color). Under the Borders tab, set the Setting to Box and leave everything else as it is (see Figure 16.9). Under the Shading tab, set the Background Color to Silver (see Figure 16.10). Click OK.

FIGURE 16.9
The Borders tab lets you set the border style and color.

Did you Know?

The Borders and Shading options under the Change Property dialog can be confusing because the names and functionality differ from the Add and Modify Style dialogs. (In fact they look more like the Borders and Shading dialogs from Microsoft Word.) Despite this apparent difference, the functions within the two dialogs are the same as the ones in the Add and Modify Style dialogs, and the output is the same as if you were to style the element with CSS.

4. The dialog now lists the style changes you made; as you can see from Figure 16.11, they are CSS code. Make further changes if you like using the other functions. When you are done, check the Restore on Onmouseout Event box and click OK to apply the behavior.

FIGURE 16.10
The Shading tab lets you set the background color or a background image.

FIGURE 16.11
The Change Property dialog lists the styling changes as CSS code.

When you save and test the page in your browser, you see that when you hover over the paragraph, a black border and silver background appear behind it just as if you created a :hover pseudostyle in CSS.

Should I Use CSS or Behaviors?

The preceding examples raise this question: If I can apply both CSS and behaviors to achieve the same result, which one do I use and why? Although CSS and behaviors can perform many of the same tasks, there are different reasons to use (or not use) them. For instance, CSS is a great tool for layout, especially if you have a certain style you are going to use many times throughout your site. But when one particular element requires a certain style or behavior, using behaviors can be the better choice because they leave the arguments attached to the element rather than in the style code. For instance, if you create a series of image-based buttons that all require different images, creating separate styles for every button is cumbersome and create a lot of style code. One way to circumvent this is by creating an overall style for the buttons and inline styles for each of the backgrounds. But that still requires a lot of specialized styling. In contrast, applying behaviors to achieve the same result requires only one function per behavior in the head of the page and the arguments will be attached to each element.

A caveat: Although JavaScript is prevalent throughout the Web, not everyone supports it. In particular, some people and companies block JavaScript in their browsers to prevent malicious scripts from attacking their computers. For those users, and on computers that do not have Java installed, behaviors will not work.

Change Property Restore

As its name suggests, the Change Property Restore behavior restores the property changed by the Change Property behavior to what it was before the behavior was applied. When you apply the Change Property behavior, you have the option to also automatically apply the Change Property Restore behavior from within the dialog, as you saw in the earlier example.

Check Browser

The Check Browser behavior checks what browser the visitor uses and redirects the visitor to a specific page based on this information. This behavior is useful if you have certain scripts or styles within your page that you know will not show up correctly in a particular browser. Applying this behavior, you can redirect users with this browser to an alternative page that doesn't contain this script.

The Check Browser behavior can detect multiple versions of the following browsers:

- ▶ Microsoft Internet Explorer
- ▶ Netscape Navigator
- ▶ Opera
- ▶ AOL
- ▶ WebTV

▶ AOLTV

▶ HotJava

> Despite the popularity of the Mozilla Firefox browser and the discontinuation of Netscape Navigator, the browser selection lists the latter. Firefox and Navigator are always grouped together due to similar signatures, so if you want to target Firefox, you have to select Netscape Navigator.

Did you Know?

In this example, you add the Check Browser behavior to the button you previously inserted:

1. Select the button you previously inserted, and click Insert in the Behaviors panel to open the Behaviors menu. Select Check Browser from the menu. This opens the Check Browser dialog (see Figure 16.12).

FIGURE 16.12
The Check Browser dialog.

2. In the If the Current Browser Type Is drop-down menu, select Microsoft Internet Explorer. Leave the Version option set to Any. Check the Go to URL box and set the target page to http://www.getfirefox.com. Check the box under Otherwise; for all other browsers, go to and set the target page to http://expression.microsoft.com (see Figure 16.13).

FIGURE 16.13
The Check Browser dialog lets you specify a particular browser and set a different target page for that browser.

3. Click OK to apply the new behavior. The Check Browser behavior now shows up in the list in the Behaviors panel above the two you previously created. Save the

page and test it in your browser. If you click the button while in Internet Explorer, you will be taken to the Mozilla Firefox download page. If you do the same in any other browser, you will be taken to the Microsoft Expression website.

> This behavior is great if you have a web page that you know will not display correctly in certain browsers and you want to redirect these browsers to a different page. However, because it is JavaScript based, it loads a bit slower than the rest of the page. This means that, depending on the visitor's computer and connection speed, parts of the page could already be loaded before the behavior redirects the browser. To avoid this problem, designers often build a separate front page that contains only this behavior so that the visitor doesn't get a flash of a broken page before the browser loads the modified one.

Check Plug-In

The Check Plug-In behavior works in much the same way as the Check Browser behavior, except that it checks for installed plug-ins instead of browsers. This behavior is extremely useful if your page features content that requires a particular plug-in to function properly. You have probably encountered this behavior in the past because designers frequently use it to test whether a browser has either the Flash or the Shockwave plug-in.

The Check plug-in behavior can check whether your browser has the following plug-ins installed:

▶ Flash

▶ QuickTime

▶ RealPlayer

▶ Shockwave

▶ Windows Media Player

Bizarrely, it does not give you the option to check whether the browser has the Microsoft Silverlight plug-in installed.

As with the Check Browser behavior, you can select to redirect the browser based on whether it has a particular plug-in installed. In this example, you make a button that points to the popular video-sharing website YouTube. If a user's browser does not have the Flash plug-in installed, she cannot view videos on YouTube, so redirect her to the Flash plug-in download site instead.

1. Select the button you previously inserted, and press Ctrl+C on your keyboard to copy it. Create a new paragraph on the page, and press Ctrl+V to paste the button in the new location.

2. With the new button selected, click the Check Browser behavior in the Behaviors panel to highlight it and delete it by clicking the Delete button in the panel, as shown in Figure 16.14. (Pressing the Delete button on your keyboard

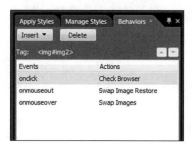

FIGURE 16.14
When you select a behavior in the Behaviors panel, you can delete it from the element by clicking the Delete button. Doing so affects only the current element.

also deletes the button, not the behavior.) Doing so deletes the behavior from only the selected element and not the other button.

3. With the new button still selected, click Insert and select Check Plug-In to open the Check Plug-In dialog.

4. In the If the Current Plug-In Is menu, choose Flash. The wording is somewhat strange, but it means "if the current plug-in is installed." Check the box below and set the target page to http://www.youtube.com. Check the Otherwise, for All Other Plug-Ins box, and set the target page to http://www.adobe.com/go/ EN_US-H-GET-FLASH (see Figure 16.15).

FIGURE 16.15
The Check Plug-In dialog lets you pick a particular plug-in and set the target of the browser to different pages depending on whether the user's browser has the plug-in installed.

Go to URL

The Go to URL behavior does exactly what it says: If the behavior is applied, the browser goes to the specified URL. In other words, it is a JavaScript method of creating hyperlinks. You can use this behavior with other behaviors if you want to make buttons and so forth. When you apply the Go to URL behavior to an element, the Go to URL dialog opens, as shown in Figure 16.16, and you insert the target address.

FIGURE 16.16
The Go to URL
dialog has only
one field where
you insert the
target address.

The Go to URL behavior enables you to make hyperlinks that are triggered by events other than the regular clicking of a button. For instance, you can set the event to onmouseover so that the browser navigates to the new address when an element is touched. Or you can set the event to onload to force the browser to navigate to the new address when the element or the page loads.

Jump Menu

The Jump Menu behavior adds a drop-down menu with a Jump Menu behavior to the page wherever you place the cursor. This behavior is actually a "two birds with one stone" approach to making a drop-down box with some functionality. Technically, the jump menu part of the behavior is just the onchange event and Jump Menu action. Separately, the Jump Menu behavior inserts a drop-down box to which you attach the behavior. The result is a drop-down box with a set of choices that link to different pages just like the menu that appears when you hover over the events in the Behaviors panel.

1. To create a new jump menu, place the cursor where you want the jump menu to appear, click Insert in the Behaviors panel, and select Jump Menu from the menu. This opens the Jump Menu dialog.

2. The Jump Menu dialog is where you define the different menu options. To add a menu option, click the Add button. This opens the Add Choice dialog. The Choice is the text that appears as an option within the jump menu. The Value is the target URL navigated to when the user selects the choice. This menu lists a series of news sources, so start with CNN as the Choice setting and

http://www.cnn.com as the Value setting. Click OK to add the item to the jump menu (see Figure 16.17).

FIGURE 16.17
The Add Choice dialog appears when you click Add in the Jump Menu dialog and lets you insert new menu items and their corresponding links.

3. Add a series of new links to other news sources to create a list. When the list has several items, you can modify each item, remove them, or move them up and down in the list with the buttons on the side.

4. When you are satisfied with your list, you can decide whether the new pages should open in the current window or a new window using the Open URLs In drop-down menu (see Figure 16.18). Set this option to New Window. You can

FIGURE 16.18
The Jump Menu dialog as it appears with multiple menu items inserted.

also check the Select First Item After URL Change option. Doing so resets the jump menu to the first item on the list after a URL change. Otherwise, the last selected item appears in the jump menu. Click OK to insert the jump menu.

If you save and preview the page in your browser, you can test the new jump menu. Because you set the URL to open in a new window, a new window opens every time you make a selection from the menu. If you had unchecked the Select First Item After URL Change box, the last selection you made would appear in the jump menu when it is not activated.

To change the properties of the menu items, double-click the jump menu in Design view and the Drop-Down Box Properties dialog opens. From here you can add, remove, modify, and reorganize the different list alternatives and even change options such as tab order (for visitors using the Tab key on their keyboard) and whether the visitor can make multiple selections. This is because you are now editing the menu as a drop-down box, not a jump menu. Note that you don't have the Open URLs In and Select First Item After URL Change options in this dialog.

Jump Menu Go

The default setting of the Jump Menu event is onchange. That means whenever the user selects a menu item, the action triggers. But sometimes you want the user to make a selection first and then press a separate button to trigger the action. You can do so with the Jump Menu Go behavior by removing the event and action from the menu itself and giving it to a separate element.

To make this scenario work properly, you have to create a new button with the Jump Menu Go event attached and then change the event of the jump menu.

1. You need to attach the Jump Menu Go behavior to a different element than the jump menu itself. Go to the Toolbox panel and find the Form Control called Input (button). Drag an instance of the Input (button) and drop it below the Jump Menu. With the new button selected, click the Insert button in the Behaviors panel and select Jump Menu Go from the menu. This opens the Jump Menu Go dialog (see Figure 16.19).

FIGURE 16.19
The Jump Menu Go dialog lists the available jump menus you can control with the new behavior.

2. Because there is only one jump menu on the page, you have only one option. Had there been several jump menus, you could choose which one the Jump Menu Go behavior would affect. Click OK to apply the new behavior.

3. The jump menu still has the Jump Menu behavior attached. To get the new button to work properly, you have to remove this behavior. Select the jump menu

and delete the Jump Menu behavior from the Behaviors panel by selecting it and clicking the Delete button. This might seem counterintuitive but, as you just learned, the Jump Menu behavior and the drop-down box are two separate entities. Now the button you created in step 1 controls the menu. Save and preview in your browser to test the new behavior.

Open Browser Window

In Hour 5, "Getting Connected with (Hyper)Links: The Cornerstone of the World Wide Web," you learned how to make hyperlinks open in a new window. The Open Browser Window behavior takes this to a whole new level by letting you create hyperlinks that open in new windows in which you set the parameters for how the window should look and behave. This gives the designer much more control of the experience the visitor has after clicking the link. This behavior is especially useful when you want to open a separate window that displays an image and you want it to be the same size as the image. Previously, you created a thumbnail of the detail photo of the damage done to the EOS 1 camera in the page named eos1.html. Now you use the Open Browser Window behavior to make the thumbnail open a new window that fits that photo exactly.

1. Open the eos1.html page and find the detail thumbnail in the third paragraph.

2. Right-click the thumbnail, select Hyperlink Properties from the pop-up menu, and click Remove Link in the Edit Hyperlink dialog to remove the original link. Click OK.

3. With the thumbnail selected, click the Insert button in the Behaviors panel and select Open Browser Window from the menu. This opens the Open Browser Menu dialog.

4. In the Open Browser Window dialog, use the Browse button to navigate to the eos1Detail.jpg image in the Images folder.

5. In the Window Name box, define a unique name for your window. This name will not be visible, but the browser uses it to identify the window so that you can target it with other behaviors or functions. The window name can contain only numbers and letters, no spaces or symbols. Name the window **image**.

6. The Window Width and Window Height setting define the physical width and height of the new window. The default value is 200px by 200px, which is very small. The eos1Detail.jpg image is 600px wide and 600px high, so match these values in your window.

7. The window's attributes make up the final set of options in the Open Browser Window dialog. By checking and unchecking these boxes, you turn various features of the window on and off. Leaving all of them unchecked means you get a stripped window with no navigation or other features (see Figure 16.20). Click OK to apply the new behavior.

FIGURE 16.20
The Open
Browser Window
dialog with all
the new settings
completed.

After saving and previewing the page in your browser, click the thumbnail and a new window opens to the size specified (see Figure 16.21). Note that because you didn't

FIGURE 16.21
The new win-
dow's size is
according to
specifications
and stripped of
all the extra fea-
tures a browser
window normally
has.

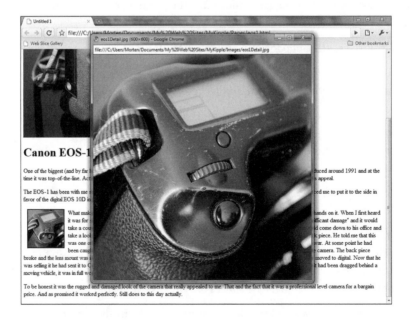

check any attributes, the window has no navigation, scrollbars, or any other features. Furthermore, you can't resize the window.

Play Sound

The Play Sound behavior plays back a sound file when the desired event triggers. The supported sound file types are

- ▶ AIFF sound files (files ending with .aif, .aifc, and .aiff)

- ▶ AU sound files (files ending with .au and .snd)

- ▶ MIDI sequencer files (files ending with .mid)

- ▶ RealAudio files (files ending with .ram and .ra)

- ▶ Wave files (files ending with .wav)

When you apply the Play Sound behavior to an element, the Play Sound dialog opens to allow you to insert the location of the sound file (see Figure 16.22). Keep in

FIGURE 16.22
The Play Sound dialog lets you browse to the sound you want to play when the event triggers.

mind that just like image files, this file needs to be available on the Web either from your own site or an external site. If you insert a link to a file on your local hard drive, only visitors using your computer can hear it.

Popup Message

When an element with the Popup Message behavior applies triggers, a warning box with the warning of your choice appears on the screen. Designers often use this behavior to warn visitors about the content about to display, that they are leaving the site, or that they are submitting information to the site. Because you are in complete control of the warning message, you can have it say whatever you want.

To create a pop-up message, simply add the behavior to an element and the Popup Message dialog opens (see Figure 16.23). There you type out your message and click OK to insert it into the page.

FIGURE 16.23
The Popup Message dialog lets you insert the text you want to display in the warning box.

FIGURE 16.23
The Popup Message dialog lets you insert the text you want to display in the warning box.

When triggered, the Popup Message behavior creates a warning box with the text you inserted, and the visitor has to manually close it to move on (see Figure 16.24).

FIGURE 16.24
The pop-up message as it appears when triggered in the browser.

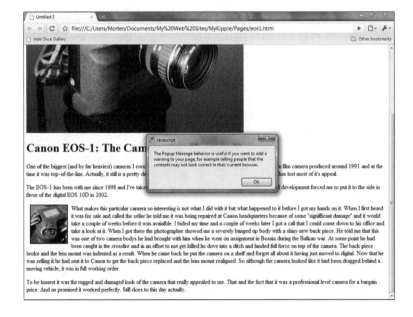

Preload Images

The Preload Images behavior loads images that are not actually present on the page into the browser memory for future retrieval. This is a useful function if your page contains images that appear when the user performs an action (such as hovering the mouse over a button), and you don't want there to be a lag between the action and the image switching out. You saw the Preload Images behavior both when you created the interactive buttons in Hour 15 and when you used the Swap Image behavior in this hour.

The Preload Images behavior is usually applied to the page as a whole (under the <body> tag) with an onload event so that it loads with the rest of the page.

1. There is already a Preload Images behavior present in your page. (You inserted it along with the Swap Image behavior.) But if you want to insert one, you simply click anywhere within the page and select the <body> tag from the Quick Tag Selector before inserting the behavior from the Behaviors panel. Because you already inserted a Preload Images behavior, simply select the <body> tag and double-click the behavior from the Behaviors panel. This opens the Preload Images dialog.

2. When the Preload Images dialog opens, it has one image listed and only the Remove button is active. To add a new image, you first have to use the Browse button to find it. Select any image in your site and click OK. The new image location appears in the Image Source File area and the Add button activates. Click the Add button to add the new image to the list (see Figure 16.25).

FIGURE 16.25
To add a new image to the Preload Images list, you first have to browse to the image source file location and then click the Add button.

Behavior Pitfalls and Expression Web 3 Idiosyncrasies

Watch Out!

Like CSS styles, a behavior always applies to the closest tag. That means if you highlight a portion of text and use the Behaviors panel to apply a new behavior to it, you attach the behavior to all the content within the same tag as the text, not just the highlighted selection. If you want to attach a behavior to a selection of text, you must first wrap it inside a set of <span> tags in Code view and give it a unique ID. However, for some reason, Expression Web 3 treats <span> tags differently from all other tags. So, when you apply a behavior to a <span> tag, Expression Web 3 inserts it without an event! To make the behavior work properly and show up in the Behaviors panel, you need to manually insert the event ahead of the action in Code view.

Set Text

Set Text is the only behavior with a submenu. This behavior changes the text or HTML content of various fields within the page. To fully understand how this behavior works, you first need an introduction to frames, layers, and text fields. Therefore the Set Text behavior will be covered in Hour 17, "Frames and Layers."

Summary

Behaviors are small programs you can attach to elements within your page to create a more interactive experience for your visitors. They can produce many of the same effects you already created using CSS and some that you can't produce using CSS. Therefore, behaviors are an important and valuable tool for designers.

In this hour, you learned how to apply behaviors to different elements within a page and how to edit them. More important, you got a complete walkthrough of all the available behaviors and learned how each one works. Knowing the behaviors in Expression Web 3 is your first step on the path to understanding JavaScript. Looking at JavaScript in more detail is beyond the scope of this book.

In the upcoming hours, you apply what you learned about behaviors to some of the content in the MyKipple site to create a more interactive experience for the visitor.

Q&A

Q. *When I click the last button with both an Open Browser Window and a Popup Message action, the new browser window opens behind the main window while the pop-up message appears on top. Why is that?*

A. JavaScript is handled in sequence from top to bottom. That means if an object has several actions attached, they will be triggered in the order they appear in the Behaviors panel. If the Open Browser Window action appears above the Popup Message action, the button tells the browser to create a pop-up window on top and then return to the main window and perform the other action. To change the order of the two actions, simply click on the Open Browser Window action and click the down button (with an arrow pointing down) in the Behaviors Panel. This moves the behavior down in the order. Now when you preview the page in your browser, the pop-up message shows up first, and only after you click OK does the new window with the image appear. As you can see, this organization of a pop-up message and a new window can warn visitors that a new window is about to be opened.

Workshop

The Workshop has quiz questions to help you put to use what you just learned. If you get stuck, the answers to the quiz questions are in the next section. But try to answer the questions first. Otherwise you'll be cheating yourself.

Quiz

1. What two components are behaviors composed of?

Answers

1. A behavior consists of an event and an action. The event defines the trigger that causes the action to engage. The action contains the small JavaScript program that makes the behavior what it is.

Exercise

Later in this book, you learn how to use Behaviors to create an interactive menu. Here is a preview: Create a table with one row and four columns, and place a new button in each of them. Use the different behaviors you learned about in this hour to make the buttons do different things, such as changing the properties of a block of text, creating a new window pointing to your favorite website, or simply changing color when you click on it.

HOUR 17

Frames and Layers

What You'll Learn in this Hour:

▶ How to create a frameset to separate the contents of a page

▶ How to edit the frameset and its individual frames

▶ How an inline frame differs from a frameset and how to use it

▶ How to change the content of a frame using the Set Text of Frame behavior

▶ What layers are and how they differ from frames

▶ How to create and edit layers to create an interactive experience

▶ How to use layers and inline frames together to make a preview of a hyperlink

Introduction

So far you learned how to create page layouts using Cascading Style Sheets (CSS). But there are times when CSS just doesn't cut it, and times when you want some added functionality you just can't get with a style sheet. In this hour, you learn about frames and layers and see how making smart use of these layout tools can improve the functionality of your websites.

Frames and layers are layout tools that have been around for quite some time, and at one time each was the hot new thing in web design. In this hour you take a closer look at both these techniques and learn when to use (and when *not* to use) them.

Frames: An Introduction

Frames (plural) are a group of web pages displayed together in a web browser. A separate Hypertext Markup Language (HTML) file, commonly referred to as a *frameset*, controls the frames. The frameset creates a group of frames, gives a name to each frame, and tells the browser how to position the different frames in relation to one another. There is also a subset of frames called an *iFrame*. The *i* is short for *inline*, which as its name suggests, is a box in which a different HTML page displays inside the current page—more on that later.

For the most part, designers use frames to separate the navigational tools from the content. That way you can let the user scroll through lists of navigational links or large documents independently of other page elements. The Microsoft Developer Network (MSDN) Library uses frames in this manner to separate the header and sidebar navigation from the document content (see Figure 17.1). That way the visitor has

FIGURE 17.1
The MSDN Library demonstrates an effective use of frames and is also a good resource for further information on Microsoft applications and services including Expression Web.

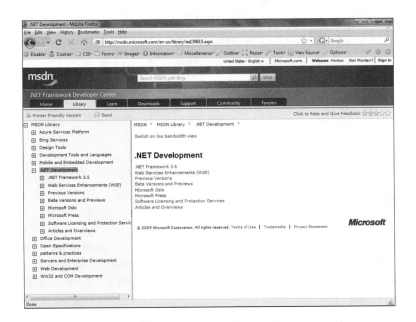

immediate access to the navigational tools in the header and can scroll through the library archive to the left without losing her place in the document she is currently reading. Likewise she can scroll through the document without either the header or the sidebar moving away from its current location.

The MSDN Library page consists of three separate frames that each display different web pages. This layout hints at one of the major problems when using frames:

Because the actual page content is separate from the overall layout, the content pages don't contain any navigational tools. As long as they display as intended within the frameset, this is not a problem. But if a user accesses them from outside the frameset, the visitor loses the ability to navigate to the rest of the site. This is especially problematic because search engines usually index individual pages and not framesets, so a visitor that finds a certain page in a search engine is likely to land on just the content page without any of the navigation attached.

Try It Yourself

Creating a Web Page with Frames

As it does with CSS layouts, Expression Web 3 comes with a series of preconfigured framesets for you to use. This makes the initial process of building a frames-based web page much easier.

1. In the Folder List panel, create a new folder called **Frames** and double-click it to select it. Select File, New, Page from the menu bar to open the New dialog.

2. In the New dialog, select Frames Pages from the menu. This opens the preset frames layouts in the next window and gives you a short description and a preview of each frameset (see Figure 17.2).

FIGURE 17.2
By selecting Frames Pages in the New dialog, you get a list of preconfigured frames layouts with a short description and a preview.

3. Select Banner and Contents and click OK to build the frameset. This opens the frameset in Design view, and Expression Web 3 asks you to set an initial page or create a new page for each frame (see Figure 17.3).

4. Before you continue, press Ctrl+S to save the frameset. Name the file **frameset.html** and save it in the Frames folder. Click the New Page button in the top banner. This changes the banner to a white page with a cursor in it.

FIGURE 17.3
After building the frameset, you define the contents of each frame by either inserting the address of an existing page or creating a new page.

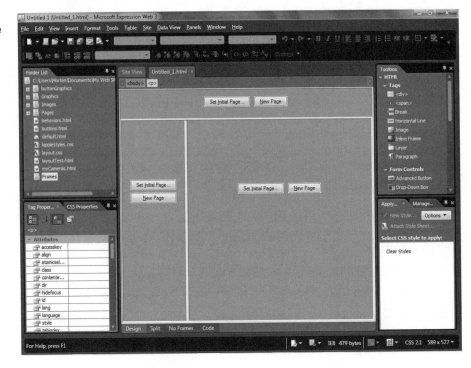

Now you are actually looking at two separate HTML pages: the frameset that defines the overall layout, and the new page that is visible only in the banner area. Do the same for the sidebar and the content area, as shown in Figure 17.4.

5. Place your cursor in the top frame and press Ctrl+S again to save the new frame pages. This opens the Save As dialog for the top frame (the banner). Name this page **banner.html** and click Save. Expression Web 3 creates the file, and the Save As dialog opens again—this time for the left bar. Name this page **navigation.html** and click Save. The Save As dialog opens for a third time, this time for the main content area. Name the final page **camera.html** and click Save. You saved all the pages, and you can now start editing each one individually.

The Frames folder now has four files in it: **frameset.html**, **banner.html**, **navigation.html**, and **camera.html**. The three last pages you created are normal HTML pages that you can open separately. frameset.html is an HTML file that contains only information about the spatial relationship between the different frames.

FIGURE 17.4
By clicking the
New Page but-
tons in all three
frames, you cre-
ate three new
pages.

Beyond that, it is empty. If you press F12 to preview the page in your browser, you see the three frames, but the address bar tells you that you are actually looking at the frameset.html file—the other pages are embedded.

Editing Individual Frames

Now that you have created the frames pages, it's time to insert some content into the frames. Because each frame contains a separate HTML page, you can edit it in the same way you have done throughout this book—by inserting text and images and applying styles or style sheets.

> Because you are now working with a frame layout, you need to consider the over-all layout of the frameset, not just the individual pages. For instance, applying the layout.css style sheet to each frame means they all will have the top background graphic applied to them individually, which will look strange.

This frameset will be a simple archive with a list on the left and pages for each of the items on the right. Start by placing the cursor in the banner frame and typing **Kipple Archive**. Set the font style to H2, and create a body style with font-family set to

Arial, Helvetica, sans-serif; `text-transform` to uppercase; `color` to #FFFFFF; and `background-color` to #3399FF. Expression Web 3 applies the new style to only the top frame. In the left frame, create an unordered list and give the first list item the text **Canon EOS 1**. In the final frame, insert the eos1.jpg image from the Images folder.

Using the CSS skills you learned throughout this book, you can now make styling changes to the individual pages: Create a `li` style in the page in the left frame, and change the List-Style-Type setting to None. Create a `ul` style in the same frame and set the borders and margins to 0px. Create a new class called `.alignCenter` in the right frame. Change the Margin-Left and Margin-Right settings to Auto and change the Display setting under Layout to Block. Apply the new class to the `<img>` tag using the Quick Tag Selector. Now you have three different style sets for the three different pages, all working together to create an overall layout (see Figure 17.5).

FIGURE 17.5
The contents of each page within the frameset are styled separately by the styles defined in each page.

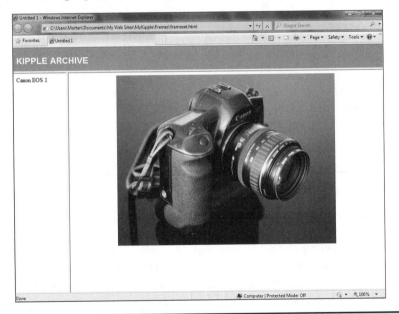

▼   **Try It Yourself**

Edit the Frames Layout

The actual layout and functionality of the frameset as a whole are contained within the frameset.html file, not the individual frames. So, to change the layout and/or relationship between the different frames, you have to edit frameset.html.

There are many ways in which to change the layout of the frames. The simplest one is to grab the frame borders with the mouse and drag them to a different size. But for more detailed control, it is better to use the Frame Properties dialog.

1. To open the Frame Properties dialog, right-click inside the frame you want to change (in this case the left frame), and select Frame Properties from the context menu. This opens the Frame Properties dialog (see Figure 17.6).

FIGURE 17.6
The Frame Properties dialog lets you configure the properties of the frame in relation to the other frames. These properties have no direct effect on the page within the frame, only how the browser displays it.

2. In the Frame Properties dialog, you can set various different attributes. The Name attribute is the identifying name of the frame. This is the name you use when targeting the frame with links. Change the name to **sidebar**.

3. Initial Page is the first page displayed when a browser opens the frameset.html page. Because this is the navigation frame, leave it the way it is.

4. Long Description and Title are fields used by screen readers to describe the contents of the frame for visitors that cannot see the content. Long Description links to a file with a long description. Title is a short description of the frame. These two attributes work in the same way as the alternative text and long description attached to image files. Leave the Long Description field blank and insert Kipple Archive list-menu in the Title field.

5. Frame Size defines the physical size of the frame in relation to the other frames on the page. The Width and Row Height attributes can be set to a numeric value that is relative (in relation to the other frames), percent (of the entire width or height of the page in the browser), or pixels. To give the menu some more room, set the Width attribute to 200 pixels.

6. *Margins* refer to the space between the walls of the frame and the content within it in much the same way that the padding in CSS relates to the box. Changing the margin values in the frame properties creates a smaller or larger

buffer zone for the content. Setting the margins to zero can look strange but might be exactly what you want if you style the individual frame content with CSS. For this example, leave the values as they are.

7. Under Options, if the Resizable in Browser box is checked, the visitor can grab the frame borders and change the size of the frame in the browser. (This affects only the page in the browser, not the actual page on the server.) In this case, and almost every case, this option should be unchecked. Show Scrollbars gives you the option to decide whether scrollbars should be visible if the content doesn't fit on the screen. It can be set to Always, If Needed, or Never. In most cases, the If Needed option is the right way to go. The user has no way to see any content that spills outside the frame if this option is set to Never and the visitor has a small screen or the content is too large to fit. Set Show Scrollbars to If Needed for this frame.

8. The last function in the Frame Properties dialog is the Frames Page button. This button opens the page properties for the frameset page (see Figure 17.7). When the visitor opens the frameset page, the browser considers this file to be the page and regards the pages within the frames as displayed information. In other words, all the information sent to the browser, such as title, page description, keywords, and so forth, comes from the frameset page. By clicking the Frames Page button, you have access to all these properties. This is also where you control the frame borders. Their width is defined in pixels by the Frame Spacing value, and they can be turned on and off with the Show Borders setting. Set the Frame Spacing value to 1px, and click OK twice to apply the changes.

FIGURE 17.7
By clicking the Frames Page button, you can access the page properties for the frameset page. From here you can control the thickness and visibility of the frame borders, among other things.

You can also split and delete frames just as you would with table cells. To split a frame into two frames, either horizontally or vertically, select the frame by clicking anywhere inside it and choose Format, Frames, Split Frame from the menu bar. This opens the Split Frame dialog where you can choose whether to split the frame in two horizontally or vertically. To delete a frame, select it in the same way and choose Format, Frames, Delete Frame from the menu bar.

Making Framed Navigation

As you previously learned, the main reason you would use frames is to separate the navigation from the content. After the frameset is set up, this is a simple operation as long as you keep tabs on what you are doing. This is where the frame name comes in. When you create a hyperlink in one frame that you mean to open in a different frame, you target that frame using the frame's name. In the past you had to remember the names of the different frames, but Expression Web has taken away that barrier and made the process much easier:

1. Before you can create a hyperlink to a new page, you need a new page to which you can link. In the Folder panel, open the Frames folder and open the camera.html file. Click File on the menu bar, select Save As, and change the filename to **eos1detail.html**. This creates a new HTML file, shown in the Folder List, called eos1detail.html (see Figure 17.8). Open the new file, right-click the image, select Picture Properties, and change the picture file to the **eos1detail.jpg** file found in the Images folder. Save the file and close it.

FIGURE 17.8
Creating a new file can be as easy as clicking Save As and changing the name in the Save As dialog. After you create the new file, you can make changes to it without having to worry about the old file.

2. In the frameset.html file, add a second list item to the left frame and type **EOS 1 Detail**. Highlight the first line item, right-click, and select Hyperlink from the context menu to open the Insert Hyperlink dialog. Navigate to the camera.html page in the Frames folder, and then click the Target Frame button to open the Target Frame dialog (see Figure 17.9). There you can pick what frame the hyperlink should open the new page in, either by clicking the frame in the Current Frames Page area or selecting one of the Common Targets. Click the left

FIGURE 17.9
The Target Frame dialog lets you pick what frame to target by clicking a visual representation of the current frameset or selecting one of the common targets.

frame in the Current Frames area, and the Target setting changes to Main (the name of the right frame). Click OK twice to create the hyperlink.

3. Repeat the same process with the second line item and link it to the eos1detail.html page you created earlier. Save and preview the page in your browser.

When you click the two hyperlinks in your browser, you see that the right frame changes between the camera.html page and the eos1detail.html page whereas the banner and sidebar frames remain unchanged.

Creating and Modifying Inline Frames

Unlike the frameset, which is a series of frames that contain the content, the inline frame (often referred to as the *iFrame*) is a frame inserted into a page to display the contents of a different page. An easy way to understand how an inline frame works is to imagine the frame as a hole cut into the page and filled with the contents from a different page.

Inline frames can be inserted anywhere within an HTML page and, as their name suggests, they work as other inline items. That is, they line up alongside the current line of text. Inline frames are a great way to insert content from other websites into a page without having to either copy the content over or link to it.

1. Create a new page and call it **inlineFramePage.html**. In the page, insert a headline and two paragraphs of text.

When web designers and developers work with unfinished pages, they often need some dummy text to work with. The most common dummy text is Lorem Ipsum, and you can find it at http://www.lipsum.com. You define how many paragraphs, words, or bytes you want, and the website generates it for you.

Did you Know?

---

2. Place the cursor at the beginning of the second paragraph, and press Enter to create a new paragraph. Move the cursor to the new empty paragraph in the middle. Insert an inline frame in one of two ways: Select Insert, HTML, Inline Frame from the menu bar, or drag-and-drop an inline frame from the HTML submenu in the Toolbox panel.

3. When you insert the inline frame, Expression Web 3 gives you the same two choices you saw with the frameset: Set Initial Page and New Page. Select Set Initial Page and the Insert Hyperlink dialog opens. The hyperlink you set in this dialog becomes the content of the inline frame. Set the address to http://www.designisphilosophy.com and click OK. Because this is a live website, Expression Web 3 navigates to the site and inserts the page into Design view if you have an open Internet connection (see Figure 17.10).

4. To change the size of the inline frame, select it by clicking close to the outer edge of the inline frame, and then drag the handles to the desired size.

Inline frames can be tricky to handle because if you click anywhere inside the frame after loading the content, you are actually selecting the content within the frame—not the frame itself. To select the inline frame, hover your mouse close to the outer border, and click so that you see the Tag Selector iframe appear.

Watch Out!

FIGURE 17.10
When you set the inline frame hyperlink to an external site, Expression Web 3 loads the external site into Design view.

To make more advanced changes to an inline frame, you can change the inline frame properties by right-clicking the inline frame and selecting Inline Frame Properties from the context menu. As you can see from Figure 17.11, the Inline Frame Properties dialog and its functions are similar to the Frames Properties dialog you encountered earlier (refer to Figure 17.6).

FIGURE 17.11
The Inline Frame Properties dialog gives you detailed control of all aspects of the inline frame.

From here you can change the initial page URL, the size, whether to use scrollbars, the alternative text (if the browser does not support inline frames), and a host of other options. You can also give the inline frame a unique name just like the earlier frames so that hyperlinks and actions can target it.

Set Text of Frame Behavior

You learned about behaviors in Hour 16, "Using Behaviors," but a couple behaviors were not covered: specifically, the Set Text behaviors which make little sense without first understanding frames and layers. Now that you know how to use frames, you can take a closer look at the Set Text of Frame behavior.

The Set Text of Frame behavior sends a block of predefined HTML code to the defined frame and replaces the current content of the frame with this code. You can use it to target any frame, whether in a frameset or an inline frame. Because the Set Text of Frame behavior works only on frames displaying pages from the current site, before starting this tutorial you need to change the hyperlink of the inline frame to one of the other pages in the MyKipple site, for example default.html. This can be done from the Inline Frame Properties dialog previously described.

1. First you need an element in which you can attach the behavior. Place the cursor below the inline frame and create a new button, either using the interactive button feature or by dragging an Input (button) instance from the Toolbox panel. Set the button text to **Change Text** but don't attach a link to it. Click OK to insert the new button (see Figure 17.12).

FIGURE 17.12
The Set Text of Frame behavior must be applied to a button or another interactive element.

2. If it's not already visible, open the Behaviors panel by clicking Panels, Behaviors from the menu bar. With the new button selected, click Insert in the Behaviors panel, and select Set Text of Frame from the Set Text submenu. Doing so opens the Set Text of Frame dialog (see Figure 17.13).

FIGURE 17.13
The Set Text of Frame dialog lets you control what frame to target, what text to insert (in HTML code), and whether you want the frame to retain its background color.

3. In the Set Text of Frame dialog, you can choose what frame to target from a drop-down menu. (In this case there is only one frame on the page and, therefore, only one option.) In the Text area, you can insert plain text, HTML code, or a combination of both. The Preserve Background Color check box lets you decide whether you want to keep the background color from the last content visible in the frame. Insert some text with basic HTML coding such as <strong> or <em> and click OK to apply the behavior to the button. A new onclick event appears in the Behaviors panel with the Set Text of Frame action attached.

4. Save the page and any embedded files if, you used the interactive buttons feature, and test it in your browser.

When you click the button you just inserted, the content of the inline frame changes to the text you inserted in the Set Text of Frame dialog (see Figure 17.14).

As an example, you could use the Set Text of Frame behavior with the jump menu to display different messages to the user depending on his selections in the menu.

Set Text of Frame Only Works with Local Pages!

The Set Text of Frame behavior works by telling the browser to modify the content in the frame. This is why you can retain the background color of the original content when replacing the text. However this also causes a problem: Most browsers do not let you modify the contents of external pages, even if it is just done locally in the browser! As a result, if your frame links to an external page (that is, a page that doesn't have the same domain name as the current page), browsers including Internet Explorer and Opera return an Access Denied error, and the behavior will not work. As a result the Set Text of Frame behavior should be used only on frames that contain pages from your own domain.

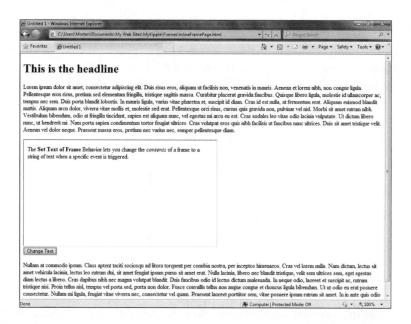

FIGURE 17.14
When triggered, the Set Text of Frame behavior changes the text content of the targeted frame to what the designer defined.

Creating Advanced Functionality Using Layers

Another advanced layout technique is the use of layers. Whereas inline frames are inserted into the content of the page, layers contain boxes that float on top of the content in the page. This can be a useful tool when you want to create a more interactive experience for the visitor. One of the reasons layers are used is the ability to make them invisible. As a result, you can create advanced elements such as pop-up menus or boxes that the user can trigger.

By default, Expression Web 3 places all layers within an absolutely positioned <div> tag so that you have complete control of the position of the layer within the page. Because the layer is absolutely positioned, three attributes control the layer's physical placement. Left controls the distance between the left side of the layer and the left side of the page; Top controls the distance between the top of the layer and the top of the page; and Z-Index controls the imagined position of the layer in three-dimensional space if you stack several layers on top of one another.

When setting the z-index, 0 represents the bottom layer. The element with the highest z-index number is always on top.

By the Way

Creating a Layer

To help create and edit layers, Expression Web 3 has a specialized panel just for this layout tool. To open it, select Panels, Layers from the menu bar. The Layers panel opens in the same area as the Behaviors panel (see Figure 17.15).

FIGURE 17.15
The Layers panel gives you full access to all the layers and layer functionality on the page.

1. In the inlineFramePage.html page, place the cursor at the beginning of the first paragraph. Click the Draw Layer button in the Layers panel, and draw a small box by clicking and dragging the mouse in Design view (see Figure 17.16).

FIGURE 17.16
To draw a layer, simply click the Draw Layer button and then click-and-drag the layer to the desired size in Design view. You can always resize it later.

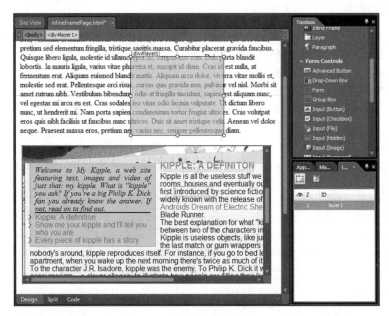

2. When the layer is drawn, the cursor should appear within it. If not, click it with your mouse to activate it. Drag-and-drop the eos1Detail_small.jpg image into the layer. The image should now hover over the rest of the content.

3. In the Layers panel, right-click the layer1 instance and select Modify ID from the context menu. Change the ID of the layer to cameraThumb.

4. In the Layers panel, click twice on the layer just underneath the eye to set the Visibility attribute to Hidden. (No eye means default, open eye means visible, and closed eye means hidden, as shown in Figure 17.15.) The image disappears from the screen. If you look in the CSS Properties panel, you see that the Visibility attribute has been set to Hidden.

5. Highlight a word in the first paragraph next to the layer you just inserted, and create a hyperlink that points to the eos1.html file under the Pages folder.

6. With the new hyperlink selected, go to the Behaviors panel and insert a new Change Property behavior.

7. In the Change Property dialog, check the Select Element option, and set the element type to <div> and the element ID to cameraThumb. Doing that means the Change Property behavior will affect the layer you just created.

8. Click the Visibility button and set the visibility style to Visible. Click OK. Check the Restore on Mouseout Event option and click OK to apply the behavior (see Figure 17.17).

FIGURE 17.17
You can use the Change Property behavior to change the visibility of layers.

9. The default event for the Change Property behavior you just added is onclick. Change it to onmouseover so that the image becomes visible when a visitor hovers over the hyperlink. Save and test the page in your browser.

When you open your browser and hover over the hyperlink you just created, the layer with the image becomes visible and hovers on top of the text.

To move the location of the layer, click the layer in the Layers panel to select it and hover the mouse over the tag selector to turn it into a four-way arrow. By clicking the tag selector, you can move the layer anywhere on the page. As you previously learned, the layers have absolute positioning, so the distance from the left and top edges of the page or a containing tag with its position defined form the basis for the layers' final position (see Hour 14, "Harnessing the Power of CSS Layouts").

> The reason you need to place the cursor at the beginning of the paragraph you insert the layer into is that Expression Web 3 wraps the layers in a `<div>` tag. As you previously learned in this book, `<div>` tags are block tags that create a new separate line to be on. So, if you place the cursor in the middle of a paragraph, the layer creates a new line that remains empty and breaks up the text. Placing the layer at the beginning of the paragraph doesn't change its position but ensures that the paragraph does not split in two.

▼   **Try It Yourself**

Create a Layer Containing an Inline Frame

You can use layers with inline frames to make a fancy pop-up effect in which the user previews the linked page in real-time without going to the actual page.

1. To do so open the default.html page and find the text Do Androids Dream of Electric Sheep? that contains a hyperlink to the Amazon.com page for the book. Right-click the text, choose Hyperlink Properties, and copy the hyperlink address by highlighting it and pressing Ctrl+C. Close the Edit Hyperlink dialog without making any changes.

2. With the hyperlink copied, place the cursor at the beginning of the paragraph that contains the hyperlink. Open the Layers panel and use the Draw Layer function to draw a medium-sized layer directly underneath the hyperlink. From the Toolbox panel, drag-and-drop an iFrame into the new layer (see Figure 17.18).

3. Click the Set Initial Page button in the inline frame and paste the Amazon.com link you copied earlier into the address bar. Expression Web 3 might tell you that the content on the page requires extra software to display properly. If it does, just click No. The page might not display properly inside Design view, but it will in a browser. Select the inline frame by clicking close to the outer border and resize it to fit the layer.

4. Change the Layer ID to `amazonPreview` by double-clicking the layer name in the Layers panel. Set the `Visibility` attribute of the layer to Hidden by clicking twice on the area underneath the eye (see Figure 17.19).

FIGURE 17.18
Layers can contain any kind of HTML element, including inline frames.

FIGURE 17.19
Even after setting the layer's visibility to hidden, the inline frame might still be visible in Design view. But when you preview the page in a browser, you see that the browser hides the frame.

5. As in the earlier example, to make the layer appear only when the visitor hovers over the link select the hyperlink and use the Behaviors panel to attach a Change Property behavior to it. In the Change Property dialog, select the div element `amazonPreview` and set the `Visibility` attribute to Visible. Check the Restore on Onmouseout Event box, and click OK to apply the behavior.

6. Finally, with the hyperlink still selected, change the event of the `Change Property` action to **onmouseover**. Save the page and preview in your browser.

When you hover the mouse over the hyperlink in your browser, the layer opens with the inline frame inside it and shows you what the linked page looks like in real-time (see Figure 17.20).

FIGURE 17.20
With the Change Property behavior attached to the hyperlink, the layer with the inline frame opens only when the visitor hovers over the hyperlink.

Visibility is set to Hidden

Set Text of Layer Behavior

The Set Text of Layer behavior works the same way as the Set Text of Frame behavior. When applied, it changes the content of the selected layer to the text or HTML content inserted into the Set Text of Layer dialog (see Figure 17.21).

FIGURE 17.21
The Set Text of
Layer behavior
works exactly
the same way as
the Set Text of
Frame behavior
except it targets
layers rather
than frames.

Summary

Frames and layers have been, and still are, important components of advanced web design. In this hour, you got a thorough walkthrough of how you can use these layout elements to add interactivity to your sites.

This hour was packed with a lot of information, so it is not surprising if you feel a little bit overwhelmed by all the new things you learned. To help you make sense of it all, think of it this way:

▶ A frame (and an inline frame) is a *hole cut in the page*, and you fill it with the contents of a different page.

▶ A layer is a box placed *on top of* the page, and you fill it with HTML content including inline frames.

In this hour, you learned how to set up and use a frameset to completely separate the contents from the navigation. You learned how to define and configure framesets, how to change and resize the individual frames, and how to make hyperlinks that target the other frames.

You also learned how to make and use inline frames, and saw how they can enhance your site. Inline frames differ from framesets in that they are placed inside a page rather than alongside other frames. Designers often use them to display external content, such as other web pages, and interactive content, such as Silverlight applications.

To top off the frames portion of this hour, you learned how to use the Set Text of Frame behavior to change the contents of a frame. You can use this behavior to target both inline frames and framesets.

In the second half of the hour, you learned about layers—more specifically how to create them and edit them. One of the most important features of layers is the ability to hide them and their content and then use behaviors to make them visible again. This technique enables you to make some highly interactive and impressive features easily.

This hour scratched only the surface of what is possible when using layers. In the next hour, you create a full-fledged drop-down navigation menu using the same techniques you learned here.

Q&A

Q. *I created a new hyperlink in the frameset, but when I clicked it in the browser, the contents in the same frame changed rather than the one I wanted to change.*

A. When you click a link and the current frame changes (or a different frame from the intended one changes, for that matter), something is wrong with your targeting. Most likely you simply forgot to change the target frame, or you clicked the wrong target frame in the Target Frame dialog. To fix this problem, open the Hyperlink Properties dialog and ensure that the target frame is correct.

Q. *When I click one of the links, the entire frameset appears in the right frame. Now the entire site is doubled up!*

A. A common problem when using framesets is *nested frames*, which means that the entire frameset opens inside one of the frames. This is because you created a hyperlink to the frameset rather than the actual page you wanted to link to. To avoid this problem, always include the word *frameset* in the filename for your framesets and the word *frame* in the filename for single frame pages.

Q. *I created several different layers, but there is no real system to which one appears on top. What is going on?*

A. If you create multiple layers in one location and you want them to appear in a particular order, you need to change the z-index of each of the layers so that the lowest layer has the lowest number and the highest layer has the highest number.

Workshop

The Workshop has quiz questions and exercises to help you put to use what you just learned. If you get stuck, the answers to the quiz questions are in the next section. But try to answer the questions first. Otherwise you'll be cheating yourself.

Quiz

1. What is the difference between a frame and a layer?

2. When should you use a frameset rather than a single HTML file to create a page?

3. How do you set the position of a layer on your page?

Answers

1. A frame can be thought of as a hole cut in your page that contains another page. A layer by contrast can be thought of as a box that is placed on top of the content of the page that contains HTML.

2. A frameset should be used if you need to keep the navigation or other elements completely separate from the content so that when the visitor scrolls through the content, the other element stays put. A good example would be to use layers to create an index page where the index itself is in one frame and the pages it points to appear in a different frame.

3. By default the layers inserted by Expression Web 3 are placed inside absolutely positioned `<div>` tags. Therefore they are positioned in relation to the top left corner of the closest element with a position other than static. To position a layer you can either drag it to the desired location using your mouse or set the X and Y values manually using CSS. You can also change the positioning of the `<div>` tag to any of the other values for a different effect although setting it to static defeats the purpose of a layer.

Exercise

Create a new frameset with four frames and create new files for each frame. Select one of the frames as the navigation frame and create a series of hyperlinks that change the contents of each of the other three frames to different pages on the Web. Use percentages in setting their widths and heights to resize the frames so that they take up the same amount of space.

Create a series of layers slightly offset from one another and insert different images into each layer. Change the z-index for each layer to set the order. Preview the page in your browser to see how the images stack on top of one another. Go back to Expression Web 3 and change the z-index for some of the layers to change the order. Preview the page in your browser again to see what happened.

Create a new button and use the Set Text of Layer behavior to change the top layer to predefined text when you click the button.

Building a Functional Menu

What You'll Learn in This Hour:

▶ How to build a vertical menu using CSS

▶ How to build a horizontal menu using CSS

▶ How to convert the horizontal menu to a standards based drop-down menu using only unordered lists and CSS

Introduction

Menus are a great tool for simplifying navigation in a website. They enable you to group several different pages or links together visually and give the user an intuitive and interactive experience when surfing your site. There are many types of menus—from the standard vertical list menu to horizontal menus to drop-down menus of all shapes and sizes. And all of them can be built using standards-based code and CSS. You just have to know how.

Participating in web design forums and answering comments on my blog and emails, I've realized that creating menus, and especially drop-down menus that work properly, is a common challenge for new designers and developers. Much of the confusion seems to stem from the myriad of different techniques available and a lack of understanding of the processes behind them and the problems created by browser inconsistencies. This is unfortunate because the principles behind creating functional drop-down menus are simple.

This hour shows you how to make proper, functional, and lightweight CSS-based menus of the vertical, horizontal, and drop-down variety that you can implement into any site. You see how using some simple CSS tricks seemingly boring text-based menus can be made to look both inviting and interactive.

Making the Basic Vertical Menu Exciting

The most basic standards-based menu available is the vertical unordered list. Not only is it easy to build (all you need to do is create an unordered list in which each list item is a link) but it is also easy to maintain, and it works no matter what browser the visitor uses. That said there is no good reason why it should look bland and boring. Using the CSS techniques you have picked up by reading the preceding chapters of this book, you are well equipped to make the good old vertical menu look modern and stylish.

Throughout this hour you learn to make three different kinds of menus. To keep it all in one central location so that you can go back to it at any time to look at what you did (and copy the code into future pages), create a new folder called **menus** with a page called **menus.html** to work from.

1. If you haven't already done so, open the menus.html page in Design view.

2. Create a standard unordered list with five menu items named Menu Item One, Menu Item Two, and so on.

3. Directly above the unordered list insert a new paragraph, type **Basic Vertical Menu**, and change the style to **H2**.

4. Press Enter to create a new paragraph, and insert a couple of lines of text explaining that this is a basic vertical menu based on an unordered list. You should now have a page that looks like Figure 18.1.

5. The whole idea of a menu is to create navigation. To do so, make each of the menu items a hyperlink back to the menus.html page.

6. Switch to Split view and create a div to wrap the heading, paragraph, and list. Give the div the ID `vertMenuBox`.

7. Now it's time for the styling. First, create a new ID style for #vertMenuBox and set `font-family` to Arial, Helvetica, sans-serif; `color` to #333333; `background-color` to #EBEADF; and all four borders to solid, 1px, and #C4C2AB. To give the content some breathing space, set `top` and `bottom` `padding` to 5px and right and left padding to 10px. Finally, to constrain the size of the menu, set `width` (found under Position) to 250px. Click OK and you see that the menu is now contained in a nice box with a beige color (see Figure 18.2).

8. Now for the menu itself. To remove the list bullets and align the menu items with the left side of the box, create a new style with the selector #vertMenuBox

FIGURE 18.1
To start, the menus.html page should have an H2 heading, a paragraph, and an unordered list with five items.

FIGURE 18.2
By styling the #vertMenuBox ID alone, the menu already looks much better.

ul and set the padding and margin values to 0px and the list-style-type under List to none. Click OK to apply the new style.

9. Next you want to style each of the list items to space them farther apart. Create a new style with the selector #vertMenuBox ul li and set the top and

bottom padding to 5px. To create a further visual separation, set border-bottom to dotted, 1px, and #333333. Click OK to apply the new style.

10. Next up is the links. Create a new style with the selector #vertMenuBox ul li a and set font-size to 0.8em, text-transform to uppercase, color to #666666, and check none under text-decoration. Click OK to apply the style.

11. Finally create a new style with the selector #vertMenuBox ul li a:hover and set color to #333333. Click OK, save the page, and test it in your browser.

Now you have a basic vertical menu with some styling that makes it look less boring. But it's still pretty basic. To make it stand out, let's add a couple of extra style tricks to the menu:

1. Open the Modify Style dialog for the #vertMenuBox ul li style and set padding-left to 5px. Click OK to apply the change.

2. Create a new style with the selector #vertMenuBox ul li:hover and set the background-color to #FAFAF5. Click OK to apply the new style, save, and test the page in your browser.

With the addition of the :hover pseudoclass to the list item, you are adding a visual guide for the visitor to see what list item she is hovering over even before she touches the actual link button (see Figure 18.3). This effect highlights list items and other

FIGURE 18.3
The :hover pseudoclass added to the li style adds a sophisticated interactive experience to the menu with only minor effort.

elements without, at the same time, having to make them into links. Note that the link itself changes only to the hover state when the mouse touches it.

The Horizontal Menu—Laying a List on Its Side

As you saw in the preceding exercise, making a vertical menu based on an unordered list look interesting with CSS isn't all that hard. But you don't always want your menus to be vertical. In many cases a horizontal menu looks better and is more functional. But how do you create a horizontal menu from an unordered list when the unordered list by its very nature is a list, and therefore vertical? The answer is simple: Lay it on its side:

1. Below the Basic Vertical List box you just created (and outside the box), create a new unordered list with the same five list items as before, and make each a link back to the current page.

2. In Split view, wrap the new list in a div with the ID #horizontalMenuBox. Create a new style with the selector #horizontalMenuBox and set font-family to Arial, Helvetica, sans-serif; background-color to #EBEADF; border to solid, 1px, #C4C2AB; and margin-top to 10px to create some space between the Basic Vertical Menu and the new one you are about to create.

3. Create a new style with the selector #horizontalMenuBox ul and set padding and margin to 0px for all sides.

4. To get the menu items to appear on one line instead of as a list, create a new style with the selector #horizontalMenuBox ul li and set display to inline under the Layout category. Click Apply and you see that the list items are now on one line (Figure 18.4).

5. To give the menu some more weight, you want to create some vertical space above and below the links. But if you go to Box and set padding-top and padding-bottom to 10px and click Apply, you see that nothing changes. To change the line height and thereby the vertical space above and below the list items, go to the Block category and set line-height to 25px. Click OK to apply the style.

6. Right now the menu items are stacked almost on top of one another. To give them some breathing room, create a new style with the selector #horizontalMenuBox ul li a and set padding-right and padding-left to 10px. To match the vertical space created earlier, set padding-top and

FIGURE 18.4
To make the items of an unordered list appear next to one another, simply set the li style to display:inline.

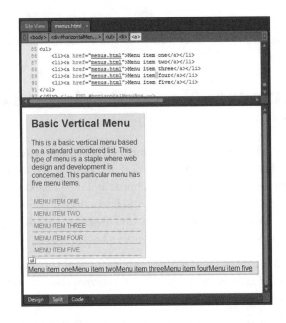

padding-bottom to 5px. At the same time, set the font-size to 0.8em, text-transform to uppercase, color to #666666, and text-decoration to none. Click Apply to see the changes take effect.

7. Finally to make the menu items react when the visitor hovers her mouse over them, create a new style with the selector #horizontalMenuBox ul li a:hover and set color to #333333 and background-color to #C4C2AB. Click OK to apply the new style, save, and test the page in your browser.

As you can see in Figure 18.5, the items in the horizontal menu reacts in much the same way as the vertical one with one major difference; the entire hover area is a link. This is because you used the padding in step 6 to expand the link area to cover an area larger than the text itself. You can use the same technique to make the entire area of the vertical menu into a link.

Pure CSS Drop-Down Menus: A Clean Alternative

Now that you've created a vertical and a horizontal menu, it is time to merge the two into a more advanced drop-down menu in which the main menu is horizontal and the submenus are vertical. As you have learned, if you want your page to be as accessible as possible and standards-compliant and cross-browser compatible, base

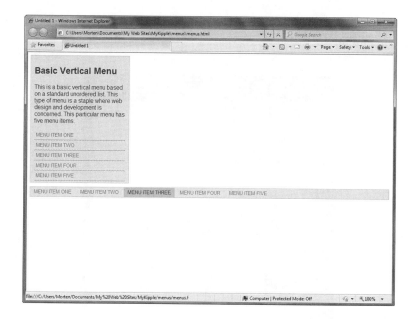

FIGURE 18.5
With some basic styling, the unordered list is turned into a functional horizontal menu.

all your menus on ordered or unordered lists. That way, the menu is still meaningful if the visitor is on an old computer or uses a text-only or text-to-speech browser. The ideal solution for making drop-down menus should be to create an unordered list with sublists styled using CSS. And in an ideal world, this wouldn't be that much of a problem. Unfortunately the idiosyncratic nature of the most prolific browsers (especially Internet Explorer 6) has made it all but impossible to make a CSS drop-down menu without using some form of custom coding for these browsers or adding JavaScript or behaviors to make everything work properly.

As new versions of the many different browsers emerge, these problems with inconsistencies become less and less prevalent. Sometime in the foreseeable future, they will likely disappear completely or at least diminish to the point where they are no longer a concern. In the meantime, designers have to live with one of two options: create pure CSS drop-down menus that might have problems in older browsers, or make menus that have JavaScript built in to fix the browser problems.

Here we focus on merging the preceding two menus to create a drop-down menu using only CSS and no special browser-specific code. As a result, it might not work properly in Internet Explorer 6.

Step 1: Make a Menu List

1. In the menus.html page, insert a new div underneath the code for the horizontal menu and give it the ID #dropDownMenu. Inside the new div create another

copy of the unordered list menu from above by copying and pasting everything within the <ul> tags (see Figure 18.6)

FIGURE 18.6
You can duplicate the basic unordered lists by copying and pasting them within Code view.

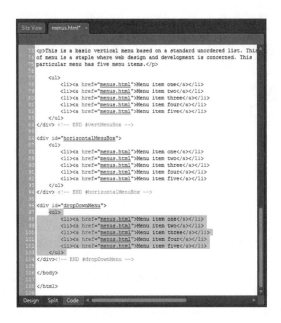

2. Create sublists for three of the new menu items. In Split view, select the Menu Item Two list item. In Code view, place the cursor right before the closing </li> tag, and press Enter to create a new line. Type **<ul>** to create a new unordered list (IntelliSense closes the tag for you), press Enter again to create a new line, and create a sublist item by typing **<li>**. Create three sublist items named **Sub List Item One** and so on (see Figure 18.7).

3. Now that you have a sublist, go back to Design view make all of the new items into links that point back to the current page.

4. Repeat steps 2 and 3 for two of the other main menu items (see Figure 18.8).

Step 2: Styling the Main Menu

Now you have a working set of hyperlinks, but it looks nothing like a menu. The next step is to turn the menu into a horizontal one like you did in the menu previously in this chapter.

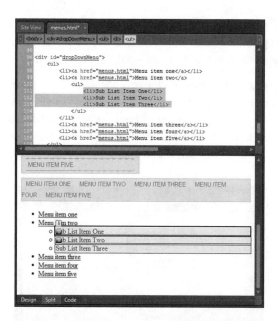

FIGURE 18.7
To create a list within a list, you need to edit the code in Code view. Although doing so is not necessary, splitting up the tags and spacing them as shown in this screenshot helps with readability.

FIGURE 18.8
The lists within lists appear as subsets of their parent list items.

1. Create a new style with the ID #dropDownMenu. Set font-family to Arial, Helvetica, sans-serif; background-color to #EBEADF; border to solid, 1px, #C4C2AB; and margin-top to 10px to create some space.

2. Create a new style with the selector #dropDownMenu ul and set padding and margin to 0px for all sides. Note that in Design view all the list items line up to the left side of the box regardless of what level they are at.

3. Create a new style with the selector #dropDownMenu ul li and set display to inline under the Layout category. In the preceding menu, this was enough to align the menu items left to right rather than top to bottom, but if you click Apply you see that the list items still stack vertically. This is because the sublists are too wide to fit on one line and are considered one item (see Figure 18.9).

FIGURE 18.9
Even with the li style to display:inline the list still stacks vertically.

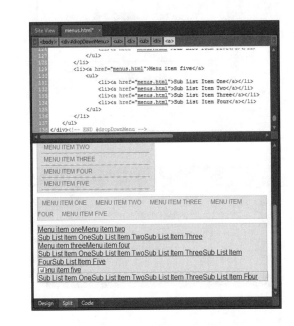

4. To get the new menu to stack properly, you need to do two things: Define a specific width for each list item and make them float to the left. Still in the #dropDownMenu ul li style, set width under Position to 150px. You can set it wider if you want, but any narrower and the text in the submenu items won't fit. Then go to the Layout category and set float to left. Click Apply again, and you see that now the main menu items line up from left to right, and the submenu items appear as vertical lists under their respective parent item (see Figure 18.10).

5. Because we are operating with two layers of list items, the basic font styling should be done in the li style: Still in the #dropDownMenu ul li style, set the font-size to 0.8em and text-transform to uppercase. To give the buttons

FIGURE 18.10
With the width
and float attrib-
utes set, the list
starts to look
like a drop-down
menu.

some breathing space, set `height` under Position to 25px. Click OK to apply the changes.

6. Next you need to style the links like you did earlier. Create a new style with the selector #dropDownMenu `ul li a`. Under Font set `color` to #666666 and set `text-decoration` to none. Go to Background and set `background-color` to #EBEADF manually, or you can use the Eyedropper tool and pick the background color from one of the other menus. Click Apply and you see that the links now have the right font and background color but that the background is visible only directly behind the links, as shown in Figure 18.11.

7. For the menu to look and function properly, the link area needs to extend beyond the text to cover the allotted area in the boxes the `li` style has created. In the earlier horizontal menu, you used the `padding` attribute to do this, but this time you use the `line-height` and `display` attributes: Still in the #dropDownMenu `ul li a` style, go to Block and set the `line-height` attribute to 25px to match the height you set in the #dropDownMenu `ul li` style earlier. Next go to Layout and set `display` to block. Finally set `padding-left` to 8px to create some space between the left edge and the text. Click OK and the backgrounds now fill out the correct areas, as shown in Figure 18.12.

8. Now that the buttons extend to fill the required area, create a new pseudoclass with the selector #dropDownMenu `ul li a:hover` and set `color` to #333333 and `background-color` to #C4C2AB. Click OK, save the page, and test it in your browser.

FIGURE 18.11
Unless otherwise defined, the background color only appears directly behind the link text.

FIGURE 18.12
With the line-height and display properties set properly, the link backgrounds extend to "fill out" the menu boxes.

Previously in the book, you learned that the `block` attribute caused the element to which it was applied to appear on its own line and fill out that line. The same thing happens when the attribute is applied to the style in step 7, but because the list item style (`li`) has already been set to inline with a fixed width, the block is constrained by the `li` box and fills out only the area within it.

Step 3: Making the Drop-Down Menus Drop Down

As you can see in Figure 18.13, the main menu and submenus line up correctly, but the submenus are all visible all the time. But the whole point of drop-down menus is that they drop down only when the visitor hovers over them. To achieve this you are going to use the :hover pseudoclass with the visibility attribute to hide the submenus.

FIGURE 18.13
Although the menus line up correctly, all the submenus are visible all the time.

1. First hide the submenus so that they are invisible unless the user triggers them. To do so, create a new style with the selector #dropDownMenu ul li ul. This style affects only the unordered lists contained within a list item, aka the submenus. Under the Layout category, set the visibility to hidden. Click OK to apply the modified style. Now the submenus are no longer visible in Design view.

2. Create a new style with the selector #dropDownMenu ul li:hover ul. This style is a pseudoclass that triggers when the visitor hovers over a main menu list item and affects any unordered list contained within that list item. Under the Layout category, set visibility to visible. Click OK to apply the new style.

Save and preview the page in your browser; you see that the drop-down menus now work the way they should (see Figure 18.14). Furthermore the menu is 100% CSS-based, which means it works without any code additives such as JavaScript. But, most important, it is fully legible if the visitor uses a text-only or text-to-speech browser.

FIGURE 18.14
The pure CSS
drop-down menu
now works prop-
erly in all mod-
ern browsers.

As you can see in Figure 18.15, with styles turned off in Firefox, the CSS-based menus revert to their original form, which is standard unordered lists with sublists. Not only is the menu easier to read, but also the layout and ordering is intuitive to the visitor even without styles.

FIGURE 18.15
With styles
turned off, the
CSS-based
menus revert
back to standard
unordered lists
for easy reading.

Not All Browsers Like the Pure CSS Drop-Down Menu

Watch Out!

As previously mentioned, the pure CSS drop-down menu is not a perfect solution because not all browsers support it. For unknown reasons, Internet Explorer 6 does not support pseudoclasses attached to items other than simple anchors (a style). Because you used the `li:hover` style to create the drop-down effect, it will not work properly in Internet Explorer 6. To solve this problem, you have to either employ a custom JavaScript that simulates the `li:hover` pseudoclass for IE6 or create a separate menu that replaces the pure CSS drop-down menu for IE6 users. One clever workaround is to place the pure CSS drop-down menu in one layer and a custom IE6 menu in another, and then use the Check Browser behavior to choose what layer to show in the page based on what browser the visitor uses.

The Internet Explorer 6 compatibility issue is a diminishing one because more and more users are upgrading to newer versions of the browser (Internet Explorer 7 has been out for some time and Internet Explorer 8 was rolled out in the spring of 2009), and most, if not all, other browsers support the `li:hover` property. With that said, you always have to consider the lowest common denominator and whether you should "dumb down" your sites to accommodate it.

Styling the Submenus to Make Them Stand Out

Right now there is no visual difference between the main menu items and the submenus. But depending on the design of the site, it can sometimes be a good idea to give the visitor visual clues that separate different types of content from each other. A simple way of doing this is to give the submenu items a different set of styles than the main menu items.

1. Create a new style with the selector #dropDownMenu ul li ul li a. This style affects only the links inside list items that are housed inside another list item. Under Font set `color` to #FFFFFF and under Background set `background-color` to #3399FF. This gives the submenus a blue background color. Click OK to apply the new style.

2. Because of the cascade, unless you specify something different, the hover state of the submenus is styled by the #dropDownMenu ul li a:hover pseudoclass. To change the hover state, you need to create a new pseudoclass with the selector name #dropDownMenu ul li ul li a:hover. Set the `color` to #FFFFFF and set the `background-color` to #0065CA. Click OK, save and test the page in your browser.

With the new styles applied, the submenu now has a distinct look that is different from the main menu (see Figure 18.16).

FIGURE 18.16
The submenu styling produces a visual cue that tells the visitor these buttons are different from the ones on the main menu.

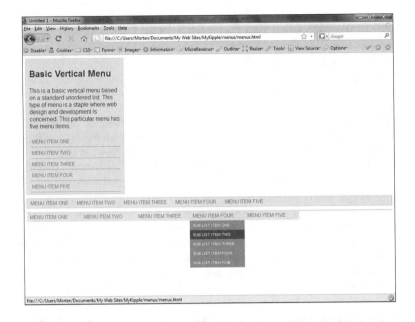

Try It Yourself

Create an Image-Based Menu for the MyKipple Site

Now that you know how to make a functional menu, let's apply that knowledge to the MyKipple site and, in the process, make it even more advanced by applying image-based backgrounds.

1. With the default.html file open in Split view, find the #mainMenu div housed inside the header. In Code view create a new unordered list with three buttons named **Home**, **Gallery**, and **Contact**. Make each of them a link pointing back to default.html.

2. Create a new style in kippleStyles.css and give it the selector #mainMenu ul. Set width to 100% so that the box spans the entire width of the header box.

3. Create a new style in kippleStyles.css and give it the selector #mainMenu ul li. Under Block set line-height to 30px and under Layout set display to inline. This aligns the buttons on one line.

4. Create a new style in kippleStyles.css and give it the selector #mainMenu ul li a. Set color to #000000, text-align (found under Block) to center, width to 110px, height to 35px, and under Layout set display to block and float to left.

5. Create a pseudoclass for a:hover and set color to #FFFFFF and text-decoration to none.

At this point you should have a basic three-item menu along the bottom left side of the #header div, as shown in Figure 18.17. The buttons work but there

FIGURE 18.17
The menu items are now styled so that they appear on a horizontal line, but they have no backgrounds and are transparent.

are no backgrounds. Now you assign separate graphic backgrounds to each of the three buttons using custom classes.

6. Import the three files green.png, blue.png, and purple.png from the lesson files for this hour and place them in the Graphics folder.

7. In kippleStyles.css create a new style with the selector .blue. Set background-image to blue.png, background-repeat to no-repeat, and height to 35px.

8. In the Manage Styles panel, right-click the new .blue style and select New Style Copy from the pop-up menu. This creates an exact copy of the style. Rename it **.green** and change the background-image to green.png. Click OK to save the new style, and use the exact same technique to create a third style with the selector .purple.

9. In Code view, find the anchor tag for the first of the three buttons and place your cursor directly after the letter a. Press spacebar and type **class="blue"**. This applies the .blue class to the first button.

10. In Design view, click the second button, and use the Quick Tag Selector to select the <a> tag. In the Manage Styles panel right-click on the .green style, and select Apply Style from the pop-up menu.

11. In Design view click on the third button, and make sure the <a> tag is highlighted in the Quick Tag Selector. In the Apply Styles panel, click the .purple style to apply it.

As you can see in Figure 18.18, you now have three buttons with three different backgrounds. And if you paid attention to the earlier lessons in this hour, you noticed that the styling of this menu is the same used to create the drop-down menu, which means that if you want to, you can expand the menu to include drop-down features later!

FIGURE 18.18
The menu items now have individual colored backgrounds applied using custom classes.

Summary

Menus are important elements for navigation and design. A website with functional and well-designed menus gives the visitor a more interactive experience and the website a feeling of professionalism. For this reason and many others, it is important to know how to make different types of menus including drop-down menus that look great and work properly across browsers and platforms.

There are many approaches to creating menus, and in this hour you learned what I think is the best and most-solid approach: the pure CSS menu. Not only is this type of menu standards-based but it is also easy to manage and future proof (not to mention accessible).

At the end of this hour, you have three different menus: The basic vertical menu, the basic horizontal menu, and the advanced horizontal drop-down menu. All three were based on simple standards-based unordered lists and styled with fairly basic CSS. Hopefully what you learned by following these lessons is that if you have a firm grasp of some basic CSS concepts including the `display`, `float`, and `visibility` attributes, you can create advanced layout elements with only minimal style code.

The drop-down menu at the end of the hour is as pure and simple as I can make it. Its basis is a simple unordered list with sublists. This is done for several reasons: It makes the contents of the menu accessible regardless of what type of browser the visitor is using; it keeps the styling separate from the content; and it is easy to manage because all you need to do is edit the lists themselves—the design follows automatically.

The styling you applied to the different menus in this hour was very basic and can easily be expanded and elaborated on to create much more advanced looks and designs. The backgrounds can be replaced by images, you can attach borders, and even classes to make each button different from the rest. And all this is made possible by the standards based approach.

There is no right or wrong when it comes to creating menus, and there are other techniques available. In Appendix A, "Building Layers-Based Menus," you can find a tutorial on how to use layers and images to create a drop-down menu. I have deliberately taken the tutorial out of the main body of the book because I do not want you to use layers-based menus. They are not standards-based; they are cumbersome; they require JavaScript support; and most important they are hard to modify and redesign. Nevertheless, if you want to use this type of menu or if you want to get a better understanding of how you can use layers to create some fairly advanced visibility effects, the tutorial is there for you to read.

Like I previously said, the menus you made in this hour are as clean as possible, and they are the ones I use in all the sites I design (with more advanced styling, of course). You can find a more advanced version of the pure CSS drop-down menu that incorporates the necessary JavaScript to solve the IE6 problem by going to http://www.alistapart.com and searching for Suckerfish menu.

Q&A

Q. *You say that the pure CSS drop-down menu doesn't work in Internet Explorer 6. Is that something I should worry/care about?*

A. The answer to this question depends on who your target audience is. If you assume your audience is up-to-date where technology is concerned and is using equipment that is less than 8 years old (i.e., running Windows XP or a newer operating system), chances are they have upgraded their browser to either Internet Explorer 7 or 8, in which case this really doesn't matter. However, there are certain corporations and users who for one reason or another do not upgrade their browsers, and for those people, the drop-down menu won't work. So if you are creating a website targeted at users with old systems or a corporation that uses Internet Explorer 6, you need to add some JavaScript to your menu to make it work for your target users.

Workshop

The Workshop has quiz questions and exercises to help you put to use what you just learned. If you get stuck, the answers to the quiz questions are in the next section. But try to answer the questions first. Otherwise you'll only be cheating yourself.

Quiz

1. What CSS attribute is used to make the items in an unordered list appear side-by-side rather than under one another?

2. If you have a menu with a submenu, what selector name do you give to the style that controls the links in the list items of the submenu?

Answers

1. `display: inline;`

2. `#menuName ul li ul li a`

Exercise

Create a new submenu for the Menu Item Five buttons. Make at least five new menu items for the submenu. Link the buttons in the different menus to random websites to see how they work.

HOUR 19

Dynamic Web Templates

What You'll Learn in This Hour:

▶ How to create a Dynamic Web Template

▶ How to create a new page from a Dynamic Web Template

▶ How to apply a Dynamic Web Template to an existing page

▶ How to edit a Dynamic Web Template and the files created from it

Introduction

Most websites consist of more than a single page. The whole idea behind creating the World Wide Web was the ability to make numerous documents available and then link them together rather than presenting them all at the same time. But this causes a problem: If you have a website with multiple pages and you want to make a design change to all these pages, you have to update each page individually. If your site has only a few pages this is not a problem, but what if it has tens or even hundreds of pages?

In the past, updating large sites was a daunting task because each page contained all the styling information. As a result, webmasters rarely updated designs and sites quickly became outdated. The introduction of Cascading Style Sheets (CSS) solved many of these problems because the designer could now put the styling code in a separate document and modify this file for sitewide changes. This was a huge step forward and paved the way for a new generation of site models, including blogs.

But wouldn't it be great if you could take that principle one step further and set your site up so that one file controlled not just the styles but also the common elements of all the pages such as headers, footers, and main menus? This question is already answered in the form of Dynamic Web Templates (commonly known as *DWTs*).

A DWT is a special type of file built using Hypertext Markup Language (HTML) and CSS to define which areas of a page a publisher might edit and which areas are off limits to regular page building. After a DWT exists, you can use it to build new pages in which all you need to do is input new content in the predefined areas without having to worry about all the common elements present in every page. More important, when you have multiple pages built using a DWT, you can change the composition and layout of all the pages by making changes to only the DWT file. In other words, using DWTs makes global alterations to a website a snap.

In this hour, you learn how to build a DWT and create new pages based on it. You also learn how to make changes to the DWT and its children, and how to apply a DWT to an existing page. The most important lesson of this hour is that using DWTs wisely can have a huge positive impact on your workload and make updating multi-page websites nearly as easy as editing a single page.

Dynamic Web Templates

When you design a website, you should always consider the following question: "How do I make sure it is easy to update the look and functionality of every page within the site?" Depending on the scale of the project and the kind of content you are presenting, the answer to this question is different:

▶ If you are creating a small-scale site with only a few pages (fewer than 10) and multiple different layouts and designs, you can go with straightforward HTML pages with one or several style sheets attached.

▶ If your site is (or could become) larger and you have one or two layouts to implement sitewide, creating pages based on DWTs is an effective solution.

▶ If your site has a high number of pages or constantly updated dynamic content (think an online paper or magazine, a forum, a blog, or a site with multiple authors), the best solution is to use a Content Management System (CMS) that generates pages dynamically with server-side script and a database—this option is for advanced users only.

For the large majority of sites, the second option is the best choice because it makes for easy page construction and quick sitewide design changes.

Blogs, Forums, and Content Management Systems

If you are ready to move beyond the basics, you should take some time and familiarize yourself with the most common Open Source blogging platforms, forums, and CMSs. With these technologies in your toolkit, you will be well equipped to provide clients with a wide range of services and options for their websites.

One of the great things about Open Source software is that because it is developed by the users, the programs are always evolving, and someone is always out there with an answer for you when you run into a difficult problem. For this reason the best place to start learning about these technologies is the home page of the project.

If you are new to web design, entering into the world of dynamic web technologies can be a seemingly daunting task. But it isn't as complicated as it seems. If you want to learn about CMSs and how database-based dynamic websites work, a good place to start is actually the blogging platform WordPress.

WordPress (www.wordpress.org) was originally a basic blogging platform that over time has grown into a full-fledged publishing platform or CMS. I use it as the base of most of my clients' sites and for blogs. The benefit of using WordPress is the seemingly endless variety of plug-ins that enable you to expand the platform to do whatever you want as well. What is great about WordPress is that it is built with the user in mind, so it can be as easy or as complicated as you want it to be. Furthermore it can work as either a blogging platform, a CMS, or both—it's totally up to you. Finally the look and feel of WordPress is created using standards-based code and CSS, meaning that you can use the techniques learned in this book to completely redesign your WordPress-based sites. For more information on how to do this visit, my blog at http://www.designisphilosophy.com where I have created an ongoing series called "WordPress as CMS" where I explore how to rework and redesign WordPress to do whatever you want.

As an added bonus, WordPress has excellent Search Engine Optimization (SEO) built in, meaning that sites built using the platform are easily found on Google and other search engines. That in itself is a huge selling point.

WordPress is not the only option available, and it might not be the platform you are looking for. Other popular platforms include PHPBB Forum (www.phpbb.com) on which the large majority of web forums are built and the two full-scale CMSs Joomla! (www.joomla.org) and Drupal (drupal.org) both of which also offer extensive customization and expandability.

Try It Yourself ▼

Creating a Dynamic Web Template

To get a firmer grasp on what a DWT is and how it works, you build a DWT for the MyKipple.com website based on the default.html page.

Before you begin, replace the current default.html, kippleStyles.css, and layout.css files in your site with the new ones found in the lesson files for this hour. The new files include more styling to make the overall look and feel of the pages more polished. All the changes to the files are based on the lessons you have already completed. If you take a closer look at the code in the kippleStyles.css file, you see that you can recognize most, if not all, of the different styling elements. Also, import the two images menuBG.png and footerBG.png and place them in the Graphics folder.

1. With the new default.html page open in Design view, click File, Save As on the menu bar. In the Save As dialog, change the file type to Dynamic Web Template (.dwt) and name the new file **mykippleMaster.dwt**. This creates a new DWT.

2. With the mykippleMaster.dwt page open in Split view, delete all the text content in the #mainContent div (see Figure 19.1). You can do this by highlighting the text and deleting it in Design view, or by highlighting all the content

FIGURE 19.1
After deleting the content within the #content div, you should still see the #centeredBG, #header, #menu, #content, and #footer divs in Design view.

between the beginning and end <div id="mainContent"> tags and deleting it in Code view. Make sure you leave the #centeredBG, #wrapper, #header, #mainMenu, #content, and #footer divs intact.

3. Place the cursor on the first line inside the #mainContent div, and use the Style drop-down menu from the Common toolbar to set the style of the line to Heading 2 (h2). Press Enter to create a new paragraph underneath (see Figure 19.2).

FIGURE 19.2
Add two empty
text lines in the
#mainContent
div—the first
one with the h2
style and the
second one with
the p style.

4. Place the cursor inside the first line (h2) and from the menu bar select Format, Dynamic Web Templates, Manage Editable Regions.

5. The Editable Regions dialog lets you add and remove editable regions within your DWT. Under Region Name, type **heading** and click the Add button (see Figure 19.3). This creates a new editable region called heading. Click Close to apply the changes.

FIGURE 19.3
The Editable
Region dialog
lets you add and
remove editable
regions.

6. Place your cursor inside the paragraph on the next line, and click the <p> tag in the Quick Tag Selector to select the entire line, including the tags. From the

menu bar, select Format, Dynamic Web Template, Manage Editable Regions to open the Editable Regions dialog again.

7. Create a new editable region called content and click Close to apply the changes. You now have two regions within the page, outlined in orange in Design view (see Figure 19.4).

FIGURE 19.4
The Editable
Regions heading
and content are
inserted into the
DWT.

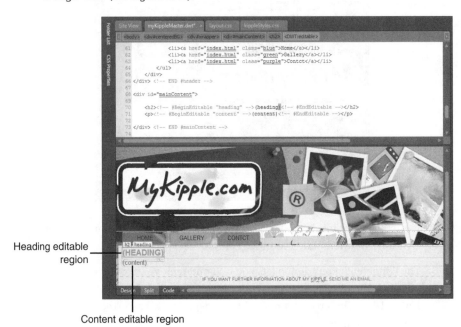

Heading editable
region

Content editable region

How Dynamic Web Templates Work

Now that you have created a DWT, let's take a closer look at how it works. Looking at the page in Code view, you see that it looks pretty much the same as the original file with the exception of a few new lines of commented-out code. The new elements tell Expression Web 3 that a specific DWT controls the page. The elements are commented out because they are not HTML code but rather custom script designed specifically to work with Expression Web 3. As a result, they have no actual function when a browser displays the page and, like other commented content, the code is ignored. But when the application opens the page, they link the DWT and its children together.

In the body of the document are several code segments that tell Expression Web 3 which areas are locked and which areas are editable. When you create a DWT from scratch, you get a standard HTML page with two editable regions: doctitle and body. As the names suggest, the doctitle region holds the <title> tag in the head portion of the page, and the body region holds the body of the page. The same thing happened when you converted the default.html page to a DWT: Expression inserted the doctitle region into your page at the end of the <head> tag.

The beginning and end codes are commented out because they are not HTML and their sole purpose is to help Expression Web 3 to define the editable regions. For example, the doctitle editable region looks like this in Code view:

```
<!-- #BeginEditable "doctitle" -->
<title></title>
<!-- #EndEditable -->
```

Expression Web 3 considers anything within these two code snippets editable. Because code that is invisible to browsers defines the editable regions, you can choose how much you want to micromanage the content within them. The two editable regions you inserted in the mykippleMaster.dwt page serve as good examples of this.

If you select the heading region in Design view and look at the code, you see that the editable region is contained within the h2 tags:

```
<h2><!-- #BeginEditable "heading" -->(heading)<!-- #EndEditable --></h2>
```

That means whatever content you place inside the editable region will be styled with the h2 style. As a result, when building a page based on this DWT, the designer cannot change the style of this content. Expression Web 3 placed the editable region inside the <h2> tags because you placed the cursor inside the h1 area before inserting it.

Alternatively you can manually place the content region on the outside of the style tags like this:

```
<!-- #BeginEditable "content" --><p>(content)</p><!-- #EndEditable -->
```

As a result, the content within the region is not yet styled and the designer can apply other tags and styles at will.

Understanding the difference between these two methods of inserting editable regions means that the designer of the DWT has almost unlimited control of the output that comes from pages created with the template.

▼ **Try It Yourself**

Create a New Page from a DWT

When you have a DWT, creating new pages for your project becomes much easier. The DWT contains all the common elements that all pages should feature, and all you need to do is insert the page-specific content. Because HTML is the basis for the DWT, all the CSS styling you attach to the DWT is available in your new page.

1. To create a new page from a DWT, select File, New, Create from Dynamic Web Template from the menu bar.

FIGURE 19.5
Select the DWT you want to base your page on in the Attach Dynamic Template dialog.

2. When you create a page from a DWT, the Attach Dynamic Template dialog opens. Select the mykippleMaster.dwt file and click Open (see Figure 19.5). An information box opens to report that a number of files updated—this refers to the content of the DWT populating the new file.

3. With the new page open in Design view, you now have only two clickable areas in the page: the heading and the content. If you move your cursor anywhere else, all you get is a stop sign. Place your cursor in the heading area and type **About Me** (see Figure 19.6). Note that Expression Web 3 automatically applies the h2 style. If you press Enter to create a new line, a warning pops up to tell you that you can't make the change because a DWT is locking the code.

4. Place your cursor in the content region, and write a short bio about yourself or insert some other content of your choice. Because this region is not contained within a tag, it is not constrained in the same way the heading region is, so

you can add several paragraphs, images, or any other HTML content as you place and style it using the styles and classes in the attached style sheet (see Figure 19.7).

FIGURE 19.6
With the DWT attached to the new page, you can make changes only to the editable regions. The template locks the rest of the page.

FIGURE 19.7
The content created inside the regions can be styled with any of the styles available in the attached style sheet and new styles.

5. When you finish inserting content in the page, press Ctrl+S to save the file. In the Save As dialog, go to the Pages folder and give the new page the name about.html.

By previewing the new page in your browser, you see that although all you did was insert the heading and main content, the page looks and works just like the default.html page. That is because all the common components are the same.

▲

Understanding Dynamic Web Templates

The preceding example should give you a good idea of what happens when you create a new page from a DWT. When you attach a DWT to a new page, what actually happens is that Expression Web 3 takes the code content from the DWT and places it in your new page. But unlike a "normal" page, the application knows that only the editable regions within the page should be available for changes, so it looks for the editable regions and blocks all the other content. After inserting content in the editable regions, the result is the same as any other HTML page except that the code contains the commented-out code calls for the editable regions. But because they are commented out, the browser ignores them.

▼   **Try It Yourself**

Update Your Site by Editing the DWT

The reason the editable regions code remains in the page is to give you the ability to change the DWT and by doing so to change all the pages created from it.

1. Open the mykippleMaster.dwt page in Split view. Find the unordered #main-Menu list in Code view.

2. Create a new list item before Contact to create a new button. Type **About Me** as the text, and create a hyperlink that points to the new about.html page you just created.

3. Like the three other buttons, attach a color class to the new button (see Figure 19.8).

4. Save the mykippleMaster.dwt page. An information dialog opens to tell you that there is one page attached to mykippleMaster.dwt and asking whether you want to update it now (see Figure 19.9). Click Yes. Expression Web 3 now updates all the files built based on the DWT.

FIGURE 19.8
It is usually easier to edit lists in Code view than Design view because you have more control of how the different elements relate to one another.

FIGURE 19.9
After updating the files connected to the DWT, Expression Web 3 opens an information dialog telling you how many files were updated and if any files were skipped.

5. When it finishes, another information dialog opens to tell you how many pages Expression Web 3 updated. If you check the Log box, the dialog expands to provide a more detailed log of the update process including a list of what pages the application updated (see Figure 19.10).

FIGURE 19.10
By changing the DWT and updating the files it attaches to, you change the contents of all the pages in the site without ever opening them.

If you test the about.html page in your browser, you see that the main menu now has an About Me button in addition to the three original ones even though you didn't make any changes to the page.

This example showcases the true power of DWTs: By making a website where a DWT is the basis for all the pages, you can make consistent changes to the common content in every page by editing just one page.

▲

▼   **Try It Yourself**

Attach a DWT to an Existing Page

Sometimes you want to add the new DWT designs to old pages that you already built. Your initial hunch might be to copy-and-paste the contents from this page into a new one, but that is not necessary. Just as you attached a DWT to a new page, you can also attach a DWT to an existing page. In Hour 9, "Getting Boxed In, Part 1: Using Tables for Tabular Content," you created a page called myCameras.html that contained a table listing all my cameras. Now you want this page to match the rest of the pages in the MyKipple site.

1. Open the myCameras.html file in Design view. From the menu bar, select Format, Dynamic Web Template, Attach Dynamic Web Template. In the Attach Dynamic Web Template dialog, select mykippleMaster.dwt.

2. A warning appears telling you that content outside of the <html> tag will be deleted and that if you want to preserve it, you need to move it into an editable region or into the <head> tag. This warning is to alert designers who have attached code, such as a script, outside of the main content of the page. If that is the case, you can click No and move the script. For most situations this is not necessary, so click Yes.

3. Because you did not create the myCameras.html page using the DWT, there are no editable regions defined within the page. Instead of just erasing the content not already defined in the page, Expression Web 3 makes an educated guess as to where you want your content and lets you correct its choices. When there are no matching editable regions or there is another conflict, the Match Editable Regions dialog opens (see Figure 19.11). From here you can tell Expression Web 3 what content should go in what region. In this example, the <body> tag contains only one block of content, and Expression Web 3 is guessing that it should go in the heading region. To change this, select the list item by clicking it and clicking the Modify button.

FIGURE 19.11
When the regions in the current page don't match the editable regions, Expression Web 3 lets you match them manually.

4. When you click the Modify button, the Choose Editable Region for Content dialog appears. There you can define which new region should receive the content from the old region. Use the New Region drop-down menu to select the `content` region for the `<body>` content (see Figure 19.12). Click OK twice to attach the DWT.

FIGURE 19.12
The Choose Editable Region for Content dialog lets you pick which editable region to put different content from the old page in.

As you can see, the conversion to the new look is not flawless. Among other things you now have some stray divs and tags (most important, one called #wrapper0) that you need to remove, and you also need to move the heading up into the heading area and delete the entire #sidebar div. All of these fixes can be done in Split view, and after some tidying up, the page will look the way it should (see Figure 19.13). Now if you make any changes to the DWT, the myCameras.html page changes automatically, too.

FIGURE 19.13
With some tidy-
ing up, the
myCameras.html
page fits in
nicely with the
new design.

Editable Regions Outside the Body

As mentioned in the beginning of this hour, Expression Web 3 inserts an editable
region called doctitle by default in all pages attached to a DWT because the application assumes (as it should) that every page has its own distinctive title. Because the
<title> tag is contained within an editable region by default, you can edit it as you
normally would either through the Page Properties dialog or directly in Code view.

Using the same technique, you can also predefine other head content (editable or
locked) for your pages. Moreover you can use the editable content area in the DWT
to give the page predefined common properties that you or other designers can edit,
add to, or replace when building new pages.

▼   **Try It Yourself**

Create Common Editable Keywords for All Pages

To make a page easier to find for people who search the Web using search engines, it
should always contain keywords and a description that describes the page and its
contents.

1. With the mykippleMaster.dwt page open in Split view, right-click in Design view and select Page Properties from the drop-down menu. This opens the Page Properties dialog.

2. In the Title area, enter **MyKipple.com**. In the Page Description area, enter a short description that is common to all the pages. In the Keywords area, insert the keywords **kipple**, **philip k dick**, **junk**, **trash**, **treasure** (see Figure 19.14). Click OK to apply the changes.

3. Toward the top of the page in Code view (most likely around line 15) are two new lines of code that start with <meta content=".... These lines define the keywords and description for the page. In this example, you want the keywords

FIGURE 19.14
Inserting content in the Page Properties dialog is an easy way to create the header code.

to be editable but not the description. To do so, place your cursor at the beginning of the first line in Code view containing the keywords and manually add the following line of code: **<!-- #BeginEditable "keywords" -->** (see Figure 19.15).

4. Press the End key or use the mouse to place the cursor at the end of the line. Add the following line of code after the last tag: **<!-- #EndEditable -->**.

5. Save the DWT and click Yes when asked whether you want to update the attached pages.

After applying the changes, open the about.html page, right-click, and select Page Properties from the context menu. In the Page Properties dialog, you see that the Title and Keywords areas are editable, but the Description and other areas are

FIGURE 19.15
You need to manually add the editable regions outside of the <body> tag in Code view.

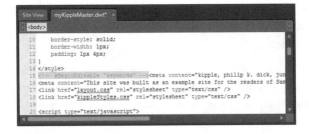

grayed out (see Figure 19.16). It is also important to note that even though the Keywords section remains editable, Expression Web 3 still inserts the words you added in the DWT. After the application creates the new page, you can edit, add to, or delete those words without the changes affecting the DWT or the other pages.

FIGURE 19.16
The Description meta tag was not defined as an editable region in the DWT and is, therefore, inaccessible in the Page Properties dialog of the pages created with this DWT.

Watch Out!

You can insert and edit only the editable regions in the DWT that are outside the <body> tag in Code view. If you highlight code outside of the <body> tag and use the Manage Editable Regions dialog to add a new editable region, Expression Web 3 places the new region inside the <body> tag and wraps all the content. There is also no support for this particular code set in IntelliSense, so you have to write all the code. On the upside, there are only two variations of the editable region code: the begin editable region code (<!-- #BeginEditable "regionName" -->) and the end editable region code (<!-- #EndEditable -->). If you can't remember these two code segments, scroll down further in the document, copy the code from a different editable region, paste it where you want the editable region, and change the region name.

Editing Content Outside the Editable Regions in Individual Pages

Although I do not recommend it, you can manually change the content outside of the editable regions in individual pages. While in Design view, the only selectable areas are the editable regions. But if you switch to Code view, you can modify the code manually.

In a page created from a DWT, Expression Web 3 highlights all the code defined by the DWT in yellow in Code view. The highlighting tells you exactly which areas the template controls externally and which areas are open for editing. Nevertheless you can place your cursor anywhere within the code and make all the changes you want. But if you make changes to the highlighted code, Expression Web 3 tells you that you are now changing code defined by the DWT.

When you save the file or switch back to Design view after changing the code outside the editable regions in Code view, Expression Web 3 displays an alert dialog with a warning that the changes you have made are in the code defined by the DWT (see Figure 19.17). The Dynamic Web Template Alert dialog gives you two options: either

FIGURE 19.17
If you change code inserted by the DWT in your page, Expression Web 3 gives you a warning and asks you to explicitly verify that these changes are intentional.

restore the noneditable content (in other words, discard any changes made to the code defined by the DWT) or keep the changes. If you choose the latter, you have the additional option of detaching the page from the DWT.

The ability to change the code in individual pages comes with a strong warning because if, later, you choose to make changes to the DWT and update the files attached to it, you permanently erase the changes you made in the individual page code.

If an area within a page requires individualization for each page, it is always advisable to place this area within an editable region and place the default content in the DWT. That way, if you do nothing to the code, it remains the same across every page, but you retain the ability to change the individual pages if you choose to do so. The most obvious example of this would be if you wanted to change menu options for some pages, but not others. To do so, simply place the menu list items within an editable region called menu, and you now have the ability to change the menu in individual pages if necessary without making those changes sitewide.

Summary

One of the major challenges for web designers and developers is tackling the task of sitewide design updates. If the site's creators do not design it with this in mind, updating it could easily become a large and difficult task.

In this hour, you learned about Dynamic Web Templates and you saw how you can use them to create sites that are easy to expand and update. The DWT is a great tool if all your site's pages have common elements and only certain portions of the page have unique content.

The DWT function inside Expression Web 3 works by linking the DWT to the files it is attached to either because they were built based on the DWT or because the DWT was attached later. These pages contain small segments of code that define editable regions that are accessible to the designer or whoever is creating or editing the page. Likewise all the content outside of the editable regions is off limits, and no one can edit it without going directly into the code. This is to ensure that when a developer updates the site by changing the DWT, none of the individual page content gets lost in the process.

After a DWT exists and creators have based a number of pages on it, a change in the DWT spreads through all the other pages, making the new changes sitewide. Rather than having to make changes to all the content in every page, you just change the DWT, and Expression Web 3 asks whether you want to update the other pages automatically.

By defining editable (and noneditable) regions within the layout, you can micromanage the contents, both visual and nonvisual, of your pages. In addition, within the editable regions, you can add predefined content for insertion into every page and can edit the individual pages later.

A website designed using DWTs makes life easier for not only the designer but also for the client. In many cases, a client asks to have a site designed where she can add or edit the pages herself. By creating a DWT and building all the pages based on it, the client receives a set of pages in which she can edit only the informational content of the site and can't accidentally damage or destroy design elements such as menus and so forth. This makes for a far less intimidating end-user experience because the pages have clearly marked and named regions that the client can edit using principles familiar to anyone who has worked with a word processing application.

Q&A

Q. *I removed one of the editable regions from my Dynamic Web Template, and when I told Expression Web 3 to update the attached pages, the Match Editable Regions dialog popped up. What do I do?*

A. If you remove or rename an editable region, Expression Web 3 asks you where to place the content that used to be in that region. Whether you removed or renamed the region, you have to explicitly tell the program where to place the temporarily orphaned content. If the region has been removed and no new region has been created to take the content, select the item from the list, click Modify, and change the New Region setting to None. If you create a new region or rename the old one, change the New Region attribute to the correct region. This situation occurs because all the files that have the DWT attached have code segments calling for the old regions, and you need to redefine the code segments for the page to work properly inside Expression Web 3.

Q. *Can I open and use a DWT created in Expression Web 3 in a different web authoring application?*

A. Yes, as long as they support DWTs, you can open your DWT and make changes to both the template itself and its children from other web authoring applications.

Workshop

The Workshop has quiz questions and exercises to help you put to use what you just learned. If you get stuck, the answers to the quiz questions are in the next section. But try to answer the questions first. Otherwise you'll be cheating yourself.

Quiz

1. What is the main benefit of using a Dynamic Web Template to design your web site?

2. What happens if you manually change the code outside of the editable regions in a page generated using a Dynamic Web Template?

Answers

1. By using a Dynamic Web Template as the basis for all the pages in your web site, you are effectively placing all the controls of the look and functionality of your site in one file so that when you want to make sitewide changes to the layout, design, or functionality of your site, you can make those changes in one file and see them implemented throughout all the pages.

2. If you change the code outside of the editable regions, the page will work with the new code just like any other HTML page. The major concern with doing this is that if you update the page using the DWT, all the changes made outside the editable regions will be deleted and replaced by the original code in the DWT. Therefore, if you are planning to have custom code that differs from page to page, you should create an editable region to contain this code so that it won't be deleted when the site is updated.

Exercise

In the mykippleMaster.dwt file, change the Description metatag to an editable region so that you can have individual descriptions for each page.

The MyKipple project contains a number of pages that you have already built. Using what you have learned in this hour, attach the mykippleMaster.dwt template to all the pages you have created so far and give them all individual titles, keywords, and descriptions.

Getting Interactive with Forms

What You'll Learn in This Hour:

▶ How to create a form
▶ How to insert and configure form controls in Design view
▶ How to change the properties of forms and form controls
▶ How to make an email form using the built-in features of Expression Web 3

Introduction

The last few years have seen the emergence of the interactive web or "Web 2.0" as people like to call it. The interactive web is an evolution from one-way communication to two-way (or three- or four-way) communication where the content becomes a conversation rather than an information session.

At the core of this evolution lies a simple group of tools introduced shortly after the World Wide Web came into existence. These tools are Hypertext Markup Language (HTML) forms, and they give the visitor the ability to input information and communicate with the site rather than just ingest the information on it.

In its most basic form, an HTML form is a group of elements that together gather information such as text or choices from the visitor and sends it off to a predetermined location for further processing. A form can be anything from a simple email generator or newsletter subscription signup tool to a fully interactive commenting feature in a blog, a posting feature in a forum, or even a checkout page for an online store. In fact, every time you input information in a web page, whether it be your address when purchasing a book or a status update in your favorite social networking site, you are using forms.

Harnessing the power of HTML forms means that you can create immersive experiences with true interactivity for the visitor and facilitate communication between the owner of the site and those who use the site.

Creating Forms in Expression Web 3

HTML defines all the different form elements and form controls. As a result, when you place these elements inside `<form>` tags in an HTML page, the browser automatically knows what they are and how they are supposed to behave; all you need to do is tell the browser what to do with the information gathered.

FIGURE 20.1
All the form controls are available under the Form Controls section in the Toolbox panel.

To make the creation of forms as easy as possible, Expression Web 3 provides all the available form controls in one convenient location: the Toolbox panel (see Figure 20.1). From here you can drag and drop any of the form controls directly into either Code view or Design view without writing a single line of code.

By hovering the mouse over each form control, Expression Web 3 provides a Screen-Tip with a short explanation of what each control does. These explanations are sometimes a little too short, so here is a more detailed explanation of each of the form controls.

▶ Advanced Button ▣ creates a button whose actions are defined by the designer by embedding HTML code.

▶ Drop-Down Box ▦ creates a drop-down box where you can define the different options. Hour 16, "Using Behaviors," introduced you to the drop-down box when you used the Jump Menu behavior.

▶ Form ▦ is the outer tag that defines the form as a whole. The group of all the elements contained within the `<form>` tags makes up the form. A page can have multiple independent forms.

▶ Group Box ▦ creates a separate subgroup or box within the form. You can use this control to visually separate different sections of a form and still preserve the form's integrity by keeping it together. This is a purely visual tool without any actual function.

▶ Input (Button) ▦ creates a standard HTML button with an `onclick` event that can trigger JavaScript. (Think back to Hour 16.) This function is most often used to create Submit, Cancel, and Reset buttons but can be used for any other purpose as well. The Input (Button) function works in much the same way as the interactive button except that you don't control what it looks like—only what the button text is.

▶ Input (Check Box) ▦ creates a check box. The check box lets the visitor make yes-or-no choices such as Send Copy of the Information to Your Own Email address?.

▶ Input (File) ▦ creates a text box with a Browse button attached that lets the user input a location or browse for a file on her computer to submit along with the rest of the information in the form.

▶ Input (Hidden) ▦ creates a hidden text box that is invisible in the browser window but present in the code. This function is often used to insert extra content into a form without giving the visitor a chance to change it.

▶ Input (Image) ▦ makes an image click-sensitive, meaning you can use it as a button. The function also collects the x and y values of where on the image you clicked. This information can be used for added interactivity.

▶ Input (Password) ▦ creates a text field where you can input a password. When the visitor enters text into the field, each character is replaced by an * symbol.

▶ Input (Radio) ▦ creates a radio button. These buttons are similar to check boxes, but rather than being stand-alone yes/no units, they are connected and work as multiple choice.

▶ Input (Reset) ▦ creates a Reset button that when pressed sets the value of each element in the form to its default setting.

▶ Input (Submit) ▦ creates a Submit button that submits the form.

▶ Input (Text) ▣ creates a single-line text box that can collect text such as a name or an address.

▶ Label ▣ associates a label with a form control, meaning that you can create a line of text, image, or other element connected to and working as a description of a specific form control. The Label can also set keyboard shortcuts for specific form controls.

▶ Text Area ▣ creates a multiline text box for longer segments of text. You can define how many lines of text the box allows.

Because form controls are a bit cryptic in their description, it is easier to understand how they work by seeing them in action. The following exercise uses some of the form controls to make a simple email form.

▼   **Try It Yourself**

Create an Email Form

One of the most basic and most useful applications of an HTML form is to create an email form for your website. In addition to giving the user the ability to send emails to you directly from your website, an email form can also help reduce the amount of spam you receive every day. If you leave a mailto: hyperlink in your page, spam bots (computers that automatically sift through the Web looking for email addresses and then inundate them with spam) will find the address and use it. If you place an email form on the page instead, the spam bot will have a much harder time finding your address and you will most likely receive less spam.

1. Create a new page from the DWT you created in Hour 19, "Dynamic Web Templates," by selecting New, Create from Dynamic Web Template on the menu bar and save it as contact.html.

2. Change the Heading to **Contact Me** and place the cursor in the contents editable region.

3. In Split view, remove the <p> and </p> tags in Code view. Go to the Form Controls in the Toolbox panel and find the Form control. Anything contained within this control is considered part of the same form. Double-click the Form control to place it in the editable region of the page.

4. Place the cursor inside the new form area in Design view and select Table, Insert Table on the menu bar to open the Insert Table dialog. Set Rows to 5 and Columns to 2. Under Specify Width, check the In Pixels radio button and set the width to 780 (see Figure 20.2). Click OK to insert the table.

FIGURE 20.2
To keep forms structured, they are usually placed inside tables.

5. With the cursor placed in the first cell of the table, type **Your Name:**. Press the Tab key to move to the next cell.

6. Go to the Form Controls on in the Toolbox panel and find the Input (Text) control. Place it in the cell either by dragging and dropping it or by double-clicking it in the Toolbox (Figure 20.3).

7. In Design view, right-click the new form control and select Form Field Properties from the context menu. This opens the Form Field Properties dialog for this form control. Set the Name to fullName, the Width in Characters to 30, and the Tab Order to 1. Click OK to apply the changes (see Figure 20.4).

8. Back in Design view, place the cursor in the second left cell and type **Your E-mail Address:**. Press the Tab key to move to the next cell and insert another Input (Text) control there.

9. Open the Form Field Properties dialog for the new form control and set the Name to **email**, the Width in Characters to 30, and the Tab Order to 2 to match the first field.

10. Place the cursor in the third left cell and type **Type of Inquiry:**. Press the Tab key to go to the next cell and insert a Drop-Down Box control. Right-click the Drop-Down Box and select Form Field Properties from the context menu to open the Form Field Properties dialog.

FIGURE 20.3
The form controls can be inserted by dragging-and-dropping them into Design or Code view or by placing the cursor where you want them to be placed and double-clicking them in the Toolbox panel.

FIGURE 20.4
By right-clicking a form control and selecting Form Field Properties from the context menu, you get access to the various attributes and features provided for this particular form control.

11. In the Drop-Down Box Properties dialog, set the Name to **options**. Click the Add button to create a new choice. In the Add Choice dialog, type **Question** as the choice, and click the Selected radio button under Initial State (see Figure 20.5). Click OK to add the new choice.

12. Use the Add button to create three more choices: Comment, Suggestion, and Random Thought. Set the initial state for all of them to Not Selected.

13. When all the choices are created, set the Tab Order to 3 and click OK (see Figure 20.6). The Drop-Down Box automatically resizes itself to fit the longest choice.

FIGURE 20.5
The Drop-Down Box Properties dialog lets you define the default choice and what choices the visitor can select from.

FIGURE 20.6
All the choices are added to the Drop-Down Box.

14. In the fourth left cell, type **What's On Your Mind?** Press the Tab key to move to the next cell and insert a Text Area form control.

15. Open the Form Field Properties for the Text Area. Set the Name to **comment**, Width in Characters to 70, Number of Lines to 8, and Tab Order to 4 (see Figure 20.7). Click OK to apply the changes.

16. Place the cursor in the bottom-left cell and type **Finished?** Press the Tab key to move to the lower-right cell and insert an Input (Submit) and an Input (Reset) form control. This creates two buttons that say Submit and Reset, respectively.

17. Open the Form Field Properties for the Submit button. In the Push Button Properties, change the Name to **submitButton**, change the Value/Label to **Submit** (with an uppercase S), leave the Button Type set to Submit, and set the Tab Order to 5 (see Figure 20.8). Click OK to apply the changes.

FIGURE 20.7
In the TextArea
Box Properties
dialog, you can
set the width
and height of the
text area by
defining the
number of char-
acters and num-
ber of lines.

FIGURE 20.7
In the TextArea
Box Properties
dialog, you can
set the width
and height of the
text area by
defining the
number of char-
acters and num-
ber of lines.

FIGURE 20.8
The Push Button
Properties dialog
lets you change
the text that dis-
plays on the but-
ton and its
function.

18. Repeat step 17 for the Reset button, but change the Name to **resetButton**, the
Value/Label to **Reset**, and set the Tab Order to 6.

Now all the basic components for the email form are in place. Save the page and test
it in your browser (see Figure 20.9).

FIGURE 20.9
The contact.html
page with the
email form as it
appears in the
browser.

As you can see, the form already looks pretty good even though you haven't applied any styling to it yet. And if you test the different elements, you can see that they all work properly: You can insert text into the text boxes and make a selection from the drop-down menu, and all the info resets when you click the Reset button. And because you set the tab order for each element, if you select one and press the Tab button on your keyboard, the next one is automatically selected.

▲

But there is still one major issue yet to be resolved: What happens to the information after you click the Submit button?

Making Use of Form Results

To make an HTML form work, you need two main components: the form itself, which you just created; and the functions that collect the info or results from the form and send them off to be processed. And although building the form is a relatively simple task, getting the form to perform the required actions is a bit more complicated.

After results are submitted from a form, the browser passes on the information to whatever process has been defined by the designer or developer. These processes are called server-side scripts, and they take the information, make the necessary alterations to it, and send it off to a file, a database, or an email account. And this is where things get complicated:

To process, or parse, the results from the form, the server that hosts the page has to perform some actions. Unfortunately there are several different server languages available, and they are for the most part mutually exclusive. As a result, a function that works perfectly on one server might generate only errors on another server. So, before you start applying functionality to your forms, you have to find out what language the hosting server speaks.

> **By the Way**
>
> Most web servers run one of the two main server architectures: Linux Server or Microsoft's Windows Server. Both servers support a programming language called PHP, whereas only Windows servers support the application framework called ASP.NET. If you have a Windows server, there is a good chance it has FrontPage Server extensions installed but there is no guarantee. Therefore it is imperative that you find out what architecture the server you plan to put your page on is running and what languages and extensions it supports. If you follow the next tutorial and upload the page to a Linux server or a Microsoft server without the FrontPage Server extensions installed the form will not work properly.

Did you Know?

> If you are hosting your page on a Linux server, you need to use PHP to create the email form functionality. Hour 22, "Beyond the Basics, Part 1: PHP in Expression Web 3," talks about PHP and has a full tutorial on how to make the email form work using this programming language.

▼ **Try It Yourself**

Send Form Results

Now that you have a basic form built into your page, you need to connect it to the functions that make it work. Provided your server has FrontPage Server extensions installed, Expression Web 3 has built-in functions that make it easy to create forms to send results directly to a predefined email address, file, or database.

1. Right-click anywhere inside the email form and select Form Properties from the context menu. This opens the Form Properties dialog (see Figure 20.10).

FIGURE 20.10
You can change and configure the different functions of a form from the Form Properties dialog.

2. Because you want the form to generate an email, select the Send To radio button at the top of the dialog.

3. In the Send To area, you have two options: You can enter a filename and you can enter an email address. If you enter a filename, the results of the form will be sent to a file stored on the server. The two options can be used separately or together. Saving the results to a file and sending them to an email address is an easy way to make sure the message doesn't get lost.

   Click the Browse button next to the File Name area to open the browser and create a new folder called Contact. Click Cancel and enter **Contact/emails.txt** in the File Name area.

Step 3 asked you to use the Browse button to create a new folder without actually selecting a file inside this folder. This is a trick you can use to create new folders while inside a dialog without having to close the dialog.

4. In the E-mail Address area, enter your own email address (see Figure 20.11).

FIGURE 20.11
With the Send To function, you can choose whether to send the results of the form to a file on the server, an email address, or both.

5. To further configure the output generated by the form, click the Options button. This opens the Saving Results dialog.

6. The first tab of the Saving Results dialog deals with the file to which the content is saved (see Figure 20.12). From here you can change the location of the

FIGURE 20.12
When saving the results to a file, you have a choice of many different file formats.

file and the file format (how the content is displayed within the file). For most purposes, Formatted Text is the best option, but there are many alternatives including HTML and XML and text database variants. Below the File Format option, you can check whether you want to include the form field names and whether you want to generate an optional second file. Leave everything as it is in this tab.

7. Under the E-mail Results tab, you can configure what the email sent by the form will look like. The email address bar is self-explanatory, and the E-mail Format menu provides the same options as the File Format menu in the prior tab. Under E-mail Message Header, you can set the Subject line and the Reply-To line for the email generated. Each of these can be set to a standard line of text or to a form field name by checking the Form Field Name box. Check the Form Field Name box for the Subject line and insert the field name **options** (the drop-down menu). For the Reply-to Line, check the Form Field Name box and enter the field name **email**. That way the Reply-To address matches the address the visitor entered in the form (Figure 20.13).

FIGURE 20.13
You can set the Subject line and Reply-To addresses to either a predetermined line of text or get the info from one of the form fields.

8. The Confirmation Page tab provides you with the option of sending the visitor to a specific page in your site after the file has been stored, email has been sent, or both. This can be any page on your site, but it is normal to create a page with a message telling the visitor the process was successful. If you do not insert a link, the server generates a page for you automatically. (But this page does not match the rest of your site.) Even though the page does not exist yet, set the URL of Confirmation Page to Contact/Confirmed.html (see Figure 20.14). If you have inserted validation scripts in your form (such as scripts to ensure that certain fields are filled out), you can also create a custom page to redirect the visitor to if the form is not properly filled out.

FIGURE 20.14
With the Confirmation Page option, you can send the visitor to a specific page after sending the form.

9. The last tab in the Saving Results dialog is Saved Fields. From here you can decide what fields should be saved and submitted from the form. By default Expression Web 3 inserts all the fields including the Input (Submit) button. In almost every case, you want to remove this last instance because it is unnecessary. (The fact that the file has been saved or the email sent means that the Submit button was pressed.) To remove it, simply highlight the submitButton instance in the window and delete it (see Figure 20.15). The Saved Fields tab also allows you to save the date and time of the form submission in various different formats that you can select from the drop-down menus. Finally, you can choose to save additional information about the user including the remote computer name, username, and browser type. (Note that the username will be saved only if the user is required to log in before submitting the form.)

10. When you click OK to save the changes, a warning appears and tells you that the file you are trying to link to does not exist and asks you whether you want to save the link anyway. This is because in step 8 you entered a hyperlink to a page you have not created yet. Click Yes.

11. When you click OK in the Form Properties dialog, another warning will likely appear, telling you that this form cannot be configured to send emails because it is at a disk-based location or on a server that has not been configured to send emails. This is because the email functionality you have configured requires server-side scripting in the form of FrontPage Server extensions. Your local computer will not have these capabilities installed. The warning asks

FIGURE 20.15
You can decide what fields are to be saved and submitted from the Saved Fields tab. From here you can also include new fields that contain the date and time and information about the user.

whether you want to remove the email recipient. Click No to keep the email address in the script. After the page is uploaded to a server with FrontPage Server extensions, it will work properly.

The email form with all the necessary functionality is now complete.

Other Uses for Form Results

Creating an email form using forms is just the tip of the gigantic iceberg of possibilities that are available. Forms can be used for a wide range of functions that go far beyond simple text communication.

If you open the Form Properties dialog again, you see that in addition to the Send To option, you can also Send to Database or Send to Other Scripts. These functions let you use forms to communicate with and make alterations to databases. The databases can, in turn, manage content on a website or an online store or even keep track of warehouse stocks for a company. The possibilities are virtually endless.

Setting up a form with a database or script connection requires both a server that supports the chosen script language and a deeper understanding of the use of databases on the Web. For this reason, it is outside the scope of this book.

Forms in Code View

As explained in the beginning of this hour, forms and form controls are simple HTML elements. To get an idea of just how simple these elements are (and through that an understanding of why they are so heavily used), let's peek behind the curtain and look at the form in Code view.

To start, click anywhere inside the form while in Split view and look at the Quick Tag Selector. Depending on where you placed the cursor, the last few tags differ, but the main <form> tag should be the first one in the series (see Figure 20.16).

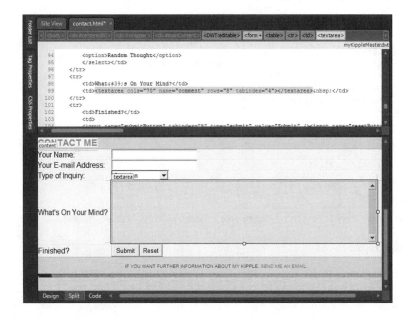

FIGURE 20.16
The <form> tag encapsulates all the elements that make up the form.

The <form> tag was the first element you inserted into the page, and all the form controls are contained within this tag. By looking at the form code in Code view, you can see that Expression Web 3 has organized it in such a way that it is easy to read.

A closer look at each form control shows you that they are all based on a basic code formula. Click the first text box as an example. The code highlighted in Code view is simple to read:

```
<input name="fullName" size="30" tabindex="1" type="text" />
```

As you can see, the form function is no different from any other HTML tag, and you insert the different attributes in the same way as any other tag. This also means that you can use the Tag Properties panel to make changes to the form functions.

More than that, it also means you can apply CSS styles to the form controls just as you have done with other tags throughout this book. For example, by making a new style with the selector name form, you can set the font family, font size, background color, box, or any number of other style attributes for the forms. Or you can set individual styles for each different form elements separately by applying classes to them.

Put next to one another you can get a clear idea of how exactly the code for each of the form controls works:

Text box:

```
<input name="fullName" size="30" tabindex="1" type="text" />
```

Drop-down box:

```
<select name="options" tabindex="3" >
        <option selected="selected">Question</option>
        <option>Comment</option>
        <option>Suggestion</option>
        <option>Random Thought</option>
</select>
```

Text area:

```
<textarea cols="70" name="comment" rows="8" tabindex="4"></textarea>
```

Input (Submit):

```
<input name="submitButton" tabindex="5" type="submit" value="Submit" />
```

Input (Reset):

```
<input name="resetButton" tabindex="6" type="reset" value="Reset" />
```

As you can see, each tag starts with the type of function followed by the name you gave each instance, the tab index, and if necessary the type of control it is.

In Hour 22, when you use the same form you just built to create a PHP-based email form, you see that to unlock the true potential of HTML forms you need to have a basic understanding of the code behind form controls. This is because the Form Field Properties dialogs give you access to only a select few of the many attributes and properties available. As a result more advanced functions have to be added manually with the help of the Tag Properties panel or IntelliSense.

Summary

Forms are key components in taking your sites from being one-way monologues to two-way dialogues. By including forms in your site, you provide the visitor with a way to interact with the site and make choices or send and receive information based on what she wants. You could go as far as saying that without forms there would be no search engines, social networking sites, or blogs, and the Web would be little more than a long list of boring archival material.

To get an idea of how prevalent and varied the use of form controls is throughout the Web, think about this: Every time you see a text box, check box, radio button, or any of the other main form elements, you are actually looking at a form. In fact, every time you enter a word into a search engine and click the Search button, you are using a form connected to a massive database!

In this hour, you learned how to build a simple form that lets the visitor input information that is sent to a file on the server and to your own email address. You saw that building the form itself is as easy as dragging and dropping the elements into place and using the Form Field Properties dialogs to make them do what you want them to.

You also learned that when dealing with forms, you have to take into consideration what kind of server the form will reside on. Because static HTML pages can run on any web server, the transformation of text and selections in a form on a web page to a readable file or email requires server-side scripts, and these scripts have to be written in a language the server understands and allows.

By including forms in your website, you are moving beyond the basics and into more advanced territory. That means there are more things to consider and understand, but the payoffs are also far greater. For an online vendor, the difference between providing an email address and providing the ability to ask questions or communicate with the website owner from inside the website can be the difference between a visitor dropping by and a visitor actually purchasing the services offered. In truth, something as simple as the email form you just created elevates the perceived level of professionalism many times over and makes the visitor feel like you take her seriously.

HTML forms in their most basic form are easy to build and use, and because they are HTML elements, they are not tied to any particular kind of server-side script, so they can be used for all sorts of different applications.

Q&A

Q. *I created the email form and tested it in my browser, but I am not receiving any emails. What am I doing wrong?*

A. For the actual email functionality to work, the pages have to placed on a web server that has FrontPage Server Extensions installed. Because you are testing the pages from your local hard drive through the Expression Development Server, no such extensions are running. In fact you are testing only the form itself, not the server-side scripts. To get the form to work properly and send emails, it needs to be uploaded to a web server with FrontPage Server Extensions installed.

Workshop

The Workshop has quiz questions to help you put to use what you just learned. If you get stuck, the answers to the quiz questions are in the next section. But try to answer the questions first. Otherwise you'll be cheating yourself.

Quiz

1. Give a brief description of what form controls are and what they do.

2. What is the number one requirement for using the email form created using the functionalities demonstrated in this hour?

Answers

1. Form controls are a group of standard HTML components that can be inserted into any web page that gives the visitor the ability to interact with the site. Form controls come in many shapes and functionalities; from text boxes to buttons to check boxes and drop-down menus. Form controls can be grouped in a web form that when filled out and triggered sends information to the browser memory for further processing. Every time you input information in a web page whether it be a search string in Google, a bid on eBay, a message on Facebook, or a blog entry, you use form controls contained in a web form.

2. For the email form you created in this hour to work, the server it is placed on has to have FrontPage Server Extensions installed. This is a requirement because all the email functionality is based on this technology. Before building and refining this form, it is imperative that you contact your web host and ensure that your hosting plan includes FrontPage Server Extensions. If not you need to use a different technology such as PHP to create the email form.

HOUR 21

Working with Flash and Silverlight

What You'll Learn in This Hour:

► How to place a Flash Movie in your web page

► How to configure the embedding code for Flash movies to ensure cross-browser compatibility

► How a Silverlight application works

► How to place a Silverlight application in your page using the JavaScript and the iFrame methods

Introduction

One of the major turning points in the evolution of web design was the introduction of Flash. By designing interactive components in this new animation platform, designers were no longer restricted by simple roll-overs and straight page changes. All of a sudden there was a way to make incredibly advanced animated buttons, sliding screens, and whatever else the designer could come up with.

Unlike everything else you have been introduced to so far, Flash is not a native web language. To run Flash content, visitors must have the Flash Player plug-in installed in their computer. On your end it means that any Flash element has to be inserted into a page as a replaced item, much like an image. This puts some restrictions on how you can and should use Flash content in your pages.

For many years Flash has been one of the only options for interactive animation in websites. With the proliferation of video-sharing sites, such as YouTube, the platform has become as ubiquitous as regular television sets. But that is changing. Silverlight, Microsoft's newcomer, is now challenging Flash's reign of supremacy.

Silverlight is an animation platform, just like Flash, that enables the designer to create highly interactive and animated user experiences. Unlike Flash it is entirely code-based, meaning that instead of having a compiled file that contains all the elements, Silverlight applications consist of a series of files, including a new file type called Extensible Application Markup Language (XAML), which is pronounced "zamel," that are read and compiled on the spot by the browser and the Silverlight plug-in.

Because both Flash and Silverlight applications behave differently than regular HTML elements they need special attention when they are included in a website. To make this process easier, Expression Web 3 includes specialized tools to handle these files. In this hour you learn how to insert and configure both Flash and Silverlight applications into your pages.

Flash: An Introduction

When you encounter Flash content in a web page, what you see is actually an external file called a Flash movie. A Flash movie is a file with the suffix .swf and it plays through the Flash Player.

A Flash movie can be anything from a simple button with a hyperlink to a complete web experience with buttons, pages, videos, audio, dynamic content, and links to internal and external pages. All Flash movies are created using the Adobe Flash application, and they cannot be altered after they are compiled into an SWF file.

> Flash movies were originally created and published using the Flash application from Macromedia. Adobe bought Macromedia in late 2005, so today when you speak of Flash, you refer to Adobe Flash.

Because the Flash movie itself is a static file, designers build dynamic fields much like the form fields you created in Hour 20, "Getting Interactive with Forms," that obtain data from external files. This allows otherwise static Flash content to become dynamic and interactive for the user and the designer and content handler.

As mentioned before, Flash movies are not native web content and require a special plug-in to play. As a result, including Flash movies in your web pages requires the use of special code. The Flash movies are inserted by placing them inside elements that work much like inline frames. There are actually two such tags: `<object>` and `<embed>`. In the past the `<object>` tag worked in Internet Explorer, whereas other browsers used the `<embed>` tag. Both tags work in newer browsers, but because not every visitor has a newer browser, the norm is to use both tags by placing the

`<embed>` tag inside the `<object>` tag. Expression Web 3 inserts only the `<object>` tag, so you have to insert the `<embed>` tag manually if you want to use both.

Try It Yourself ▼

Publish a Flash Photo Gallery

To give you an idea of how Flash movies can work with external content and to provide you with a component you can use in your design projects, the lesson files for this hour contain a simple Flash-based photo gallery that is controlled by an external data file and that sources images from external folders. The Flash movie was built using Macromedia Flash MX 2004 Professional, and the slideshow was based on an excellent plug-in, SlideShowPro, that you can buy at www.slideshowpro.net. Of course, as with all other Flash content, you need the Flash application to create and modify the movie.

1. In the MyKipple project create a new folder called **Gallery**.

2. Open the Import dialog by selecting File, Import, File on the menu bar.

3. Click on the Add Folder button in the dialog and select the Flash folder found in the lesson files for this hour. When you click on Open, the Import dialog lists all the files with their current and new location (see Figure 21.1). Click OK and

FIGURE 21.1
When you use the Add Folder option, the Import dialog lists all the files with their current and new location.

make sure the new Flash folder ends up in the Gallery folder. If not, drag and drop it into the Gallery folder.

4. With the Flash folder selected in the Folder List panel or the Web Site view, create a new HTML page from the myKippleMaster.dwt template by selecting File,

New, Create from Dynamic Web Template on the Menu bar. Select File, Save As on the menu bar and give the new page the name **flashGallery.html** and save it under the Flash folder (see Figure 21.2).

FIGURE 21.2
With the new HTML page, the Flash folder should now contain three files and two folders.

5. With the new page open in Split view, give it the heading **Flash Gallery**. To insert a Flash movie into the page, you need to use the built-in media functions in Expression Web 3 that you can find in the Media submenu under Insert on the menu bar and in the Toolbox panel under Media (see Figure 21.3).

FIGURE 21.3
The insert Media options enable you to easily insert Flash movies, Silverlight applications, and Windows media files from the Toolbox panel and the Insert menu.

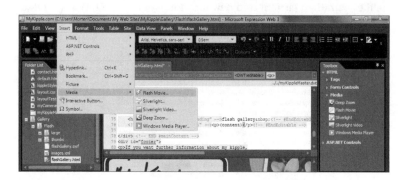

6. Click on the + sign next to Media in the Toolbox panel to open the media options. Click and drag the Flash Movie option into the content section of the page.

7. The Select Media File dialog opens to ask you to specify what Flash movie you are inserting (see Figure 21.4). Select the flashGallery.swf file in the gallery/flash folder and click on Insert.

8. A new gray box appears in Design view with a lightning logo and the name of the Flash movie file you just inserted. To play the Flash movie in Design view,

FIGURE 21.4
When inserting a
Flash movie,
Expression Web
3 asks you to
specify what file
you want to
insert.

right-click on the movie and select Play Movie in Flash Format from the context
menu (see Figure 21.5). Now you should see a small image gallery playing
inside the box you just inserted.

FIGURE 21.5
To play a Flash
movie in Design
view, you have to
select Play Movie
in Flash Format
from the context
menu. Otherwise
all you see is a
gray box.

Now that the Flash movie is inserted into the page, you can start working with it to
make it look the way you want. Unless otherwise specified, Flash movies resize to fit
whatever area you insert them into. Note that even though Flash movies contain
information about their intended size, Expression Web 3 insists on setting the width
and height of all inserted Flash movies to 200 by 200 pixels and scaling the content
accordingly.

▼ **Try It Yourself**

Customize the Appearance of the Flash Movie

Right now the photo gallery is small and off to the left side of the page. To make it more appealing, you need to resize it to the intended size and center it on the page. To do this you use the Flash properties and some Cascading Style Sheets (CSS) styling.

1. When Expression Web 3 inserted the Flash movie for you, it defaulted the width and height to 200 by 200 pixels and the photo gallery scaled itself accordingly. The Flash movie is actually 600 pixels wide and 400 pixels in height. To change this, open the Flash SWF Properties dialog by either right-clicking on the Flash movie and selecting Flash SWF Properties or simply double-clicking on the Flash movie.

2. From the Flash SWF Properties dialog, you can make changes to many different settings. For most purposes, the default settings (sans the sizing) are what you want. Make sure the Keep Aspect Ratio box is unchecked and change the width to 600px and the height to 400px (see Figure 21.6). Click OK to apply the changes.

FIGURE 21.6
The Flash SWF Properties dialog gives you control of the playback functionality connected to the Flash movie including size, position, and image quality.

The Flash movie now has the correct size, but as you can see in Design view, it is positioned to the left of the page. To make it more visually pleasing, it should be positioned in the center.

3. To position the Flash movie in the center of the page, click anywhere inside the Flash movie in Design view to select the `<object>` tag and apply the `.alignCenter` class from the Apply Styles panel by clicking on it.

Because Flash movies are always contained in an `<object>` tag, you can apply regular styles, classes, and IDs to this tag to further style the content. When applying styles, it might be easier to imagine the Flash movie as a simple image and apply your styles to it that way. Using CSS to position Flash content is one good example. Another is using CSS to give the Flash movie margins so that it doesn't bump up right next to the other content.

▲

Did you Know?

The contents inside an `<object>` tag can appear either inline or as a block, depending on how you style it. This is important to remember if you insert Flash movies commingled with the text in your page. If no styling is applied, the movie appears alongside the text content just like an image. This can cause your layout to be broken as is often the case when bloggers insert Flash-based ads in their posts without applying styles to them first. As with images, the `.alignLeft`, `.alignCenter`, and `.alignRight` classes are lifesavers for placing Flash movies in your page without ruining the text flow in the process.

Adding the <embed> Tag for Full Cross-Browser Compatibility

As you learned earlier in this hour, there are two tags used to place Flash content in a page, and some older browsers (more specifically Internet Explorer 6 and lower) use only one or the other. Even though most new browsers don't have this problem, it is always a good idea to include both tags to ensure full cross-browser compatibility so that everyone can see your Flash content.

Because Expression Web 3 inserts only the `<object>` tag for Flash movies, you need to insert the `<embed>` tag manually in Code view. For a Flash movie, the `<embed>` tag syntax is simple to remember:

```
<embed src="flashMovie.swf" quality="high" type="application/x-shockwave-flash"
width="size in pixels" height="size in pixels" />
```

In the current case, the embed code would therefore be

```
<embed src="flashGallery.swf" quality="high" type="application/x-shockwave-flash"
width="600" height="400" />
```

Watch Out!

The <embed> Tag Doesn't Comply with Web Standards!

As explained earlier in this book, Expression Web 3 was created as an application that produces standards-based code out of the box. That means it does not insert nonstandard or deprecated code. The <embed> tag was deprecated in favor of the <object> tag and as such it is not supported by the World Wide Web Consortium (W3C). For that reason, when you include the <embed> tag in your code, a warning about incorrect code appears in the status bar, and if you press F9, the <embed> tag is highlighted. Even so, I recommend that you include the <embed> tag when you insert Flash movies in your page if you want to keep it accessible for as many visitors as possible.

To prevent the browser from displaying two copies of the same Flash movie, *always* place the `<embed>` tag at the end of the `<object>` tag on the line above the `</object>` end tag, as in Figure 21.7.

FIGURE 21.7
The `<embed>` tag should always be placed inside the `<object>` tag to avoid having two consecutive Flash movies appear in browsers that support both tags.

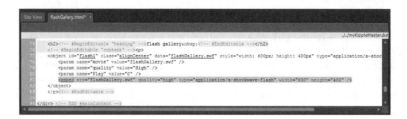

YouTube and Other External Flash Content

Until a few years ago, Flash content was primarily a design element, and you needed to worry about how to include it in your pages only if you designed the site with Flash elements in mind. But then out of nowhere a new video-sharing service called YouTube appeared, and all of a sudden the ability to include Flash content in your site became a must if you wanted to stay current.

Today there are hundreds of different video-sharing sites, and almost all of them use Flash as their player platform. These sites build their client base (and revenue) by getting people to embed the videos into their pages. To make doing so as easy as possible, they all provide the complete embed codes for you to copy and paste into your page. Despite that, many novices still have trouble getting the players to work because they don't understand the difference between Design view and Code view.

If you go to YouTube and find a video you like and want to place on your site, all you have to do is copy the embed code (placed on the right side of the page) and paste it into Code view at the location you want the video to appear. You immediately notice that the code looks almost identical to the one Expression Web 3 inserts except that the actual link to the movie itself is different. When the code is in your page, you can change the size and apply styles to it just as you did with the photo gallery.

Silverlight: An Introduction

Silverlight is the newcomer in the world of animation-based web elements. It is based on Microsoft's new code language XAML and is intended to be not only an alternative to Flash but also to introduce new types of functionality to the web and offline applications such as presentation software, desktop applications, and so on.

What sets Silverlight apart from Flash is that it is entirely code based, and the code is open. That means instead of using a precompiled movie similar to what Flash offers, Silverlight applications are dynamic elements that are created on the spot by the server, browser, and the Silverlight plug-in.

Silverlight applications are built with .NET-based code languages using a combination of Microsoft Visual Studio and a new program called Expression Blend 3, which is included in the Microsoft Expression Studio. One of the driving forces behind Silverlight was to create a work environment where code-based developers and visual designers could work together on the same project at the same time. Because Silverlight applications are 100% code-based, you now have that option. For the code-based developer, the entire application can be written in both Visual Basic and C# code languages. For the visual designer, the same application can be edited in Expression Blend without ever looking at the code. In short, Silverlight could be the ultimate amalgamation of two technical fields that, until now, have had a hard time finding a common language.

Placing Silverlight Applications in Your Page

Although Silverlight is a relative newcomer, there is little doubt that it will become important enough that you, as a designer, need to know about it or at least know how to place its contents in your pages.

> Just like Flash, you need to install the free Silverlight plug-in to view Silverlight content. It is a simple one-time browser install, and you can find it at www.silverlight.net.

Did you Know?

Because this is an emerging technology, understanding the basics of how Silverlight works gives you an advantage for when the technology and its applications become more mainstream. To get a glimpse of how powerful this new technology is and a better understanding of how and why it works, you build a photo gallery application, similar to the Flash gallery from earlier in this chapter and place it in your site.

Try It Yourself ▼

Create a Photo Gallery Using Slide.Show

As a part of the launch of Silverlight, Microsoft contacted a group of .NET developers and asked them to create custom applications that would be released on an open license so that anyone could download and use them for their purposes. One of these projects, called Slide.Show, was developed by Vertigo (www.vertigo.com) and is published on the Microsoft CodePlex website for public download. This application is a perfect example both of how Silverlight works and how you can use two entirely different methods to place Silverlight content on your page. As a bonus it is an excellent and highly customizable application that lets you build a great-looking photo gallery with little work. You can get the entire source code along with templates, demos, and customization information by visiting http://www.codeplex.com/SlideShow. To make things easier for you, I compiled the core files in the lesson files for this chapter, but if you want you can start from scratch by getting the entire application from the Code-Plex site.

1. In Expression Web 3, create a new folder under the Gallery folder and call it **Silverlight**.

   You can use several different methods to add a Silverlight application to a web page. In this example you use two: first the object method and then the iFrame method. The differences and different usage situations become apparent as you progress.

   For a Silverlight application to work, you previously added several different files to the server. But as the platform has evolved, it has become a lot easier to handle. As a result, all you need to add to your site is a single code file and an object tag, not unlike the one you just added for the Flash movie.

2. Use the Import File option to import the files from the Silverlight folder into the Silverlight folder you just created. There are only two: Vertigo.SlideShow.xap and Data.xml (see Figure 21.8).

FIGURE 21.8
The two files, Vertigo. SlideShow.xap and Data.xml, must be under the Silverlight folder for the application to work.

3. In the Silverlight folder, create a new page based on myKippleMaster.dwt and give it the name **SlideShow.html**. Open the page in Split view.

4. Set the heading to Silverlight Gallery

5. Place the cursor in the content area and select Insert, Media, Silverlight from the Main menu. This opens a file browser. Navigate to the gallery/Silverlight folder and select the Vertigo.SlideShow.xap file; click OK to insert the Silverlight application.

As you can see from Figure 21.9, the inserted Silverlight gallery looks similar to the Flash gallery when it was inserted—a gray box with some non-functional content in it (refer to Figure 21.5). The <object> tag also looks similar.

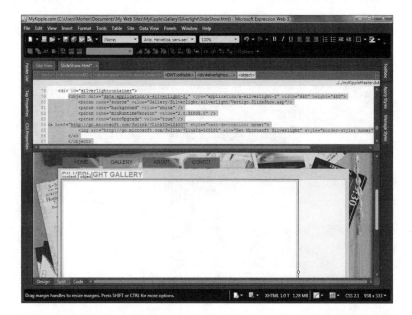

FIGURE 21.9
The Silverlight.html page as seen in Code view.

6. To get the Silverlight gallery to work, you still need to make a couple of changes to the code. First, for whatever reason, Expression Web 3 creates a relative link that sets the address of the .xap file as if the current page is in the root folder and the .xap file is in a different folder. That is not the case here, and you need to remove all the extraneous folder information from the code to get it to point to the right file. In Code view, change the source param value to look like this: `<param name="source" value="Vertigo.SlideShow.xap"/>`.

7. Finally you need to set some parameters for the Slide.Show application. This is one of the true powers of Silverlight applications: You can set custom parameters for the application right in the embed code so that each instance of the same application looks and works differently. Under the other <param> tags create a new <param tag with the name **initParams** and the value

ConfigurationProvider=LightTheme,DataProvider=XmlDataProvider;Path
=Data.xml. It should look like this: `<param name="initParams" value="`
`ConfigurationProvider=LightTheme,DataProvider=XmlDataProvider;Path`
`=Data.xml"/>`. This parameter sets the theme (look) of this instance of the
Slide.Show application to LightTheme and tells the browser that the data file
pointing to the content of the gallery is called Data.xml. Save the page.

8. Rename the page to **SlideShow.aspx** and preview the page in your browser.
    You should see the Slide.Show application running with the images and infor-
    mation from the Flash slideshow you created earlier, as shown Figure 21.10. If

FIGURE 21.10
After you apply
some small
changes to the
code, the
Slide.Show Sil-
verlight applica-
tion runs
properly in your
browser.

not, you might be missing the Silverlight plug-in, or you are not running the
page through Expression Development Server. If you have problems, look at the
Q&A for this hour to see whether you can find the answer there.

Previewing Silverlight Applications in Your Browser

To make sure everything is working properly, you should preview the page in your
browser. But if you do, all you see is the page with an empty white box in the content section. This is because Silverlight is a server-side script that to work properly
must be running on a web server. In other words, technically, you need to upload
your files to a web server and test them from there. Fortunately, there is a way

around this problem: Because a big part of Expression Web 3 is the ability to create advanced dynamic websites using Microsoft's server-side script language ASP.NET, the program comes equipped with a small application called Expression Development Server. This application creates a virtual server on your computer that behaves like a web server and lets you run server-side scripts in pages even though they are stored only on your computer. You will be introduced to the Expression Development Server in more detail in Hour 22, "Beyond the Basics, Part 1: PHP in Expression Web 3."

The problem here is that the Silverlight script runs only on a web server. So, to preview the application, you need to make Expression Web 3 think that the page you are currently working with is actually an ASP.NET page. That way it will be previewed using Expression Development Server, and the Silverlight script will run properly. Doing so is surprisingly simple: Open the HTML file that contains the Silverlight application you want to preview; select File, Save As on the menu bar, and change the file extension to .aspx—the extension for ASP.NET pages that can contain regular HTML code. Now when you open the page, it will be previewed in the browser through Expression Development Server and the Silverlight application will run properly.

Try It Yourself ▼

Make the New Galleries Available

Now you have two galleries, naturally you want people to open and watch them. To do so you need to add links to them in the main menu of the site.

1. Open the mykippleMaster.dwt file in Split view.

2. Click on the menu and go to Code view.

3. Change the button that now says Gallery to say **Silverlight**. Change the href attribute to point to the new SlideShow.aspx file you just created.

4. Copy and paste the list item for the Silverlight button directly under the Silverlight button. Change the text to **Flash** and point the href attribute to the flashGallery.html file in the Flash folder.

5. Save the DWT file and click on Yes when you are asked to update all the associated pages.

Now the visitor can choose to view either the Flash or the Silverlight gallery directly from any of the pages.

▲

> Earlier you saved the SlideShow.aspx and SilverlightGallery.aspx pages as ASP.NET files to preview them through Expression Development Server. Now that you have finished the pages, you should change their extensions back to HTML. This is because ASP.NET files run only on Microsoft servers, whereas HTML files run on all servers, and the files do not actually contain any ASP.NET content. After it's on a server, the Silverlight application works regardless of what the file extension is.

Bonus: Making the Galleries Your Own

You can customize both the Flash gallery and the Silverlight gallery introduced in this hour with your own images and descriptions. As you previously learned, all the images are placed under the Flash folder, thumbnails in the thumbs folder, and the full images in the large folder. Both galleries use XML files to define the image locations, titles, and descriptions. You can change these using Expression Web 3 and make the galleries feature your own images.

The Flash image gallery is controlled by the images.xml file found in the Flash folder. The syntax of that file is simple:

```
<album
        title="Random Kipple"
        description="Some random photos of my kipple"
        lgPath="large/"
        tnPath="thumbs/"
        tn="thumbs/bagOpennies.jpg">
                <img
                        src="bagOpennies.jpg"
                        title="Bag O' Pennies"
                        caption="A small hemp bag filled with pennies" />
</album>
```

To add another image, all you need to do is add another `<img>` tag with the `src`, `title`, and `caption` attributes defined. To add another album, just create a new `<album>` tag and insert the new information. To add more images, simply place the large version in the large folder and the thumbnail in the thumbs folder.

One caveat: The images.xml file and image folders need to stay in the same folder as the Flash movie. Otherwise the movie will not work.

The Silverlight image gallery is controlled by the Data.xml file found in the Silverlight folder. The syntax is similar to that of the Flash gallery:

```
<album
        title="Random Kipple"
        description="Some random photos of my kipple"
        image="../Flash/thumbs/bagOpennies.jpg">
                <slide
```

```
                       title="Bag O' Pennies"
                       description="A small hemp bag filled with pennies"
                       image="../Flash/large/bagOpennies.jpg"
                       thumbnail="../Flash/thumbs/bagOpennies.jpg" />
</album>
```

Likewise, to add another image, just add another <slide> tag with the title, description, image, and thumbnail attributes defined. To add another album, just create a new <album> tag and insert the new information. In this example, the URL that points to the images starts with ../ to make the browser go down one folder and then into the correct folders.

In addition to changing the images in the Silverlight gallery, you can change many of the look and behavior attributes. To get further information, check out the many demos in the application folder you downloaded.

Summary

Both Flash and Silverlight are technologies that can add an unparalleled level of visual impact and interactivity to web pages. These applications are created using dedicated programs (Adobe Flash for Flash files; Microsoft Visual Studio and Microsoft Expression Blend for Silverlight) and inserted into your pages as finished elements.

Because the files are external content, Expression Web 3 is mainly used to position and style the boxes they are inserted into: Flash movies are inserted into the page using either the <object> or the <embed> tag. In most cases you want to use both, with the <object> tag surrounding the <embed> tag, even though the <embed> tag has been deprecated. This is because many older browsers do not fully comprehend or support the <object> tag yet.

Flash movies are placed in boxes on the page, and you can apply standard CSS styling to their <object> tags to set the placement, borders, backgrounds, and whatever else you feel like. If you ignore the Flash content, an inserted Flash movie acts just like any other replaced item (such as an image). In other words, you have full control of where the movie appears. In this hour, you learned how to embed a Flash movie into your page and use CSS to change its position and styling.

Silverlight is a new technology that has been on the market for only a couple of years. It offers a great alternative to Flash and has many features you can't get with Flash. Most important, Silverlight is entirely script based, so both developers and designers can work on the application at the same time without having to compile and decompile them repeatedly.

In this hour you used the Microsoft CodePlex project Slide.Show, created by Vertigo, to get a feel for how Silverlight applications work. By adding a couple of files and making some alterations to the default Silverlight embedding code and the object tag, you placed a slideshow application much like the one in the Flash example directly into your page.

Silverlight is a server-side script, so it will not run properly on your computer unless you use a virtual server. In this hour, you learned how to trick Expression Web 3 into previewing the pages with Silverlight content through Expression Development Server by changing the file extensions of the pages to .aspx.

Q&A

Q. *When I preview the FlashGallery.html page in Internet Explorer, I get a warning that the program has restricted the website from running ActiveX controls that could access my computer. What do I do?*

A. Embedded content such as a Flash movie uses ActiveX controls to play. For some reason, when you view a local web page, Internet Explorer blocks this type of content, and you actively have to tell the browser to accept it by clicking on the warning bar at the top of the page and selecting Allow Blocked Content. This happens only for local files; after the page with the Flash movie is on a web server, you no longer receive this warning.

Q. *I tried previewing the SlideShow.html file in my browser, but all I got was a blank page.*

A. Silverlight is a server-side script, meaning that the server actually performs operations with the script when it is displayed. When you preview HTML pages in your browser through Expression Web 3, no server is used. To preview Silverlight content, you need to run the page through the virtual server called Expression Development Server that is built in to Expression Web 3. To do so, rename your file by changing the extension to .aspx. This tricks Expression Web 3 into thinking the file is a dynamic web page that requires server-side scripts to work and Expression Development Server kicks in.

Q. *The Flash image gallery/Silverlight image gallery shows up, but there are no images!*

A. Both the Flash and the Silverlight image galleries source their content from outside the application itself. They get their data from the images.xml and Data.xml files, respectively, and the images are stored in the Flash folder under the large and thumbs folders. For the galleries to work properly, it is imperative that the folder structure described in the hour be retained. The Gallery folder should contain two folders: Flash and Silverlight. All the Flash files should be in the Flash folder, and all the Silverlight files should be in the Silverlight folder. If your folder structure is correct and you are still not seeing anything, go to the finalized version found in the lesson files and replace your files with the ones provided.

Workshop

The Workshop has quiz questions and exercises to help you put to use what you have just learned. If you get stuck, the answers to the quiz questions are in the next section. But try to answer the questions first. Otherwise you'll be cheating yourself.

Quiz

1. What are the two methods of embedding Flash movies in a HTML page, and which one is the correct one?

2. Which is better? Flash or Silverlight?

Answers

1. The two methods are using the `<object>` tag and using the `<embed>` tag. Although technically the `<object>` tag is the correct standards-based method, it is advisable to also place an `<embed>` tag within the `<object>` tag to account for the lack of support for the latter in older browsers such as Internet Explorer 6. Always remember to nest the `<embed>` tag inside the `<object>` tag, or you will get two instances of the Flash movie in browsers that support both.

2. If you ask Adobe, the answer is Flash. If you ask Microsoft, the answer is Silverlight. In reality, they are completely different applications that both have advantages and disadvantages. Flash is well established and has a high penetration rate (meaning most computers can play Flash movies). Silverlight is relatively new on the market but offers a whole new range of functionalities. All things being equal, the real question you should ask yourself is what programming language you are most comfortable with. If you already know ActionScript and have worked with Flash in the past, you can always "be safe" and stick with that platform. If you come from or work with a development team that uses .NET architecture, you already have an advantage when starting to work with Silverlight. So to answer the question: There is no "better," just different.

Exercise

Use CSS positioning to change the location of the embedded Flash and Silverlight applications. Give them a white background and a thin gray border by setting the `padding` and `border` attributes.

Embed a YouTube video into one of your pages, and use the `<object>` and `<embed>` tags to resize the video so that it fits half the page. Use CSS to restyle the video and change its positioning so that the text flows around the video.

Open the images.xml and Data.xml files in Expression Web 3 and change the order of the images. Use copy and paste to create new albums for both galleries and test them to see how the applications react to the new content.

HOUR 22

Beyond the Basics, Part 1: PHP in Expression Web 3

What You'll Learn in This Hour:

▶ How to install PHP on your computer

▶ How to configure and use the Expression Development Server to test PHP scripts locally on your computer

▶ How to create a PHP-based email form

▶ How to use PHP to test whether form fields are filled out and that the email was successfully sent

Introduction

If you have surfed the World Wide Web for any length of time, you probably noticed that not all web pages have the .html suffix. When you visit more advanced sites, you often see that the filenames in the address bar end with .asp, .php, or any number of other suffixes. All these file types hint at the server-side technology that generates the pages.

Although Hypertext Markup Language (HTML) is a great code language with a wide variety of applications, it is capable of making only static pages. A static page is one in which the designer or developer inserts all the content, and it remains the same until someone manually edits the file. In contrast, most large websites including news sources, blogs, social networks, and so on consist of dynamic pages. A dynamic page is one in which the page contains only the framework, and content is gathered from other sources such as databases, other sites, or visitor input. The one thing all these dynamic pages have in common is that they all use some form of server-side scripting language to generate their content.

One of the most prevalent and popular open source server-side script languages is PHP, which is a direct competitor to Microsoft's application framework, ASP.NET. Until recently they have often been mutually exclusive because the Windows Server support for PHP has been unreliable and slow, forcing many web hosts to remove the option altogether. However, with the release of Windows Server 2008, full PHP support is now available on Microsoft servers, giving you the choice to use ASP.NET or PHP. Parallel to this, Expression Web 3 was equipped with PHP support giving designers and developers the ability to build sites and applications without looking elsewhere for their PHP scripting.

As you learned in Hour 20, "Getting Interactive with Forms," the type of server hosting your site determines what kind of server-side scripts you can use. In Hour 20, you built an email form that utilized FrontPage Server Extensions for its functionality. This form required Windows Server architecture to work. In this hour, you learn how to use the new PHP features built in to Expression Web 3 to create a PHP version of the same form that can be used in sites hosted on a Linux server.

PHP: An Introduction

PHP is a code language used to create dynamic web pages; that is, pages whose content is generated by the web server rather than stored in the pages. Advanced PHP pages are little more than frameworks with a bunch of design elements and boxes populated with content as the visitor clicks different buttons. You could say it is an advanced version of the Dynamic Web Template in which the template is the page itself and the content comes from a database or other external sources.

PHP can also perform other tasks such as processing form results, submitting content to databases, and editing files. To get an idea of just how powerful PHP is, consider that the vast majority of the millions upon millions of blogs floating around the Internet these days run off PHP. Because of this, many new PHP applications customized for blogging are developed every day.

The power of PHP lies in its capability to work alongside standard HTML code. That means you can choose whether you want to place your PHP scripts in a separate file or place them within your HTML pages inside the HTML code. In practical terms, this means you can create an HTML page with dummy content and, when you finish with layout, you can replace the placeholder content with a PHP script that grabs the real content from an external file, database, other website, Really Simple Syndication (RSS) feed, or a form. To make the file with the PHP script work, it needs the extension .php rather than .html, but even with this extension, all the HTML code renders normally. In fact, if your site is hosted on a server with PHP installed, you can save all your HTML files as .php files without any difference in how the pages display in a browser.

What Does PHP Stand for Anyway?

If you look up the definition of PHP, you get the following explanation: *"PHP" is a recursive acronym for "PHP: Hypertext Processor."* But that doesn't explain anything because the long version of the acronym contains the acronym itself! This phenomenon is referred to as a *recursive acronym* and is fairly common in the geeky world of programming. More than anything, the use of recursive acronyms in programming is a tongue-in-cheek way to deal with the fact that for the most part these acronyms don't mean anything. In PHP's case, however, the acronym originally had a meaning: PHP used to stand for *Personal Home Page tools* (without the t), but as the language morphed into a more advanced scripting language, this description became obsolete and the new recursive acronym was adopted in its place.

Other examples of ridiculous recursive acronyms are LAME, which stands for "LAME Ain't an MP3 Encoder (LAME is, in fact, an MP3 encoder) and Wine, which stands for "Wine is Not an Emulator." (Likewise Wine is an emulator that allows Windows software to run in Linux environments.) For more examples from the geeky world of recursive acronyms, take a look at the list found at http://en.wikipedia.org/wiki/Recursive_acronym.

Installing PHP on Your Computer to Test PHP Scripts

Because PHP is a server-side script, pages with PHP, code will not work properly if you test it in your browser as you have with HTML pages. This is because unlike HTML, which renders in the browser, PHP renders in the server, and it sends the resulting information to the browser for display. One way to work around this problem is to upload your PHP files for testing on a web server that has PHP installed and test them live, but that is a cumbersome and ineffective method requiring time, a live Internet connection, and available server space. Another way to approach the issue is to run a web server with PHP installed on your local network. This solution is common in larger companies but is not feasible (or economical) for smaller companies and those just starting out with web design.

The ideal solution would be if you could test your PHP scripts locally on your computer in the same way that you test your HTML pages. To answer this call, the Expression Development Server you were introduced to in Hour 20 can be set up to include PHP as a testing environment.

The Expression Development Server can preview ASP.NET and PHP scripts, but for the PHP scripts to function properly, you first need to install PHP on your computer. PHP is free open source software that you can legally download and install on your computer.

1. In your web browser, go to http://windows.php.net/download/, as shown in Figure 22.1, to find the latest release of PHP. (p.t. is the latest stable PHP release is version 5.3.0).

FIGURE 22.1
The PHP website found at www.php.net provides new and old versions of PHP for download.

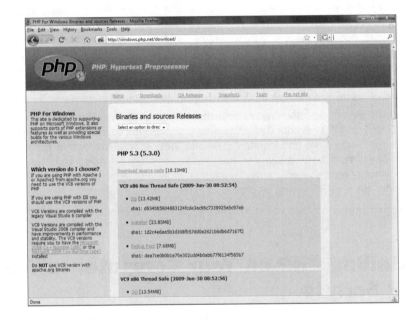

2. Download the installer and save it on your computer.

3. Run the installer and install the application to the suggested location (in my case C:\Program Files\PHP).

4. In the Web Server Setup dialog (see Figure 22.2) you do not need to set up a web server (that's what the Expression Development Server is for), so select Do not setup a web server unless you plan to use the web server for something else.

5. Open Expression Web 3 and select Tools, Application Options on the menu bar to open the Application Options dialog (see Figure 22.3).

6. In the PHP section at the bottom of the Application Options dialog, use the Browse button to navigate to the location in which you installed PHP

FIGURE 22.2
Unless you want to set up a web server on your computer, select Do Not Set up a Web Server when asked.

FIGURE 22.3
To be able to preview PHP scripts in your browser via the Expression Development Server you need to tell Expression Web 3 where the php.exe file is located in the Application Settings dialog.

(C:\Program Files\PHP). Expression Web 3 looks for a PHP CGI Executable file, but the newer versions of PHP don't have this file type. Change the File Type search to All Files and select the file named php.exe. Click OK to apply the changes.

Now PHP is installed on your computer, and when you restart Expression Web 3, it uses this installation of the program when testing PHP pages.

As you previously learned, you can place PHP script directly inside the code of an HTML page or in a dedicated file. When a browser opens a file containing PHP code, the browser looks for special PHP tags called *delimiters* that define which

Did you Know?

> portion of the code is PHP and which is not. The regular HTML code then processes normally while the code inside the PHP delimiters goes to the server for interpretation.

Using PHP and HTML to Create a Contact Page

PHP is a fairly simple code language when you know how to read it. But for a novice it can be rather intimidating. Therefore, let's create some basic examples of how you can use PHP alongside HTML to build a contact page.

1. Create a new page from the mykippleMaster.dwt Dynamic Web Template and save it in the Contact folder as PHPcontact.php either by changing the Save As type or simply changing the file extension manually.

    ▶ All PHP code has to be contained within PHP delimiters. Unlike the regular HTML tags you previously used, all PHP content is included inside the tag itself; that is, between the < and > brackets rather than between the beginning and end tag sets. The standard syntax for PHP code is <?php ?>, in which the PHP code goes in the space between.

    ▶ Expression Web 3 not only has full IntelliSense support for PHP but also has a series of common PHP scripts built in to the Insert menu for easy access and use. Many of these code segments come equipped with the beginning and end delimiters. The most basic command of any code language is the one that prints a line of text on the screen. In PHP, this command is echo. To insert a heading using PHP, you need to insert the echo command.

2. In Code view, erase the (heading) text and place the cursor in the heading editable region.

3. Select Insert, PHP submenu on the menu bar and choose Echo (see Figure 22.4). This inserts the PHP delimiters and the echo command.

    The echo command displays any text inserted inside quotation marks as regular HTML text in a browser:

4. With the cursor placed after the echo command (in green) in Code view, type **"Contact Me"** with the quotation marks included (see Figure 22.5).

Save the page and press F12 to test it in your browser through the Expression Development Server. If this is the first time you are using PHP under Expression Web 3, you

FIGURE 22.4
Expression Web 3 has a set of built-in PHP scripts accessible from the PHP submenu under Insert.

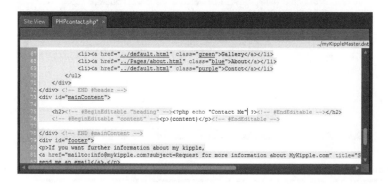

FIGURE 22.5
You insert the echo command with delimiters and a value in Code view, but they do not show up in Design view.

get an error message telling you the php.ini file is not configured correctly and asking if you want Expression Web to configure it for you. Click Yes and the page is previewed in your browser. If PHP installed and configured properly, the page appears with the text Contact Me in the header.

Using PHP you can define variables that display using the echo command. You can define these variables with the PHP command somewhere else on the page (such as the head) or even in a separate file or database.

Try It Yourself ▼

Use PHP Variables to Display Content

To define a variable, you give it a name that starts with a dollar sign ($). The name must start with a letter and can consist of only letters, numbers, and underscores. It is also important to know that PHP is a case-sensitive language.

1. Place the cursor before the echo command in Code view and press Enter to create a new line. Insert the following line of code:

   ```
   $heading = 'Contact Us';
   ```

   The first part of the code ($heading) is the name of the variable. The content of the variable is contained within single quotation marks, and the semicolon marks the end of the variable definition just as in CSS.

   To call a variable to display, all that's needed is to insert the variable name after the echo command.

2. Press Enter to move the echo command to a new line and delete the "Contact Me" text. In its place, insert the variable name $**heading** (see Figure 22.6).

FIGURE 22.6
A variable replaces the echo text.

Save and test the page in your browser, and you see that it looks the same as before.

PHP in Design View

You probably have noticed by now that the results of the PHP code do not appear in Design view. This is because Design view is a web browser emulator and does not have a web server simulator connected to it. As a result, the only way to preview your PHP code is to test it in your browser locally through the Expression Development Server, on a local web server, or on a live web server on the World Wide Web.

Creating an Email Form Using PHP

In Hour 20, you created an email form using the built-in functionalities of Expression Web 3. This email form generated an email sent to a specified address by way of the FrontPage Server extensions on the web server. But not all web servers have FrontPage Server extensions installed, and on those servers the email form generates code only errors. If your site is hosted on a Linux server, a PHP-based email form is a rock-solid alternative.

The first step is to create a new email form for the contact page.

1. With the PHPcontact.php page in Split view, remove the <p> and </p> tags in the content editable region. Go to the Form Controls on in the Toolbox panel and insert the Form control.

2. Place the cursor inside the new form area in Design view and select Table, Insert Table on the menu bar to open the Insert Table dialog. Set Rows to 5 and Columns to 2. Under Specify Width, check the In Pixels radio button and set the width to 780.

3. Insert the names for each of the five form boxes in the left columns. From top to bottom they are Your Name:, Your E-mail Address:, Type of Inquiry:, What's On Your Mind?, and Finished?.

   ▶ When you click the Submit button on a form, all the form fields are sent to the browser memory. To identify which content comes from which form field, you need to give each form field a unique name. You can do that from the Tag Properties panel or with the help of IntelliSense in Code view.

4. In the first right cell, insert an Input (Text) control. Click the box to highlight it in Code view. Find the Name value and change it to **fullName**.

5. Use the Tag Properties panel to set the tab index to 1 and the size to 30 (see Figure 22.7).

FIGURE 22.7
You can use the Tag Properties panel to define all available variables for any form control.

6. Insert a new Input (Text) control in the next cell below, and use the Tag Properties panel to set its name to emailAddress, size to 30, and tab index to 2.

7. In the third right cell, insert a Drop-Down Box control. Right-click the Drop-Down Box and select Form Field Properties from the context menu to open the Form Field Properties dialog.

8. In the Drop-Down Box Properties dialog, use the Add button to create four choices: Question, Comment, Suggestion, Kipple Story, and Random Thought. Set the initial state for Question to Selected and the other choices to Not Selected.

9. Use the Tag Properties panel to set the name to inquiryOptions and the tab index to 3.

10. In the fourth right cell, insert a Text Area. Use the Tag Properties selector to set cols to 55, name to thoughts, rows to 8, and tab index to 4.

11. In the bottom-right cell, insert an Input (Submit) button and an Input (Reset) button. Use the Tag Properties selector to change their values to Submit and Reset, respectively. Set their tab index orders to 5 and 6.

You now have an email form that looks the same as the one you created in Hour 20 (see Figure 22.8). But as with the other form, this one does nothing until you attach some functionality.

FIGURE 22.8
The email form is built.

Try It Yourself ▼

Making the Email Form Work

When the visitor clicks the Submit button in the email form you just created, four strings of text with the names fullName, emailAddress, inquiryOptions, and thoughts are created and sent to the browser. In the form in Hour 20, code inserted by Expression Web 3 intercepted the strings, and all the necessary actions performed by that code was instead done by the FrontPage Server extensions. Now you want to re-create those same functions using PHP instead.

To perform the actions needed to send the email to the desired address, make a new PHP file that contains the code that writes and sends the email.

1. Create a new PHP file by selecting File, New on the menu bar and choosing PHP under the General option.

2. Delete all the code in the new file so that it is completely blank, and save it as **emailProcessor.php** in the Contact folder.

   Now you need to send the information from the contact.php file to the new file. By default the Form form control has a built-in action triggered by the onclick event attached to the Submit button. You use this action to send the contents of the form to the new file.

3. With the PHPcontact.php file open in Design view, click anywhere inside the form and select the <form> tag from the Quick Tag Selector.

4. In the Tag Properties panel, click the action tag to activate it and click the ... button. Doing so opens the Select File dialog. Navigate to the Contact folder and select the emailProcessor.php file. Click Open to set the action (see Figure 22.9). Save PHPcontact.php.

   Now you need to set up the PHP functions that generates the email.

5. Open the emailProcessor.php file in Code view. Place the cursor at the top of the page, and click Code Block in the PHP submenu options under Insert on the menu bar. Doing so inserts the PHP delimiters <?php ?>.

6. With the cursor between the delimiters, press Enter several times to create some space.

   To get a PHP script to send an email, you use the mail() function. The syntax of this function is as follows:

```
mail(to,subject,message,headers,parameters)
```

FIGURE 22.9
By setting the `action` attribute of the form to a file, you send the information from the form to that file.

Of these, the `to`, `subject`, and `message` variables are mandatory, whereas the `headers` and `parameters` variables are optional. For the email form you create, you use the `to`, `subject`, `message`, and `headers` variables.

To help you remember the order, IntelliSense displays a ScreenTip with the different sections as you insert them.

7. On a new line, type **mail**(. This brings up the IntelliSense ScreenTip for the `mail()` function (see Figure 22.10).

FIGURE 22.10
IntelliSense helps you keep track of the many variables necessary when using PHP functions.

8. IntelliSense asks for the names of each of the variables, but you haven't created the variables yet. To keep track of what the different variables are supposed to contain, type out the function of each variable as its name, and end the line with a parenthesis and a semicolon. When finished the line of code should look like this: `mail($to, $subject, $message, $header, $parameter);`.

The next step is to create new variables that contain either predefined information or information received from the form.

9. First you need to create a $to variable to tell the program where to send the email. Create a new line above the mail() function and type the variable name $to followed by your email address, like this:
$to = 'you@yourdomain.com';.

When an HTML form is submitted, all the contents are sent using a method called POST. To capture that content, you need to use a form variable. A form variable looks like this:

```
$_POST[];
```

The original variable name is inserted in single quotation marks between the two brackets.

10. Create a new line. The $subject variable should contain the choice the visitor made in the Type of Enquiry field in the form. The name of that field was inquiryOptions. To insert that content into a variable, you need to create a form variable: $subject = $_POST['inquiryOptions'];.

Skip the $message variable for a moment. The $header variable can have several different headers, including From, Cc, and Reply-to. In this case, you want the From header to match the email address of the sender.

11. Create a new line. Set the $header variable to receive the content from the emailAddress form field: $header = $_POST['emailAddress'];.

Now all that is missing is the message, or body, of the email. Before you create the $message variable, you need to learn a few more things about PHP syntax. First, PHP enables you to mix clean text and code as much as you want. Second, to make a line break in PHP, you need to insert the line break code, which is a backslash followed by a lowercase n, like this: \n. PHP understands that this is a line break, even if it is sandwiched between two lines of text or other code without spaces.

For the emails generated from your website to make as much sense as possible, it is a good idea to space the content properly. Ideally you want your email body to look something like this:

```
From: Sender Name
Sender e-mail address: sender@senderdomain.com
Regarding: The selection made from the drop-down box.
Message:
Message entered in the box goes here.
```

12. The $message variable will be somewhat different from the rest of the variables. Start by making the variable: $message =''; .

13. On the first line of the email body, you want the text From: followed by the name of the sender. Place the cursor between the two single-quotes and type **From: $fullName\n.**

14. On the next line you want the text Sender e-mail address: followed by the email address. The sender's email address was stored in the $header variable in step 11. Directly after the \n, without any space between, type **Sender e-mail address: $header\n.**

15. The third line of the email body should read Regarding: and have the selection the visitor made from the drop-down box. This information was stored in the $subject variable in step 10. Directly after the last piece of code you inserted, write **Regarding: $subject\n\n.** Note the double line shift to create a space between the sender info and the message.

16. Finally, you want the actual message to appear below the rest of the content. The word Message: should also appear on its own line. Directly after the last \n, type **Message:\n$thoughts\n.**

The entire variable should now read

```
$message = "From: $fullName\nSender e-mail address: $header\nRegarding:
$subject\n\nMessage:\n$thoughts\n";
```

17. To make the sender's email address appear in the From field in your email reader, you need to make a small change to the mail() function: Replace $header with **"From: <$header>".**

<table>
<tr><td>Watch
Out!</td><td>I'm Not Receiving Any Emails from the Form!
If you test the page in your browser and try to send an email to yourself, you quickly discover that nothing happens. This is because in addition to having PHP running on your computer, the email() function requires a working email server. To test this functionality, you need to upload the contact.php and emailProcessor.php files to a server with working email functionality.</td></tr>
</table>

18. Because you will not be using the $parameter variable, remove it from the mail() function.

The final code, as shown in Figure 22.11, generates emails laid out exactly as the earlier example from the contents of the email form.

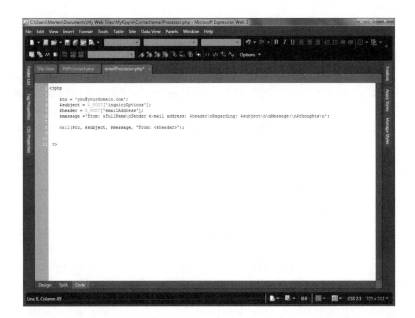

FIGURE 22.11
The finished emailProcessor. php file as it appears in Code view.

Added Functionality

There are still a couple of things to add before the email form is complete. For one, the visitor has no way to know whether the email was sent. Additionally, the form currently sends an email even if there is no information entered. You can fix both these issues by adding some simple PHP code.

Try It Yourself

Create Landing Pages for Success and Failure

As a courtesy to your visitor, you should always tell her whether the email was sent. You can do so by using "landing pages" that the browser navigates to depending on whether the email was sent.

To start, create three new HTML pages called success.html, failure.html, and error.html that have messages telling the visitor whether the email was sent, if it was not sent, or if something went technically wrong in the sending process. Place all three files into the Contact folder in your site.

PHP is actually a scripting language you can use to create small programs that behave according to your input. One of the many things you can do with PHP is define a set of conditions that have to be met for some specific action to occur and also say what happens if the conditions are not met.

1. If the email is sent successfully, you want the browser to be redirected to the success.html page. To do this, you use the echo function with an HTML meta tag called Refresh to redirect the browser. Still in the emailProcessor.php file, on a new line, type **echo "<meta http-equiv=\"refresh\" content=\"0;URL= success.html\">";**. The Refresh meta tag can be used to delay the redirection to a new page. The delay, measured in seconds, is defined by the content variable. The backslashes in front of the quotation marks tell the PHP interpreter that they are not PHP code but HTML.

2. Likewise if the email is not sent, you want the browser to be redirected to the failure.html page. On a new line, type **echo "<meta http-equiv=\"refresh\" content=\"0;URL=failure.html\">";**.

3. To let the server know when to say the email was sent, you first have to define what you consider a success. In the case of the email form, a success would mean that the `mail()` function executed properly. To define the `mail()` function executing properly as a success, place the cursor at the beginning of the line that has the `mail()` function and type **$success =**.

   Now that you have a way to measure whether the email was sent and you have the resulting actions for what should happen in either case, you need to make a small program that tells the server when to do what. This is done by using the `if` and `else` statements. Like the names suggest, the `if` statement checks whether a certain condition is met. If it is, the attached action takes place. The `else` statement kicks in whenever the `if` condition is not met. In this case, you want the `if` condition to be the $success variable. If it is met, the success.html page should display, and if not, the failure.html page should display.

4. Create a new line above the `redirect` meta tag that leads to the success.html page and type **if ($success){**.

5. Create a new line directly below the redirect meta tag and close the curly bracket **}**.

6. Create a new line under the last one and type **else {**. Close this curly bracket on a new line after the redirect meta tag that leads to the failure.html page.

Figure 22.12 shows the emailProcessor.php file as it appears in Code view with the new conditional redirects added. The browser now directs to either the success.html or failure.html pages depending on whether the email is sent.

FIGURE 22.12
Add the conditional
`redirect` tags
to tell the visitor
whether the
email was sent.

Try It Yourself

Create a Filter to Stop Empty Messages

The easiest way to weed out nonsense emails and accidental clicks is to set up the email form so that if the visitor doesn't enter an email address, the message is not sent. To do this, you need to test whether the $header variable, which contains the contents of the emailAddress field from the form, is empty.

1. Create a new line above the $success variable. To see whether the $header variable is empty, type **if ($header =="")** {. (In programming, a single equal sign means "is the same as," whereas two equal signs mean "is identical to".)

2. If the $header variable is empty, the browser should be redirected to the error.html page in which the visitor is told to enter an email address. Create a new line and type **echo "<meta http-equiv=\"refresh\" content=\"0;URL=error.html\">";**.

3. Insert one more line and type **exit;** to stop the script from executing further. Close the curly bracket }.

The final version of the emailProcessor.php file should now look like this:

```php
<?php

    $to = 'morten@pinkandyellow.com';
```

```
$subject = $_POST['inquiryOptions'];
$header = $_POST['emailAddress'];
$message = "From: $fullName\nSender e-mail address: $header\nRegarding:
$subject\n\nMessage:\n$thoughts\n";

if ($header=="") {
        echo "<meta http-equiv=\"refresh\" content=\"0;URL=error.html\">";
        exit;
}

$success = mail($to, $subject, $message, "From: <$header>");

if ($success){
        echo "<meta http-equiv=\"refresh\"
content=\"0;URL=success.html\">";
        }
        else{
        echo "<meta http-equiv=\"refresh\"
content=\"0;URL=failure.html\">";
        }

?>
```

To sum up, here is what happens step by step: When the visitor enters information into the email form and clicks the Submit button, the different variables are sent to the emailProcessor.php file. From here each value is given a variable name and inserted in various sections of the email body. Then the script tests to see that an email address was entered. If no email address was entered, the browser is redirected to the error.html page. Otherwise the script continues on to send the email. If the email is successfully sent, the browser is redirected to the success.html page. If for some reason the email was not sent, the browser is redirected to the failure.html page.

Summary

If you want to move beyond static pages and add dynamic content and true interactivity to your sites, you need to employ server-side scripting. And when you consider server-side script languages, many argue that PHP reigns supreme. Even though PHP is technically a direct competitor to Microsoft's application framework, ASP.NET, Expression Web 3 comes equipped with an extensive range of tools to create, write, edit, and deploy PHP-based pages.

To test your PHP scripts locally on your computer, you first need to install PHP. In this hour, you learned how to install this free open-source software and set up Expression Web 3 so that it deploys when you test your scripted pages through the Expression Development Server.

One of the major benefits of PHP is that the scripts can live alongside HTML code, which means you can build your pages as you normally would and substitute your static content for dynamic content without breaking HTML. It also means that even with PHP scripts installed, you still have full control of the layout and functionality of your pages through the use of tags, CSS, and other techniques you learned by reading this book.

In this hour, you learned about basic PHP scripts and saw how a script can insert content into a page. You built an email form based on PHP that can be uploaded to a Linux server. (The form from Hour 20 works only on Microsoft servers.) Using PHP scripts, you went beyond simply generating an email and created conditional rules that sent the visitor to different pages depending on whether the email was sent. Finally, you created a conditional rule that tested whether the visitor inserted an email address before submitting the form.

PHP is an advanced coding language, and in this hour you saw only a fleeting glimpse of what can be done with it. By using the PHP tools in Expression Web 3, including the full IntelliSense support, you are well equipped to dive into the world of server-side scripting. If you want further information about PHP, including tutorials, visit the official PHP website at www.php.net or the W3C schools at http://www.w3schools.com/PHP/.

Q&A

Q. *When I tested my PHP page in the browser after installing PHP, the address in the address bar changed to http://localhost: and some number. What happened to my original address?*

A. When you run a page through the Expression Development Server, the application creates a temporary simulated server on your computer. The address changes because the page is not merely read from its original location as it is when you test an HTML page but is rendered through the server. Thus the browser is displaying the server output, and because the server is hosted on your computer, it is a local host.

Q. *When I tested the email form using the Expression Development Server, all I received was a page displaying the PHP code.*

A. This problem could be caused by two different things. Either you didn't change the suffix of the contact page to .php but left it as .html, in which case the Expression Development Server will not deploy, and the page will be rendered as straight HTML, or PHP is not running properly. First check that your contact page is named contact.php. If so, make sure you followed all the steps when installing PHP on your computer.

Workshop

The Workshop has quiz questions to help you put to use what you just learned. If you get stuck, the answers to the quiz questions are in the next section. But try to answer the questions first. Otherwise you'll be cheating yourself.

Quiz

1. What is the difference between the email form you created in this hour and the one you created in Hour 20?

2. How does the browser know what part of a PHP page is PHP code and what should be considered standard HTML?

Answers

1. The email forms you created in the two hours are virtually identical. The difference lies in how the data or information generated from the forms is handled after the visitor presses the Submit button. In the form created in this hour, the data is sent to a PHP file that parses the information and creates an email message that is sent to the defined address. In the form from Hour 20, the data is processed by the FrontPage Server Extensions on the server and the email is generated by them. One of the biggest distinctions between the two is that while the PHP functions are contained in a separate file in this example, the FrontPage Server Extensions code is contained within the form code itself.

2. One of the many benefits of PHP is that it can live alongside regular HTML code without any problems. When the browser opens a PHP page, it reads all the regular HTML code as it normally would and sends only the PHP code contained within the PHP delimiters <?php ?> to be processed by the server before being displayed. This way the server helps out only when needed, and the browser does the rest of the work. In the extreme this means that you can create PHP pages that contain nothing but HTML, and the browser reads them as if they were HTML pages.

HOUR 23

Test Twice, Publish Once: Introducing SuperPreview

What You'll Learn in This Hour:

▶ What SuperPreview is and how it came about

▶ How to use Snapshot to get instant in-browser previews of your pages

▶ How to use SuperPreview as a standalone application

▶ How to diagnose and fix problems uncovered by SuperPreview

▶ How to create a warning telling Internet Explorer 6 users to upgrade their browser

Introduction

As I have previously mentioned several times in this book, cross-browser and cross-platform testing of your web pages and sites is paramount if you want to ensure that all your visitors have the same experience. This has two reasons: First, even though the browser producers are converging on an agreement about how to interpret CSS and JavaScript (and in spite of the W3C conventions on the topics), there is still no absolute truth about how to do this; as a result all browsers available have idiosyncrasies that can cause your pages to render improperly. This is further complicated because the same browsers running under different platforms (most notably Safari running under Mac OS and Windows) render different results. Whatever the reason, cross-browser testing is a necessary evil where web design is concerned. And it has been an annoying and time-consuming process that developers and designers alike would give a lot to go without. (So annoying, in fact, that many simply turn a blind eye to the problems and pretend they doesn't exist!)

The biggest hurdle for all involved has been to test against old and outdated browsers. It is a well-known fact that older versions of Internet Explorer, and in particular Internet Explorer 6 (IE6), turn layouts and designs that work perfectly in pretty much every other browser into a garbled mess. The problem is that to test for IE6, you need a working version of IE6 to test against. But if you run an updated version of Windows XP, Windows Vista, or Windows 7, IE6 is long gone and you can only have one version of the browser installed on your computer at one time. The only way to do proper IE6 testing would be to have an old computer running an old operating system with the browser, to run a virtual PC inside your operating system, or to use one of the many online browser screenshot services available. And even if you did somehow get to test your page against IE6, all you'd end up with would be a screenshot telling you that something is wrong. Finding out exactly what went wrong is a trial-and-error game.

Knowing the pains designers and developers went through to test their pages and sites against as many browsers as possible, the Expression Web team developed an application dedicated to not only perform proper cross-browser testing but also provide more detailed information about what goes on behind the scenes to help in diagnosing and fixing problems. The result is Microsoft Expression Web SuperPreview—a standalone application integrated into Expression Web 3 that makes cross-browser testing a one-stop-process.

Having the Right Browsers

SuperPreview comes with Internet Explorer 6 built in. But to get the most out of this application, you also need to be up-to-date on your other browsers. In particular you need the latest version of Firefox (to get it visit http://www.getfirefox.com) and Internet Explorer (to get it visit http://www.microsoft.com/ie).

Snapshot—Instant Browser Previews Inside Expression Web 3

SuperPreview is a powerful standalone application, but it also lends some functionality to Expression Web 3 in the form of a panel called Snapshot. With Snapshot you get instant and up-to-date screen shots of your current page from your different browsers. The functionality is quite basic, but it gives you a quick-and-easy way to check if your latest style change is current with all the necessary browsers. It is also a great tool for on-the-spot testing during the process of debugging browser problems.

Snapshot itself doesn't require a lot of explanation. To activate it go to Panels on the main menu and select Snapshot. This opens a new panel that floats above the work-space or in the View panel below Design view (see Figure 23.1).

FIGURE 23.1
The Snapshot panel works along side the Code and Design view panels. You can dock it to an area of the work-space or float it like any of the other panels.

The Snapshot panel can hover over the workspace like it does by default, or it can be docked to any of the panel zones by simply grabbing the top of the panel and drag-ging it to the desired location. As the panel hovers over potential zones, they are highlighted with a blue line. Personally in my dual-monitor setup, I place and size the Snapshot panel to cover the entire left monitor while keeping the Expression Web 3 workspace on the right. On my laptop I place the Snapshot panel below (or some-times in place of) the Design view.

Snapshot Functionality

Snapshot has two drop-down menus with options: The browser menu, which lets you pick what browser you want the snapshot to be taken from (see Figure 23.2), and the

FIGURE 23.2
The browser menu lets you pick which browser the snapshot should be taken from.

size menu, which lets you define what size the imagined screen the snapshot is taken from should have (see Figure 23.3).

FIGURE 23.3
The size menu
lets you pick the
imagined size of
the browser win-
dow the snap-
shot should be
taken from.

The size menu requires a little further explanation: Snapshot works by passing the page info to a browser and taking a screen grab of the output the browser generates. To allow you to see what the page looks like in different browser window sizes, you can define the size of the browser output. That way, even if you don't have a 30-inch 2560 x 1600 pixel widescreen monitor, you can still see what the page would look like on that monitor.

To display page output in Snapshot, you need to have a page open in Expression Web 3. If you already have Snapshot open and you open a page, that page is displayed automatically. Depending on the content of the page and whether it is linked to online content and so on, the actual process of taking the snapshot might take some time, so you will probably encounter a spinning clock graphic quite frequently.

The refresh button (circular arrows) toggles the Always Preview Active Document function on and off. With the function active Snapshot will update every time you switch between different pages. With the function inactive Snapshot is only updated when the currently open page is saved.

The Snapshot is just that—a snapshot or a picture of what the page looks like in the selected browser on a selected size screen. The page is nonfunctional, so you can't click to select any elements or buttons. In other words, Snapshot is in no way a replacement for Design view or viewing and interacting with your page in a web browser.

Because it is a picture of the browser output, Snapshot is not dynamically updated as you make changes to your files. To refresh Snapshot, you need to save the page to which you have made changes. This automatically triggers Snapshot to update. That means if you make a change in your CSS file only, you still need to resave the page it relates to if you want to see the change reflected in Snapshot. Another more round-about way to refresh Snapshot is to change the browser from the browser menu. Changing the size does not trigger Snapshot to refresh, so if you want a different size you have to first change the size in the menu and then either save the page in question or change the browser.

Try It Yourself ▼

Preview default.html in Snapshot

To see how easy it is to preview pages in multiple browsers at different sizes and learn how Snapshot works, preview default.html.

1. Open default.html in Code view.

2. Go to Panels on the main menu and select Snapshot. The Snapshot panel opens as a hovering panel above the workspace.

3. If the new panel floats above the workspace, grab the top of the Snapshot panel with your mouse and drag it toward the bottom of the View pane until you see a blue line appear on the bottom. Let go of the panel, and Snapshot docks underneath the View panel showing default.html as it appears in your default browser (refer to Figure 23.1).

4. Use the browser menu to change the browser to Internet Explorer 6.

5. Use the size menu to change the browser size to 1600 x 1200. Save the page to refresh Snapshot.

Note that when the Snapshot panel is docked below Code view, the Design, Split, and Code buttons shift up accordingly. This is because Snapshot is an independent panel, not part of the View panel. So if you click on the Split button, Split view appears above the Snapshot panel. ▲

Using SuperPreview for Cross-Browser Testing

As I said before, Snapshot is a basic version of SuperPreview that can be used from inside Expression Web 3. The full-featured version of SuperPreview is a standalone application that has been integrated into Expression Web 3 for ease of use. To use SuperPreview you can either use the SuperPreview button next to the browser preview button on the Common toolbar, as shown in Figure 23.4, or launch it from the start menu of your operating system.

FIGURE 23.4
SuperPreview can be launched from the Common toolbar by clicking the SP button to the left of the browser preview button.

Do not run Snapshot and SuperPreview at the same time!

Both Snapshot and SuperPreview are complicated applications that put a lot of stress on your operating system. Running them both simultaneously can lead to your system getting sluggish or Expression Web 3 crashing. To avoid this problem, be careful to use only one of the applications at one time. If you think about it, they do the same thing, so it superfluous to use them both anyway.

When you open SuperPreview, you are see a menu and two preview panels, each with a series of browser buttons (see Figure 23.5).

FIGURE 23.5
SuperPreview as it appears in its default state.

The easiest way to understand how the application works is to simply use it. If you haven't already done so, open the default.html page in Expression Web 3 and press the SuperPreview button on the Common toolbar. If this is the first time you've opened SuperPreview, you need to select your baseline browser and the browser you want to test against. This is done by simply clicking the appropriate browser in the two view panels. The left panel contains your baseline browser—the browser you normally test all your pages against. Mine is Firefox, but you can choose any of the other ones if you like. The right panel contains the browser you are testing against. You can assign multiple browsers to this panel but only one shows at a time. More on that later. After you select your baseline and testing browser, click the green Submit arrow next to the location box on the menu. This tells SuperPreview to generate previews of the selected page in all the browsers you defined. While SuperPreview is working, you see a spinning clock in each of the view panels (see Figure 23.6). Depending on the complexity and location of the page you load, this process can take anywhere from a couple of seconds to several minutes.

FIGURE 23.6
Creating browser previews in SuperPreview takes time, so you'll have to get used to the spinning clocks.

When the pages are loaded, you can start using the different functions of SuperPreview to identify and diagnose problems.

The Tools of SuperPreview

SuperPreview has a series of different tools designed to help you diagnose problems. Most of them are actually variations of the same tool, but they each have a slightly different use and purpose.

The majority of the tools are placed on the toolbar (see Figure 23.7). From here you control what kind of information the application provides and how the application displays your page in the different browsers.

▶ In Selection Mode when you click on an element within the page, the selected element is highlighted in your view panels.

▶ In Panning Mode, you can click and drag the page in the view panel. If you have two view panels open, the page in the other view panel moves in sync with the one you are moving.

FIGURE 23.7
The menu bar in
SuperPreview
helps you select
how the pages
are to display
and how you
want to interact
with them.

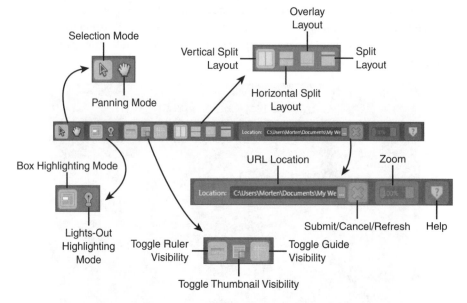

In Box Highlighting Mode, SuperPreview draws a colored and outlined box highlighting the affected area of the selected content. If both view panels are open, the box is highlighted in both panels with different colors (see Figure 23.8).

FIGURE 23.8
Box Highlighting
Mode highlights
the selected box
element with an
overlay color and
an outline.

▶ Lights-Out Highlighting Mode highlights the same area as the Box Highlighting Mode by darkening all other content surrounding it (see Figure 23.9).

FIGURE 23.9
Like the name suggests, Lights-Out Highlighting Mode highlights the selected box element by darkening everything not selected.

▶ Toggle Ruler Visibility turns the rulers on and off.

▶ Toggle Thumbnail Visibility turns the thumbnail navigator on and off (see Figure 23.10). The thumbnail navigator is a box in the bottom-right corner of each view panel that provides a thumbnail of the entire page with the currently visible area highlighted. You can use your mouse to drag the highlighted area around inside the thumbnail for quick navigation.

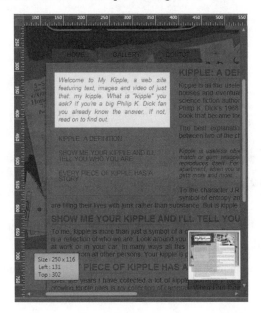

FIGURE 23.10
The thumbnail navigator provides a quick way to navigate inside large pages.

▶ Toggle Guide Visibility turns guides on and off. Guides can be placed anywhere in the view panels by dragging and dropping them from the rulers. If you have both view panels open at the same time, a guide dragged into one panel will be duplicated in the other. The guides can be used to measure differences in size and position of elements. Note that you cannot make new guides if Toggle Ruler Visibility is turned off.

▶ Vertical Split Layout is the default view panel layout in which the two browsers display side by side.

▶ In Horizontal Split Layout, the two view panels display one on top of the other. This display is useful if you want to compare wide elements of a page across browsers.

▶ Overlay Layout is the most unusual of the layout modes. This function displays the two selected layouts one on top of the other through what is often referred to as "onion skinning," meaning you can see one shining through the other (see Figure 23.11). This function is particularly useful to identify minute changes in positioning.

FIGURE 23.11
Overlay Layout allows you to place two browser outputs one on top of another to see if the content shifts between the two.

▶ Single Layout displays only one browser at a time giving you a full screen view of the output.

▶ The URL Location bar lets you enter any URL, local or external to be previewed in SuperPreview. Because the application is standalone, there is no limit to what page you can preview: If you can visit it in your browser, you can open it in SuperPreview (as long as the website doesn't require you to log in first)!

▶ The Submit/Cancel/Refresh buttons relate to the URL Location bar and require no further explanation.

▶ The Zoom menu lets you zoom in and out in your view panels. As with the other functions, the zoom function affects both view panels identically.

On the bottom of the window, two more tools are worth mentioning: the Preview Browser button and the DOM button.

The Preview Panel(s)

When you opened SuperPreview, you had to pick a baseline browser and a testing browser. But as I said before, you can define several testing browsers. To add another browser, simply click the + symbol next to the testing browser. When you do, the testing browser view panel changes back to the browser selection page, and you can pick another browser.

Because many designers create image mock-ups of their pages, SuperPreview also enables you to test the real browser output against images. To do so, select the Open Image option (see Figure 23.12) and browse to the image you want to preview

Open Image ...

FIGURE 23.12
The Open Image option lets you import an image file such as an original mockup from a design application or a screen grab from another browser.

against. The function supports all the standard image formats (.bmp, .gif, .jpg, .png) and Photoshop files (.psd). The image function can also be used to import screen grabs of other browsers not supported by SuperPreview. As with the browsers, there is no limit to how many images you can test the page against (see Figure 23.13).

Keep in mind that SuperPreview compares only two browsers at a time, so to switch between the different testing browsers and images, you need to actively select them.

FIGURE 23.13
SuperPreview enables you to test your pages against a multitude of browsers and images at the same time.

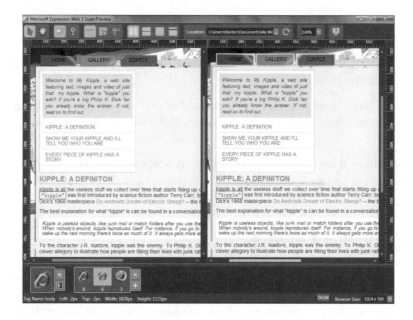

The DOM Tree View

The final and most-advanced feature of SuperPreview is the DOM Tree View that you can open by clicking the DOM button on the bottom of the window.

Did you Know?

> DOM or Document Object Model is the name of the code used in HTML and other web code to allow programs, applications, and scripts to access specific elements of the content and modify, style, update or do other things to it. It sounds confusing but the term DOM refers to the tags that contain the content inside HTML and other web documents. So basically if someone talks about the DOM, what they mean is quite literally the beginning and end tags that surround content.

When you click to select an element in your preview pages with the DOM Tree View open, SuperPreview provides a full breakdown of the entire DOM or tag structure for that element (see Figure 23.14). As a result you can see every tag that affects the content and, if anything, what code is interpreted differently between the browsers. This is an advanced function that has limited usefulness unless you know what you are doing. Even so it can be a quick-and-easy way to find out why elements start behaving strangely when they are opened in different browsers. The key to using the DOM Tree View is to remember that different browsers have different DOMs, so when something goes awry, it's a fair bet that there might be something amiss in the tag tree.

FIGURE 23.14
The DOM Tree View displays the DOM or tag tree of the selected element.

Identify, Diagnose, and Solve Cross-Browser Issues with SuperPreview

By following the lessons in this book, you have created a fully working version of the MyKipple.com site. And if you followed my previous advice, you tested it against your browsers at every step along the way, and you probably have a fairly good idea of what, if any, cross-browser issues exist. But that applies only to current browsers. For older browser versions such as Internet Explorer 6 and 7, you don't know unless you have a fairly advanced setup, or you have deliberately avoided updating your browser for some time.

Now that the site is done, it is time to make sure it looks the same across all browsers. To do so, open default.html in SuperPreview with Firefox as the baseline browser and IE8, 8->7 and 6, respectively, as the testing browsers. As you can see from clicking through the different testing browsers and from Figure 23.15, a couple of elements look different between the browsers: In IE8 and Firefox the sidebar is next to the content, but in IE7 and 6 the content appears below the sidebar. In addition, in IE6 everything seems slightly shifted, and the transparency is gone.

Now that you know the main issues, it is time to do some browser triage: What problems are most important and should be fixed, and what problems are either unimportant or hard to fix without a massive amount of work? This requires a bit of knowledge of the different browsers.

FIGURE 23.15
Default.html
looks surpris-
ingly different
depending on
what browser
you use.

Technically, Firefox and IE8 should look almost exactly the same. Any noticeable difference between the two most likely means there is an actual error either in the HTML markup or the CSS styles. We already know that IE6 does not support PNG transparencies without some serious JavaScript workarounds. But apart from the transparencies and some slight shifting in the size and spacing of the text, there doesn't seem to be anything else dramatically wrong with the IE6 output. For those reasons, there is no point in trying to fix the page for IE6, but we should probably add a warning on the page telling IE6 users they should upgrade to a new version of the browser.

In SuperPreview, you can see that the heading and content appear on the right side of the sidebar in Firefox and IE8 and their positions are almost identical. (According to the position pop-ups, they are only 2 pixels apart.) But if you click on IE7 or IE6 the heading along with the rest of the content appears below the sidebar rather than beside it (see Figure 23.16)!

The explanation for this discrepancy lies in Hour 13, "Getting Visual, Part 3: Images as Design Elements with CSS," when you created a custom H2 style to ensure that the background image appeared behind the text rather than to the extreme left of the containing box. One of the things you did was to set the `clear` attribute to both to ensure that no other text appeared on the same line as the heading. Now it turns out the two older versions of Internet Explorer interpret the `clear` attribute a little too strictly and force the content down below the sidebar.

FIGURE 23.16
Small browser inconsistencies can have big consequences. In this case the content is shifted down below the side-bar in IE7.

This is a typical situation when dealing with browser incompatibilities: To fix a problem in an older browser or one that doesn't play nice with web standards, you have to start chipping away at your code and remove elements that are there for a reason. So for each such instance, you have to ask yourself a couple of questions: Is the discrepancy bad enough that I need to fix it? Is the fix going to adversely affect the design in browsers that interpret my code correctly to begin with? For this page, the answer to the first one is yes. For the second question, in most cases you need to do some trial and error to find the answer.

Back in the default.html page in Expression Web 3, find the H2 style in the Manage Styles panel and open the Modify Styles dialog. Go to Layout and delete the clear:both attribute. Click OK, save the page, and save the attached CSS page. Save and open the page in SuperPreview.

Clicking through the different testing browsers and testing the page in your other browsers, you see that the change fixed the problem without any undesired consequences for the rest of the content.

Troubleshooting and Fixing the Sidebar in Internet Explorer 7

With the heading issue resolved, a new and much more serious problem emerges: Part of the sidebar is now blocked in Internet Explorer 7. Because this problem is visible only in IE7, it is likely one of those idiosyncrasies I previously mentioned in which the browser doesn't interpret web standards properly. But because IE7 is still the most prevalent version of the browser, it is a problem we have to fix. Unfortunately, because it is a web standards-compliancy issue, the fix might result in the page looking a bit different—in other words, we might have to "dumb it down" to work in the broken browser. Using the tools in SuperPreview to select and highlight the different sidebar elements, you can see that the content isn't merely blocked by the blockquote box, but it is cut off at the bottom. What makes this problem even stranger is that it appears only in IE7 but not IE6, meaning this is an isolated issue for that browser only.

Because there is no obvious reason why the sidebar is interrupted by the blockquote, the only way to find the problem and fix it is through trial and error. Based on what you see in SuperPreview, it seems logical that the culprit is the blockquote, so let's start there:

1. In Expression Web 3, open the kippleStyles.css file in Code view and find the blockquote style.

2. Use CSS comments to disable all the styling inside the curly brackets. The syntax for a CSS comment is forward slash + star (/*) for the beginning and star + forward slash (*/) for the end. When you comment out CSS, the affected code turns gray, as shown in Figure 23.17.

FIGURE 23.17
Like in HTML, you can use special code to comment out sections of CSS. This is an easy way to turn CSS code on and off without deleting it.

```
106      color: #808080;
107  }
108  blockquote {
109  /*  background-color: #FFFFFF;
110      padding: 8px;
111      text-align: justify;
112      font-size: 0.8em;
113      color: #333333;
114      margin-bottom: 10px;
115      font-style: italic;
116  */
117  }
118  #sidebar {
```

3. Save the style sheet and reload default.html in SuperPreview. Without any of the style code, the sidebar appears as it should in IE7.

4. Back in kippleStyles.css move the beginning comment tag down one line so that the background-color attribute becomes active. Save the style sheet and

reload default.html in SuperPreview. The background color is added, but the sidebar menu is still visible.

5. Continue moving the beginning comment tag down one line, save the style sheet, and test the new style in SuperPreview until you find the style attribute that causes the problem.

Going down the list of attributes, you find that it is `font-style: italic;` that is the culprit. For whatever reason, it looks like IE7 doesn't like this particular style combination, and as a result the other elements are affected. The reason why I say it doesn't like this style combination is because the problem isn't actually caused by the `font-style` attribute alone: If you leave the `font-style` attribute active and comment out the `background-color` attribute, the menu is also visible. So it seems it is the combination of a background color (or a border for that matter) and italicized or oblique text that together cause the problem. That leaves you with a decision to make: What matters more to you? The background color or the italicized text? You can choose one or the other but not both.

This, I'm afraid, is a typical browser-compatibility conundrum, and I built it in just to show you how weird things can get. Sometimes you are forced to make choices you don't like because things don't work the way they are supposed to. There are always ways around it, but they are usually complicated and time-consuming, and applying them becomes a question of whether the return on investment is good enough.

Solve IE6 Problems by Telling Visitors to Upgrade Their Browsers

As you can see by testing your site in IE6, things just don't work properly in this old browser. The problem becomes blatantly obvious when you use the Overlay Layout mode in SuperPreview: Not only are the PNG transparencies not working but also the content positioning and text alignments are off. IE6 has been a thorn in the side of web developers and designers since day one, and there are no turnkey solutions to solve all the problems the browser creates. In many cases, designers are forced to either clutter their code with custom IE6 code (commonly known as IE hacks) or create whole separate style sheets just for this browser.

Internet Explorer 6 was released in 2001, alongside Windows XP. It was replaced by Internet Explorer 7 in 2006, and Internet Explorer 8 was released in April 2009, so you would think that people had moved on to the newer browsers. But for myriad reasons, this has not happened. There are still a large percentage of web-faring users visiting your sites with this old-and-outdated dinosaur of a browser.

Since IE6's release in 2001, designers and developers have bent over backward to make their sites look and work properly in the browser. But over the past couple of years, more and more of us have decided that enough is enough and started working to educate people about why they should upgrade to a newer browser and how to do so. If you search the web for anti-IE6 campaigns, you'll find a long list of campaigns that all have the same goal in mind: to phase out IE6 for good by getting people to upgrade.

I started a campaign on my own back in January 2009, called StopLivingInThePast.com, and as part of that campaign, I created a small script anyone can add to their site. This script displays a warning to visitors using IE6 that they need to upgrade their browsers. Now that you know why IE6 is such a bad browser, I encourage you to add an IE6 warning to your sites to help your visitors get out of the rut and experience the web the way it was meant to be, through newer and better browsers. In the process, you'll learn a simple-and-easy trick to target specific browsers through the use of CSS!

▼   **Try It Yourself**

Use Conditional CSS Comments to Target Specific Browsers

In Hour 16, "Using Behaviors," you learned how you can use JavaScript to target specific browsers. But there is another way to do this using a cool but little-known CSS trick. It involves a conditional CSS comment tag and some basic programming language:

1. In Expression Web 3, open myKippleMaster.dwt in Code view.

2. Find the <body> tag and create a couple of new lines below it to make some space.

3. Below the <body> tag, insert the following code: <!--[if IE 6]>.

4. On the next line, type <p>You are using Internet Explorer 6</p>.

5. On the line below, insert the closing tag: <![endif]-->.

6. Create a new line and duplicate steps 3 to 5, substituting the number 7 for the number 6 (see Figure 23.18).

FIGURE 23.18
The <!--[if IE 6]> <![endif]--> tags can be used to target specific browsers.

```
56  <body>
57
58  <!--[if IE 6]>
59      <p>You are using Internet Explorer 6</p>
60  <![endif]-->
61  <!--[if IE 7]>
62      <p>You are using Internet Explorer 7</p>
63  <![endif]-->
64
```

7. Save the DWT and the linked pages, and test default.html in SuperPreview.

Now when you open default.html in IE6 and IE7 in SuperPreview, you see the text you just entered at the top of the pages (Figure 23.19). These conditional CSS comments

FIGURE 23.19
The conditional tags insert the browser-specific code in the pages.

work only on Internet Explorer and can be used to target any of the browsers by changing the if statement to match the browser version (5, 5.0, 5.5, 6, 7) or by setting a less than or equal (lte) or greater than (gt) value like this: [if lte IE 6] or [if gt IE 6].

The great thing about this conditional CSS comment trick is that there is no limit to what you can put inside the commented-out sections. And because it doesn't use JavaScript or other custom code to trigger, it works even on the most basic and stripped-down browser.

To add a full IE6 warning to your site, go to http://www.stoplivinginthepast.com/get-the-code/, copy the code from that page, and paste it into the DWT in place of the code example you just created. This adds a nice blue box at the top of your page (see Figure 23.20) that tells your visitors to upgrade their browser and provides links both directly to the upgrade page under Microsoft.com and also to more information about why they should upgrade.

FIGURE 23.20
When inserted into the DWT, the StopLivingInThe Past.com box appears only when people visit the site using Internet Explorer 6.

Summary

Throughout this book, I told you to keep testing your pages against as many browsers as possible to ensure that they look the same across all of them. Not only is this a cumbersome process, but it is also not 100% accurate because you need to test against old and outdated browsers you most likely don't have on your computer.

To solve this problem, Expression Web 3 comes complete with a new and revolutionary application called SuperPreview. SuperPreview lets you do cross-browser testing in one central location and provides you with detailed information about the elements on your page and how they interact in different browsers.

SuperPreview is a new feature with Expression Web 3, and because it is such an important tool in your web development toolkit, an entire hour has been devoted to helping you understand how to use it. The application actually has two components: Snapshot, which is a browser-based screen grab panel inside Expression Web 3; and SuperPreview, which is a standalone application that works with Expression Web 3. In this hour, you learned how to use Snapshot to get instant browser previews of your current page from multiple browsers and browser versions at the click of a button. This function is a quick-and-easy way to test to make sure your code and style changes are not going to have adverse effects on your layouts and designs.

Most of this hour was spent learning how to use SuperPreview to test your pages against different browsers and browser versions and use the tools to identify, diagnose, and correct problems. Even though the actual operation of SuperPreview is quite basic, the information the application provides in terms of cross-browser issues is invaluable and can help you identify problems and make decisions on whether they are worth fixing or should be ignored.

In this hour, you learned how to use all the functions in SuperPreview, and you used the different views and tools in the application to identify and solve several cross browser issues that you probably wouldn't have known about if it weren't for the application.

One of the things you discovered when using SuperPreview was that Internet Explorer 6 does not play nice. Unfortunately, solving IE6 issues is an uphill battle that often leads nowhere. So rather than delving into a complicated trial-and-error process to try to fix these problems, the last part of this hour was dedicated to show you how to create conditional CSS comments that target only certain browsers and use these to display a warning to all users of IE6 that they need to upgrade their browser. This same technique can be used to target any version of Internet Explorer and provide custom code to just that browser without the use of JavaScript or other advanced code.

Q&A

Q. *I have a page open in the Snapshot panel but when I try to click on the different elements to get more information nothing happens. Why is that?*

A. Snapshot represents the most basic form of browser previewing, where all you get is a literal snapshot of what the current page will look like in a browser. The purpose of this function is to give you a quick way of testing changes in your code on-the-fly against multiple browsers instead of having to leave Expression Web to do so. To get more detailed feedback and information on individual components in your design, you need to use Expression Web SuperPreview.

Q. *When I run Snapshot and SuperPreview at the same time my computer starts acting up, working slowly, or crashes. What am I doing wrong here?*

A. The answer is actually in the question: Snapshot and SuperPreview run off the same system processes, and if you try to preview the same page in both applications at the same time, you can overload your computer. A good rule of thumb is to close Snapshot if you are going to use SuperPreview and vice versa.

Q. *Why does my page look so different in Snapshot and Design view?*

A. Design view is not a browser but an approximation of a conglomerate of browsers and thus it doesn't necessarily show you what the true output of a browser would be. Snapshot, on the other hand, does give you accurate renderings of what the page will look like in the real browsers.

Workshop

The Workshop has quiz questions and exercises to help you put to use what you just learned. If you get stuck, the answers to the quiz questions are in the next section. But try to answer the questions first. Otherwise you'll be cheating yourself.

Quiz

1. Why is cross-browser testing so important?

2. Should you care if your page looks terrible in Internet Explorer 6 if it looks great in all the other browsers?

Answers

1. For whatever reason, the many different browsers available all display web content slightly differently. Cross-browser testing is essential to ensure that if not perfect your pages appear as similar as possible no matter what browser they are viewed in.

2. There is no correct answer to this question: The decision on whether or not to make a web page or site compliant with Internet Explorer 6 relies on what the owner of the site wants and what browsers the projected visitors of the site use. If there is a predominance visitors to the site using older computers that may run IE6, the site should be designed with this compliance in mind. But if the vast majority of visitors are using more modern browsers this becomes less important. A good analogy is full-screen vs. widescreen TV shows: If the majority of your viewers own older full-screen TV sets you are best suited to film and broadcast your show in 4:3 (full-screen) format. But if the majority of your viewers have widescreen HDTV sets, you are better off filming and broadcasting the show in 16:9 (widescreen) format and leaving the few that still have

full-screen TVs to either clip off the sides of the widescreen picture or watch the show with letterboxing.

Exercise

Expression Web SuperPreview is a great tool to test your own sites against multiple browsers simultaneously and check for browser incompatibilities in your scripts. But it is also a great tool for learning about the challenges of cross-browser compatibility and see that even the best designers and developers out there sometimes get things wrong. Take a moment to test some of your favorite sites in SuperPreview. All you have to do is enter the site URL in the Address box and the site will open in the browsers you choose. I suggest testing famous sites like http://www.microsoft.com, http://www.cnn.com and even the new http://www.whitehouse.gov. Use the different view tools to see how the content shifts around and formats differently in the different browsers. And then test my own blog http://www.designisphilosophy.com against IE6 to see how bad things can get when the designer deliberately creates a site that does not take this browser into consideration at all. (A hint: It's not pretty and doesn't work.)

HOUR 24

Publishing Your Website

What You'll Learn in This Hour:

▶ What the six different publishing options are and how they differ
▶ How to set up your site for publishing using FTP
▶ How to use the Publishing view to publish and update your site
▶ How to change the publishing and HTML optimization settings

Introduction

The final and arguably most important step to create a website is publishing it so that it is available to your intended audience, whether it is on a local network, an intranet, or the World Wide Web.

In practical terms, publishing a website means taking the files you have been working with on your computer and putting them on a server so that others can access them. There are many ways to do, this and which method works best for you depends on where the files go, what software the server runs, and several other considerations.

In the publishing phase of the website building process, Expression Web 3 goes from being a developer and designer tool to a file management tool. When you publish files to an external host, the application keeps track of which files were published and when they were published. That way you can easily see whether a file has already been published, or if you have a newer version of the file on your computer that needs to be published in place of an older one.

In this hour, you learn how to use the different publishing methods to manage files on your computer and on the final location and discover how to decide which method works best for you. You also learn how to configure Expression Web 3 to automatically update new versions of your files for you and keep tabs on what you have done in the past.

A Word on Domains and Web Hosting

In most cases, a website is intended to be published on the Web for everyone to see. In that case, you need a web server connected to the Web on which to place your files and a web domain that takes the visitors to your site. The most common way to do this is to use a web-hosting service that provides both domain name registration and web hosting.

The All-Important Domain Name

Buying a domain name can be a harrowing and frustrating experience because so many names are already taken, and it is important to get an easily spelled and memorable name that reflects positively on your company or service. In addition, thousands of companies out there prey on designers looking for a specific domain name. If you're not careful, they might snap up your preferred name right before you buy it and ask for a ridiculous fee (or ransom if you will) to release it to you. A common mistake people make when looking for a new domain name is to search on Google for it. What they don't know is that people monitor Google and other search engines for those searches. When they pop up, those people buy the domain names so that you have to pay them to get the names released. If you are looking to see whether a domain name is taken, you should always use a trusted Whois service such as www.whois.net rather than a search engine. Such services not only tell you whether a domain is taken, but if so, also who holds the rights to it and when those rights expires.

After you find a domain name you like, you can buy it from any number of vendors. The price of a domain name depends on the extension you want (.com, .ca, .net, .tv), and some domain extensions (.edu, .gov, and so on) are not available to the public. As of this writing, a .com domain should run between $10 and $20 per year. Pay any more and you are being ripped off!

Did you Know?

> Most web hosts offer free or discounted domain names with the purchase of a hosting plan, but you don't need to register your domain name with your web host unless that is what you want.

After you decide on a domain name, you need to find a place to host your site. Depending on the size of your site, what primary web technology you want to use (ASP.NET or PHP for example), and the estimated traffic your site will receive, you have many options to choose from. A small site with limited traffic will do fine with a basic shared-hosting plan, whereas a high-traffic site might need a virtual private server or even a dedicated server. In most cases, you can start with a small shared-hosting plan and upgrade when it becomes necessary.

An important thing to consider when buying hosting is what kind of applications you will run on your site. As you learned in this book, if you plan to run ASP.NET applications, you need a host that supports ASP.NET. Likewise if you run PHP applications, like the popular WordPress blogging software, you need a host that supports PHP. Before buying hosting anywhere, always make sure that the hosting plan includes all the features you plan to use.

A bit of research can save you lots of money! There are millions of web hosts, and their services and prices differ greatly. By doing some research and asking around, you can quickly find that the same service can be up to 10 times more expensive from one host to another. And the most famous hosts are not always the best ones. I have used five different hosts, and they have been progressively cheaper yet offered better service. For your convenience I placed up-to-date links to my hosting recommendations on the front page of the website for this book: http://expression.pinkandyellow.com.

Did you Know?

Six Different Publishing Options

Expression Web 3 offers several different publishing options to choose from, all with advantages and drawbacks. Which option you should use depends on where you are publishing the site to, what software the server runs, and your own personal preferences.

To select a publishing option, you need to set up your Publishing properties. This is done from the Site view (see Figure 24.1). On the bottom of the Site view are four

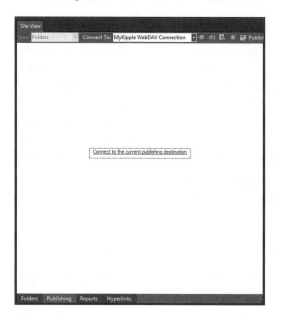

FIGURE 24.1
Publishing Settings can be accessed from the Publishing area under the Site view.

options: Folders, Publishing, Reports, and Hyperlinks. To set up your remote website properties, click the link in the middle of the panel with the text Add a Publishing Destination. This opens the Connection Settings dialog.

The Publishing view is new to Expression Web 3, and among the new features is the Connection Settings dialog (see Figure 24.2), which gives you more options than in

FIGURE 24.2
The Connection Settings dialog lets you define the different settings for each of your connections.

earlier versions of the application in terms of how you want to publish your files. One of the most important features is that you can now set up several different publishing options for the same site, so you can publish the same site to different servers or other locations without having to change your settings every time. You can also choose which one to use each time you make a change. For this reason the first element you need to define for your connection setting is a name. This name is just an identifier, so you can call it whatever you want, but it is a good idea to give the connection a name that makes sense and is easily understood and identifiable.

After you decide on a name, you need to select a connection type. Expression Web 3 offers six different types that all fit different scenarios:

▶ File Transfer Protocol (FTP)

▶ Secure Shell File Transfer Protocol (SFTP/SSH)

▶ File Transfer Protocol over Secure Sockets Layer (FTPS/SSL)

▶ Front Page Server Extensions

▶ Web Distributed Authoring and Versioning (WebDAV)

▶ File System

These six methods are quite different and serve different purposes. Depending on your server, you might choose from several or be restricted to just one. Knowing the difference between them means you can make the right decision now and not run into trouble in the future.

File Transfer Protocol (FTP)

Of all the methods offered, FTP is the most well known and frequently used. File Transfer Protocol (FTP) is an old file transfer method that dates back to 1971. Because of its age, FTP is a simple protocol that is firmly rooted and supported in networking and the World Wide Web. For this reason, FTP can be considered the standard for file transfer between computers.

In spite of FTP's reliability and ubiquitous support, it has some significant drawbacks; the most important is that the protocol is not secure by default. Without using an added layer of security, it is relatively easy for outsiders to monitor an FTP connection and pick up both usernames and passwords.

Did you Know?

When Expression Web originally appeared, the FTP performance was sporadic at best, and the many bugs associated with this feature became a major hang-up for early adopters. The release of Expression Web 2 saw significant improvements on this front, and the FTP option worked at an acceptable level. Even so, the Expression Web development team took criticism seriously, and for the release of Expression Web 3, they rewrote the entire publishing portion of the application from the ground up. As a result, the FTP option in this new version of the application is solid and works properly across the board.

To set up FTP as the publishing method, select FTP from the Connection Type list and insert the destination address in the Location field. With FTP, you also have the Directory option to specify a destination folder that the files will be sent to. That folder must already exist on the server.

Next, set your FTP username and password under Credentials. Your web host supplies the FTP username and password, and if you use FTP as your method for transferring files, you should change the password frequently.

In the Settings section, you can set the maximum number of simultaneous connections from 1 to 10. A higher number can speed up the time it takes to push data from your computer to the server and vice versa, but not all Internet service providers and web hosts allow multiple connections (therefore the term "maximum connections"). Figure 24.3 shows the FTP setup for the MyKipple.com site with the username blocked

FIGURE 24.3
When selecting FTP as the publishing method, you need to insert the address with the FTP protocol in place of the regular HTTP protocol.

out. Note that the FTP protocol is specified in the prefix of the address, so the address starts with ftp:// instead of http://.

Finally you have the option to turn on passive FTP if active FTP is not available. (Active FTP is often blocked by firewalls but you can normally get through using passive FTP.)

Secure Shell File Transfer Protocol (SFTP/SSH)

In spite of what the name suggests, Secure Shell File Transfer Protocol is not regular FTP run under Secure Shell (SSH) but rather a file transfer protocol in its own right. Whereas FTP transfers all your file content and other data (including your username and password) in plain text between your computer and the server, SFTP transfers this information under encryption making it extremely hard to intercept or exploit. That said, for you, the user, there is no discernable difference between the two. The setup for SFTP is almost identical to that of FTP with the exception of SFTP not having the option of using Passive FTP.

File Transfer Protocol over Secure Sockets Layer (FTPS/SSL)

FTPS is an FTP protocol that uses a Secure Sockets Layer (SSL) for added security. An oversimplified explanation of the difference between SFTP and FTPS is that whereas SFTP encrypts the data as part of the transfer protocol, FTPS adds a layer of encryption on top of the FTP transfer. Another way to think of the difference is that SFTP encrypts all the data to binary code before it is transferred whereas FTPS sends the plain text data inside an encrypted connection that can be read only by the clients and servers that share the same authentication key.

As the name Secure Sockets Layer implies, FTPS employs a second layer of constant challenging and verification of the authenticity of the transfer between the client and the server. For this reason FTPS works only with hosts that have a valid SSL certificate and supports SSL. And in many cases to get this service, you have to pay extra.

Setup of an FTPS connection is identical to the setup of a regular FTP connection because with the exception of the added secure layer, there is no difference between them.

FrontPage Server Extensions

You were briefly introduced to FrontPage Server Extensions in Hour 21, "Working with Flash and Silverlight," when you used them to create an email form. FrontPage Server Extensions are a set of small programs that run on the web server and give you the ability to add functionality (such as the ability to generate and send emails) to websites. More than that, they keep tabs on your files both locally and on the server to ensure that elements such as hyperlinks are updated if a file is moved from one folder to another, and so on. They follow your web-authoring process to tell you what files have been altered either by yourself or someone else on your team and whether the files on your computer are newer or older than the ones on the server. As the name suggests, FrontPage Server Extensions were introduced with Microsoft's old web design program, FrontPage, and they have become common throughout web servers, especially those running Microsoft Windows Server software. The name FrontPage Server Extensions might be a bit confusing because you are actually talking about many different things: the extensions that run at the heart of the server, the extensions that run independently inside your files (such as the email form functions), and the extensions that run in your authoring program keeping tabs on your files and your work.

When you check the FrontPage Server Extensions option in the Remote Web Site Properties dialog, you tell Expression Web 3 that the server you are publishing the site to has FrontPage Server Extensions installed and that you want to use this technology to communicate the files to and from the server. After set up, the application uses the HTTP or HTTPS protocol to send and receive file contents. This is the same protocol you use when you surf the Internet (the http:// prefix in front of all web addresses), which means that even if you are on a computer behind a strong firewall, if you can surf the Internet, you can use FrontPage Server Extensions to publish content.

To set up FrontPage Server Extensions as your upload option, select the option from the list, and enter your Remote Web Site location in the address box along with the username and password, as shown in Figure 24.4.

FIGURE 24.4
After selecting FrontPage Server Extensions as your publishing method, enter the destination address in the address bar along with your username and password.

You can use FrontPage Server Extensions as your publishing method only if your web server supports this technology. If it does not, you immediately get a warning message saying the current settings will not work, and you are directed back to the Connection Settings dialog where you can make a different choice.

Watch Out!

FrontPage Server Extensions Are on the Way Out

Despite their popularity, Microsoft has not supported FrontPage Server Extensions for some time. For this reason, there have not been any security updates to the technology for several years, and many web hosts are now stepping away and discontinuing their support for these scripts entirely. If you plan to use FrontPage Server Extensions, it is imperative that you contact your web-hosting service to make sure it is supported now and in the future.

Web Distributed Authoring and Versioning (WebDAV)

WebDAV stands for Web Distributed Authoring and Versioning and is an extension of the HTTP protocol that provides better security in the form of encrypted transmissions (to keep your data secure), file versioning (to prevent files from being overwritten when more than one person is working on them at the same time), and authentication. Unlike FrontPage Server Extensions, which are add-ons, WebDAV is already built in to your operating system to handle external links to HTTP addresses.

Setting up WebDAV as the publishing method is done the same way as setting up FrontPage Server Extensions: Simply select the WebDAV option and insert the destination address, username, and password. Also as with FrontPage Server Extensions, WebDAV has to be supported by your web server for it to work. If it is not supported or not turned on for your specific plan, you cannot access the server, and Expression Web 3 generates an error message. Unfortunately, this message causes a lot of confusion because the first item on the list of possible reasons why the connection failed is that the server does not have the FrontPage Server Extensions installed (see Figure 24.5). This suggestion is misleading because WebDAV and FrontPage Server Extensions are mutually exclusive. In fact if WebDAV fails, it could mean that FrontPage Server Extensions is installed on the server and is blocking WebDAV. If you get this message, contact your web-hosting provider and ask whether WebDAV is supported, and if so whether FrontPage Server Extensions is interfering with your connection.

FIGURE 24.5
The error message generated when WebDAV fails can be misleading because WebDAV and FrontPage Server Extensions are mutually exclusive.

File System

The final option is to host your website in a folder on your local computer or in your local network. That option can also be used to place your files on removable devices such as data discs, USB (Universal Serial Bus) keys, PDAs (Personal Data Assistants),

MP3 players, or any other storage device that can be connected to the computer. That way you can bring the website with you without having to lug around your entire computer. The file system option is frequently used when publishing to local networks and corporate intranets in which the web server is on the same network as the computer used.

If you publish to a local drive, all you need to do is insert the folder name in the address bar. If you publish to a local network location or a mapped drive, you need to insert the Universal Naming Code (UNC) path for this location. A UNC path looks like this: \\myServer\sites.

Example: Publishing Content Using SFTP

You now have a basic idea of what the six different publishing methods offer and when to use them. After you select a preferred method, the actual publishing process is the same. The method that is most readily available and at the same time secure is SFTP; so in this example you see how to use SFTP to publish your website to an external web host.

1. With the MyKipple site open, in Site view, click the Add publishing destination link in the middle of the window, or click Publishing Settings in the top-right corner, and under the Publishing tab press the Add button to open the Connection Settings dialog.

2. In the Connection Settings dialog, set the name to **MyKipple SFTP Connection**. Select SFTP; enter the destination address provided by your web-hosting service. If you publish to a specific folder, enter the folder name in the FTP Directory box.

3. Under Credentials insert the username and password provided by your web host. Leave the Maximum simultaneous connections at 4 and click Add. If you started by opening the Publishing Settings you need to click OK in the Publishing Settings dialog to complete the process.

When you add the new connection, the blue link in the middle of the Publishing view changes to say "Connect to the current publishing destination." Clicking this link logs into your new connection automatically. Depending on your Internet connection and your web host, this initial login procedure might take a little bit of time, and while it is working the control bar at the top of the Site panel will be blurred out.

After successfully logging in, you are presented with a view like in Figure 24.6 with the local website on the left and the remote website on the right. The left column

FIGURE 24.6
When you are logged in to the web server, you can see both the local files and the remote files and move them back and forth.

shows all the files in the folder you defined as your website project in Expression Web 3. The right column shows all the files currently at the remote location you defined in the address bar in step 2.

Expression Web 3 uses icons to tell you about the status of the files in your local and remote locations. In front of every file is an arrow pointing right (file to be published to the remote location) or left (file to be downloaded from the remote location), a question mark (Expression Web 3 is unsure what to do with this file), or a red balloon with an x in it (don't publish this file). When you log in to your remote location for the first time, all the files in your local view have an arrow pointing right because none of the files are in the remote location yet.

How you proceed from this point depends on what you want to achieve. For example, if you publish your entire site to the remote location for the first time, all you need to do is press the blue arrow button in the middle going from left to right. This sends a copy of all your local files and folders to the remote location.

Depending on how many files you have in your website, publishing the entire website to a remote location can take quite a bit of time. And it might look like Expression Web 3 stalls in the process. In general, publishing large sites to a remote server is a test of patience, so I usually start the process and then leave the computer to work on its own to avoid getting annoyed at how long it takes.

If you have previously published files to your remote server and you have made changes to only some of your local files, Expression Web 3 inserts the arrow icons on only the files that have been changed, and you can use the same option as before to overwrite the old files on the remote location with the new ones.

If files on the server have been changed since you last uploaded them, Expression Web 3 signifies that by attaching an arrow pointing to the left to the files in the remote location. This usually happens if you or a colleague uploads new files from a different computer or if someone made changes to the file directly on the server. To transfer these files from the server to your local computer, you simply click the arrow in the middle pointing left.

In some cases, alterations have been made to both local files and remote files. If that is the case, you can use the Synchronize files button in the middle column (the one with two arrows pointing in opposite directions). Use this function with caution because sometimes even though the files on the server are newer than the ones in your local folder, they might not be the ones you want to keep, and you could inadvertently overwrite important files in your local version of the site.

In addition to using the publishing options from the menu, you can also drag and drop files and folders between Local and Remote view. This is actually an effective way to perform targeted updates and give you detailed control of which files are located where.

You often find that your local folder contains many files that should not be put on the remote location for different reasons. For example, there is no reason to upload the Dynamic Web Template file to the server because it is functional only within Expression Web 3. To prevent a file or folder from being included when Expression Web 3 suggests files that should be uploaded or downloaded, right-click on the file and select Exclude from publishing from the pop-up menu (see Figure 24.7). A red balloon icon is attached to the file, and it will be ignored in the publishing process.

Advanced Publishing Settings

You can change the way Expression Web 3 handles local and remote files by default and configure the application to make changes to the files as they are uploaded. This is all done from the Publishing tab in the Site Settings dialog.

Optimizing HTML

Under the Publishing tab you have an option called Optimize HTML during publishing. If you check this option and click the Customize button that becomes available,

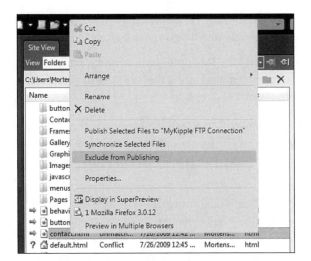

FIGURE 24.7
To prevent a file from being uploaded or downloaded, right-click on it and select Exclude from Publishing from the context menu.

you are taken to the HTML Optimization Settings dialog. From here you can instruct Expression Web 3 to remove all or part of the nonfunctional code in your HTML pages (see Figure 24.8). This option is available because both designers and

FIGURE 24.8
You can configure Expression Web 3 to remove all nonfunctional code from your HTML pages.

developers using Expression Web 3 tend to insert a lot of nonessential elements in HTML pages to make them easier to understand. Among these elements are comments explaining the different sections, Dynamic Web Template comments, and whitespace. You can also remove code generated by the application. The rationale behind removing this content is usually to either reduce the file size to improve load times (although this improvement will be negligible at best) or to make the HTML page less readable for people who take a sneak peek at the code.

There are several options for HTML optimization, and when they are checked, the selected components are removed as the files are published to the remote location. Here is a quick rundown of each option:

▶ **All HTML Comments**—All HTML comments whether inserted by Expression Web 3 or yourself will be removed. HTML comments are ignored by the web browser and are visible only in the source code. They always start with <!-- and end with -->.

▶ **Dynamic Web Template Comments**—In Hour 19, "Dynamic Web Templates," you learned that the editable regions in pages based on Dynamic Web Templates are inserted with HTML comments. These code sections relate only to Expression Web 3 and have no purpose outside the application.

▶ **Layout Tables Comments**—When you use the Layout Tables function to create layouts in Expression Web 3, the application includes comments to these tables.

▶ **Script Comments**—Expression Web 3 includes comments when inserting JavaScript and other script elements in your HTML pages. Likewise, it is common to attach comments to scripts to help remember what they do.

▶ **All Other HTML Comments**—This option covers all comments not covered by the other categories and can be used to remove only the comments you inserted without touching the comments Expression Web 3 created.

▶ **HTML Leading Whitespace**—The leading whitespace is the empty space before the first character in each line.

▶ **HTML All Whitespace**—In addition to leading whitespace, you can have inline whitespace and empty lines.

▶ **Expression Web Tracing Image and Interactive Button Attributes**—When tracing images and interactive buttons are inserted into a page, Expression Web 3 adds attributes to them for editing purposes (that is, allowing you to open and edit the interactive buttons). These attributes relate only to Expression Web 3 and have no function in a web browser.

▶ **Generator and ProgID Tags**—The Generator and ProgID tags used to be inserted in HTML pages to tell the browser what program was used to create and edit them. This is not done by Expression Web 3 but can apply to pages originally created in other web-authoring applications.

All the changes made by the Optimize HTML options are applied as the files are published to the remote location. Your local files are not changed. However, if you apply any of these options and then later overwrite your local files with ones from the remote location, all the content that was removed when the files were published will be removed locally as well.

The Publishing Tab

From the Publishing tab (see Figure 24.9), you can add, edit, or delete the publishing destinations for the current siteIn addition, and you can tell Expression Web 3 to publish subsites and generate a log file each time it publishes content.

FIGURE 24.9
You can add, edit, or delete the publishing destinations for the current site.

By default, only pages and folders contained within the main site are published by Expression Web 3. But if you have subsites defined in your project that you want published at the same time, you can check the Include Subsites option.

When you open the Publishing view of your Site, Expression Web 3 makes an educated guess as to what files it thinks you want to replace in your local and remote locations. By default it does this by comparing the modified dates of the files in both locations. However, if you work on the remote files as a team, from several different computers, or on the server itself, it can be almost impossible for Expression Web 3 to know which file is the correct one.

Finally, you can choose whether to let Expression Web 3 create a log file during publishing. If this box is checked, an HTML page is created and stored in your Temporary Internet Files folder so that you can check to see that the publishing process went according to plan.

To view the log file after publishing a site, click on the View Your Publish Log File option under Status in the Publishing view. This opens the log in your web browser for you to inspect. If you want to save the log file, select Save As under File in your browser.

At the bottom of the Publishing view panel there is a new section added in Expression Web 3 that provides information about your publishing status. This area lists the Last publish status (whether files were published successfully, and if there were problems what they were) as well as last publish time and also provides a link that says "Open destination site in Expression Web." This link opens the external site in a new instance of Expression Web 3 and sets it as the local site for that instance. That way you can work directly on the files in the remote location as if they were on your local computer.

Summary

By following the tutorials in this book, you have created a basic website with a lot of functionality. The last step of any web design process is to publish the site so that others can access it and enjoy the results of your hard work. That is when Expression Web 3 goes from being a web design and authoring tool to becoming a file and website management tool.

When your site is completed and ready for the world to see, Expression Web 3 offers you six different methods for publishing your content, all with benefits and setbacks. Those methods are FTP, FTPS, SFTP, FrontPage Server Extensions, WebDAV, and file system. In this hour, you learned what each of these options mean and when they are used.

There is no correct answer to the question "Which method should I use?" And after setup, the actual publishing and file-copying processes are the same regardless of what method you choose.

Expression Web 3 keeps tabs on what you do with your files in the program and makes educated guesses about what files you want to publish to your site. Even so, you can change these options either by selecting or deselecting files for upload or changing the publishing settings. You can also use the program to strip your HTML files of nonfunctional content such as comments and whitespace. All this is done from the Remote Web Site Properties dialog.

In this hour, you learned how to set up your site in Expression Web 3 for publishing to the desired location. And with that you have reached the end of the road of the initial design and deployment process. But this is just the beginning. When your website goes live and you start getting visitors, you probably want to make additions and changes to the site or build a subsite. Now that you know how to use Expression Web 3, you can apply the techniques you have acquired to build your knowledge of HTML, CSS, ASP.NET, PHP, and all the other technologies available to you and make informative and entertaining web experiences for the world to see.

Q&A

Q. *I tried uploading my site to my web host using FrontPage Server Extensions/WebDAV, but when I do, I get a warning saying that FrontPage Server Extensions are not installed on the server. What do I do?*

A. To use FrontPage Server Extensions or WebDAV as your publishing method, they need to be installed and supported by your server. Furthermore they are mutually exclusive; so if you can use one, you cannot use the other. The warning message Expression Web 3 generates is a bit confusing because it tells you there are no FrontPage Server Extensions installed even if you try to use WebDAV to upload your files. If you get this message using either method, contact your hosting provider and find out if either technology is supported with your plan. Most likely it is not, and you will be forced to use FTP as your method for uploading content.

Workshop

The Workshop has an exercise to help you put to use what you have just learned.

Exercise

Because this is the final hour, and you are probably tired of answering questions and doing exercises, I am giving you a challenge instead:

Take all the things you learned from reading this book and use them to create your own fantastic website. When you finish, submit it to the book website at http://expression.pinkandyellow.com, and I will post it for the world to see.

And last but not least, have fun!

Beyond the Basics, Part 2: Building a Site with ASP.NET

What You'll Learn in This Hour:

- ▶ How to use an existing ASP.NET site as a base to build a new site
- ▶ How an ASP.NET master page works and how to edit it
- ▶ How an ASP.NET web form or page works and how it relates to the master page
- ▶ How dynamic sites use source files to distribute content to different pages
- ▶ How to use CSS and HTML techniques to modify an existing ASP.NET site

Introduction

In Hour 19, "Dynamic Web Templates," you learned about Dynamic Web Templates (DWTs) and how to use them to create an easily updateable website with a consistent look. Then in Hour 22, "Beyond the Basics, Part 1: PHP in Expression Web 3," you got a first glimpse of how server-side scripting can be used to create websites with highly advanced dynamic content and interactivity. Now you put the two together to make a website controlled by a master page layout filled with dynamic content.

Even though Expression Web 3 comes equipped with script support and basic tools for PHP authoring, it is nothing compared to what the application offers from Microsoft's server-side script language, ASP.NET. Expression Web 3 is built around ASP.NET and offers extensive and unprecedented authoring and deployment tools and support for novice and advanced users.

As with PHP, the core concept of ASP.NET is to leave the generation of the content of the page to the server so that the designer or developer needs to do only minimal changes to files for maximum results. Likewise, ASP.NET code can live alongside regular HTML to simplify authoring. As a result, by deploying ASP.NET scripts, you can perform the same actions (populating text fields, sending and receiving information from forms, and so on) you did in Hour 20, "Getting Interactive with Forms," and many others as well.

Because building an ASP.NET-based site from scratch requires a relatively high level of programming know-how and skill, rather than building it from scratch you use a prebuilt site provided by Microsoft to learn about ASP.NET and how it works.

> To run an ASP.NET website, you need a server that supports this scripting language. In other words, your site needs to be hosted on a Microsoft server. Before you start working with ASP.NET, it is vital that you ensure that your server supports this language; otherwise, you are wasting your time.

Getting a Jump Start by Using a Starter Kit

Building ASP.NET applications from scratch can be quite intimidating for a novice. To help with the learning process, Microsoft has created a set of Starter Kits that you can download from the Expression website. The kits contain fully working and fully customizable sites that utilize both regular and advanced scripts to create highly functional and great-looking sites. In this hour, you use the Design Portfolio Starter Kit to get a better understanding of what ASP.NET is and how Expression Web 3 can help you build sites employing this technology in a fast and efficient manner, even without a firm understanding of the code language.

▼ **Try It Yourself**

Downloading and Installing the Starter Kit

The Expression website features learning tools such as videos, articles, tutorials, and downloads to help you start to use the different applications in the Expression Suite. For Expression Web 3, the Starter Kits can be a great help when taking your first steps with ASP.NET.

1. In your web browser, go to http://expression.microsoft.com, click on the Learn tab, and select Starter Kits. If you can't find the page, use this link: http://expression.microsoft.com/en-us/cc188682.aspx

2. From the Starter Kits page, select Expression Web Starter Kits and download the Design Portfolio Starter Kit to your computer.

3. Extract the contents of the zip archive you just downloaded (called ExpressionWebPorfolioStarterKit.zip) to a folder of your choice. The extracted folder contains a folder called Expression Portfolio Starter Kit and a Microsoft Word document. The folder contains a new folder called Portfolio Starter Kit and a Microsoft Word document that is identical to the one in the first folder.

4. Copy the Portfolio Starter Kit folder (the one inside the Expression Portfolio Starter Kit folder) to your Web Sites folder (see Figure 25.1).

FIGURE 25.1
My Web Sites folder as it appears with the MyKipple project and the new Portfolio Starter Kit folder.

5. Open Expression Web 3 and select Site, New Site from the menu bar. In the New dialog, select Empty Web Site under General, and use the Browse button to navigate to the Portfolio Starter Kit folder. Select the Portfolio Starter Kit folder, and Expression Web 3 automatically sets the name for you (see Figure 25.2).

It is vital that the site link is the Portfolio Starter Kit folder and *not* the higher level Expression Portfolio Starter Kit folder, or the site will not work properly.

Watch Out!

As you can see from the Folder List panel and the Web Site view, the Portfolio Starter Kit has a long list of pages and assets already installed (see Figure 25.3). Now that the site is properly linked from within Expression Web 3, you can open the pages, make changes, and test the site from within the program through Expression Development Server.

FIGURE 25.2
Create a new empty website located in the folder you just installed. This lets Expression Web 3 know that there is a site in the folder.

FIGURE 25.3
The Portfolio Starter Kit contains several pages along with assets that together make up the functionality of the resulting site.

The ASP.NET Master Page

Looking at the list of files in the Portfolio Starter Kit, the file that sticks out the most is arguably the most important one: Default.master. This file can be compared to a highly evolved version of the Dynamic Web Template (DWT), but this comparison hardly does it justice. The ASP.NET master page is the control center for the entire site. And whereas the DWT merely provided its child pages with static and styling content, the master page provides functionality and sitewide control.

In Hour 19 you learned that when you build a page based on a DWT, the code content of the DWT is copied over to the new page. As a result, every time you make a layout or style change in the DWT, all the associated pages need to be updated and have their code changed. In contrast, the ASP.NET master page is the source of all the layout and styling code. So, instead of this code being copied over to each individual child page, the children go back to the master page for layout, styling, and other common elements and contain only the info for the individual page contents. In other words, this is a truly dynamic site where all the files are generated from one central location.

To understand how this works, open the Default.master page in Design view. At first glance it looks like any other HTML page, but if you look closer you see two areas highlighted by a faint purple outline. By clicking on them you see that they are named NavContent and MainContent, respectively (see Figure 25.4). Each is a ContentPlaceHolder, the ASP.NET equivalent of the editable regions of the DWT.

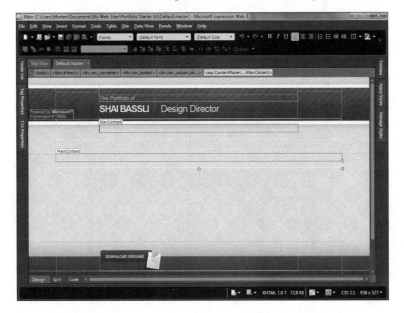

FIGURE 25.4
The NavContent and MainContent Content-PlaceHolders are highlighted with a purple outline. In this image, both are highlighted simultaneously for visual reference, and all the panels are set to AutoHide to provide more space for the Design view.

The ContentPlaceHolders (also called content regions) work in much the same way the editable regions work in a DWT: When a page is generated from the master page, only the areas within the content regions can be edited; the master page controls everything else. But unlike the pages generated by the DWT, you have no way to edit the code outside of the content regions in each individual page because the code is present only in the master page.

Managing the content regions is done the same way that you managed the editable regions: Under Format on the menu bar is a submenu called Master Page, and within that submenu is the Manage Content Regions option (see Figure 25.5).

In the Manage Content Regions dialog, as shown in Figure 25.6, you can add, rename, and remove content regions with the click of a button. In addition, you can

FIGURE 25.5
You can manage the content regions from the Manage Content Regions option found in the Master Page submenu under Format on the menu bar.

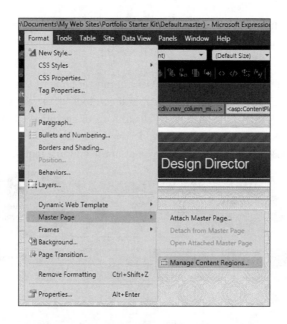

FIGURE 25.6
The Manage Content Regions dialog can also be used to quickly navigate to a particular region in Design view.

use the dialog to navigate to the different content regions. This option is especially useful when your layout has many regions and you are confused about where a certain region is placed. The Go To option works only in Design view.

The Master Page in Code View

When switching to Split view, the first thing you notice is that all the contents of the .master page are placed in a form. You can see this because wherever you click inside the page, the two first tags on the Quick Tag Selector are always <body> and

<form#form1>. That's because all ASP.NET sites that use .master pages consist of ASP.NET web forms that are populated. This will all make more sense in a few minutes.

Looking at the code, you see that for the most part it looks like any other HTML page. But if you click on one of the content regions in Design view, you see that the corresponding tags are somewhat different from what you encountered before (see Figure 25.7).

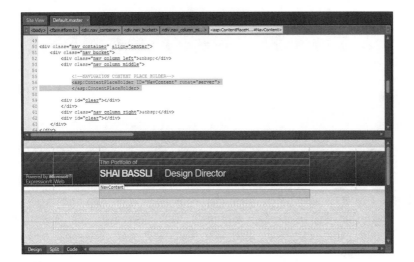

FIGURE 25.7
The NavContent Content Region in Design view with the corresponding code.

The `<asp:ContentPlaceHolder ID="NavContent" runat="server" >` tag is the ASP.NET master page equivalent of the `<!-- #BeginEditable "heading" -->` tag of the DWT with a few major differences. Whereas the DWT tag worked solely as a helper for Expression Web 3 to know what regions were to be editable, the ASP.NET tag is an actual functional part of the page just like any other tag. It tells the browser that the tag is an ASP function and that within it there will be ASP.NET-generated content. In addition it gives the area a name in the form of an ID and tells the browser where the script should run (on the server).

Try It Yourself ▼

Change a Content Region

The ASP.NET content regions work in much the same way as the DWT editable regions, and you can edit them in the same way in the master page. By default the Portfolio Starter Kit has three content regions: head, NavContent, and MainContent. But if you look at the head editable region in Code view, you see that it is empty, and the title tag is in a noneditable part of the page. As with the MyKipple project, you want the title, keywords, and description tags to be inside an editable region so that they can be customized for each individual page.

1. In Code view, find the `ContentPlaceHolder` tag for the head content. (It should be on line 9.)

2. Create a new line between the beginning and end tags and cut and paste the `<title>Main</title>` tags from line 7 into the new line (see Figure 25.8).

FIGURE 25.8
The <title>
tag is moved
into the head
content region.

3. Press Enter to insert a new line underneath the `<title>` tags and create a new `<meta>` tag like this: **`<meta content="" name="keywords" />`**. This tag will be filled with the keywords inserted in the Page Properties dialog of each individual page.

4. Insert a third line and create a new `<meta>` tag for the page description: **`<meta content="" name="description" />`** (see Figure 25.9).

FIGURE 25.9
The head con-
tent region now
contains the
title, keywords,
and description
of the page.

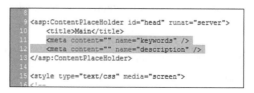

When you save the master page, you notice that unlike when you made changes to the Dynamic Web Template in Hour 19, you are not asked whether you want to update the files related to the master page. This is because rather than copying all the code over into each individual page, the pages created from the master page are built dynamically by the browser when they display; therefore, the updates happen instantly when the browser opens the pages.

ASP.NET Content Pages

As with the Dynamic Web Template, the master page serves only as the framework that tells the browser what the pages of the site should look like. To create the actual site, you need content pages. In the Portfolio Starter Kit are four such content pages: Contact.aspx, Default.aspx, Details.aspx, and Work.aspx.

Open the Default.aspx page in Design view. The page looks the same as the Default.master page, but if you click around inside it you see that you can place your cursor inside only the two editable regions, NavContent and MainContent. The NavContent area contains the navigational buttons for the page, whereas the MainContent area contains all the individualized page content. The NavContent is editable because the site is designed so that the button for the current page looks different from the other buttons. To set up the buttons for each page individually is an easy way of doing this.

Content Pages in Code View

The Default.aspx page looks the same as the Default.master page (except for the content, of course) in Design view, but Code view is a different story. If you switch to Split view, you see that the code for the page contains only the link back to the Default.master file off the top followed by the contents of the content regions. None of the styling, layout, or other code is present in this file. Only when you look at the code of a content page does the concept of web forms truly begins to make sense.

In plain English, each .aspx page is an advanced web form, just like the email form you created in Hours 20 and 22 that when opened in a browser submits its contents to the .master page, which is then displayed with the contents inserted. In fact, the actual page exists only when the server puts the content (the .aspx) file and the template (the .master) file together and then sends it to the browser. Just like in *The Matrix* when the little boy bends the spoon with his mind, the answer to the question "Where is the page?" is "There is no page!"

Websites like the Portfolio Starter Kit site are commonly referred to as dynamic websites because the pages are created dynamically on demand by the browser and the server when the visitor opens them. In contrast, a static site consists of pages that have already been built, and visitors simply download them to their browser when the pages are opened.

▼   **Try It Yourself**

Give the Page a Title, Description, and Keywords

Even though the Default.aspx page is just a web form that contains only the individual contents of the page, it is still edited just like the other web pages you have been working with whether it is HTML or PHP.

As you can see in Code view, even though you made alterations to the head content region in the master page, there is no corresponding content region in the web form. To define the content for the head region, you first have to create a new content field in the web form.

1. With the Default.aspx page open in Split view, navigate the Code view section to the top and place the cursor on line 2. Press Enter twice to create some space.

2. Place the cursor on line 2 and type **<asp**. IntelliSense immediately suggests <asp:Content, which is what you want. Press Enter to insert the code (see Figure 25.10).

FIGURE 25.10
IntelliSense has full support for ASP.NET and is a great tool when writing and editing .aspx pages.

3. Press the spacebar and IntelliSense pops up a new menu suggesting ContentPlaceHolderID. Press Enter to insert the code.

4. The cursor is now placed inside the quotation marks. Type **head** and use the right-arrow key or End to get to the end of the line.

5. Press the spacebar again and IntelliSense provides a new menu of suggested code. Use the arrow keys to select runat and press Enter to insert the code. Now IntelliSense offers only one option, server, which is the correct one. Press Enter again.

6. Finally, close the tag with a > and IntelliSense automatically inserts the corresponding closing tag (see Figure 25.11).

    After the content region has been inserted, you can make changes to the head tags using the Page Properties dialog.

```
1 <%@ Page Language="C#" masterpagefile="Default.master" title="Default" %>
2
3 <asp:Content ContentPlaceHolderID="head" runat="server"></asp:Content>
4
5 <asp:Content ContentPlaceHolderID="NavContent" runat="server">
6
```

FIGURE 25.11
The
`ContentPlace
HolderID` tag
for the head
region is
inserted with the
help of Intel-
liSense.

7. In Design view, right-click anywhere inside the content regions and select Page
   Properties from the context menu. (If you click anywhere else, nothing happens).

8. In the Page Properties dialog, change the title to **My Portfolio** or anything else
   you want. Create a description for the page and some keywords, and click OK
   to apply the changes (see Figure 25.12).

FIGURE 25.12
With the head
content region
inserted, you are
free to edit the
title, description,
and keywords for
the site using
the Page Proper-
ties dialog.

Going back to the top of the page in Code view, you can see that the title has been
changed in the first line whereas the keywords and description have been inserted into
the content region you just created. Now when a browser opens the page, the title,
description, and keywords are inserted into the correct regions in the master page.

Getting Data from External Sources

One of the major benefits of creating dynamic websites is the ability to gather content from external sources and display it in the current page without actually having
to place it there. By using an external source for your content, you can use one
source to populate multiple pages with different layouts at different times. When a

change is needed, all you need to do is change the source file, and all the dynamic pages that get their content from it automatically update, too.

To see this process in action, preview the Default.aspx page in your browser. When you press F12 or choose Preview in Browser button on the Common toolbar, Expression Development Server is engaged, and a virtual server displays the ASP.NET site as if it were hosted on a web server.

On the right side of the About (Default.aspx) page, under Featured, are three thumbnails representing projects. When you hover the mouse over each of them, a rounded corner box appears with name, description, and a link to further reading about that project. If you click on the Work button, you see the same thumbnails again; only this time there are nine of them arranged in three rows and columns (see Figure 25.13). Although the layout of the thumbnails in the two pages is dramatically different, all are gathered from the same source.

FIGURE 25.13
The About and Work pages both feature external data from the same source displayed in different ways.

Back in Expression Web 3, you see that the featured thumbnails are replaced by broken image links (a small square with a red x in them). This is because, as with PHP, Design view cannot display the results of server-side ASP.NET scripts. Nevertheless, by clicking on the images, you can see the code that generates them (see Figure 25.14).

The code put in place to display the thumbnails and all their functionality is quite complicated, but even with little to no experience with programming, you can still figure out what is going on. Take a look at the first line of code in the block:

```
<asp:DataList runat="server" ID="MyDataList" DataSourceID="MyXmlDataSource"
RepeatLayout="Flow" RepeatDirection="Vertical">
```

In plain English, it reads, "Here follows a data list to be created by the server. The name of the data list is MyDataList and it will contain items provided by a source named MyXmlDataSource. The list items will be repeated in the vertical direction."

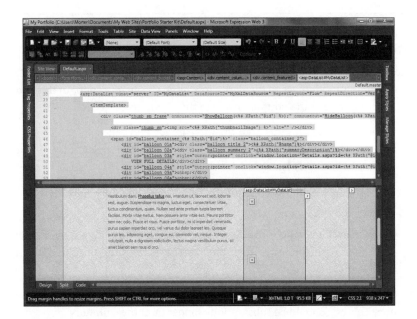

FIGURE 25.14
In place of the actual thumbnails that appeared when you previewed the page in a browser, by clicking on the Featured section, you get the ASP.NET code that gets the content from the external source.

The code that follows, wrapped in the `<ItemTemplate>` tag, describes the look and behavior of each of the list items and the server will cycle through this list for each of the items as they are placed on the page when it is displayed.

But there is still one question left unanswered: Where do the data and images come from? All we know so far is that the source is called MyXmlDataSource. To find the source, use the Find feature: Place the cursor anywhere in Code view and press Ctrl+F. In the Find dialog, type **myxmldatasource** and click Find. Doing so takes you to the next place where MyXmlDataSource is mentioned:

```
<asp:XmlDataSource ID="MyXmlDataSource" DataFile="portfolio.xml"
XPath="portfolio/portfolioItem[@featuredItem='true']" runat="server">
It is in this line of code you find the source of the list: a file called
portfolio.xml.
```

Go to the Folder List panel and open the portfolio.xml file. As you can see, this is a pure data file that contains a series of variables defined for each item in a list. The variables include `name`, `summaryDescription`, `fullDescription`, `webSiteAddress`, `fullSizeImage`, and so on. Using this information with the different web forms of the site, the browser and the server can build multiple different layouts and pages.

▼   **Try It Yourself**

Modify the External Source for Immediate Sitewide Effects

By modifying the portfolio.xml file and adding a few image files to your project, you can make dramatic changes to the Portfolio Starter Kit site in a snap. In this example, you change one of the portfolio items to the MyKipple project.

1. In the project files for this hour are three image files called mykippleFront_lg.jpg, mykippleFront_sm.jpg, and mykippleContact_lg.jpg. Import them into the images folder in the project.

2. In the portfolio.xml file, go to line 5 and change the name value to MyKipple.com.

3. On the next line, remove the dummy summaryDescription and insert a short description of the project, something like **This is the site I built by following the lessons in Morten's book.**

4. Go to the next line, remove the dummy content, and insert a new fullDescription. This one should be substantially longer than the summary.

5. Change the webSiteAddress to http://www.mykipple.com.

6. Change the fullSizeImage to images/mykippleFront_lg.jpg.

7. Change the thumbnailImage to images/mykippleFront_sm.jpg.

8. Under detailImages, remove two of the entries and change the two other to images/mykippleFront_lg.jpg and images/mykipplecontact_lg.jpg.

9. Save the file (see Figure 25.15).

FIGURE 25.15
The portfolio.xml file with the first list item changed to the MyKipple.com project.

```
 4
 5    <portfolioItem id="1" name="MyKipple.com" featuredItem="true">
 6      <summaryDescription>This is the site I built by following the lessons in
 7      <fullDescription>Vestibulum diam. Phasellus tellus nisi, interdum ut, la
 8      <websiteAddress>http://www.mykipple.com</websiteAddress>
 9      <fullSizeImage>images/mykippleFront_lg.jpg</fullSizeImage>
10      <thumbnailImage>images/mykippleFront_sm.jpg</thumbnailImage>
11        <detailImages>
12          <image>images/mykippleFront_lg.jpg</image>
13          <image>images/mykipplecontact_lg.jpg</image>
14        </detailImages>
15    </portfolioItem>
```

Without making any changes to any of the other pages, open Default.aspx in your browser. As you can see, the first portfolio item has been changed to the MyKipple. com project. The same is true for the Work page. And if you click on the View Full Details option, a new page appears and displays all the info about the project.

▲

Personalizing and Styling an ASP.NET Site

Now that you have seen how advanced the functionality of the Portfolio Starter Kit is, you might want to use all or part of the site as a basis for your own website. But to do this you need to personalize and customize the site so that it reflects you and your company and doesn't look like the many other sites built from the same files. Doing this might seem like a daunting task, but you shouldn't be too surprised to learn that even though this site uses ASP.NET, the look and feel of the site is still firmly based in the same CSS techniques you learned through reading this book. In fact, if you have a lot of time and patience, you can actually make the Portfolio Starter Kit look exactly like the MyKipple.com site!

Making changes to a dynamic site is a bit trickier than making changes to one with static pages because not all the information is contained in the same file. But by keeping your tongue level (as we say in Norwegian), you can make quick changes for maximum effect: You just need to know where to make them.

Changes that affect all pages across the site should be made in the .master file. Changes that should appear only in individual pages should be made in the .aspx files using HTML. Finally, changes to content provided by external data sources such as .xml files or databases should be made in the respective sources. To find out whether a certain item in a page is generated from an external data source, open the page in Design view and see if the content appears. If it does, it is HTML-based. If it doesn't show up, but is replaced by a tag or block of code, it is generated from an external source.

Try It Yourself ▼

Make Sitewide Changes

Not surprising, layout and style changes that should affect all the pages on the site are made by modifying the master page.

1. Open the Default.master page in Design view.

2. In the header of the page, highlight the name and change it for your name or the name of your company. Also change the title to your title or the tag line for your company.

3. Scroll down to the bottom of the page and find the footer. Change the contents so that the copyright is attributed to you or your company.

4. Highlight your name or the name of your company in the footer, and use the Insert Hyperlink dialog to turn it into a hyperlink pointing to your website.

Because the design of the site is created using regular CSS, you can make changes to the site by modifying the CSS. Now you can use your CSS skills to change the look of the header.

5. You might have noticed that regardless of what you write, the first letter of the title in the header is capitalized. To change this, click on the title to see what style is affecting it. Click on the `<span.title>` tag in the Quick Tag Selector and go to the CSS Properties panel. Here you can see that `text-transform` is set to Capitalize. Using the CSS Properties panel, change `text-transform` to none (see Figure 25.16).

FIGURE 25.16
Because the master page is controlled by CSS, you can change the design of the site by using the Modify Styles panel, the CSS Properties panel, or even by editing the style sheet directly in Code view.

6. Likewise to change the color of the heading, click the heading and find the `.name_column_middle` class in the Manage Styles panel. Open the Modify Style dialog and change the font color to a bright orange (#FF6600).

7. Save the master page and the attached CSS file. Preview any of the pages in your browser, and you see that the changes have been applied to the site as a whole.

Now that you know how to make changes to the look of the site, it's time to look at how you can make changes to the content of the different pages within the site. Making changes to the individual pages contained in the Portfolio Starter Kit allows you to further personalize the site and is also a necessary step to ensure that the people who visit the site get the message you want to convey to them. This is particularly true for the Contact page.

Configure the Contact Form

The final page of the Portfolio Starter Kit is a contact form much like the one you created in Hour 20. To personalize the contact page, you need to make changes to two files: Contact.aspx and Contact.cs.

1. Open the Contact.aspx page in Design view.

2. Each of the web forms (pages) in the site has some page-specific content. This content is created and styled using the same techniques you have used throughout this book. At the top of the MainContent region is a mailing address and an email address. Change these to your name, mailing, and email address as you would in any other HTML page.

   Below the addresses is the email form. This form was created using the ASP.NET controls, not the HTML form controls you used in previous hours. The ASP.NET controls are in the Toolbox panel in the Standard submenu under ASP.NET (see Figure 25.17).

FIGURE 25.17
Although they look similar to the HTML form, the forms in the ASP.NET site are made using the ASP.NET controls found under ASP.NET in the Toolbox panel.

3. If you look through the code of the Contact.aspx page, you notice that there is nowhere to input the email address the email should be sent to. This information is stored in the Web.config file. Open the Web.config file and find the EmailTo attribute on line 11. Change the value to your email address. You can also change the default subject line if you want.

4. Save both pages.

Summary

As websites become more advanced and you start looking for added functionality, ASP.NET gives you options that are far outside of the scope of straight HTML. With this server-side script language, you can make highly advanced dynamic websites with increased interactivity and features that are sure to impress any client.

ASP.NET is Microsoft's server-side scripting language, and as such it is an integral part of Expression Web 3. But because it is a server-side script language, it requires a whole new set of skills that reach far beyond the scope of this book. For this reason, you were introduced to the Portfolio Starter Kit, an ASP.NET-based website designed by Microsoft to give new designers a first look at ASP.NET, and you used it to learn the basics of how these sites work.

An ASP.NET site is different from everything you have encountered so far in this book because unlike the regular HTML and PHP pages and even those generated from a Dynamic Web Template, the individual pages of an ASP.NET site exist only when a visitor opens them. In other words, rather than stored on the server as individual fully programmed pages, the contents of an ASP.NET site are stored in web forms (files with the suffix .aspx) and external data sources such as XML files. When the visitor opens one of these forms, the browser and the server work together to put the contents of the form into the layout of the master page, and look through the form to see whether other content should be sourced from external data sources. It all sounds complicated, but when you work with larger websites with hundreds or even thousands of pages, this type of structure combined with a database to hold all the external content is far more feasible than making each page individually.

In this hour, you learned the basics of how an ASP.NET site works and what makes it different from other static sites. You learned how to edit the master page to change the content regions that can be defined for the individual pages. And even though it is based on ASP.NET, the layout of the master page is still nothing but HTML and CSS.

You also learned how to change the contents of individual web forms and how they interact with the master page to create a complete page. In addition, you took a closer look at how external data files are used as sources to generate content for multiple pages, and you saw how easy it is to change these external data sources for immediate and sitewide results. Finally, you learned how to customize the project to work as a basis for your own web portfolio or another project.

Now you have the basic skill set to customize the Portfolio Starter Kit site and make it your own. Even if you don't want to use it as a basis for your own or a client website, the project is an excellent tool to learn more about how ASP.NET works and how you can employ it to create richer and more interactive web experiences for the visitors.

The Expression website has other Starter Kits that introduces you to elements such as login control, calendar controls, and style sheet switches. These Starter Kits are not covered in this book but are based on the same principles as the Portfolio Starter Kit, and you can apply the same techniques learned in this hour to personalize them as well.

Q&A

Q. *The Portfolio Starter Kit doesn't work! I can open it in Expression Web 3, but when I try to preview it, all I get is a weird error message. What is going on?*

A. Unlike a website built using static HTML pages, a dynamic website like the Portfolio Starter Kit has a specific folder and file structure that must be maintained for everything to work properly. If you receive an error message when previewing the page in your browser, it is most likely because you didn't set the correct folder as the site folder when you first created the site. As previously stated, the site link must be to the Portfolio Starter Kit folder and not the Expression Portfolio Starter Kit folder or the site will not work properly.

Workshop

The Workshop has quiz questions and exercises to help you put to use what you have just learned. If you get stuck, the answers to the quiz questions are in the next section. But try to answer the questions first. Otherwise you'll be cheating yourself.

Quiz

1. What is the primary difference between a static HTML-based site and a dynamic ASP.NET-based site?

Answers

1. As the name suggests, the static HTML site consists of a series of pages that are static, meaning they can be changed only by editing the content manually on the server. The dynamic ASP.NET site, on the other hand, consists of a series of pages that are populated by the server when they are opened. They get their content from different sources and are updated by changing the sources rather than the pages themselves. This way you can make sweeping changes to many pages by altering their data sources. Dynamic pages can also gather content from sources outside of the current website.

Exercise

In this hour, you learned to insert a new title, description, and keywords in the Default.aspx page. Open the three other .aspx pages, insert the necessary content regions, and give each of them an individual title, description, and appropriate keywords. Keep in mind that the Details.aspx page displays the full information from the portfolio.xml data source, so the description and keywords need to be generic enough to describe all the different projects.

Edit the portfolio.xml file to create new portfolio items. To do so, you also need to add new image files to the Images folder. The easiest way to do this is to open existing image files in your favorite image editor, replace the contents of these files with new content, and save them with new and descriptive names just as was done with the images for the MyKipple project.

APPENDIX A

Building Layers-Based Menus

Introduction

In Hour 18, "Building a Functional Menu," you learned how to build a CSS-based menu. This is the preferred approach for building menus because it is flexible and allows for easy styling and dynamic content building. Nevertheless there is another method to build menus—and in particular drop-down menus—that is often used that involves buttons and layers. Throughout the book you learned about buttons, behaviors, and layers. In this appendix, you use that knowledge to create an advanced and functional drop-down menu for easy navigation.

The Layers-Based Menu

Using layers and child layers is a quick-and-dirty way to create drop-down menus that has been around for some time. This technique allows for great flexibility when it comes to the look and feel of the menu, but the code portion can be messy. Even so, many designers still use the layers-based menu, and you can create it in Expression Web 3 without writing or looking at a single line of code.

Creating the Main Menu

A drop-down menu consists of two groups of elements: the main menu that is always visible and the child menus triggered by the main menu. The main menu buttons can work as buttons or just as triggers for the child menus. In this lesson, you use Expression Web 3's interactive buttons to create the Layers menu.

1. Create a new Hypertext Markup Language (HTML) page and call it **layers-Menu.html**. Open the page in Design view.

2. Open the Layers panel and click the Draw Layer button. Draw a layer the width of the page and about one paragraph in height in Design view. After creating the layer, double-click it in the Layers panel and change the layer ID to `mainMenu` (see Figure A.1).

FIGURE A.1
Naming the layers as you create them is a good habit that prevents confusion when your layouts become more complicated.

3. Click the layer to place the cursor inside it and select Insert, Interactive Button on the menu bar to create a new interactive button.

4. In the Interactive Button dialog, scroll down and select one of the Linked Row buttons. Set the Text option to Home and click OK to insert the button.

5. You now have two choices of how to create more buttons: Either repeat steps 3 and 4 or copy the current button, paste a new one next to it, and double-click the new button to open the Interactive Button dialog and give the button a new name. Either way you choose, create four new buttons and call them **News**, **Gallery**, **Archive**, and **Contact** (see Figure A.2).

FIGURE A.2
The mainMenu layer now contains five buttons.

Create a Submenu

Now that you have designed the main menu, it is time to add the submenus to the page. Each submenu should reside in its own layer, and the layers should be children of the mainMenu layer. This is because when a layer is a child of a different layer, the parent layer defines its position. In practical terms, this means that if the parent layer moves, the child layers move with it.

1. To create a child layer, use the Draw Layer button to draw a new layer anywhere on the page. (You will position it later.) After drawing the layer, click and drag the new layer instance on top of the mainMenu layer instance in the Layers panel so that the mouse pointer changes to include a superimposed box and a + sign. When you let go, the new layer appears slightly indented under the mainMenu layer in the list. The indentation indicates the new layer is a child of the mainMenu layer (see Figure A.3).

FIGURE A.3
The – (minus sign) in front of the mainMenu layer and the slight indentation of the new layer indicate that the new layer is a child of the main-Menu layer.

2. Change the layer ID of the new layer to newsSub.

3. Place the cursor inside the new layer and select Insert, Interactive Button from the menu bar to create a new interactive button.

4. Choose the Simple Block button and set the button text to New News. Under the Font tab, set the Horizontal Alignment to Left. As you can see from the preview, you have to insert a space before the words to separate them from the box graphic. To do so, simply place your cursor at the beginning of the text and press the spacebar once. Click OK to insert the button into the new layer.

5. Press Enter to go to the next line, copy and paste the first button into the second line, and give it the name **Old News**. Repeat the process and make two more buttons called **Good News** and **Bad News**.

6. Resize the layer by clicking it and dragging the handles so that the layer borders fit the content (see Figure A.4).

7. Finally, reposition the layer directly under the News button on the main menu where you want it to appear when the visitor triggers it (see Figure A.5). To reposition the layer, hover your mouse over the Tag Selector until the four-direction arrow shows and then drag and drop the layer to the location of your choice.

FIGURE A.4
After creating all the buttons, you can resize the layer using the handles.

FIGURE A.5
Because the pop-up layer is likely to overlap parts of the mainMenu layer, it is a good idea to wait until you finish the layer before moving it to its final position.

When you save the page, you get a long list of embedded image files that you must save. Click the Change Folder button in the Save Embedded Files dialog and create a new folder called **layerMenuButtons** for all the button images.

After saving the page, preview it in your browser. As you can see, the main menu buttons and the submenu buttons are working properly, but the submenu is visible all the time. To create the drop-down effect, you need to apply a series of behaviors to the different elements.

Try It Yourself ▼

Use Behaviors to Make the Drop-Down Menu Drop Down

The whole idea of a drop-down menu is that the submenus are not visible until you trigger them. In Hour 17, "Frames and Layers," you learned how you could use the `Visibility` property to hide and show layers in the browser. Now you are going to use this technique to trigger the new submenu.

1. The newsSub layer should not be visible unless the user triggers it. Use the eye column in the Layers panel, or right-click the newsSub layer and select Set Visibility: Hidden from the pop-up menu (see Figure A.6).

FIGURE A.6
You can set the visibility of a layer by using the eye icon in the leftmost column in the Layers panel or by right-clicking it and setting it from the pop-up menu.

The newsSub layer should become visible when the visitor hovers over the News button on the mainMenu layer.

2. Click the News button in the mainMenu layer and apply a Change Property behavior from the Behaviors panel.

3. In the Change Property dialog, check Select Element and set the element type to Div and the element ID to newsSub. Click the Visibility button and set the visibility to Visible. For this behavior, do not check the Restore on Mouseout Event box (see Figure A.7). If you do, the submenu becomes invisible when you move your mouse away from the News button and into the menu. Click OK to apply the behavior.

4. In the Behaviors panel, change the event of the Change Property behavior to onmouseover by clicking it and selecting onmouseover from the drop-down menu.

Now the newsSub menu appears whenever the visitor hovers over the News button. But if you test the page in your browser, you see that after submenu triggers, it doesn't disappear again.

5. Select the newsSub layer either by clicking it in Design view or selecting it from the Layers panel, and go to the Behaviors panel. Apply a Change Property behavior to the newsSub layer.

FIGURE A.7
Use the Change
Property behavior
in the News but-
ton to trigger the
drop-down menu.

6. In the Change Property panel, leave Current Element checked and set the Visibility to Hidden. Again, do not check the Restore on Mouseout Event box. Click
   OK to apply the behavior.

7. In the Behaviors panel, change the event of the Change Property behavior to
   onmouseout. This tells the browser that the menu should be invisible when the
   mouse is no longer hovering over it.

   Save and test the page in your browser, and you see that the drop-down menu
   now stays put when you hover over the first button but disappears again if you
   move further down. To fix this, you need to tell the browser that as long as the
   mouse is in the newsSub layer it should remain visible.

8. With the newsSub layer still selected, add a new Change Property behavior and
   set the Visibility property for the layer to Visible. Click OK to apply the new
   behavior and change the event to onmouseover (see Figure A.8).

   Now the drop-down menu works almost the way it should, with one exception:
   If the visitor moves the mouse to one of the other main menu buttons instead
   of somewhere else on the page, the submenu stays visible.

9. To hide the submenu when the visitor moves from the News button to one of
   the other buttons on the main menu, click the mainMenu layer in the Layers
   panel layer and apply a Change Property behavior to it. Check Select Element
   and set the element type to Div and the element ID to newsSub. Click the Visibility button and set the visibility to Hidden. Click OK twice to apply the
   behavior to the layer and change the event to onmouseout.

FIGURE A.8
The newsSub layer needs two Change Property behaviors to work properly: one for when the mouse hovers over it and one for when the mouse moves away from it. Note that I have placed the Behaviors panel in the top-right panel area so that I can have both Behaviors and Layers open at the same time.

Now, finally, the drop-down menu for the News button works properly.

Adding and Managing Several Drop-Down Menus

As you saw in the prior section, to get the drop-down menu to work properly, you need to apply multiple different behaviors to different elements within the page. Unfortunately, there is no quick way to automate this process: You need to apply the same set of behaviors to every new submenu.

1. To create a new submenu for the Gallery button, click to select the newsSub layer in the Layers panel and press Ctrl+C to copy it and Ctrl+V to paste it. The new layer should appear with the name newsSub0 in the Layers panel and on top of the original newsSub layer in Design view.

2. Double-click the layer in the Layers panel to rename it. Give it the name **gallery-Sub** (see Figure A.9).

3. Grab the new gallery-Sub layer in Design view and move it so that it is directly under the Gallery button on the main menu. Toggle the layer visibility to visible by clicking the eye icon in the Layers panel.

4. Double-click the first button and give it the name **My Kipple**. Rename the two other buttons to **Other Kipple** and **Found Kipple** (see Figure A.10).

FIGURE A.9
You can copy and paste layers from within the Layers panel. They become independent entities, and it's a good idea to rename them immediately to keep track.

FIGURE A.10
The new button titles are longer than the ones in the original layer, so you need to extend the gallery-Sub layer to the right to fit them in.

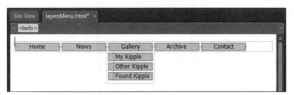

5. With the gallery-Sub layer selected, go to the Behaviors panel. The behaviors from the newsSub layer are still visible, but if you double-click the onmouseout behavior to open the Change Property dialog, you'll be notified that it is no longer working (see Figure A.11).

FIGURE A.11
The Previous Target Element Was Not Found warning tells you that although the behavior appears in the Behaviors panel, it no longer works.

6. Click OK to close the warning box, and you see that the behavior is empty. The event is still present but the action is gone. Set the element ID to gallery-Sub and the visibility to Hidden. Open the onmouseover behavior and do the same except set the visibility to Visible.

7. To link the new layer to the main menu, select the Gallery button on the main menu and apply a Change Property behavior to it. In the Change Properties dialog, set the element ID to gallery-Sub and the visibility to Visible. Click OK to apply the new behavior and change the event in the Behaviors panel to onmouseover.

8. To finalize the process, set the gallery-Sub layer visibility to Hidden in the Layers panel by clicking the eye icon twice to get the closed eye. Create a new behavior that sets the visibility of the gallery-Sub layer to Hidden and attach it to the mainMenu layer. Change the event of this behavior to onmouseout. The mainMenu layer should now have two onmouseout events that both have Change Property actions.

Save and preview the page in your browser, and you see that you now have a menu with two fully working drop-down submenus under the News and Gallery buttons.

Basing Drop-Down Menus on Layers and Behaviors Is a Double-Edged Sword

Although making a drop-down menu using layers and behaviors might seem easy because you can do it all by pointing and clicking different elements, there are some serious drawbacks to this technique. You are required to apply a long list of behaviors to each element just to make the menu work properly, and you have to add even more if you want the buttons to do something. In addition, if you switch the page you have been working with to Split view, you can see that the code generated for this menu is complicated and hard to read, even for seasoned professionals (see Figure A.12). As a result, a small error or omission on the part of the designer or developer can have catastrophic consequences for the functionality of the menu as a whole.

FIGURE A.12
Although the menu looks great in Design view, the code that makes it work is complicated and hard to read.

On the upside, this technique enables you to use fancy graphic elements as buttons and gives you an easy way to create and control highly interactive menus. Although this book does not cover the topic, for a more customized look you can create graphic buttons outside Expression Web 3 that work the same way as the interactive buttons.

The drop-down menu tutorial serves as a demonstration of what is possible when you use layers and behaviors together. When applied properly, this technique produces robust, attractive, and interactive menus that work both as navigation and eye candy. But as you saw, the code is complicated, and you have to keep tabs on a lot of buttons and behaviors, not to mention that the menu works only if JavaScript is enabled.

> If JavaScript is enabled in the browser used to visit the page, layers-based menus are 100% nonfunctional, meaning they do not work at all!

Summary

The layers-based drop-down menu gives you complete control of the look of your menu both in terms of buttons and functionality. Because you construct it using images as buttons, you have unlimited options for what each button should look like. In this appendix, you built the menu using the interactive buttons built in to Expression Web 3, but you can do the same operation using buttons created in a different design application. You can also open the interactive button images created by Expression Web 3 in a design application and edit them individually. Just keep in mind that if you do, you can't change them in Expression Web 3 without losing the new design.

The downside of the layers-based drop-down menu is that it depends on behaviors and JavaScript to work properly. For most visitors, this is not a problem. But for those who do not have JavaScript activated or use text-only or text-to-speech browsers, it can cause unwanted results. In addition, the layers-based menu can be hard to handle because you must keep track of a long list of behaviors that work together to make the menu function properly. Forgetting just one of these behaviors can have fatal results for the overall function of the menu.

Index

swap-images, creating, 260-262

synchronizing files, **438**

syntax, formatting hyperlinks, 71. *See also* fonts

T

Table AutoFormat dialog box, 139

Table Layout Tool, 139-141

Table Properties panel, 134-136

tables, 28-29, 126

AutoFormat option, 138-139

creating, 129-130

editing, 140

forms, formatting, 351

modifying, 130-139

navigating, 128

Tables toolbar, 130

tabs, 126

Button, 245

Confirmation Page, 358

Font, 246

Publishing, 441-442

Saved Fields, 359

Tag Properties panel, 13, 391

tags, 56, 167

body, 153

classes, applying, 188-193

ContentPlaceHolderID, 454

div, 191-193

DWTs, 340

embed, 370-372

forms, 348. *See also* forms

h1, 236

meta, 185

modifying, 62

pseudoclasses, 176-178

Quick Tag Selector, 450

Quick Tag tools, 155-158

redirect, 399

span, 191, 254

titles, 45

Target Frame dialog box, 74, 292

technical specifications, 6

templates, 41

DWTs, 438, 448-450. *See also* DWTs

PHP. *See* PHP

testing, 402-404

Check Browser behavior, 267-270

compatibility, 50

cross-browser, SuperPreview, 407-409

font sizing methods, 150

hyperlinks, 69

PHP, 399

web pages, 47-49

text

areas, 350

editing, 58-62

frame behaviors, 295-296

hyperlinks. *See* hyperlinks

importing, 57-58

managing, 246

Set Text behavior, 279

X

Y–Z

SAMS

REGISTER

THIS PRODUCT

informit.com/register

Register the Addison-Wesley, Exam Cram, Prentice Hall, Que, and Sams products you own to unlock great benefits.

To begin the registration process, simply go to **informit.com/register** to sign in or create an account. You will then be prompted to enter the 10- or 13-digit ISBN that appears on the back cover of your product.

Registering your products can unlock the following benefits:

- Access to supplemental content, including bonus chapters, source code, or project files.
- A coupon to be used on your next purchase.

Registration benefits vary by product. Benefits will be listed on your Account page under Registered Products.

About InformIT — THE TRUSTED TECHNOLOGY LEARNING SOURCE

INFORMIT IS HOME TO THE LEADING TECHNOLOGY PUBLISHING IMPRINTS Addison-Wesley Professional, Cisco Press, Exam Cram, IBM Press, Prentice Hall Professional, Que, and Sams. Here you will gain access to quality and trusted content and resources from the authors, creators, innovators, and leaders of technology. Whether you're looking for a book on a new technology, a helpful article, timely newsletters, or access to the Safari Books Online digital library, InformIT has a solution for you.

informIT.com

THE TRUSTED TECHNOLOGY LEARNING SOURCE

Addison-Wesley | Cisco Press | Exam Cram
IBM Press | Que | Prentice Hall | Sams

SAFARI BOOKS ONLINE

informIT.com
THE TRUSTED TECHNOLOGY LEARNING SOURCE

InformIT is a brand of Pearson and the online presence for the world's leading technology publishers. It's your source for reliable and qualified content and knowledge, providing access to the top brands, authors, and contributors from the tech community.

Addison-Wesley   Cisco Press   EXAM/CRAM   IBM Press.   QUE®   PRENTICE HALL   SAMS   Safari Books Online

LearnIT at InformIT

Looking for a book, eBook, or training video on a new technology? Seeking timely and relevant information and tutorials? Looking for expert opinions, advice, and tips? **InformIT has the solution.**

- Learn about new releases and special promotions by subscribing to a wide variety of newsletters.
  Visit **informit.com/newsletters**.

- Access FREE podcasts from experts at **informit.com/podcasts**.

- Read the latest author articles and sample chapters at **informit.com/articles**.

- Access thousands of books and videos in the Safari Books Online digital library at **safari.informit.com**.

- Get tips from expert blogs at **informit.com/blogs**.

Visit **informit.com/learn** to discover all the ways you can access the hottest technology content.

Are You Part of the IT Crowd?

Connect with Pearson authors and editors via RSS feeds, Facebook, Twitter, YouTube, and more! Visit **informit.com/socialconnect**.

informIT.com
THE TRUSTED TECHNOLOGY LEARNING SOURCE   PEARSON

Addison-Wesley   Cisco Press   EXAM/CRAM   IBM Press.   QUE®   PRENTICE HALL   SAMS   Safari Books Online

Try Safari Books Online FREE

Get online access to 5,000+ Books and Videos

 Safari Books Online

FREE TRIAL—GET STARTED TODAY!
www.informit.com/safaritrial

Find trusted answers, fast
Only Safari lets you search across thousands of best-selling books from the top technology publishers, including Addison-Wesley Professional, Cisco Press, O'Reilly, Prentice Hall, Que, and Sams.

Master the latest tools and techniques
In addition to gaining access to an incredible inventory of technical books, Safari's extensive collection of video tutorials lets you learn from the leading video training experts.

WAIT, THERE'S MORE!

Keep your competitive edge
With Rough Cuts, get access to the developing manuscript and be among the first to learn the newest technologies.

Stay current with emerging technologies
Short Cuts and Quick Reference Sheets are short, concise, focused content created to get you up-to-speed quickly on new and cutting-edge technologies.

FREE Online Edition

Your purchase of **Sams Teach Yourself Microsoft Expression Web 3 in 24 Hours** includes access to a free online edition for 45 days through the Safari Books Online subscription service. Nearly every Sams book is available online through Safari Books Online, along with more than 5,000 other technical books and videos from publishers such as Addison-Wesley Professional, Cisco Press, Exam Cram, IBM Press, O'Reilly, Prentice Hall, and Que.

SAFARI BOOKS ONLINE allows you to search for a specific answer, cut and paste code, download chapters, and stay current with emerging technologies.

Activate your FREE Online Edition at www.informit.com/safarifree

> **STEP 1:** Enter the coupon code: CWCIPXA.

> **STEP 2:** New Safari users, complete the brief registration form.
> Safari subscribers, just log in.

If you have difficulty registering on Safari or accessing the online edition, please e-mail customer-service@safaribooksonline.com

         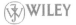